Social Movements

Social Movements
An Introduction

Donatella della Porta and Mario Diani

BLACKWELL
Publishers

First published 1999
Reprinted 1999, 2000

Blackwell Publishers Ltd
108 Cowley Road
Oxford OX4 1JF
UK

Blackwell Publishers Inc.
350 Main Street
Malden, Massachusetts 02148
USA

British Library Cataloguing in Publication Data

A CIP catalogue record for this book is available from the British Library.

Library of Congress Cataloging-in-Publication Data

Della Porta, Donatella, 1956–
Social movements: an introduction / Donatella
della Porta and Mario Diani
p.   cm.
Includes bibliographical references and index.
ISBN 0–631–19212–3 (alk.paper). — ISBN 0–631–19213–1 (pbk.: alk.paper)
1. Social movements. I. Diani, Mario, 1957–.
II. Title.
HN17.5.D523   1998
303.48'4—dc21
                                                                    98–28669
                                                                    CIP

Typeset in 10½ on 12pt Palatino
By Graphicraft Limited, Hong Kong
Printed in Great Britain by MPG Books Ltd, Bodmin, Cornwall.

This book is printed on acid-free paper

Contents

Figures and Tables

Figures

Tables

Acknowledgements

This book originates from the fortuitous and timely coincidence of a conversation we had in Florence in November 1991, when we first explored the possibility of writing a general text on social movements, and a request along the same lines which kindly came from Simon Prosser, then editor for social sciences at Blackwell, in February 1992. That in the meanwhile Simon has managed to move to Blackwell, USA, become a father, return to England, and take up two more jobs, speaks volumes about our failure to quickly convert favourable opportunities into collective action. Thanks, therefore, for their patience and encouragement, to Simon, and to Jill Landeryou who has replaced him as our liaison at Blackwell, as well as to Gian Luca Mori of Nuova Italia Scientifica, the equally supportive editor of the Italian edition of the book.

We are particularly indebted to Alessandro Pizzorno, Chris Rootes and Sidney Tarrow for their critical remarks. Sections of the book have also been read and commented upon by Ron Eyerman, Marco Giugni, John McCarthy, Alberto Melucci, Nicola Negri, Luca Ricolfi and Loredana Sciolla. Chapter 8 in particular was written after a stimulating discussion at a workshop on the 'Political opportunity structure' at the Wissenschaftszentrum Berlin für Sozial Forschung, with Hanspeter Kriesi, John McCarthy, Friedhelm Neidhardt and Dieter Rucht. While stating that these friends and colleagues are not responsible for any shortcomings in our work may sound rather conventional, our gratitude to them is definitely not. We are also grateful to the publishing press *il Mulino* for granting permission to reproduce materials they originally published (Bianchi and Mormino 1984: 159–60). The Harry Frank Guggenheim Foundation, The Alex von Humboldt Stiftung and the Ministery of the University in Italy provided material support for Donatella della Porta's research activities. Finally, thanks to our translators: Johanna McPake for chapters 1 to 5, and John Donaldson for chapters 6 to 9.

We obviously accept full responsibility for the book as a whole. However, for the record, Mario Diani has written chapters 2 to 5, and Donatella della Porta chapters 6 to 9; the first chapter has been jointly written.

D. d. P.–M. D.
Florence–Glasgow

1

The Study of Social Movements: Collective Behaviour, Rational Actions, Protests and New Conflicts

From the 1960s onwards, social movements, protest actions and, more generally, political organizations unaligned with major political parties or trade unions have become a permanent component of western democracies. There has been considerable fluctuation in the intensity of movement mobilization over this period, as there has been in its degree of radicalism, and in its capacity to influence the political process. However, forecasts that the wave of protest in 1968 would quickly subside, and that 'business as usual', as represented by interest-based politics, organized according to traditional political divisions, would return in its wake, have largely been proved wrong. In different ways, and with a wide range of goals and values, various forms of protest have continued to emerge in recent years (Kriesi et al. 1995). Describing these as 'unconventional' – as observers did originally – is increasingly inappropriate. On the contrary, the mention of a 'movement society', in some interpretations (Neidhardt and Rucht 1991), now seems a plausible, albeit controversial, hypothesis.

In this book we introduce the reader to some of the principal issues raised by the growth of social movements. Although we focus on some of the approaches which have been elaborated since the mid-1970s, the intellectual roots of recent debates (and not only those concerned with collective actors) can be traced to the 1960s. In fact, the revival of interest in the study of movements, collective action and protest, dates back to that period, and has developed subsequently in the studies discussed in this volume. The movements of 1968 raised, first, questions of a practical nature, relating to the evaluation of emerging forms of social and political participation, and the response to them. These were, in fact, the most widespread mass mobilizations since the 1930s (and the earlier mobilizations were, in many cases, largely antidemocratic in nature). Furthermore, actors engaged in the new conflicts (youth, women, new professional groups and so on) could only partly be characterized in terms of the principal political cleavages of the industrial societies. It was even less appropriate to view these actors in terms of class conflicts, which certainly constituted the principal component of these cleavages.

Movements of that period revealed the difficulties experienced by the two principal theoretical models of interpretation of social conflict – the Marxist model and the structural–functionalist model – in explaining the revival of collective action. Different reactions to these theoretical lacunae developed on each side of the Atlantic. In America, the critique of structural–functionalism emerged within three main perspectives: collective behaviour (in its interactionist version),[1] resource mobilization and political process. From different starting points, each explored the mechanisms which translate various types of structural tension into collective action (the 'how' of collective action: Melucci 1982). In Europe, however, dissatisfaction with Marxism led to the development of the 'new social movements' perspective, concerned with transformations of the structural bases of conflict (the 'why' of action: Melucci 1982). What have conventionally come to be known as the 'American' and the 'European' approaches to the study of movements took shape in this way (Klandermans and Tarrow 1988).

The origins of these developments lie not only in the differences between American and European intellectual traditions – though these are marked. Another factor was the diversity of the objects of study.[2] Although they developed at the same time and were in close contact with each other, student movements at the end of the 1960s and those which followed on from them (from feminist to ecological movements) differed to a certain extent on the two continents. In the United States, organizations born during waves of protest rapidly became pragmatic, and were structured, in most cases, as interest groups (McCarthy and Zald 1987a; Gelb 1989); in contrast, movements which were antagonistic to the system had a strong countercultural character and were – in many cases – explicitly religious in nature (Gerlach and Hine 1970; Roszak 1976; Yinger 1982; Rochford 1985). In Europe, emerging social movements borrowed many characteristics from workers' movements, including a heavy emphasis on ideology (Tarrow 1989a; della Porta 1995).

In this chapter we present the principal analytical perspectives which have given rise to reflection and research into movements and non-institutional collective action since the 1960s. As will become clear from this presentation, these various perspectives are not mutually exclusive but, rather, approach the issue of social movements from different directions. Subsequently, we consider some elements which are useful in defining the concept of social movement in the way it has been employed in sociology and political science. These elements also constitute the basic framework of this book, which is presented at the end of this chapter.

1.1   Theoretical and Research Perspectives on Social Movements[3]

It is possible to identify four currently dominant perspectives in the analysis of collective movements: collective behaviour; resource mobilization; political process; and new social movements. Of course, any attempt to reduce the heterogeneity of positions adopted in a given field of study to a limited number of approaches is subject to a certain unavoidable arbitrariness. Our case is no different. Therefore, before moving on to the analysis of these approaches, three points need to be made. First, these are not homogeneous intellectual currents, and it is possible to distinguish within each a multiplicity of concerns which cannot altogether be assimilated.[4] Second, individual scholars have often borrowed concepts and insights from several theoretical perspectives.[5] Lastly, it is important to bear in mind transformations which have taken place over time in the course of the intellectual development of individual scholars.[6] When we speak of approaches we do not therefore intend to suggest the existence of real 'schools' but rather of a shared attention to a series of theoretical questions which have virtually dominated recent debate. The collective behaviour perspective has drawn the attention of analysts to collective action as an activity concerned with meaning.[7] Resource mobilization stressed the importance of the

rational and strategic components of seemingly irrational phenomena. Questions relating to the importance of the transformations which have occurred in industrial society, and their
implications, can be explored through the new social movements
approach. The political process approach has focused attention
on social movements as new protagonists in the aggregation and
representation of different interests. [8]

1.1.1 Collective behaviour as the producer of cultural change

In the 1960s, the structural-functionalist school – and in particular Neil Smelser (1962) who had dedicated considerable attention to collective behaviour – considered social movements to be
the side-effects of over-rapid social transformation. According to
Smelser, in a system made up of balanced sub-systems, collective behaviour reveals tensions which homoeostatic rebalancing
mechanisms cannot, temporarily, absorb. At times of rapid, large-
scale transformations, the emergence of collective behaviours –
religious cults, secret societies, political sects, economic Utopias
– had a double meaning: reflecting on the one hand the inability
of institutions and social control mechanisms to reproduce social
cohesion; and on the other attempts by society to react to crisis
situations through the development of shared beliefs, on which
to base new foundations for collective solidarity.

If Smelserian theory represented the most organic formulation of the structural-functionalist approach, other approaches
shared his vision of collective action as crisis behaviour. Having
reduced collective phenomena to the summary of individual
behaviours, psychologically derived theories defined social movements as the manifestation of feelings of deprivation experienced
by actors in relation to other social subjects, and of feelings of
aggression resulting from a wide range of frustrated expectations. Phenomena such as the rise of Nazism, the American Civil
War or the movement of black Americans, for example, were
considered to be aggressive reactions resulting either from a
rapid and unexpected end to periods of economic well-being
and of increased expectations on a worldwide scale; or from
status inconsistency mechanisms (Davies 1969; Gurr 1970). From
a somewhat different but compatible point of view, the emergence of political extremism was associated with the spread of
mass society in which social ties – the family, the community –
tended to become fragmented (Kornhauser 1959; Gusfield 1963).

Isolation produced individuals with fewer intellectual, professional and/or political resources, who were particularly vulnerable to the appeal of antidemocractic movements of the right and the left.[9]

As James Coleman recalled (1990: 479), the hypothesis that situations of frustration, rootlessness, deprivation and social crisis automatically produce revolts reduces revolt to an agglomeration of individual behaviours. This perspective ignores the importance of the dynamics by which feelings experienced at the (micro) level of the individual give rise to (macro) phenomena such as social movements or revolutions. There have been numerous responses to these theoretical gaps. The first has developed by symbolic interactionists through the revitalization of the collective behaviour perspective, stating that collective phenomena are not simply the reflection of a social crisis but rather an activity aimed at producing new norms and new solidarities.

Attention to social movements as engines of change, primarily in relation to values systems, began with the work of some scholars of the so-called 'Chicago School', credited with having developed the analysis of collective behaviour as a specialist field within sociology, in the 1920s. The concept of collective *behaviour* – contrasted with that of collective psychology which was then in fashion – indicates the shift of attention from the motivation of individuals to their observable actions (Gallino 1978a). Leading figures in this approach to the study of social movements were Robert E. Park, Ernest W. Burgess and, most importantly, Herbert Blumer. Subsequently, other students of collective behaviour, such as Ralph H. Turner, Lewis M. Killian (Turner and Killian 1987)[10] and Joseph Gusfield (1963), were to make reference to the tenets of the Chicago School, focusing their attention on situations of rapid change in social structures and prescriptions (Blumer 1951). Tendencies towards large-scale organizations, population mobility, technological innovation, mass communications, and the decline of traditional cultural forms were all considered to be emerging conditions pushing individuals to search for new patterns of social organization. Collective behaviour was in fact defined as behaviour concerned with *change* (for example, Blumer 1951: 199), and social movements as both an integral part of the normal functioning of society and the expression of a wider process of transformation.[11]

Rooted in symbolic interactionism, the contemporary school of collective behaviour sees particular relevance in the meaning actors attribute to social structures; and the less structured the situations faced by the individual, the more relevant this aspect appears to be. When existing systems of meaning do not constitute a sufficient basis for social action, new norms emerge, defining the existing situation as unjust and providing a justification for action (Turner and Killian 1987: 259). As an activity born outside pre-established social definitions, collective behaviour is located beyond cultural norms and ordered social relations. The study of collective behaviour thus concentrates on the transformation of institutional behaviours through the action of emergent normative definitions. These definitions appear when the traditional normative structure comes into conflict with a continually evolving situation.[12] Change, in fact, is conceived of as part of the physiological functioning of the system: social movements are accompanied by the emergence of new rules and norms, and represent attempts to transform existing norms.[13]

The genesis of social movements is in the co-existence of contrasting values systems and of groups in conflict with each other. These are regarded as distinctive parts of social life (Killian 1964: 433). Changes in the social structure and in the normative order are interpreted within a process of cultural evolution through which new ideas emerge in the minds of individuals. When traditional norms no longer succeed in providing a satisfactory structure for behaviour, the individual is forced to challenge the social order through various forms of non-conformity. A social movement develops when a feeling of dissatisfaction spreads, and insufficiently flexible institutions are unable to respond.

The sociology of social movements owes many of its insights to students of the collective behaviour school. For the first time, collective movements are defined as meaningful acts, driving often necessary and beneficial social change. Observations of processes of interaction determined by collective action moreover constitute important foundations for those who, in more recent times, have taken on the task of understanding movement dynamics. The emphasis on empirical research has led to experimentation with new techniques, providing through the field observation method, a valid integration of archive data. Lastly and most significantly, the interactionist version of the theory of collective behaviour has stressed the processes of symbolic production and of construction of identity, both of which are essential components of collective behaviour.[14]

It is necessary to say, however, that especially in the 1950s and 1960s, students of collective behaviour tended to classify under the same heading phenomena as diverse as crowds, movements, panic, manias, fashions and so on. Two problems arose from this. On the one hand, although many of them defined movements as purposeful phenomena, students of collective behaviour placed more attention on unexpected dynamics – such as circular reactions – rather than on deliberate organizational strategies or, more generally on strategies devised by actors. On the other hand, focusing on the empirical analysis of behaviour, they are often limited to a description – albeit detailed – of reality, without devoting much attention to the structural origins of conflicts which subsequently well up in particular movements. Analyses of collective action as rational conduct address the former problem; and the new social movements deal with the latter.

1.1.2   Collective mobilization as rational action

While the interactionist version of the collective behaviour school emphasized the role of social movements in the construction of new values and meaning, functionalist theories of collective behaviour also came under fire for regarding collective movements as irrational actors, and collective action as the exclusive product of malfunctions of the social system or, more specifically, of its integrative apparatus. Action thus came to be devalued as reactive behaviour, incapable of strategic rationality, isolated from the conflicts it sought to express. In deliberate contrast to this way of conceptualizing social movements, American sociologists initiated, in the 1970s, a current of research centred on the analysis of processes by which the resources necessary for collective action are mobilized. In their view, collective movements constitute an extension of the conventional forms of political action; the actors engage in this act in a rational way, following their interests; organizations and movement 'entrepreneurs' have an essential role in the mobilization of collective resources on which action is founded. Movements are therefore part of the normal political process. Stressing the external obstacles and incentives, numerous pieces of research have examined the variety of resources to be mobilized, the links which social movements have with their allies, the tactics used by society to control or incorporate collective action, and its results. The basic questions which they seek to answer relate to the evaluation of costs and benefits of participation in social movement organizations.

In early theories related to this issue, Mayer Zald (Zald and Ash 1966; McCarthy and Zald 1987a, 1987b), Anthony Oberschall

(1973; 1978) and Charles Tilly (1978) defined collective movement as a rational, purposeful and organized action. Protest actions derive, according to this perspective, from a calculation of the costs and benefits, influenced by the presence of resources – in particular by organization and by the strategic interactions necessary for the development of a social movement. In a historical situation in which feelings of unease, differences of opinion, conflicts of interest and opposing ideologies are always present, the emergence of collective action cannot be explained simply as having been caused by these elements. It is not enough to discover the existence of tensions and structural conflicts, but necessary also to study the conditions which enable discontent to be transformed into mobilization. The capacity for mobilization depends either on the material resources (work, money, concrete benefits, services) or on the non-material resources (authority, moral engagement, faith, friendship) available to the group. These resources are distributed across multiple objectives according to a rational calculation of costs and benefits. Beyond the existence of tensions, mobilization derives from the way in which social movements are able to organize discontent, reduce the costs of action, utilize and create solidarity networks, share incentives among members, and achieve external consensus. The type and nature of the resources available explain the tactical choices made by movements and the consequences of collective action on the social and political system. In the analysis of a group's internal resources, attention has focused above all on forms of organization and mobilization of material and symbolic resources, such as moral engagement (Tillock and Morrison 1979) and solidarity (Fireman and Gamson 1979).

The existence of solidarity networks calls once again into question the hypothesis which was, at the time, widespread, namely, that movement recruits are mainly isolated and rootless individuals who seek to immerse themselves in the mass as a surrogate for their social marginalization. According to rational approaches, mobilization can thus be explained as being more than the gratification of pursuing a collective good; it also promotes the existence of horizontal solidarity links, within the collective, and vertical links, integrating different collectives. On the basis of a wide range of empirical research, one can therefore foresee that 'participants in popular disturbances and activists in opposition organizations will be recruited primarily from previously active and relatively well-integrated individuals within the collectivity, whereas socially isolated, atomized, and uprooted individuals will be underrepresented, at least until the movement has become substantial' (Oberschall 1973: 135).

This leads us to concentrate our attention on the ways in which these collective actors operate, on the methods they adopt to acquire resources and mobilize support, both within and outwith their adherents' group. While viewing collective movements as agents of change, along the lines of the collective behaviour approach, scholars of resource mobilization consider them also to be protagonists in the normal workings of the system. The definition of social movements as conscious actors making *rational choices* is, therefore, among the most important innovations of the resource mobilization approach. This characterization of social movements has, however, been the target of several criticisms. It has been charged with indifference to the structural sources of conflict and the specific stakes for the control of which social actors mobilize (Melucci 1982; Piven and Cloward 1992). Its emphasis on the resources controlled by a few political entrepreneurs, at the cost of overlooking the self-organization potential by the most dispossessed social groups, has also been criticized (Piven and Cloward 1992). Finally, it has been noted that in its explanation of collective action this approach overdoes the rationality of collective action, not taking the role of emotions adequately into account (Marx Ferree 1992; Taylor and Whittier 1995).

1.1.3 Protest and political system

A rational view of collective action is also found in the perspective which we have defined as 'political process'. However, this approach pays more systematic attention to the political and institutional environment in which social movements operate. The central focus of 'political process' theories is the relationship between institutional political actors and protest. In challenging a given political order, social movements interact with actors who enjoy a consolidated position in such an order.[15] The concept which has had the greatest success in defining the properties of the external environment, relevant to the development of social movements is that of 'political opportunity structure'. Peter Eisinger (1973) used this concept in a comparison of the results of protest in different American cities, focusing on the degree of openness (or closedness) of the local political system. Other empirical research indicated important new variables, such as electoral instability (Piven and Cloward 1977), the availability of influential allies (Gamson 1990 [1975]) and tolerance for protest among the elite (Jenkins and Perrow 1977). Sidney Tarrow integrated these empirical observations into a theoretical framework for his study of protest cycles in Italy, singling out the degree of openness or closure of formal political access, the degree of stability or instability of political alignments, the availability and strategic posture of potential allies (1983: 28) and political conflicts between and within elites (1989a: 35).

To these variables have been added others, relating to the institutional conditions which regulate agenda-setting and decision-making processes. Characteristics relating to the functional division of power and also to geographical decentralization have been analysed in order to understand the origins of protest and the forms it has taken. In general, the aim has been to observe which stable or 'mobile' characteristics of the political system influence the growth of less institutionalized political action in the course of what are defined as protest cycles (Tarrow 1989a), as well as the forms which these actions take in different historical contexts (Tilly 1978). The comparison between different political systems (Kitschelt 1986; della Porta 1995; Kriesi et al. 1995; Rucht 1994) has enabled the central theme of relationships between social movements and the institutional political system to be studied in depth.

The 'political process' approach succeeded in shifting attention towards interactions between new and traditional actors, and between less conventional forms of action and institutionalized systems of interest representation. In this way, it is no longer possible to define movements in a prejudicial sense as phenomena which are, of necessity, marginal and anti-institutional, expressions of disfunctions of the system. A more fruitful route towards the interpretation of the political dimension of contemporary movements has been established.

One should not ignore, however, some persisting areas of difficulty. On the one hand, supporters of this perspective continue to debate delicate problems such as the choice of the most appropriate indicators to measure complex institutional phenomena. On the other hand, this line of thinking has been criticized externally for its tendency to adopt a kind of 'political reductionism' (Melucci 1987, 1989). In effect, theorists of political process have paid little attention to the fact that many contemporary movements (of youth, women, homosexuals or minority ethnic groups) seem to have developed within a political context and in a climate of cultural innovation at the same time (Melucci 1984a; Rupp and Taylor 1987; Canciani and De La Pierre 1993). Lastly – as we have already noted when introducing resource mobilization theories – rationalist approaches to the study of collective action have tended to neglect the structural origins of protest. Other scholars, associated with the new movements approach, have explored this area.

1.1.4 New movements for new conflicts

The response of European social sciences to the rise of the movements of the 1960s and the 1970s was a critique of the Marxist models of interpretation of social conflict. Such models have encountered a number of problems in explaining recent developments. First, the social transformations which occurred after the end of the Second World War put the centrality of the capital–labour conflict into question. The widening of access to higher education or the entry *en masse* of women into the labour market had created new structural possibilities for conflict, and increased the relevance of social stratification criteria – such as gender – which were not based on control of economic resources. Problems posed by Marxist interpretations did not, however, relate only to doubts about the continued existence of the working class in post-industrial society: they concerned also the logic of the explanatory model. The deterministic element of the Marxist tradition – the conviction that the evolution of social and political conflicts was conditioned largely by the level of development of productive forces and by the dynamic of class relations – was rejected, as was the tendency, particularly strong among orthodox Marxists, to deny the multiplicity of concerns and conflicts within real movements, and to construct, in preference, outlandish images of movements as homogeneous actors with a high level of strategic ability (for a critique: Touraine 1977, 1981). Certainly, scholars of the new movements were not the only ones to be aware of these problems. The same difficulties had been raised by those who had studied class action from a non-economistic position, when considering an 'old' class actor such as the workers' movement (Thompson 1963). Nevertheless, scholars associated with the 'new social movements'[16] made a decisive contribution to the development of the discussion of these issues.

Scholars of new movements agreed that conflict among the industrial classes is of decreasing relevance, and similarly that representation of movements as largely homogeneous subjects is no longer feasible. However, there were differences of emphasis in relation to the possibility of identifying the new central conflict which would characterise the model of the emerging society, defined at times as 'post-industrial', 'post-Fordist', 'technocratic' or 'programmed'. An influential exponent of this approach, Alain Touraine, was the most explicit in upholding this position: 'Social movements are not a marginal rejection of order, they are the central forces fighting one against the other to control the production of society by itself and the action of classes for the shaping of historicity' (Touraine 1981: 29). In the industrial society, the ruling class and the popular class oppose each other, as they did in the agrarian and the mercantile societies, and as they will do, according to Touraine, in the programmed society, where new social classes will replace capitalists and the working class as the central actors of the conflict.[17]

The break between movements of the industrial society and new movements was also stressed in the 1980s by the German sociologist Claus Offe (1985). In his view, movements develop a fundamental, metapolitical critique of the social order and of representative democracy, challenging institutional assumptions regarding conventional ways of 'doing politics', in the name of a radical democracy. Among the principal innovations of the new movements, in contrast with the workers' movement, are a critical ideology in relation to modernism and progress; decentralized and participatory organizational structures; defence of interpersonal solidarity against the great bureaucracies; and the reclamation of autonomous spaces, rather than material advantages. New social movements are characterized, in Offe's view, by an open, fluid organization, an inclusive and non-ideological participation, and greater attention to social than to economic transformations.

Another contribution to the definition of the characteristics of new movements in the programmed society has been made by Alberto Melucci (1982, 1989, 1996). Drawing upon the image proposed by Jürgen Habermas of a colonization of lifeworlds, Melucci described contemporary societies as highly differentiated systems, which invest increasingly in the creation of individual autonomous centres of action, at the same time as requiring closer integration, extending control over the motives for human action. In his view, new social movements try to oppose the intrusion of the state and the market into social life, reclaiming the individual's identity, and the right to determine his or her private and affective life, against the omnipresent and comprehensive manipulation of the system. Unlike the workers' movement, new social movements do not, in Melucci's view, limit themselves to seeking material gain, but challenge the diffuse notions of politics and of society themselves. New actors do not, therefore, ask for an increase in state intervention, to guarantee security and well-being, but resist the expansion of political-administrative intervention in daily life and defend personal autonomy.

This approach has several merits. First, it draws attention to the structural determinants of protest, re-evaluating the importance of conflict. Compared with Marxism, the theoreticians of new social movements have two specific advantages: they place importance once again on the actor; and they have the ability to capture the innovative characteristics of movements which no longer define themselves principally in relation to the system of production. Nor should the existence of the notable area of research largely inspired by their original hypotheses be ignored (Maheu 1995). The main problem which this approach leaves unresolved is the analysis of mechanisms which lead from conflict to action (with the exception of Melucci's work: 1984a, 1988, 1996). Furthermore, there is the risk of positing certain coincidental traits – in particular the illustration of novel elements among actors in new collective movements – as absolutes.[18] This has been a particularly strong element of the critique put forward by those who have studied social movements primarily as political processes (Rootes 1992; Rüdig 1990; Koopmans 1995; Tarrow 1994; della Porta 1996a: ch. 1).

1.2 What are Social Movements? Towards the Integration of the European and American Traditions[19]

Stimulated by empirical phenomena which were not homogeneous, the four perspectives discussed above have boosted research on social movements. If, at the end of the 1940s the 'crudely descriptive level of understanding and a relative lack of theory' (Strauss 1947: 352) was criticized, and, in the 1960s, the fact that 'in the study of social changes, social movements have received relatively little emphasis' (Killian 1964: 426) was a matter for complaint, by the mid-1970s, research into collective action was considered rather to be 'one of the most vigorous areas of sociology' (Marx and Wood 1975). At the end of the 1980s, commentators talked of 'an explosion, in the last ten years, of theoretical and empirical writings on social movements and collective action', underlining the way in which 'these writings have stimulated debate, a new school of thought, defence of old schools of thought and a deepening theoretical awareness. Furthermore, important research into social movements has been carried out by various disciplines, including sociology, political science, history, economics and communication sciences' (Morris and Herring 1987: 138; see also Rucht 1991a).

The expansion of the field of study has corresponded with an intensification in contacts between American and European scholars. Opportunities to compare the merits and the limitations of the various paradigms have increased, and attempts to meld different theoretic perspectives into a new synthesis have multiplied (Klandermans et al. 1988; Eyerman and Jamison 1991; Tarrow 1994; Melucci 1996; for a sceptical view, Cohen 1985). If it is still premature to speak of an integrated theory of social movements, it is, however, possible to note that scholars from varying theoretical and territorial backgrounds, share a concern for at least four characteristic aspects of movements:

1   *Informal interaction networks*. Movements may be conceived of as informal interaction networks between a plurality of individuals, groups and/or organizations. The characteristics of these networks may range from the very loose and dispersed links described by Gerlach and Hine (1970) in their seminal book, to the tightly clustered networks which facilitate adhesion to terrorist organizations (della Porta 1988). Such networks promote the circulation of essential resources for action (information, expertise, material resources) as well as of broader systems of meaning. Thus, networks contribute both to creating the preconditions for mobilization and to providing the proper setting for the elaboration of specific world views and lifestyles.

2   *Shared beliefs and solidarity*. To be considered a social movement, an interacting collectivity requires a shared set of beliefs and a sense of belonging. Indeed, social movements condition and help constitute both new orientations on existing issues and also the rise of new public issues, in so far as they contribute to 'the existence of a vocabulary and an opening of ideas and actions which in the past was either unknown or unthinkable' (Gusfield 1981: 325). The process of symbolic redefinition of what is real and what is possible is linked to the emergence of collective identities, as a shared definition of a collective actor. Because of the development of collective representation and shared feelings, it has become clear that 'elements which have all been present for some time, without, however, having been combined,

suddenly become part of a well-integrated movement' (Kriesi 1988a: 367).[20] New collective identities and value systems may persist even when public activities, demonstrations and the like are not taking place, thus providing some continuity for the movement over time (Melucci 1989; Turner and Killian 1987).

3 *Collective action focusing on conflicts.* Social movement actors are engaged in political and/or cultural conflicts, meant to promote or oppose social change at either the systemic or non-systemic level. By conflict we mean an oppositional relationship between actors who seek control of the same stake. In order for social conflict to occur, it is necessary, first, that this is defined as a shared field, with actors who perceive each other as different, but who, at the same time, are linked by reference to interests and values which both sides see as important, or as high stakes desired by two or more adversaries (Touraine 1981: 80–4). Furthermore, it is necessary that interaction should lead, on the part of each of the actors involved, to negative claims, or demands which, if realized, would damage the interests of the other actors, not to mention threats of sanctions explicitly directed at the latter.

4 *Use of protest.* Until the early 1970s debates on social movements were dominated by considerable emphasis on the non-institutionalized nature of their behaviour (Alberoni 1984). Even now, the idea that social movements may be distinguished from other political actors because of their adoption of 'unusual' patterns of political behaviour is still very popular. Several scholars maintain that the fundamental distinction between movements and other social and political actors is to be found in the contrast between conventional styles of political participation (such as voting or lobbying political representatives) and public protest (Rucht 1990a). Although public protest plays only a marginal role in movements concerned with personal and cultural change, it is undoubtedly a distinctive feature of political movements, on which we shall largely focus in this book. It is more debatable, perhaps, whether protest can still be considered an 'unconventional' activity, rather than explicitly violent or 'confrontational'. Effectively, various forms of political protest have become, to an increasing degree, part of the consolidated repertoire of collective action, at least in western democracies. Nor does it seem possible to consider violence as a distinctive trait of movements taken as a whole. It seems more useful, rather, to look at the relevance of violent and radical tactics in order to differentiate between different types of movement or different phases in the life of one movement.

The categories which we have just reviewed can help us to define the field of phenomena which we intend to consider in this book. We will consider social movements – and, in particular, their political component – as (1) informal networks, based (2) on shared beliefs and solidarity, which mobilize about (3) conflictual issues, through (4) the frequent use of various forms of protest. These elements will enable us to distinguish social movements from various forms of collective action which are more structured and which take on the form of parties, interest groups or religious sects, as well as single protest events or ad hoc political coalitions.

1.2.1   Social movements versus political or religious organizations

Social movements, political parties and interest groups are often compared with each other, on the assumption that they all embody different styles of political organization (for example, Wilson 1973). At times, they are identified with religious sects and cults (for example, Robbins 1988). However, if the definition we propose here is correct, the difference between social movements and these and other organizations does not consist primarily of differences in organizational characteristics or patterns of behaviour, but of the fact that social movements are not organizations, not even of a peculiar kind (Tilly 1988 and Oliver 1989). They are networks of interaction between different actors which may either include formal organizations or not, depending on shifting circumstances. As a consequence, a single organization, whatever its dominant traits, is not a social movement. Of course it may be part of one, but the two are not identical, as they reflect different organizational principles.

Indeed, many influential scholars in the field continue to use the term 'social movement' to mean both networks of interaction and specific organizations: citizens' rights groups like Common Cause, environmental organizations like the Sierra Club, or even religious sects like Nichiren Shoshu (McAdam et al. 1988: 695). Yet, this overlap is a source of analytical confusion, in so far as it fosters the application to social movement analysis of concepts borrowed from organizational theory, concepts that only partially fit the looser structure of social movements. As Pamela Oliver puts it: 'all too often we speak of movement strategy, tactics, leadership, membership, recruitment, division of labor, success and failure – terms which strictly apply only to coherent decision-making entities (that is, organizations or groups), not to crowds, collectivities, or whole social movements' (1989: 4).

Talking of Common Cause or the Sierra Club or Nichiren Shoshu as 'social movements' leads one to formulate concepts like 'professional social movement' (McCarthy and Zald 1987a) or 'single-organization movements' (Turner and Killian 1987: 369–70) to emphasize the obvious differences between these cases and the nature of social movements as informal networks. But qualifying Common Cause as a 'professional social movement' does not add very much to the understanding of it, that cannot be provided by concepts like 'public interest group' (see, among others, Etzioni 1985). Similarly, a religious organization like Nichiren Shoshu or Hare Krishna may be conveniently analysed as a 'sect'. This concept takes into account the greater organizational rigidity and the more hierarchical structure that these organizations display by comparison with social movement networks (see Robbins 1988: 150–5). It also recognizes the higher degree of social control that is exerted over members. In contrast, what both 'public interest group' and 'sect' do not really capture are the interaction processes through which actors with different identities and orientations come to elaborate a shared system of beliefs and a sense of belonging, which exceeds by far the boundaries of any single group or organization, while maintaining at the same time their specificity and distinctive traits.

The instability of the relationship between organizational and movement identities means that movements are by definition fluid phenomena. In the formation and consolidation phases, a sense of collective belonging prevails on links of solidarity and loyalty which can exist between individuals and specific groups or associations. A movement tends to burn out when organizational identities come to dominate once more, or when 'feeling part of it' refers primarily to one's organization and its components, rather than to a broader collective with blurred boundaries.

To shift the emphasis from single organizations to informal networks allows us, furthermore, to appreciate more fully the space reserved for individuals within movements. Individual participation is essential for movements, and one of their characteristics is, indeed, the sense of being involved in a collective endeavour – without having automatically to belong to a specific organization. Strictly speaking, social movements do not have members, but participants.[21] The participation of the individual, detached from specific organizational allegiances is not necessarily limited to single protest events. It can also develop within committees or working groups, or else in public meetings.[22] Alternatively (when the possibility arises) one may support a movement by promoting its ideas and its point of view among institutions, other political actors, or the media. However, the existence of a range of possible ways of becoming involved means that the membership of movements can never be reduced to a single act of adhesion. It consists, rather, of a series of differentiated acts, which, taken together, reinforce the feeling of belonging and of identity (see also Gusfield 1994: 62).

If we accept that social movements are analytically different from social movement organizations we have also to redefine our notion of what is part and what is not part of a movement. Indeed, any organization which fulfils the requirements we have indicated (interactions with other actors, conflict, collective identity, and recourse to protest) may be considered part of a given movement. This may also hold for bureaucratic interest groups, and even political parties. By saying that political parties may be part of social movements we do not mean to suggest that 'social movements' is a broader theoretical category in which several type of organizations (interest groups, community groups, political parties and so forth) are represented as many sub-types. Rather, we suggest that under certain and specific conditions some political party may feel itself to be part of a movement and be recognized as such both by other actors in the movement and by the general public. This is likely to be the exception rather than the rule, and to be largely restricted to parties whose origins lie in social movements, such as the green parties (Kitschelt 1989; Richardson and Rootes 1994).

One could reasonably object that no matter how strong their identification with a movement, political parties actually perform specific functions at the level of interest representation and in this sense are different from social movements. That differences exist at the functional level is beyond question. Yet, the main peculiarity of social movements does not consist of their specific way of performing the function of interest representation. Of course, their networks of interaction favour the formulation of demands, the promotion of mobilization campaigns and the elaboration and diffusion of beliefs and collective identities. These factors all, in turn, contribute to redefining the cultural and political setting in which the action of interest representation takes place. However, when we focus on the function of interest representation in strict terms, we do not look at the way 'the movement' performs this function. We look at the way different specific social movement organizations do this. Whether or not they decide to include participation in elections within their repertoire of action is dependent upon several factors including external opportunities, tactical and/or ideological considerations and their links to other actors in the movement. The mere fact that they decide to do so, however, will not automatically exclude them from the movement. Rather, they will be part of two different systems of action (the party system and the social movement system), where they will play different roles. The way such roles are actually shaped will constitute a crucial area of investigation (Kitschelt 1989).

1.2.2   Social movements, protest events, coalitions

If social movements do not coincide with organizations, neither do they coincide with other types of informal interaction. In particular, social movements differ from both loosely structured protest events and political coalitions. Under what conditions may a protest against the construction of a motorway run by informal citizens' action groups, a 'wildcat' strike for higher wages in a firm or a demonstration for better nursing facilities in a neighbourhood be considered part of a social movement? And when are they merely simple, isolated 'protest events'?

The aspect which enables us to discriminate is the presence of a vision of the world and of a collective identity which permit participants in various protest events to place their action in a wider perspective. In order to be able to speak of social movements it is necessary that single episodes are perceived as components of a longer-lasting action, rather than discrete events; and that those who are engaged feel linked by ties of solidarity and of ideal communion with protagonists of other analogous mobilizations. The course of the movement for the control of toxic waste in the United States provides a good example of the importance of cultural and symbolic elaboration in the evolution of collective action. From a series of initiatives which developed from a local base and in relation to specific goals such as blocking the construction of waste disposal plants in particular areas, the movement gradually developed into a collective force with a national base, concerned with numerous aspects of the relationship between nature and society, and with a much more sophisticated cultural elaboration (Szasz 1994: 69–99).

The presence of identities also means that a sense of collective belonging can be maintained even after a specific initiative or a particular campaign has come to an end. The persistence of these feelings will have at least two important consequences. First, it will make the revival of mobilization in relation to the same goals easier, whenever favourable conditions recur. Movements often oscillate between brief phases of intense public activity and long 'latent' periods (Melucci 1984b; Taylor 1989), in which activities involving inner reflection and intellectual development prevail. Ties of faith and solidarity activated in the European anti-nuclear movements during the mobilizations of the second half of the 1970s, for example, represented the base on which a new wave of protests gathered momentum in the wake of the Chernobyl incident in 1986 (Flam 1994d). Second, representations of the world and collective identities which developed in a certain period can also facilitate, through a gradual transformation, the development of new movements and new solidarities. For example, the close relationship existing in several countries between movements of the new left of the early 1970s and successive political ecology movements has been noted on a number of occasions (Diani 1988, 1995a; Dalton 1994).

Reference to other examples of informal networks of collective action, such as coalitions,[23] clarifies why collective identity is such a crucial feature of social movements. Coalitions share some features with social movements, in so far as they imply the existence of conflict and of collective activity. However, interaction and coordination between different actors occur mostly at an instrumental level, as actors try to maximize their outcomes by establishing alliances with other actors. In contrast to social movements,[24] interaction in coalitions does not result necessarily in the emergence of collective identities, nor does it imply necessarily any sort of continuity beyond the limits of the specific conflictual situation, let alone a global redefinition of the issues at stake. For these reasons, it is impossible to reduce movements to purely instrumental coalitions (Pakulski 1988).

Industrial action in countries like Italy, where there are several competing trade unions, illustrates the point well. The defence of workers' interests is usually undertaken by single organizations, which may or may not form alliances, but which, fundamentally, maintain unchanged their own identities. These identities have priority over identification with a broader workers' movement. For several years after 1968, however, the sense of belonging to the new workers' movement became more important than pre-existing loyalties to specific organizations (Pizzorno et al. 1978; Regalia et al. 1978).

1.3   The Structure of This Book

In this chapter we have, first of all, briefly presented the main issues explored in four theoretical perspectives which developed (or emerged) from the 1960s onwards in response to the deficiencies of the Marxist and functionalist traditions: the reformulation of the 'collective behaviour' approach in an interactionist perspective; the rationalist line, concentrating on a vision of collective action as strategic action; the perspective of the 'new social movements'; and the approach which focuses on political process. In these theoretical perspectives we have then tried to trace elements which are useful in defining the specificity of social movements in relation to other more or less structured forms of collective action. We have then identified four levels of analysis which we hold to be fundamental for the study of movements: the conflicts of which they are protagonists, and their structural bases; the production of shared beliefs and collective identities; organizations and social networks; and political opportunities for protest to develop. The structure of this book reflects our interest in these processes.

In speaking of the structural bases of contemporary movements we refer, on the one hand, to mechanisms by which new social groups and new interests take shape, while other groups and interests which previously held centre stage see their relevance declining; and on the other, to the impact which structural changes such as the growth of public welfare and the expansion of higher education have on forms of political participation and, in particular, on non-institutional participation. In the next chapter, we will discuss a few interpretations of recent changes in forms of social conflict.

There follow two chapters dedicated to symbolic production. Chapter 3 shows how cultural elaboration facilitates the definition of social problems as the product of asymmetries of power and conflicts of interest, and the identification of their causes in social and political factors which are subject to human intervention. In the fourth chapter, we show how the creation and reinforcement of symbols represents also the base for the development of feelings of identity and solidarity, without which collective action cannot take place.

A third important level of analysis consists of organizational factors which allow both the production of meaning and the mobilization of resources necessary for action. We take into consideration both informal networking and the more structured component of the organizational dimension, crystallized in more stable group forms. Chapter 5 deals in particular with the analysis of the networks – interpersonal as well as interorganizational – in which individuals and organizations active in a movement are rooted. Chapter 6 concentrates on certain properties of movement organizations, discussing the factors – internal and external – which influence the adoption of certain organizational models, and the consequences which follow for mobilization.

The fourth crucial dimension is the interaction between movements and the political system. Movements represent innovative, sometimes radical, elements both in the way in which the political system works, and in its very structure. The characteristics of the political system offer or deny essential opportunities for the development of collective action. It is, furthermore in reference principally, if not exclusively, to the political system that it becomes possible to value the impact of protest movements and their consequences in the medium term. In chapter 7, we reconstruct some of the properties of protest cycles which have marked the history of recent decades, and the repertoires of collective action which were formed within these. In chapter 8, we present certain aspects of the relationship between the configurations of political opportunities and the development of mobilization. In chapter 9 we discuss, finally, the problem of the effects of movements. While the centre of our analysis is represented by political change, we will try, however, to pay attention also to the impact of movements on the social and cultural spheres.

The issues with which we are concerned are undoubtedly central to the analysis of collective action. Our treatment, however, is anything but comprehensive. First, the studies to which we refer were largely inspired, as has already been noted, by the experience of 'new movements', or, in other words, by mobilizations which were not directly reducible to the principal political divisions of contemporary society, or tied to the emergence of the industrial society and to the construction of the nation state. In our analysis, there is no lack of reference to work dedicated to working-class conflict or, even more obviously, to ethno-nationalist movements, or to mobilizations which developed in the last century, but we focus on contributions which have analysed phenomena such as nationalism (Johnston 1991a; Jenson 1995) or working-class solidarity in America (Fantasia 1988) by borrowing concepts from analysts of 'new' movements; or which have become essential reading for all those concerned generally with collective action (such as Tilly 1978). We are not concerned in any systematic way with the enormous body of literature dedicated to collective phenomena which are somehow related to 'new' social movements.[25]

More generally, our work is not a reconstruction of the 'state of the art' in this field, or capable of recognizing the worth of all significant contributions in this line of research.[26] It is, rather, an attempt to present certain central problems of recent debates. We have chosen, in addition to essential studies relating to the analysis of movements, a selection of other works which, for various reasons we feel to be useful illustrations of our line of argument. From this point of view, we have paid particular, though not exclusive, attention to studies which have combined theoretical analysis and empirical research (understood in its widest and most inclusive sense: Diani and Eyerman 1992). Among the best-known works we have concentrated on those which, to some extent, have broken with the tradition of analysis and preceding research. In order to make our treatment more coherent, we have chosen, moreover, to introduce the issues covered by each chapter with examples drawn from a particular movement, focusing our attention in a selective way on the relevant research.

Several reasons forced us to devote only scattered attention to many perspectives which nevertheless contained indications of considerable interest to the questions we posed. These are partly practical, from lack of space, to our difficulty in controlling a particularly extensive literature. However they are also partly theoretical. They reflect the heterogeneity of the conceptual instruments with which movements and collective action have been analysed up to now. The range of social and political contexts in which movements develop makes it even more problematic to elaborate models which are capable of dealing with such a high level of variation among 'local' conditions for action. It is certainly true that overcoming these difficulties represents, for students of movements, a central concern (McAdam et al. 1996); but to incorporate all these lines of thinking would have required an effort of translating concepts and theories into a homogeneous language which seemed beyond our possibilities (or at least, our current possibilities, we might optimistically argue).

2

Social Movements and Structural Changes

Since the 1970s, conflicts relating to environmental issues have been among the principal examples of transformations in the course of collective action. According to some estimates, protests on environmental and nuclear energy issues have amounted to 24 per cent of the total protest activities (including those by labour and nationalist movements) promoted in Germany between 1975 and 1989, 18 per cent in Switzerland, 17 per cent in France, and 13 per cent in the Netherlands (Kriesi et al. 1995: 20; see also Rüdig 1990). The strength of environmental organizations has dramatically increased throughout the 1980s: in the UK, members of Friends of Earth have risen by 533 per cent (18,000 to 114,000) between 1981 and 1991; members of Greenpeace by 1,260 per cent (30,000 to 408,000); members of the Royal Society for the Protection of Birds by 93 per cent (441,000 to 852,000). Rates of growth in the USA have been similarly impressive, with Greenpeace jumping to 2,350,000 from 800,000 (up 194 per cent) and the Sierra Club registering an even higher increase (181,000 to 630,000, up 248 per cent) (Jordan and Maloney 1997: 12). Data about other European countries confirm this trend (van der Heijden et al. 1992; Dalton 1994; Diani 1995; Kriesi 1996). Despite a certain degree of volatility in their electoral support, Green parties have emerged and consolidated in most western democracies as well as in other parts of the globe (Richardson and Rootes 1994). This also confirms the status of environmental actors among the protagonists in the politics of the final years of the twentieth century.

Many different approaches have underlined the innovative qualities of environmental movements. Here, we are primarily interested in recalling the difficulty of analysing environmentalist conflicts in terms of class or national divisions and allegiances, which so forcefully characterized politics up until the 1960s. When a new wave of environmental activism emerged in the 1970s, along with other movements on issues such as peace, women's and human rights, it was difficult for political analysts to relate it directly to previously dominant conflicts.[1] Such difficulty has largely persisted to date. First, it has not been easy to identify the social base of the actors who are protagonists in the conflict. Both opinion polls and analyses of specific episodes during the course of mobilization have revealed the considerable diversity of views among supporters of ecological initiatives. Sympathizers and activists have come, in fact, from the new middle classes employed in intellectual professions and in social services, from the traditional middle class and the rural and urban bourgeoisie, and from the working class (even if support from this last group has been more limited). It has been equally difficult to identify the movement's adversaries. Attacks on industry have certainly been a recurring element, but this has been in relation to an industrial philosophy aimed at limitless growth rather than to the legitimacy of the control which the industrial sector exercised over the productive process; furthermore, ecologists' criticism has often included the working class and its organizations, seen as sharing with the business sector a purely quantitative vision of development.

One further problem for analysis concerns the fact that the goals pursued by these movements may not automatically be associated with specific socio-economic groups or strata. Environmental movements often reflect the common interest in public goods (Olson 1963) such as air quality and reduction of traffic: 'public', because no class or social category can monopolize access to them, and enjoy them exclusively. In the case of animal rights, indeed, mobilization has developed to protect 'non-human' beings.

Environmental interests and conflicts have also proved difficult to relate to the other major structural basis of political conflict in industrial society, the nation state. Environmental problems by definition tend to exceed the boundaries of single states and take, rather, the form of global, transnational issues (as for example in the case of global warming, acid rain, toxic waste disposal and so on: Porter and Brown 1991; Taylor 1995; Yearley 1996). When they can be associated to a specific territory, this is usually quite localized and rarely overlaps with the state (the most obvious examples being local populations' resistance to projects perceived as environmentally threatening, from nuclear power plants to dams, roads and quarries: Rüdig 1990; Taylor 1995). Although ethno-nationalist and regional autonomy movements have often addressed ecological concerns (Barcena et al. 1995; Dawson 1996), and despite the linkages between nineteenth-century nationalism and romanticist environmentalism (Worster 1994), the relationship between environmentalism and the nation state has been in the last decades far from straightforward.

A further reason why environmentalism has not fitted traditional models of political conflict has been the intersection between private and public experiences that involvement in environmental politics has generated. Since its revival in the 1960s, and with increasing vigour since the early 1980s, the growth of environmentalism as a political phenomenon has gone along with a parallel development of environmentalism as a peculiar lifestyle. Sometimes, this has assumed the form of countercultural experiences, either conducted on a private basis, through the adoption of strict ecological lifestyles, or on a collective basis, such as in the agricultural communes which spread across Europe between the 1960s and the 1970s. More often, especially recently, this has taken a less demanding form, implying the adoption of some form of eco-friendly personal behaviour, or even the mere conversion to some form of green consumerism (Elkington and Hailes 1988; Donati 1989; Dobson 1990: ch. 3; Yearley 1991: ch. 3; Lalli 1995). In all cases, the view of politics as a public activity with hardly any direct bearing on private conduct, incorporated within the dominant framework of both liberal democratic and socialist politics, has been called into question.

Environmentalism represents a useful starting point for the discussion of the relationship between changes in the social structure and collective action. Structural interpretations of social movements in industrial society have normally associated them with two fundamental processes. The first relates to the emergence of the market, the second to the creation of the nation state and of modern citizenship (Rokkan 1982; Lipset and Rokkan 1967; Giddens 1990). Initially, the advent of the market economy resulted in the centrality of conflicts between capital and labour.

However, it also produced another cleavage, opposing urban and agrarian social sectors. The construction of nation states can be seen, on the one hand, in terms of territorially based conflicts which set the central areas of new states against peripheral areas; on the other hand, in terms of conflicts between the social bloc recognized in the formation of new states and that which denied its legitimacy, supporting instead the temporal power of ecclesiastical structures (church–state conflict).

The principal conflicts which have characterized contemporary society have developed around these tensions: the consolidation of cleavages and their institutionalization have produced for political systems (and, in particular, their party systems) a configuration which has remained stable until the last decades of the twentieth century (Rokkan 1982; Bartolini and Mair 1990). The general relevance of the capital–labour cleavage has been, in various countries, supplemented by others. These have sometimes referred to the territorial dimension of conflicts. For example, in Belgium, opposition between Flemish and Francophone regions has reached the stage where the party political system has segmented along ethno-territorial lines. At other times, politics has been shaped by conflicts between the power of the church and the state, for example in Italy, with the presence of a strongly denominational party such as the Christian Democracts. Under yet again different circumstances, the major cleavage has run between urban and rural interests. In Scandinavia, specific agrarian parties have occupied a central position, in terms of political allegiances, until recent times.[2]

Political cleavages have traditionally been associated with a model of collective action in which actors: (1) fought against each other in order to protect material or political interests relating to the control either of economic activity or of the state; and (2) defined themselves (as members of a class, a faction or a national group) in relation to these interests. How should we interpret the rise of the ecology movement and others which, in contrast to their working-class and nationalist predecessors, seem to lack a specific social base and to be largely indifferent to the goal of conquering the power of the state? Is it possible to interpret these phenomena as evidence of the weakening of the link between social structure and forms of collective action? Or are we, more simply, confronting social transformations capable of creating space for new kinds of conflicts which, however, have their own structural base? In the pages which follow, we shall explore these issues.

Social change may affect the charateristics of social conflict and collective action in three ways at least. It may facilitate the emergence of new social groups with a specific structural location and potential specific interests, and/or reduce the importance of existing ones, as the shift from agriculture to industry and then to the service sector suggests. It may also increase the amount of social resources which are conducive to participation in collective action, such as education, and/or facilitate the articulation of interests. Finally, it may modify patterns of relationships between people, and therefore again facilitate or constrain the development of solidarity between people engaged in similar activities: the fragmentation of industrial activities has played against workers' capacity to act as a class, while women's increasing access to higher education and the job market has facilitated the development of new ties between them, and their emergence as a new collective actor.

In the light of these criteria, we shall focus on three types of transformation which have interested western societies since the Second World War: in the context of production, in the role of the state, and in the relationship between private and public spheres. We shall make no attempt to provide an adequate coverage of the innumerable processes which make up what is usually regarded as the transition to post-industrial (or postmodern, disorganized, post-Fordist and so on) society.[3] We shall stress here those processes of change on whose importance there is substantial consensus among scholars – including those who are sceptical of the genuine novelty of the so-called 'new movements'. We shall then discuss the broader implications of these changes for the analysis of the relationship between structural change and innovation in forms of collective action. In particular, we shall focus on two problems: how does the experience of 'new' movements affect our understanding of concepts like 'class conflict' and 'class action'; how should we interpret the overwhelming presence of members from the so-called 'new middle class' in social movements at the end of the twentieth century.

2.1 Social Structure, Political Cleavages and Collective Action

Structure affects collective action not only by creating forms of dependence between social groups, and thus the potential for conflicting interests. Consolidated forms of the organization of social life (from economic to political action, from family life to associations) also influence the make-up of collective actors. Collective action on the part of particular social groups is in fact easier when these groups are: (1) easily identifiable and differentiated in relation to other social groups; (2) endowed, thanks to social networks among their members, with a high level of internal cohesion and with a specific identity. Collective action will depend therefore on the simultaneous presence of specific categorical traits and of networks which link the subjects sharing such traits (Oberschall 1973; Tilly 1978).

From this perspective, the central question for the analysis of the relationship between structure and action will be whether change has made it easier to develop such social relationships and feelings of solidarity and of collective belonging, as these make it possible to identify specific interests and promote related mobilization. The move towards capitalism did not only create aggregates of individuals joined together by the fact that they possessed the means of production (the capitalists) or their own labour force (the proletariat); it also created systems of social relationships which facilitated the development of an internal solidarity in these aggregates and their transformation into collective actors. The integration of the capitalist class was facilitated by its limited size, the overlapping of family relationships and relationships of an economic nature, and by access to – and control of – communications. The concentration of the proletariat in large productive units and in urban areas produced a network of relationships on whose base a specific class identity developed along with a capacity for collective mass action (Thompson 1963; Lodhi and Tilly 1973; Snyder and Tilly 1972; Calhoun 1982; Lash and Urry 1987; Fantasia 1988; Urry 1995). Many of the structural changes described in the following pages – for example those relating to transformations in the organization of work and in the localization of productive activities – have important consequences for the organization of relationships and of interaction within social groups.

2.1.1   Economic change, collective action and movements

The working class was a central actor in the conflicts of the industrial society not only because of its size or the relevance of its economic function, but also as a consequence of a wider range of structural factors. Vast numbers of workers found themselves in a situation where everyone had similar tasks to perform within large productive units, where labour mobility was limited, and within labour markets whose openness to the outside world was, in global terms, modest. These factors certainly facilitated identification of a specific social actor and reinforced internal cohesion.

The bases of industrial conflict have been weakened by modifications affecting the conditions described above. First, the importance of different productive sectors has shifted, with a noticeable decline in industrial work in favour of administrative and service occupations. Highly qualified work in the tertiary sector has grown throughout the world, creating a professional 'new middle class' which is very different from traditional clerical workers in industry or public bureaucracies. The change has affected both the private sector, with a marked increase in 'producer services', and the public sector, with a strong expansion of 'social services' related to education, health and social care (Castells 1996: 208–20). The new middle class is however far from a homogeneous group; indeed, there appear to be considerable differences in terms of social rewards within it. The status of the 'new professionals' is not always comparable with that of the traditional middle-class professionals (lawyers, doctors and so on). For example, in the new producer service sector (such as advertising, marketing, communications) precarious and low-paid forms of work are fairly widespread and constitute marked discrepancies between the cultural capital which individuals have at their disposal, and the recognition – in terms of earnings as well as of social prestige – which is obtained from these.[4]

Within industry, the ways in which work is organized have changed. First, automated technologies and small work groups have replaced the Fordist conveyor-belt approach and the related mass-worker model. Collective solidarity, derived from the carrying out of the same duties, and once a potent factor of solidarity, has been weakened, as a result. Second, production has in many cases passed from large factories to smaller ones, leading to significant decentralization of production processes within a geographical area and to the growth of the hidden and informal economy (Castells 1996: chs 2–3; Amin 1994). This has also contributed to a breakdown of the relationship between productive activities and the area where they traditionally took place, accentuating mobility within urban areas. The proximity of home and the workplace has become less significant. The physical closeness of the factory and the neighbourhoods inhabited by the working classes, which once represented a source of solidarity, is now lacking (Lash and Urry 1987; Hirsch 1988).[5]

The relationship between economic activities and geographical area has changed too in the sense that such activities are increasingly 'transnational', in both 'strong' and 'weak' sectors. Thus the importance of the multinationals has grown: the emphasis on the international division of labour has facilitated the transference of activities which carry high environmental risks to the poorest areas; at the same time, the contractual capacity of trade unions has been weakened, as a result of the possibility of moving the activities of a certain group to places where the political regime and the labour market are more favourable (Castells 1996: ch. 2). On the other hand, demographic pressure and other difficulties in an increasing number of areas in the southern hemisphere have triggered significant migrations towards the stronger economies, promoting the expansion in western societies of a sub-proletariat with a strong ethnic character (Castells 1996: ch. 4, especially 233–4). While the existence of an ethnic sub-proletariat is by no means a new phenomenon (O'Sullivan See 1986; Olzak 1992), the scale of migrations towards the end of the twentieth century has certainly increased the potential for racial conflict within western democracies and created opportunities for the resurgence of extreme right groups (Hainsworth 1992; Wrench and Solomos 1993; Wieviorka 1995; Koopmans 1996a, 1997).

The relationship between the employed and the unemployed has also changed, in more general terms: entry into the labour market is delayed more and more, excessively prolonging a non-adult lifestyle; increasingly fewer sectors of the population can count on stable and protected forms of work. If it is difficult to determine effectively the level of unemployment, and its structural determinants, it is nevertheless the case that the incidence of precarious and temporary work has risen (Castells 1996: ch. 4). Overall, the size of social groups which lack full access to citizenship and its entitlements has grown, whether because they are marginal, in the strict sense of the term, or because they are employed in the hidden economy, or engaged in low-paid work. The sense of general instability has been further reinforced by the growth of individual mobility, principally horizontal: and thus more people tend to change jobs several times in the course of one's life – whether out of choice or out of necessity (Esping-Andersen 1993; Castells 1996).

Another fundamental force of change has consisted of the massive entry of women into the paid labor force. Within western societies, the phenomenon has been particularly pronounced in the service sector, to suggest a relationship between de-materialization of the economy and increased opportunities for women (Castells 1997: 163). This process has affected lines of differentiation and criteria for interest definition within social groups which were previously perceived as homogeneous. Continuing wage differentials between men and women represent, for example, an obvious source of division and potential conflict within the salaried classes (Castells 1997: 169). At the same time, the combined impact of women's growing economic independence and professional commitments has shaken the base of patriarchalism both at home and within the professions and created opportunities for the development of even deeper gender conflicts in the private sphere (Walby 1997).

These processes have weakened the structural preconditions which had facilitated the emergence of a class cleavage, particularly in the working-class model of collective action. The multiplication of roles and of professions and of the related stratifications, and the (re)emergence of ethnicity or gender-based lines of fragmentation within socio-economic groups have made it more difficult to identify specific social categories. The greater frequency of job changes and the weaker relationship with territorial communities has also made relationships among those who once shared the same structural condition more unstable and fragmentary. Work seems to be gradually losing its collective nature, a process Manuel Castells has defined as 'individualization of labor' (1996: 265). It is more difficult to deduct actors' interests from their structural position, and to organize their protection on that basis (Dalton 1988: ch. 8).

Furthermore, it is hard to believe that mass organizations of a bureaucratic nature, similar to those which were developed by the working-class movement in the industrial society, will survive (Piven and Cloward 1977: xvii). Such organizations, which were centralized but, at the same time, active at local level, and were typical of trade unions or working-class parties, along with networks of cooperative and cultural associations with which these organizations identified, responded to the need to organize a base of vast dimensions, with relatively homogeneous needs, and lacking in autonomous resources. Many of the demands which previously were represented by working-class organizations – for example, those which related to living conditions in urban areas – have, at least in part, found alternative forms of protection. Since the 1960s, environmental movements have increasingly intervened on issues such as the reduction of pollution or the expansion of public transport, which, in the past, would have been the preserve of working-class movement organizations and represented as mobilizations on 'working-class conditions'. Moreover, opposition to technologies which are held to be dangerous and untrustworthy, as well as economically unsound, such as nuclear power, has also been organized. All of these cases are examples of actions aimed at obtaining 'public goods', whose enjoyment cannot be limited to specific classes or professional groups; and which are surrounded by alliances which, from the point of view of social composition, are highly diverse.

2.1.2   Political change, collective action and movements

Politics and the state have experienced equally relevant changes. State action is capable of producing collective actors in at least two ways: by fixing the territorial limits of political action; and by facilitating or blocking the development or the reproduction of certain social groups, depending on the priorities of public policy, and in particular on the destination of public spending. In relation to the first point, political action and the definition of the industrial society presupposed a specific concept of space and of territory which translated into the model of the nation state. Having the monopoly of legitimate violence in a certain area, the state fixed its borders and the 'natural' limit of that complex of much wider relationships which conventionally are defined as society. Social relationships were, in the first place, relationships internal to a particular nation state.[6] There were admittedly many communities within states, endowed with specific institutions and forms of self-government. These were, however, considered to be largely residual phenomena, destined to disappear as modernization processes advanced (Smith 1981).

Relevant collective actors were, at that time, those social groups able to influence the formulation of national policy: for example, groups with central economic and professional roles, or organized labour. Political and class conflict tended to be seen as conflict between social groups defined on a national scale, and concerned with the control of national policy. The existence of conflicts between the centre and the periphery which were not based on class issues does not belie this rule: groups bearing a particular cultural, historical and/or linguistic identity defined their strategies and their own image in reference to a central state and to the dominion which the state exercised on their territory. In this case, the goal was not concerned with national policy but rather with the modification of the borders of the nation state. But in both instances, it was in reference to the state and to its borders that actors established themselves.

This picture is still largely a realistic one today. Some of its distinctive traits have been attenuated, however. The correspondence of state and society is weaker than it was in the past. Coupled with even stronger economic interdependence, the diffusion of mass communications has certainly contributed to the delineation of a global public space, although its real traits and implications are still uncertain (Castells 1996: ch. 6; Castells 1997: ch. 5). The emergence of a civil society and public opinion of supranational dimensions has thus become plausible, though still a distant prospect.[7] Overall, the capacity of the state to regulate behaviour within a certain territory has lessened. The growing interdependence among states and the emergence of organisms of supranational sovereignty have weakened the idea of the state as a fundamental element in the international system. At the same time, the importance of territorial political structures within single states has grown. In most cases, this has been assisted by the consolidation of various forms of territorial decentralization (Keating 1988; Sharpe 1988). In some cases, moves towards autonomy have led to the emergence of genuine subnational entities, often in places where historical traditions of autonomy were strong.[8]

This does not mean that the state should lose its centrality. Analysts of the recent impressive growth of Far East economies point for example at the role of the state as a facilitator of development (Castells 1996: 89). But undoubtedly the simultaneous presence of moves towards the constitution of supranational and subnational authorities has brought about significant changes in the construction of collective actors. For example, in the case of ethno-nationalist conflicts, within multicultural states, the presence of supranational entities tends to change the criteria according to which actors define themselves, as well as their strategies. European integration has certainly contributed to the relaunch of mobilizations of historic minorities in western European states, providing them with a new interlocutor and new goals: from the construction of new states following the break-up of those already in existence, there has been, increasingly, a move towards the renegotiation of relationships between central and peripheral regions of a state, within a 'regional Europe'. At the same time, the shift from nationalist identities with a strong ethnic component to identities which combine reference to the nation with greater attention for multiculturalism and the cohabitation of diverse cultural groups has become easier (Johnston 1991b; Melucci 1996). Similar considerations may hold for other supranational organisms, for example, in the sphere of the United Nations, or for other types of policy enacted by the European Union itself, from environmental issues to human rights. In all of these cases, new opportunities for mobilization and campaigns, conducted on a supranational scale, have emerged (Tarrow 1995; Chatfield et al. 1996; Marks and McAdam 1998).

Other aspects of the weakening of the control of the state over certain portions of its territory differ markedly from those which relate to political-administrative decentralization. So called 'no-go areas' – in particular, urban areas where the sovereignty of the state is questioned by the force of criminal organizations or, more rarely, by the self-organizing abilities of active and vital countercultures – seem to be expanding (Dahrendorf 1988). In the latter case, the result is the creation of spaces for alternative lifestyles, which are, at least partially, removed from the control of the forces of law and order (Piven and Cloward 1977).[9] The phenomenon of direct involvement of citizens in the defence of public order in urban areas usually reflects values antagonistic to those of alternative countercultures but is comparable in its enactment of forms of autonomous control of territory (Taylor 1996). Lack of faith in the regulatory capacity of the state also often leads to the entrusting of control of the territory to private policing bodies, in the most affluent neighborhoods, and in various forms of citizens' self-organization in other cases. Mobilizations against deviants or nomads are not, in fact, limited to the upper classes but rather are promoted on many occasions by exponents of the lowest social classes. The potential for conflict involving actors who, once again, cannot automatically be reduced to specific structural placings has developed around the growth of deviant behaviours, on the one hand, and of demands for law and order, on the other.

Furthermore, the make-up of collective actors is not conditioned by the state exclusively through the definition of territorial boundaries to political action. It is well known that the role of the state in the economy has increased progressively in the course of the twentieth century; that the state has moved from being a guarantor of the market to the manager, in person, of economic activities through public enterprise and through nationalizations; and that it has fulfilled through its social policies a function of containment of social inequalities (for a global discussion, see Rose 1988). This has led some observers to hold that the principal social cleavage is no longer based on the control of the means of production, but relates, rather, to the procurement of the means of survival either in the private market or through public intervention (Saunders 1987, quoted in Crompton 1993: 103–4; see also Taylor-Gooby 1986; Papadakis and Taylor-Gooby 1987). Certainly, criteria for allocation of public resources, often those concerned with the satisfaction of basic needs such as housing or transport, have represented a significant area for collective action, in particular, for social groups from an urban context (Dunleavy 1980; Castells 1983; Lowe 1986: Pickvance 1977, 1985, 1986).

The existence of certain social groups and the distribution of the opportunities which are allocated to them, are seen increasingly frequently as the result of processes of a political nature rather than of market dynamics. After the Second World War, the phenomenon has become more marked, with the development of neo-corporatist patterns of interest representation (Schmitter and Lehmbruch 1979; F. Wilson 1990; Regini 1992), which involve the state and the major interests organized by capital and by labour in tripartite negotiations. These forms of concerted action have guaranteed long periods of social peace in industry, but have, however, made the protection of interests not directly linked to the world of industry more difficult, thus creating the potential for the emergence of new conflicts. In opposition to this treatment of interests, social movements have been mobilized to promote the introduction of models of direct democracy, through various forms of self-management, decentralization of decision-making, and the facilitation of popular participation. They have thus called for classic representative democracy to be overtaken by democratic populism (Kitschelt 1993; Offe 1985; Szasz 1994; Lichterman 1995a).

In recent decades, movement action has certainly contributed to the crisis of the model of the interventionist state, as well as that of the state as mediator between the forces of productivity. Various factors have contributed to a further widening of the potential for conflict. First, as the active role of the state in the distribution of resources has become increasingly evident, the opportunities for mobilization to protect ever more heterogeneous social groups and interests have also grown. Second, while the expansion of social rights has certainly brought greater opportunities for those from the lowest social classes, it has also entailed considerable fiscal redistribution. This has proved to be, in the medium term, particularly heavy for the middle classes, as well as insufficient to cover the growing costs of the welfare state, particularly in the context of an ageing population. The result has been a universal welfare crisis which is at the same time fiscal and political. The explicitly political nature of the criteria for the allocation of social resources has, in fact, stimulated mobilization among the middle classes, not only in the form of anti-tax movements, but also from a perspective which is globally critical of the welfare state (Fabbrini 1986; Brissette 1988; Lo 1982, 1990).

To summarize: the growth of the role of the state has multiplied the number of social actors whose existence and opportunities seem to be linked at least partially to political decision-making mechanisms. At the same time, the processes which we have just described have undermined the capacity of consolidated political actors to mediate effectively among the various interests. Changes in the criteria for defining actors and for determining the stakes to play for, have promoted the multiplication of collective identities and of mobilized interests, and, therefore, also their segmentation.

2.1.3   Public sphere and private sphere

The expansion of the role of the state has also contributed to the modification of the boundaries between the public and the private sphere. The state has intervened with growing frequency in areas relating to private life, in particular, through the provision of social services and the action of welfare agencies. The principal form of support offered to citizens is, however, accompanied by increased control over aspects of life which previously would have been left to the autonomous regulation of social actors. The extension of the public health service for example has favoured the standardization both of therapeutic methods, and the treatment of other crucial events in the experience of individuals, such as maternity; therapies providing support for individuals suffering from psychological disorders have also developed in the same way. A tendency towards the bureaucratization and rationalization of the private sphere has been the result (Habermas 1976, 1987; Melucci 1989, 1996).

In this way, definitions of criteria for determining normality and deviance in areas which were previously left to the regulation of other institutions, such as the church or the family, have become the object of public intervention. Thus the premises have been created for the rise of new conflicts whose protagonists are new social groups – for example, professionals and users of social services, or managers with responsibility for the coordination and running of public agencies (Hoffman 1989). Protest has related not only to the efficiency of services but also to their impersonality and their tendency to create and reproduce deviance and marginality instead of combating these (for example, the critique of psychiatric hospitals which developed in the course of the 1960s. Challenging the role of the state on this ground is often intentionally linked with a critique of actions of private groups of professionals (for example, certain sectors of the medical establishment, pharmaceutical companies and so on) accused of subordinating care for service users to internal organisational and economic logic (Scotch 1988; Desario 1988; J. Gamson 1990; Chesler 1991; Oliver and Campbell 1996).

The fact that the distinction between public and private, in the industrial society, was relatively clear, provided another advantage for those who wanted to interpret social conflict. It allowed people to define the rights of citizenship as a complex of civil opportunities (relating, for example, to freedom of expression and association), political opportunities (relating to the right to vote, for example) and social benefits (relating to access to minimum levels of well-being and education) without any further qualifications (Marshall 1976). These rights, in fact, referred to the citizen as understood generically – usually male, adult, of western culture. Mobilization aimed at extending rights of citizenship entailed provision of the same set of entitlements to social groups which had been excluded: illiterate and non affluent people, but also women and ethnic minorities (Barbalet 1988).

Towards the end of the twentieth century, however, various factors have revealed the problematic nature of this notion of citizenship. Not only it has been pointed out how Marshall's model was hardly applicable in countries other than Britain (Giddens 1983; Barbalet 1988), but a series of structural processes have undermined previously taken-for-granted understandings. With the consolidation of the presence of women in the public sphere (in both professional and political terms), the contradiction has become clear between rights formally recognized as universal, and existing forms of organization of family and professional life which have restricted women's enjoyment of those rights.[10]

Immigration waves to western countries have made the problem of how to articulate citizens' rights in such a way as to allow for the existence of different cultural groups more urgent (Bonazzi and Dunne 1994; Soysal 1994; Cesarani and Fulbrick 1996).

Numerous initiatives have also been launched in defence of the rights of children and more generally of minors. On some occasions, these mobilizations have taken a broad political meaning. In October, 1996, in Belgium, public outrage at the protection offered by some state bodies to a group of criminal paedophiles has resulted in a wave of mass protests which have questioned the legitimacy of the Belgian elites as a whole. In this case, identification with a relatively specific cause – no matter how emotionally charged – has provided the basis for mobilizations with a far broader political impact.[11]

All these examples suggest that, although the nation state and modern rights of citizenship took their inspiration from universal identities, other possible sources of collective identity and of conflict have not disappeared. Other criteria regularly appear alongside those of a functionalist or universal type, to define collective actors. These are based on 'ascribed' traits such as gender, ethnic origin or age. In consequence, citizenship appears to be less a complex of given opportunities to which one has access, and more a process of a conflicting nature, where what is at stake is represented by the criteria defining what a citizen is.[12] The fact that the state has widened its scope for intervention only goes to make the political nature of those asymmetries and inequalities more obvious. These are based not only on the control of material resources but also on the definition of the identities of individuals and social groups and on the legitimization of their ways of life and their value systems.[13] The extension of the state's scope for intervention in the sphere of cultural reproduction and in social services makes the political nature of many of these inequalities all the more evident.

It would, nevertheless, be completely inappropriate to attribute the proliferation of potential sources of identity to the increasing intervention of public agencies alone. We are witnessing a more general and progressive shift of the production of identity and of values from the places traditionally assigned to these (the family, direct relationships within the community, or educational institutions themselves) towards other social arenas.[14] Without any claim to completeness, we will limit ourselves here to recalling briefly some of the transformations which can be held up as significant indicators of forms of social conflict and their actors.

It is necessary to look, first of all, at the growing capacity of the media to fulfil a function as a source of interpretation of reality, alongside the relationships which people have directly with cultural institutions. Until now, the debate on the effectiveness of media manipulation has not been conclusive (Katz and Lazarsfeld 1955; Noelle-Neumann 1984; Gamson 1992b; Lenart 1993). Certainly, it seems improbable that, for example, exposure to television can completely replace traditional sources of formation of political opinion, such as conversations in public places, or the influence of religious or educational institutions. Nevertheless, research has suggested that the media are capable of influencing public opinion autonomously, to a degree which should not be overlooked (Lenart 1993). It is, however, plausible to hypothesize that the media play a central role in the expansion and modification of areas of individual experience. Expanding incalculably the range of phenomena of which the individual may have direct experience – however illusory this may be – the media intervene in the formation of public opinion and contribute to definitions of individual and collective identities. Control of the media and of symbolic production therefore becomes both an essential premise for any attempt at political mobilization and an autonomous source of conflict. Increasingly, control of intellectual resources, traditionally indispensable to the success of collective action, risks becoming a hopeless task, if it is not supported by access to the means of mass communication (Gamson and Modigliani 1989; Wasko and Mosko 1992; Gamson and Wolfsfeld 1993; Eyerman 1994).

Furthermore, both the diffusion of education and developments in scientific and technological research have shown significant spheres of human experience to be the fruit of contingent processes susceptible, as such, to modification and manipulation. The undermining of religious-style interpretations of the world was obviously a feaure of the enlightenment programme and is therefore anything but new. But recent developments go well beyond that. On the one hand, human capacity to manipulate 'natural' processes has developed to an unprecedented extent. The most extreme example of this 'relativization' of processes which, up till that point had been considered to be natural, is probably that of biotechnology and genetic engineering (Hannigan 1995). On the other hand, the increasing awareness of the partial, controversial, and interest-driven nature of contemporary science has become increasingly manifest (Barnes and Edge 1982; Yearley 1988). Awareness that ever-greater areas of social experiences – and even the biological heritage of the individual – are somewhat constructed has multiplied doubts as to what can really be taken for granted and what, in contrast, can become the object of human action – and, in some cases, of collective action. In particular, the limits to the use of scientific and technological knowledge, set by current power configurations are becoming clear. When it becomes evident that (almost) everything could be different, it becomes more difficult and more problematic to accept that scientific knowledge is directed towards undesirable and/or ethically unacceptable goals (for example, of an economic or military nature). Thus space for the emergence of new conflicts and new collective representations opens up (McCrea and Markle 1989; Fischer 1993; Lash et al. 1996; Lidskog 1996; Moore 1995, forthcoming).

Growing differentiation in lifestyles represents another source of 'problematization' of social identities. In a world in which class allegiances seem fragmented and political and religious ideologies are in crisis, cultural consumption, use of one's free time, ways of organizing one's emotional life, eating habits, or styles of clothes can all represent a potent factor for diversification and, in the last analysis, of stratification, among social groups (Bourdieu 1984; Eder 1993). In many cases, it is simply an issue of individual consumer behaviour, no different from other fashion phenomena. In other cases, however, lifestyle becomes the stake of conflicts, regarding the legitimacy of emerging cultural forms, the defence of traditional ones, or the protection of a new set of citizens' rights.

Youth movements and other oppositional countercultures provide an example of how individual lifestyle may take up an antagonistic character. For example, the emergence of punk at the end of the 1970s presented an element which could easily be reduced to fashion, but also a powerful symbolic antagonism, in the sense of breaking away from consolidated canons of decorum and good taste. It also had, in other words, a distinctive countercultural flavour. Similar remarks may apply to other forms of youth cultural experience, from rap to rave.[15] In the late twentieth century, various sectors of social movements have indeed reserved considerable space for action concerning consumer goods and cultural elaboration. For example, women's, squatters', or alternative movements have promoted the construction of alternative networks, offering autonomous opportunities for support and social contact to their participants (Melucci 1984a; Lyons 1988; Taylor and Whittier 1992).

In other cases, collective action on lifestyles has been concerned with the defence of values and traditions which, it was held, were threatened. Movements such as the American Moral Majority, or those against the introduction of divorce in Italy, in the early years of the 1970s, have also chosen the private sphere and the criteria by which one can define a particular lifestyle as ethically desirable as their favoured terrain for political mobilization (Wood and Hughes 1984; Wallis and Bruce 1986; Oberschall 1993: ch. 13).

The growing importance of lifestyle has also led to consumerism becoming a specific object of collective action. The consumer has been increasingly identified as a political, and not simply as an economic, actor. Consumer organizations have addressed their mobilization attempts to the public in general. Structures for the production and distribution of alternative products, for example, in the food sector, have been created; campaigns and mobilizations in favour of consumers have also been launched. They have taken forms ranging from quasi-countercultural forms (for example, in the alternative networks promoting and distributing organic food in the early stages of environmental movements) to classic public interest group action (for example, in the form of mass professional organizations like Common Cause) (McFarland 1984; Forbes 1985; Gronmo 1987; Mayer 1989; Pinto 1990; Ranci 1992).

Obviously, it is necessary to avoid hypothesizing overly close analogies between countercultural movements and those activities aimed at consumer protection. However, from different points of view, these draw our attention once again to the new importance assumed by collective action concerned with the defence of certain models of behaviour and moral codes, rather than with the conquest of political power or the protection of economic interests. Various transformations in the private sphere and in forms of cultural production appear to have increased potential for conflicts of a symbolic nature. In particular, they may have influenced the make-up of collective actors in at least two ways. First, sources of meaning and identity are multiplied. These, increasingly, are perceived as being linked to social processes which often imply asymmetries of power (for example, in the control of communication and of scientific knowledge, or in access to certain types of consumer goods). Second, the variety of life experiences to which the individual has access is a result of the multiplication of group allegiances. Each of these can provide relationship and identity resources essential in turning some of the possible sources of inequality into a social problem, potentially the basis for collective action. However, none of these succeeds in becoming the primary source of identity, able to represent the central criteria for the organization of action, comparable with that of class or national allegiance in the industrial society (see, for example, Melucci 1996).

The map of adversaries against which collective energies can, from time to time, be mobilized is equally varied: mass media, techno-scientific elites, educational and social welfare institutions, entrepreneurial classes which control mass consumption and so on. In this situation of uncertainty, instead of representing the preconditions for action concerned with economic or political goals, the definition of collective identity tends to become an autonomous problem, object of collective action as such (although this may also apply to class conflict: Pizzorno 1978). The same thing can be said for the search for lifestyles and ways of acting which are ethically desirable and appropriate. These needs do not result inevitably in the development of social movements. For example, dissatisfaction with the contemporary urban lifestyle does not necessarily lead to support for environmental movements; it can take a variety of forms, from political engagement in a traditional political party to, quite simply, the transformation of individual consumer behaviour, a sense of personal alienation, or deviant behaviour. Yet the growth of needs linked to identity represents potential for conflict around which movement action can, under favourable conditions, develop.

2.2   Structural Transformations, New Conflicts, New Classes

The processes of structural change, which are recalled briefly in the preceding pages, contribute in various ways to the weakening of the bases of traditional social conflicts. It is more debatable whether it is possible to establish a global characterization of new conflicts on this basis. The transformations we have discussed – and even more so the interpretations that different scholars have provided of them – seem to point in divergent and sometimes contradictory directions.

However, there are at least two common elements in a large proportion of the changes with which we have concerned ourselves. First, these show the marked increase of activities linked to the production of knowledge and to symbolic manipulation, and identify a major stake of conflict in the control of those activities. The development of an advanced administrative/service sector in fact reflects the growing relevance in the economic sphere of information processing, compared with the transformation of natural resources. The extension of areas of life which seem to be regulated by principles which are of an artificial nature and no longer natural is proceeding in the same direction; as is the case with the greater importance of elements linked to style and taste – objects, that is, of creative manipulation – as sources of social differentiation. The same expansion of areas of state intervention, which lead to the multiplication of identities and of politically based interests, makes the role of decision-makers and communicators able to develop efficient syntheses between heterogeneous concerns and values ever more essential.

Second, many recent transformations have produced the potential for conflicts which cut across conventional distinctions between the private and public spheres. Evidence of this includes the influence which certain styles of scientific knowledge and certain ways of organizing it have on the psycho-physical well-being of the individual (for example, in the field of therapies and the health services). Alternatively, one may think of the public and collective relevance of individual consumer behaviour and ways of life which previously would have been relegated to the private sphere. Or, again, one might consider the importance of ascribed traits such as ethnicity or gender in conflicts concerning the extension and full realization of citizens' rights.

These processes point at a specific area of conflicts, of a non-material type. Their stake is represented by the control of resources which produce meaning, and which allow actors to intervene not only in relation to their own environment but also in the personal sphere, and above all in the link between these two levels. Rather than economic or political power, contemporary social conflict has, according to this view, more to do with the production and circulation of information; social conditions for production and the use of scientific knowledge; and the creation of symbols and cultural models concerned with the definition of individual and collective identities. This thesis has been formulated in a number of ways and with various levels of theoretical generalization (Touraine 1981; Lash and Urry 1987; Melucci 1989, 1996; Eder 1993). In particular, somewhat diverse conclusions have been drawn, as far as the relationship between structure, conflict and movement is concerned.

In order to try to make sense of what is undoubtedly a highly diversified debate we must first of all keep in mind that those who investigate the relationship between structure, class and collective action sometimes move from rather different points of departure, and use the same terms in quite different ways. To begin with, we must note the difference between a 'historical' and a 'structural' (Eder 1995) or 'analytical' (Melucci 1995) concept of class. If we refer to class as a historical product of capitalist society (referring in other words to the working and the capitalist class, and to the specific structural processes which produced and reinforced their identity), we may end up with certain conclusions regarding the future of class conflict. We may reach quite different conclusions, however, if we focus on the notion that changing properties of the social system may well produce different structural preconditions for conflict and thus create the potential for class conflicts of a different type. In this case, recognizing the declining antagonistic potential of the working class will not lead us to deny that systemic properties – in particular, the 'relationships within which social resources are produced and appropriated' (Melucci 1995: 117) – may still shape social conflict. The inequalities in power and status, peculiar of post-industrial society, might well not be conducive to the reproduction of industrial class conflict, still provide the structural roots for the emergence of new collective actors.

The tension between these two different approaches has affected recent debates on the persistence of class as a factor shaping conventional political behaviour, in particular, electoral participation (Dalton et al. 1984; Dalton 1988; Heath et al. 1991; Clark and Lipset 1991; Franklin et al. 1992; Pakulski and Waters 1996; Wright 1996; Manza and Brooks 1996; Szelenyi and Olvera 1996). Among students of social movements, even those who recognize the persistent importance of structural processes differ in their use of the concept of class. Some (for example, Eder 1995) still regard it as a useful heuristic device, provided one refrains from filling it with references to the historical experience of industrial society; others (for example, Melucci 1995) reject it precisely on the ground that historical experience has infused it with meanings which prevent its useful application to a modified context.

A second issue among those who still recognize the relevance of structural interpretations regards the existence of a hierarchical structure of different types of conflicts, and the possibility to identify core conflicts comparable to those which according to dominant interpretations shaped industrial society. The most coherent attempt to identify the core conflicts of post-industrial (or 'programmed') society has been probably Alain Touraine's.[16] According to the most influential analyst of the 'new movements', the category of social movement fulfils a fundamental task, both in defining the rules by which society functions and in determining the specific goal of sociology: 'The sociology of social movements,' writes Touraine (1981: 30) 'cannot be separated from a representation of society as a system of social forces competing for control of a cultural field.' The way in which each society functions reflects, that is, the struggle between two antagonistic actors who fight for control of cultural concerns which, in turn, determine the type of transforming action which a society exercises upon itself (Touraine 1977: 95–6). It is in relation to the concept of historicity – defined by the interweaving of a system of knowledge, a type of accumulation and a cultural model – that different types of society can be identified, along with the social classes which accompany them. In contrast with Marxism, classes are not defined only in relation to the system of production (see, for example, Miliband 1989), and action is, in fact, the 'behaviour of an actor guided by cultural orientations and set within social relations defined by an unequal connection with the social control of these orientations' (Touraine 1981: 61).

Touraine identifies four types of society, each featuring a distinctive pair of central antagonistic actors: agrarian, mercantile, industrial and 'programmed' (a term which he prefers to 'post-industrial' society). A particular trait of the programmed society is the 'production of symbolic goods which model or transform our representation of human nature and the external world' (Touraine 1987: 127, 1985). It is the control of information which constitutes the principal source of social power. In consequence, conflicts tend to shift from the workplace to areas such as research and development, the elaboration of information, biomedical and technical sciences, and the mass media. The central actors in social conflict are no longer classes linked to industrial production but groups with opposing visions concerning the use and destination of cognitive and symbolic resources. Mobilizations by social movements address, therefore, the defence of the autonomy of civil society from the attempts of public and private technocratic groups to extend their control over ever-widening areas of social life.[17]

Touraine's formulation is particularly ambitious, in that it places the analysis of conflicts and movements in the centre of his general theoretical model. Other scholars have still paid attention to the structural dimension, without however attempting to identify new dominant cleavages. The emergence of new conflicts with a centrality comparable to that of the capital–labour conflict of the industrial society has been held to be improbable, for example, by a writer originally influenced by Touraine as Alberto Melucci.[18] Melucci has never denied the persistent importance of traditional conflicts based on inequalities of power and wealth, and of the political actors, protagonists of these conflicts. However, he has identified the peculiarity of contemporary conflicts in processes of individualization which still have their roots in structural dynamics, yet of a different kind – for example, the pervasive influence of caring institutions over the self, the globalization of communications and life experiences, the growth of media systems. He has denied the possibility of reducing responses to these differentiated structural tensions to any sort of unified paradigm of collective action. The latter – itself in a variety of forms – is, rather, just one of innumerable options open to individuals struggling for an autonomous definition of their self.

The relationship between structural change and new conflicts has also been viewed from another perspective. A number of scholars have stressed the fact that social change has produced a new social stratum – the so-called 'new middle class'. According to this point of view, this class is able, as a result of the resources it controls and of its position, to play a central role in new conflicts. For some time, analyses of post-industrial society have revealed, in parallel with the growth of the administrative/service sector in society, the emergence of social groups which stand out, because of their level of education, the roles they play and their specific social location, from the traditional middle classes (Bell 1973; Gouldner 1979; Goldthorpe 1982; Lash and Urry 1987; Scott 1990). The new middle class, according to these analyses, is constituted from sectors of the population which are highly educated, tend to be employed in the service sector, and yet are not comparable with managers or traditional professionals. As a result of their technical and cultural competence and of their economic-functional position, members of the new middle class are more likely to mobilize in conflicts of the new type we have just described: that is, to fight against technocrats, public and private agencies engaged in the dissemination of information and in the construction of consensus, the military and the apparatus responsible for social control. This argument has been presented on numerous occasions in recent years, and several investigations have confirmed the persistent presence of the new middle class among sympathizers and activists of the new movements.[19]

However, it is unclear whether the link between the new middle class, movements and new types of conflict effectively demonstrates the existence of a specific structural base for these types of conflict. The presence *en masse* of the new middle class in protest movements could, in fact, simply represent the traditional inclination of the intellectual middle class to participate in any type of conflict (Bagguley 1992, 1995a; Pakulski 1995). From this perspective, the reference to specific structural contradictions at the base of new conflicts somewhat loses consistency. It is, rather, the case that belonging to the middle class, on the one hand, facilitates the taking up of concerns which are generically favourable to public involvement; and on the other, it puts at one's disposal individual resources and competences which can be spent in various types of political action.

In effect, comparative analysis of political participation has revealed on numerous occasions that variables of a socio-demographic type tend to explain with equal efficacy both unconventional participation (particularly widespread among movement sympathizers and activists) and conventional participation. There is, for example, a strong correlation between two factors that are usually regarded as indicators of the new middle class – youth and a high level of education – and various types of political attitudes and/or political participation (Barnes et al. 1979; Jennings et al. 1990; Opp 1989: ch. 7). Furthermore, some comparisons between political ecology movements and more traditional environmentalist currents show that activists from the new middle class are present in equal measure in both sectors, in spite of the fact that it is difficult to identify conservationist groups as new social movements (Diani 1995a: 58).

Rather than on peculiar class dynamics, the undeniable relationship between membership in the new middle class and involvement in contemporary protest movements might well be dependent on other factors. For example, it might be the outcome of the enormous rise in access to higher education, which again originated in the 1960s. More specifically, higher education might not only provide people with distinctive intellectual skills; it might also foster the growth of an egalitarian and anti-authoritarian set of values, which are over-represented among at least some sectors of the new middle class (Rootes 1995). Alternatively, youth radicalism might be related to generational experiences, as the current members of the new middle classes have all been exposed to that particular combination of social conditions, consisting of the end of the cold war and the spread to the middle classes of unprecedented economic prosperity (Pakulski 1995: 76; Braungart and Braungart 1986, 1992). Or, there might be lifecycle effects, as younger people's political involvement might be dependent on their biographical availability, given their more uncertain status, their still unsettled professional life, and their greater independence from family and community linkages (Piven and Cloward 1992; Crook et al. 1992: 146–47; contra Inglehart 1985, 1990a).

If understood too inclusively, the notion of middle class risks then comprising somewhat heterogeneous social sectors. For example, differences between those who work in the sector of culture and personal services and those who fulfil managerial or other technocratic functions risk remaining unclear. Furthermore, it is important to be aware of the potential tensions between those sectors of the new middle class which are closer to the problems of the management of organizations (managers) and those who, instead, draw their legitimacy and their status as controllers of professional resources, independent of specific organizational structures (professionals) (Kriesi 1993: 31–2).

To evaluate appropriately the importance of the new middle class in social movements, it is useful, therefore, to differentiate between its internal components. Taking inspiration from Wright (1985), who regards classes as defined by different combinations of 'assets in the means of production, organisational assets and skills or credentials', Hanspeter Kriesi has identified the distinctive characteristic of the new middle class in the fact that it exercises some control over organizational resources and/or over professional skills, but does not possess the means of production (Kriesi 1993: 28; see also Kriesi 1989b).[20] In particular, it is necessary to look at three different sectors of the new middle class: alongside the 'socio-cultural specialists'[21] are managers and those who fulfil clearly technical roles. This last group includes administrative and commercial personnel from public and private organizations, technical specialists – some highly qualified and others less so[22] – and those working in 'protective services' (the police, the army, civil protection organizations and the like).

Awareness of the various components of the new middle class and evaluation of their impact on political participation, alongside that of those belonging to the traditional classes (the old middle class, and the working class) help to interpret more accurately the relationship between class condition and (new) forms of participation. In the case of the Netherlands,[23] the application of this conceptualization provides interesting results. Managers and socio-cultural professionals are more prone than any other socio-economic group to mobilize in new movements, even when controlling for variables which, in theory, correlate, such as education and salary levels (Kriesi 1993: 196ff). Furthermore, this tendency is stronger among people under 40 years old, a fact which supports the hypothesis of a link between movements and recent transformations of the middle classes (1993: 198). This appears even more significant if one considers that in general, class situation explains movement participation better than participation in traditional party politics;[24] and that this emerges from a context in which the impact of class variables on politics appears, to many analysts, in decline (see also Dalton 1988: ch. 8; contra Heath et al. 1991).

These data are consistent with what has emerged from the analysis of environmentalist militancy (Cotgrove and Duff 1980; Jamison, Eyerman and Cramer 1990; Dalton 1994: ch. 5; Diani 1995a). Those filling the highest positions in groups engaged in this kind of activity are not only highly educated and – in the broadest sense – members of the middle class, but also bring specific competences to bear on the work of the group. The case of environmentalism and, more generally, of new movements analysed by Kriesi, show both the continuity and the discontinuity in the relationship between the educated middle classes and political participation. The central position of intellectual groups in collective action – a constant trait in modern society – has not been challenged by recent developments. At the same time, however, the competences and the overall profile of the middle-class activist seem to adapt themselves to what is at stake in 'new' conflicts.

Analyses of the link between individual class location and political behaviour have certainly brought to light a series of relevant characteristics of new forms of political participation. They have, in particular, provided important information about old and new social movement activists and sympathizers. In doing so, however, they have postulated a direct link between the structural position of individuals and collective action which is by no means clear cut. In fact, while it is possible to look at classes as aggregates of subjects who occupy analogous positions in the system of social stratification, in terms of the resources they control, the prestige they enjoy and their social opportunities, this is not necessarily an appropriate strategy when dealing with the problem of collective action.[25]

Alternatively, it is advisable to analyse classes as collective actors with a specific identity and self-awareness, and linked to other social groups by relationships of a cooperative or conflicting nature. In this perspective, class exists only in circumstances where people mutually recognize and are recognized as part of a distinctive social group, if specific interests and solidarity between the occupants of particular social positions have been identified, and if, on this basis, specific forms of collective action are to be promoted (Thompson 1963; Tilly 1978; Touraine 1981; Fantasia 1988; Urry 1995).

This perspective maintains that structural changes (for example, in the economy, or in the private sphere) provide a basis for the development of new political identities, and new criteria for the organization of conflict, only in cases where these are the object of explicit political action (Bartolini and Mair 1990; Kriesi et al. 1995). The major class distinctions of industrial society operated as criteria for the organization of political conflict because class mobilization had been made possible by extended networks linking class-based organizations, class communities, among themselves as well as to sectors of other social groups with a more ambiguous location, in particular, the middle classes; and because two clear-cut antagonists – working class and bourgeoisie – had finally emerged out of the complex structure of pre-industrial society. Likewise, for a new cleavage to emerge, based on the new middle class – however defined – and/or providing a stable political articulation to the new structural tensions we have just discussed, specific political organizations and systems of both individual and group relationships have to develop. However, to date, this seems to have occurred only partially.

In the first place, it is still unclear to what extent the new middle class/service class will be able to consolidate as a specific collective actor, and develop a relatively stable collective identity. The question is particularly appropriate, given the multiplicity of social positions and roles in which what is defined as the new middle class is actually fragmented; and given that frequent mobility – between social positions as well as locality – is regarded as one distinctive trait of post-industrial society (hardly a property conducive to the establishment of the networks needed to turn an aggregate into a collective actor) (Crook et al. 1992: 117; Eder 1995; Urry 1995; Melucci 1995, 1996).

The relationship between new middle class and traditional middle class seems to be equally ambiguous, at least for the moment (Offe 1985).[26] Many observers have referred to traditional middle-class groups as social sectors 'threatened by modernisation and by change'. According to this reading, which is popular, for example, among scholars of the anti-nuclear movements (Rüdig 1990; Flam 1994d; see also Klandermans and Tarrow 1988), contemporary social movements also organize, in part, the protest of those social groups (such as shopkeepers or, in general, the autonomous *petit bourgeoisie*) who see their status threatened by socio-economic transformation.

From this perspective, opposition to nuclear power, and indeed to other dangerous plants, is not only the sign of a progressive shift towards battles around 'post-industrial' conflicts such as those relating to the control of development. It also shows the diffidence of the traditional middle classes towards activities and technical competence which are outside their traditional domain, such as high-tech applications; dimensions of moral revolt against the subordination of 'traditional' values such as health to the imperatives of efficiency and modernity; the reaction to the threat which derives from living with a potential source of environmental damage. Similar considerations could be applied to the propensity of the middle class to mobilize in opposition to situations perceived to be threatening for its own prestige and social decorum, such as the case of movements against crime and urban deviance, or those against immigration. These traits are not restricted to movements with a clear right-wing connotation; in contrast, many 'new' social movements (including, but not exclusively, environmentalism) also seem to present more than sporadic characteristics typical of traditional, defensive middle-class moral protest (Eder 1993, 1995).

In other words, conditions favouring the return of various forms of status politics seem to have been reproduced. In these, the central role is taken by social groups brought together by certain levels of prestige and specific moral codes (Turner 1988; Eder 1993). Consistently with what has been objected to the more structural version of the middle-class thesis, the attention paid by the middle class to its own group identity and to its own social positioning is certainly not a characteristic exclusive to recent mobilizations (Calhoun 1993; D'Anieri et al. 1990). As the historical experience of the anti-alcohol movement reminds us

(Gusfield 1963), the middle class has distinguished itself over time by its continual attention to moral codes, socially acceptable rules of conduct and principles defining the 'good life'. Reasons for this attitude are to be found in the historically ambiguous positioning of the middle classes between the industrial bourgeoisie and the working class. Indeed, the *petit bourgeoisie* came to focus on symbolic production and on the defence of its own social status as a result of its uncertain place in the class system. For similar reasons, they may have felt the need to differentiate themselves from the principal social groups, and particularly from those – the industrial proletariat, throughout this century – which most closely threatened their prestige (Turner 1994; Calhoun 1993; Oberschall 1993: ch. 13; Eder 1993, 1995). At the same time, there are reasons to argue that substantial differences separate many recent examples of lifestyle politics from the traditional version of status politics. As Featherstone (1987) notes, reference to values and lifestyles does not necessarily characterize distinctive groups with specific identities and long-established structures. Actors involved in collective action may actually share little, apart from the common reference to a given set of values and preferences (see also Wood and Hughes 1984; Crook et al. 1992, especially p. 144; Urry 1995).

The relationship between new middle class and working class is not any clearer, nor has it been the subject of massive in-depth investigation. In the case of the Netherlands studied by Kriesi, it seems, for example, that even belonging to the working class can facilitate mobilization in new movements, particularly as far as younger people are concerned. Thus there would appear to be at least a partial convergence on the new movements among those social groups which were already particularly active in 'historical' opposition movements: there is a certain continuity, in other words, between 'old' and 'new' forms of class opposition. From this point of view, 'new' movements would therefore represent a new organizational form for inter-class coalitions concerned with protest, rather than with institutional political action.[27]

In general, however, substantial barriers seem to persist against a more systematic cooperation between new social movements and working class. Although there is no obvious reasons why should concerns for public goods like a clean environment be a preserve of the middle classes, still the way these preoccupations are organized by new middle-class activists seem to prevent working-class involvement. The global failure of the post-industrial left to accommodate working-class people has been attributed to several factors. These include persistent differences in class cultures, differences in shaping the political agenda, and the difficulty for workers to be involved in networks of social relationships disconnected from the workplace – in particular the networks related to professional activity, to common educational background, to other associational commitments, which seem to be particularly conducive to involvement in non-class movements (Croteau 1995: 191ff).

Finally, one should note that political identities and cleavages need, in order to consolidate, a clear opponent (see chapters 3–4). If libertarian and 'new left' movements in the late twentieth century have certainly demonstrated their capacity for innovation, compared with traditional political identities, it is unclear whether the same applies to the right of the political spectrum. There have certainly been a number of right-wing mobilizations and campaigns which have challenged new social movements directly, on issues ranging from pro-life and abortion to taxation, from Third World immigration to law and order.[28] The insurgence of right-wing populism in the form of parties like the French National Front, or the Italian Northern League and Mr Berlusconi's Forza Italia (see chapter 3) also suggest deep changes in the political right (Betz 1994; Taggart 1996). Very conspicuous political phenomena, such as Reaganism or Thatcherism, have also been regarded as a political synthesis of the new trends emerging on the right.

However, these changes are far from homogeneous, and it is difficult to identify a common value core. In his exploration of the potential for a new political cleavage in the Netherlands, Kriesi (1993) suggests, for example, that the new right shares with the traditional right the opposition to welfare policies, but displays a more libertarian attitude on issues of individual behaviour and civil liberties. In the American context, however, the 'new religious right' appears to have operated rather in the opposite direction, that is, as a challenge not only to the progressives, but to that version of political conservatism which combined economic and civil liberalism. Nor can it be assimilated at all to other protest campaigns broadly associated to the right, such as anti-tax movements (Lo 1990). In continental Europe, it is likewise difficult to think of anti-immigration or law and order coalitions as expressions of a 'neo-libertarian' right. An additional question – and a fundamental one, from the point of view of the existence of cleavages – is if the different components of this potential pole may define some sort of shared identity beyond the electoral context; and to what extent the new right may actually differentiate itself from the traditional political right in organizational terms. With the exception of the extreme right, this is still uncertain (von Beyme 1988; Kitschelt 1995). While there are signs that a realignment on the right of the political spectrum is taking place, available studies do not yet allow solid conclusions on this point (Kriesi 1993).

In sum, if there is ample evidence suggesting the emergence of new structural conflicts, the form of these conflicts and their capacity to persist over time is far from obvious. We would like to close our discussion by mentioning a few further reasons for caution. First, there is no evidence that the material and redistributive dimension has lost all significance in conflicts in which contemporary, non-working-class movements are protagonists (Brooks and Manza 1994: 562–3). For example, mobilizations for the development of collective services in urban areas and for urban renewal have certainly been determined by powerful concerns with collective and non-material goods, such as those associated with the quality of life. However, they have also focused on the redistribution of material resources, placing the social groups most penalized by transformations in industrial activity and by processes of urban renewal in opposition to economic groups which were the protagonists and promoters of these processes (Castells 1977, 1983, 1997; Lowe 1986; Feagin and Capek 1991; Bagguley 1994). These struggles have often seen the emergence of new alliances between working-class and community groups (Brecher and Costello 1990). Furthermore, new forms of collective action have emerged, based on conditions of particular unease, concerned, for example, with the struggle against 'new poverties'. Movements and mobilizations of homeless people have developed (Cress and Snow 1996); initiatives supporting the unemployed and marginal groups have sprung up everywhere, often in close collaboration with the voluntary sector (Bagguley 1991, 1995b; Pearce 1994). In all these cases, the conflict has been concerned, once again, not only with a general notion of the quality of life, but with the allocation of material rewards among different social groups.

One should also note that, according to many observers, contemporary movements do not necessarily demonstrate a radical ongoing transformation in the stakes of collective action as well as in its actors. Movements of recent years should rather be regarded as a manifestation of the difficulties representative systems have in dealing with the new demands which social change inevitably produces. In this perspective, 'new movements' are not necessarily the reflection of global structural transformations, or forerunners of the rise of new criteria to determine the structure of political conflicts. They are, rather, the next in a long series of manifestations of the cyclical nature of political protest.[29]

This objection is a serious one, particularly when aimed at inappropriate or hurried generalizations concerning elements of 'newness' revealed in recent years. It is important to be aware that not all examples of collective action in recent decades are automatically of the new type. The 1960s and 1970s have seen not only the rise of new political phenomena but also the revival of initiatives taken by 'old' collective actors such as the working class and ethno-linguistic minorities. The latter's capacity for mobilization has been reproduced in a variety of forms in recent years (Smith 1981; Melucci and Diani 1992; Breuilly 1993; Connor 1994).

At the same time, however, as Alberto Melucci, in particular, has remarked on several occasions (1988, 1994, 1995, 1996), the question of the newness of contemporary phenomena of collective action should be treated on an analytical rather than on an empirical level. Looking at the empirical characteristics of a given, historical social movement (from the environmental movement [Jordan and Maloney 1997] to the women's movement [Roseneil 1995; Walby 1997] to the working-class movement [Calhoun 1982]) will inevitably lead to the discovery of a mix of both 'new' and 'old' actors, 'new' and 'old' conflicts (not to mention 'new' and 'old' repertoires of action: ch. 7, this volume). However, what really matters is – according to Melucci – to assess the newness of certain specific processes in terms of their centrality to the systemic properties of advanced societies. For example, emphasis on the collective identity of a social group is by no means restricted to contemporary movements. But what renders this process peculiar, and therefore 'new', in post-industrial society is its centrality, due to the current dominance of symbolic production, and of the social relationships which shape it (for a critique of Melucci's argument: Pickvance 1995).

2.3   Summary

In this chapter we have asked ourselves whether looking at the social structure and at changes in this may provide a useful key to the interpretation of collective action. We have examined a series of recent modifications to the social and political structure, and their innovative potential in relation to consolidated lines of conflict structuring. The transformation of the economic sphere – in particular, the move to a more or less advanced service and administrative sector and the decentralization of industrial production – has undermined not only the numerical consistency of the working class but also the living and working conditions which facilitated class action. Today we face greater diversity in professional roles and interests. On the political side, the legitimacy of the state is called into question both by the tendency towards globalization and by that towards localization. Furthermore, the capacity of the state to create and reproduce social groups through public intervention has led to an increasing number of demands which are fragmented and increasingly difficult to mediate. New potential for conflict originates therefore in the increasingly blurred borders between the public and the private sphere, particularly from the multiplication of criteria to define rights of citizenship and the growing capacity for intervention among public and private institutions, in areas of private life such as physical and mental health.

Mobilizations and movements have developed in recent years around interests, involving actors who can be associated in various ways with the transformations which we have just reviewed. Scholars such as Touraine have identified the central conflicts in post-industrial society in struggles for the control of symbolic production. Others have emphasized the high level of involvement of new middle-class members in new conflicts, as a result of their particular professional position and of the intellectual resources which they control.

It is important, however, to remember that collective action does not spring automatically from structural tensions. In this respect it is still doubtful that a new political cleavage, with the capacity to structure conflicts similar to that demonstrated by the capital–labour or the centre–periphery cleavage in the industrial society, has emerged, let alone been consolidated. Numerous factors determine whether or not this will occur. These factors include the availability of adequate organizational resources, the ability of movement leaders to produce appropriate ideological representations, and the presence of a favourable political context. The rest of our book is dedicated to the mechanisms which contribute to an explanation of the shift from structure to action.

3
The Symbolic Dimension of Collective Action

The late 1980s and the early 1990s have seen a dramatic resurgence of right-wing, populist movements across Europe. In Germany, a political party has emerged, the Republikaner, which has tried to give voice to the xenophobic, nationalistic and anti-immigrant sentiments still present among sectors of the electorate. In France, the Front National, led by Jean-Marie Le Pen, has become a remarkable political force, especially in the southern regions, those with the highest percentage of Maghreb immigrants, and in industrial peripheries, previously a stronghold of the Communist Party. In Italy, a coalition of regionalist parties – the Northern League – has emerged as one of the major players in the electoral arena.[1] In all these cases, the challenge posed by right-wing political groups has exceeded the boundaries of conventional left–right politics. It has, rather, taken the form of a populist challenge to democratic politics as a whole, where both the legitimacy of professional politicians and broader elites is questioned, and the rights of the most dispossessed sectors of the population (people on welfare, members of ethnic minorities, immigrants and so on) are denied.

The success of these groups has been uneven: modest in Germany, remarkable – especially in the light of an unfavourable electoral system – in France, impressive in Italy. There, despite being confined to the northern regions alone, the Northern League has secured a consistent support: in 1992, it polled 8.8 per cent of the national vote, gaining 80 seats in the parliament – they had obtained two in the 1987 elections. This outstanding result made the Northern League the fourth strongest party in Italy, a result confirmed at the 1994 and the 1996 elections (Diamanti 1996).

The electoral success of the League confirmed that traditional political identities, and traditional ways of representing political conflict were in crisis. Allegiances to class or to religion, which had constituted the heart of the political struggle over the last fifty years of the Republic, were breaking up. Observers were struck not only by the rapidity of the process but also by its unexpected focus. While clearly no one would deny the cultural heterogeneity and the marked territorial differences within Italy, until the 1990s no one would have considered these divisions a prime source of conflict and of political identity.

Various hypotheses have been put forward to explain the emergence of the League (Diamanti 1993: ch. 1; 1996). Some have stressed the importance of the socio-economic structure. The distribution of support for the League shows how since the mid-1980s the success of this kind of formation has regularly been higher in those parts of northern Italy, such as eastern Lombardy and a large part of the north east, which have the highest incidence of small businesses and, historically, fewer larger firms. Other explanations have focused on changes to the political structure: in particular, on the crisis of the centralized state – particularly serious in the Italian situation because of the high level of inefficiency and of state corruption – and on opportunities to play an autonomous political and economic role which, according to many commentators, European integration would offer the northern Italian regions.

Both types of structural explanation appear to offer only a partial interpretation of this development. The movement has gained modest support in areas, such as Emilia-Romagna, which the League itself considers an integral part of the North, and in which small businesses are as strong a feature as in the north east of Italy. In Emilia-Romagna, which has historically been, first, a PCI (Italian Communist Party) and, latterly, a PDS (Democratic Party of the Left) stronghold, a powerful tradition of political opposition has enabled frustration with the crisis of the centralized state and tensions linked to regional imbalances to be expressed through traditional political identities. The League has been able to establish itself only in areas which, historically, were dominated by the Christian Democrats and where the Catholic Church has been a significant social presence.

Furthermore, criticism from new independent middle-class groups of a state which was inefficient, over-centralized and often corrupt, should not necessarily take the form of regionalist populism. In place of the League, one might have expected other 'new' political projects to be successful, for example that of the 'Rete', or Network (Foot 1996). The Rete movement was founded in 1990 and originated out of initiatives promoted by citizens' action groups throughout the country – with centres in Lombardy and Sicily – against political corruption, criminality, and mafia powers. Based on an interclass model as the Northern League, it was equally critical of the bureaucratic degeneration of public administration and of pacts made in recent decades between the main political parties, and between the parties and major industries. In contrast to the League, it ignored territorial divisions, emphasizing, rather, the elements which linked the north and the south of Italy. Nevertheless, this message, which, in principle, would have been broadly compatible with the interests of *petit bourgeois* entrepreneurs, failed to attract support from these quarters. Instead, the self-employed middle class aligned itself *en masse* with the League – at least until Silvio Berlusconi, the media tycoon and chairman of AC Milan soccer team, decided to enter politics.

Both the failure of the Rete and, on the other hand, the success of the left in its traditional strongholds to counter the ascent of the League demonstrate the difficulty of deducing the development of collective action from the existence of structural changes and/or crises. There are indeed margins of autonomy for social actors in identifying certain themes, transforming them into relevant political problems, exploiting the available opportunities for action and creating new ones.

In the case of the Northern League, in particular, intolerance of the centralized state could have been expressed entirely through the right–left divide (thanks to the decades-long overlapping of the government, the state and the ruling Christian Democrat party); or, despite the prevalence of hostility towards the old party system as a whole, it could have been monopolized by non-territorial organizations close to the model of the 'new politics', such as the Rete itself. It was not, therefore, a foregone conclusion that disparate themes and preoccupations such as those linked to the inefficiency of public services, the

absence of suitable policies for small business, the lack of preparation on a national scale for the moment of European integration,
or new immigration from the developing world should become
linked in a project whose goal was to call into question the notion
of the unitary state.

The fact that this occurred can be attributed, among other
factors, to the abilities of League leaders and activists in terms
of symbolic elaboration. In the early 1980s, the appearance of
graffiti urging independence for Lombardy or the Veneto on
motorway overpasses represented the first sign that a new political actor was being formed. Subsequently, the spread of posters
which showed the north as oppressed and suffocated by Roman
bureaucracy and southern greed contributed to the growth of the
conviction that a powerful organization, the League, had emerged
to look after the interests of the north which, for too long, had
been neglected. Using simple, direct language, very different
from the tortuous style of official political communication, the
League's leaders took every opportunity to draw attention to a
host of values (such as honesty, commitment, hard work) described as typical of the northern regions of the country.

The emergence in Italy of the 'northern question', to which
problems and concerns which would otherwise have been considered highly disparate could be attached, therefore constitutes
a good starting point for reflection on the role of the cultural
and symbolic dimension of collective action.[2] In this context, we
must, however, bear in mind that there are two different ways
of looking at the role of culture and its relationship with action.
The first stresses above all the relationship between values and
action. The second, on the other hand, focuses on the cognitive
dimension of social action, that is, on the process through which
actors attribute meaning to their own experiences. The two
approaches are described in the first two sections of this chapter.
We then present some typologies of interpretative frames.

3.1   Culture and Action: The Role of Values

We may think of social action as driven largely by the fundamental principles with which the actor identifies. According to
this perspective, values will influence the way in which the actor
defines specific goals, and identifies behavioural strategies which
are both efficient and morally acceptable. Moreover, they will

provide the motivation necessary to sustain the costs of action. The more intense one's socialization into a particular vision of the world, the stronger the impetus to act. The characteristics of a given system of values will shape the components of action. How is this model articulated in the case of collective action in movements? How, in other words, is it possible to describe values as the central explanatory variable in the case of actions which, by definition, call into question at least some of the (culturally legitimized) assets of power in a given society? One possibility is to interpret non-institutional collective action as evidence of a lack of social integration in the system, or, alternatively, as the inability of the system to reproduce and reinforce its fundamental values. The tradition of research into movements prior to the 1960s, a tradition whose principal empirical reference point was the revolutionary movements of right and left in the first half of the century, has paid great attention to interpretations of this type (Kornhauser 1959). From this perspective, the emergence of a movement with strong separatist components, such as the Northern League, could be interpreted as evidence of the failure of the Italian elites to create and reproduce solid identification with the unitary democratic state and its fundamental principles (Rusconi 1993).

On the other hand, it is also possible to interpret collective action not just as the consequence of social disintegration processes, but also as evidence of the emergence of the opposite tendency, towards social reintegration; as proof, in other words, of the formation and consolidation of new value systems. From this point of view, the success of the Northern League could be associated with the growth, in the Italian population, of new, individualist values, oriented towards personal and professional success while barely concerned with the principles of solidarity present in both the Catholic and the socialist-communist traditions which had, up till then, dominated the country.

The link between the emergence of new conflicts and the value dimension has been stressed with considerable force in the context of various forms of 'new politics', connected with environmental issues, peace, and civil rights (Dalton 1988; Kriesi 1993: 60ff; Rohrschneider 1988). In the most ambitious formulation of this model, the rise of 'new' political movements from the 1970s onwards is associated with more general processes of value change (Inglehart 1977, 1990a, 1990b). Inglehart's argument is based on two assumptions. According to what he defines as 'scarcity hypothesis' (Inglehart 1990a: 56), there is a hierarchy of needs, and needs of a higher order (relating, for example, to the intellectual and personal growth of the individual) are conceivable only when those of a lower order (relating, for example, to physical survival) have been satisfied. Moreover, according to the 'socialization hypothesis' (Inglehart 1990a: 56), there is a continuity in adult life which leaves both fundamental principles and the order of priorities established in the formative years leading to maturity broadly unaltered.

The experiences and lifestyles of those born in the west in the period following the Second World War, and who became adults in the 1960s or later, have been very different from those of preceding generations. In particular, they have enjoyed unprecedented levels of affluence, easier access to higher education and reduced exposure to the risks of war. In Inglehart's view, this situation is likely to produce conditions which are particularly favourable to needs modification and changes in basic orientations. In particular, a gradual weakening of the system of 'material' values and their replacement by 'postmaterial' values is likely to set in. While the former reflects concerns relating to economic well-being, and personal and collective security, the latter are oriented, rather, towards the affirmation of expressive needs. They would, in other words, prioritize individual achievement in private, and an expansion of freedom of expression, democratic participation and self-government in the public domain.

The emergence of postmaterial values has been documented by an impressive amount of survey data, collected in the USA and in key European countries, from the beginning of the 1970s.[3] Since then, the gap between the number of people holding materialist values and those holding postmaterialist values has narrowed substantially, even though materialists are still in the majority. Furthermore, the younger cohorts of the population have been shown to be consistently more sensitive to postmaterialist values than older cohorts, and the data relating to this factor have been constant for the two decades covered by these surveys (Inglehart 1990b: 75).

The empirical evidence relating to value changes has been used as the basis for a notable number of analyses of the new politics, the emergence of the green parties and the characteristics of activists and supporters of new movements.[4] From these analyses, it has become clear that those with postmaterial values are strongly disposed to support new forms of collective action or to take part in some way in protest activities (Inglehart 1990b).

In particular, this has led to discussion of the emergence of new cleavages, founded on values rather than on class or religious loyalties, as occurred previously, and on the related processes of political realignment (Dalton 1988; Jennings et al. 1990).

The generalizations emerging from Inglehart's interpretative frame have provoked considerable debate around the theories he puts forward. In the first place, it has been argued that the growth of postmaterialist values is not so much a sign of profound change but, rather, a transitory phenomenon, the consequence of an unrepeatable historical conjunction such as that which took place in the 1960s. However, the data show that this tendency has resisted the force of waves of recession, such as occurred in 1973 and 1979, which might have increased support for materialist values once more.[5] Furthermore, repeated observation over time has shown how cohorts born in more recent years have maintained a greater propensity towards postmaterialist values even when they have reached adulthood. Generational replacement actually results in a steady increase of postmaterialists among western publics (see, for example, Abramson and Inglehart 1992). This also seems to support the interpretation that the adoption of postmaterialist values is not linked to lifecycle effects but, rather, reflects a fundamental cultural shift (see, for example, Inglehart 1990b; de Graaf and Evans 1996).

There are uncertainties inherent in other points of the theory of value change. It is not always clear from the formulations of its principal exponents what type of relationship they assume exists between changing socio-economic indicators and changing values. On the one hand, the scarcity hypothesis suggests a consistently positive relationship between economic affluence and the spread of postmaterialist values. For example, Dalton seems to suggest a relationship of this type when he affirms that 'if data for a longer time period were available, we would expect to find a very substantial decline in material values over the past several generations' (1988: 85). If we accepted, however, that gradual increases or reductions in economic well-being were to correspond with analogous changes in the incidence of postmaterialism, then the notion that the change in values was primed by the socio-economic transformation of the late 1950s and early 1960s would have less resonance.[6] Furthermore, it would be difficult to explain why there has not been a drastic reduction in the level of postmaterialism among generations coming of age in the 1970s and 1980s, when the climate of global optimism which developed in the 1960s had, in fact, largely dissolved. The data, however, as we have seen, appear to confirm the tendency towards an increase in postmaterial values.

In order to understand fully this phenomenon, it seems essential to characterize the 1960s as one of those rare moments in history which produced the conditions for a radical change in perspective. From this standpoint, one might argue that social transformations and events of particular relevance and impact, such as the fading away of the cold war, produced an irreversible change in conceptions of social and political life, and that a new generation[7] of citizens (and, in many cases, of militant politicians) was formed. It would thus be possible to speak of a 1960s generation, just as one speaks of generations when referring to the events of 1848, of the post-Victorian era or of the Great Depression of the 1920s and 1930s, this century (Braungart and Braungart 1986: 217; Jamison and Eyerman 1994). The 1960s generation would have passed on – at least in part – these new conceptualizations to younger groups, even although political contexts subsequently differed greatly.[8]

A second area of debate relates not only to the existence of a trend towards growth in postmaterial values but also to the relationship that Inglehart's theory posits between needs, values and the indicators used to measure them. First, the assumption that the need hierarchy is the underlying cause of materialist and postmaterialist values has met with inconclusive empirical support; so has the notion that economic conditions in pre-adult years are a powerful determinant of need and/or value priorities (Trump 1991). Second, the capacity of Inglehart's survey items to measure material and postmaterial values has been criticized. It seems legitimate to ask oneself, for example, to what extent assigning a lower priority to the goal of 'fighting rising prices' indicates a corresponding reduction in concern for the economy. Inflation did represent a problem of prime importance in the early 1970s, when this research was carried out; but it is doubtful that the same can be said for the twenty years following this, which were characterized rather by the increasing gravity of the employment crisis (Brooks and Manza 1994: 546; Duch and Taylor 1993; Inglehart and Abramson 1994).

Nor does the link between postmaterialist orientations and new social movements seem totally unambiguous. Hostility towards the politics of 'law and order' is certainly a distinctive characteristic of these movements. They have certainly mobilized on a number of occasions in support of freedom of expression and

direct democracy. But they have equally promoted other mobilizations (for example against war, nuclear energy or environmental
pollution) which it seems difficult to consider independently from
preoccupations with personal and collective security, or, in other
words, from purely 'materialist' concerns (Brooks and Manza
1994: 558–63). Likewise, it has been noted that the value distance
between the materialist and the postmaterialist camp is partially
an outcome of the way questions are posed, as they require
people to choose between items measuring one or the other
basic orientation.[9] When the possibility of a coexistence of the
two sets of value is taken into account, more complex configurations of basic orientations may emerge. For example, in their
study of grassroots activists in the Greater Vancouver area,
Carroll and Ratner (1996) found that a political economy representation of social conflict – broadly inspired by 'materialist'
concerns – often coexisted with a representation emphasizing
the importance of identity struggles, closer to a 'postmaterialist'
point of view. It has also been argued that exclusive focus on
the materialist vs. postmaterialist distinction may somewhat con-
ceal another important distinction, opposing authoritarian and
libertarian attitudes, which does not overlap with the former
(Steel et al. 1992). Despite a substantial correlation between
postmaterialism and support for new movements, the quota of
postmaterialists embracing authoritarian, right-wing values (for
example, opposing welfare spending, or advocating authoritarian
policies of nature protection) is far from insignificant (Steel et al.
1992: 350–1).

It is also necessary to ask to what extent postmaterialism can
be said to represent the basis of the new political divide. In this
context, it is important to take account of the relationship between
the materialist–postmaterialist dimension and the more general
identification with left and right. Given the tendency of political
opposition movements to identify themselves with the left, at
least since the end of the Second World War, the materialist–
postmaterialist split might be said to be simply a reworking of
the left–right division, thus denying the existence of new and
different political perspectives. As yet, there is no conclusive
evidence to support or refute this hypothesis. It is certainly the
case that, on the historic left, both party supporters and trade
unionists tend also to be postmaterialists, as are those of the new
left and the new movements (Inglehart 1990a: ch. 11; 1990b: 90).

On the other hand, it is far from clear what the left–right
dimension refers to in strict terms. At the very mimimum it

can be deconstructed into two, independent dimensions, one measuring orientations to socio-economic issues, the other, to libertarian versus authoritarian attitudes.[10] Postmaterialism has sometimes been found to be a poor predictor of both types of orientations (Middendorp 1992). Moving to the relationship between general left orientations and movements, it is only certain sectors of the left – from the non-communist tradition – which seem to be clearly sympathetic to the new movements (Inglehart 1990a: ch. 11). Furthermore, while a generic identification with the left provides an adequate explanation for interest in the issues raised by the new movements, postmaterialism offers a better explanation of the willingness of individuals to participate in these movements (1990a). One might also argue that, rather than postmaterialism being the basis for a new political cleavage, the opposite interpretation might well be true. In other words, where a new cleavage has emerged for historical, specific reasons (like in Germany), then this may well have been organized around the materialist versus postmaterialist divide; where, however, this has not been the case (for example, in the USA), then postmaterialist values may not be associated with any specific political faction (Trump 1991).

There is also a third set of objections to the theory of value change, which relates not only to the theory itself but more generally to approaches which emphasise the relationship between values and action. If an individual's values can explain his or her fundamental sensitivity to particular questions and problems, it is not, however, automatically the case that their impact can go beyond this level. The decision to act – and, specifically, to act collectively – depends not only on basic internalized principles but on a complex evaluation of the opportunities for action and of the barriers blocking the way. Values are articulated through specific goals and are associated with strategies of appropriate conduct. It is thus necessary to interpret the external situation as favourable to action, or at least as requiring the mobilization of the individual, rather than withdrawal or conformity. And it is essential to be able to transform individual values into collective ones, identifying elements of convergence and solidarity among others sharing the same values.[11] In other words, it is necessary to have a view of reality which links the values domain with the strategic and solidaristic domain, in a coherent fashion. Attention must also be paid both to the cognitive dimension of action, as we shall do in the following sections of this chapter, and to the relationship between action and collective identity – a theme which we consider in the next chapter.

3.2   Culture and Action: The Cognitive Perspective

3.2.1   Collective action as cognitive praxis

The idea that culture, and, specifically, its impact on collective action, can be reduced to the values component has been, for some time, a controversial view. In particular, it has been observed that 'culture influences action not by providing the ultimate values toward which action is oriented, but by shaping a repertoire or "tool kit" of habits, skills, and styles from which people construct "strategies of action"' (Swidler 1986: 273). That is to say, culture provides the cognitive apparatus which people need to orient themselves in the world. This apparatus consists of a multiplicity of cultural and ideational elements which include beliefs, ceremonies, artistic forms and informal practices such as language, conversation, stories, daily rituals (Swidler 1986: 273). The content of cultural models, of which values are a key component, is here seen as of secondary importance in relation to the vision of culture as a set of instruments according to which social actors make sense of their own life experiences.[12]

In relation to the study of collective action, this standpoint allows us to consider problems which an analysis focusing exclusively on values would have neglected. It helps us, therefore, to reflect on the reasons why systems of analogous values are, in certain circumstances, able to support collective action but fail to provide adequate motivation in others. Second, the flexibility and skills of actors in adapting to different environmental conditions and confronting them successfully, emerge very clearly. An important precondition for the success of movements lies in the ability of their exponents to reformulate their own values and motivations, in order to adapt them in the most efficient manner to the specific orientations of the sectors of public opinion which they wish to mobilize (Snow et al. 1986; Tarrow 1994). In the context of this need for flexibility and adaptability, strong identification with certain norms and values can even represent an obstacle to the freedom of the actor, limiting his or her capacity for action (Kertzer 1988; Swidler 1986; Lofland 1995).

It is therefore always possible to interpret the experience of the movements as cognitive praxis (Eyerman and Jamison 1991),

which includes an unceasing round of production and reproduction of cultural codes (Melucci 1989, 1991; Benford and Hunt
1992; Hunt and Benford 1994; Benford 1993). Some observers
have come to equate movements with a form of drama 'in which
the protagonists and antagonists compete to affect audiences'
interpretations of power relations in a variety of domains'.[13] One
does not need, however, to accept all the theoretical implications
of this argument in order to be able to recognise that a key
component of the activity of movements is more or less directly
related to symbolic production; and that this element is not a
precondition for conflict but, rather, one of its constituent parts.

3.2.2 Interpretative frames

In the context of the type of analysis we are discussing here,
the notion of the schema of interpretation, or frame, borrowed
from the theoretical work of Erving Goffman (1974) has had a
particularly favourable reception. Frames have been defined as
' "schemata of interpretation" that enable individuals "to locate,
perceive, identify and label" occurrences within their life space
and the world at large' (Snow et al. 1986: 464). A frame, thus, 'is
a general, standardised, predefined structure (in the sense that
it already belongs to the receiver's knowledge of the world)
which allows re-cognition of the world, and guides perception
. . . allowing him/her to build defined expectations about what
is to happen, that is to make sense of his/her reality' (Donati
1992: 141–2).[14]

Frame analysis allows us to capture the process of the attribution of meaning, which lies behind the explosion of any conflict.
In fact, symbolic production enables us to attribute to events
and behaviours, of individuals or groups, a meaning which facilitates the activation of mobilization. There are three stages to
this process, corresponding to the recognition of certain problems, of possible strategies which would resolve these, and of
motivations for acting on this knowledge.[15]

In the first place, appropriate interpretative frames allow a
phenomenon whose origins were previously attributed to natural factors, or which was the responsibility of those already
involved, to be transformed into a social or political problem. It
comes to be perceived as being determined or at least largely
conditioned by the dynamics of social order or related factors;
and precisely for this reason, the potential for modification
through collective action is recognized (Melucci 1989, 1991; Snow

et al. 1986). Social problems, in fact, do not exist as such, but only to the extent that certain phenomena are interpreted in this way, in the light of the cultural frames of those involved. Their emergence represents an autonomous social process, with unpredictable results. Problems emerge, grow and disappear, only to re-emerge periodically, transformed to a greater or lesser extent (Blumer 1971; Hilgartner and Bosk 1988; Best 1989; Gusfield 1963, 1981; Downs 1972).

The definition of reality is always, however, a process which leads to conflict. Various social actors (state agencies, political parties, groups with hostile interests, media operators) try to affirm their own control of specific issues, imposing their own interpretation of these, to the detriment of representations proposed by movements. Movements must therefore, in the first place, claim their stake as 'problem owners', or recognition of the right to deal with a particular problem, in ways compatible with their own leanings (Gusfield 1963). It is through symbolic conflict that certain actors succeed in being recognized – and, ultimately, legitimized – as being able to speak in the name of certain interests and tendencies.

A crucial step in the social construction of a problem consists of the identification of those responsible for the situation in which the aggrieved population finds itself. Effectively,

> the heat of moral judgement is intimately related to beliefs about what acts or conditions have caused people to suffer undeserved hardship or loss. The critical dimension is the abstractness of the target . . . When we see impersonal, abstract forces as responsible for our suffering, we are taught to accept what cannot be changed and make the best of it . . . At the other extreme, if one attributes undeserved suffering to malicious or selfish acts by clearly identifiable groups, the emotional component of an injustice frame will almost certainly be there. (Gamson 1992b: 32)

However, the identification of social problems is, inevitably, highly selective. The highlighting of one particular problem leads to the neglect of other potential sources of protest or mobilization which appear not to fit in with the interpretation of reality adopted. This becomes even more obvious at the point at which it is necessary to reintegrate events and structural conditions which are, at least in part, heterogeneous. For example, for a long time, the pre-eminence within western society of representations of conflict according to a functional/class or national dimension has made the identification of other sources of conflict

– such as gender differences – very difficult. Cultural development places actors in the position of being able to choose, from among various possible sources of frustration and revenge, those against which they should direct all their energies and action, not to mention their emotional identification. The process can, in this sense, be seen as a reduction of social complexity. At the same time, however, once solid interpretative frames have been established, the possibility of identifying other potential conflicts is limited and other ways of representing the same theme become necessary. In this sense, the construction of reality, created by relatively marginal actors responsible for mobilizing movements, is inextricably linked to the asymmetries of power.

The Italian regionalist leagues are a good example of the selective nature of interpretative frames. For the most part, they have adopted a frame which reduced a series of disparate social phenomena to a regionalist conflict between the north and south of the country. The inefficiency of state administration, the serious state financial crisis, the growing inconsistency between the strong economic role of small businesses in the north and their limited political weight, concerns about the spread of organized crime, mainly of southern origin, and the increase of immigration from the Third World were all incorporated – with a marked populist tenor – into this territorial type of interpretative model (Biorcio 1991, 1992; Diani 1996). Those responsible for the problems of the north – and of Italy in general – have been identified, first, in the 'Roman' political class and, second, in their allies, the politico-industrial elites.

Thus, phenomena which might initially have been thought diverse have been incorporated into the same interpretative frame. Other frames might have been devised. For example, north–south tensions might have been represented through an ethno-nationalist frame which stressed the profound cultural differences to be found in Italy. One might, therefore, have represented the north as a *nation manqué*, colonized by an administration and a people of different ethnic origins. This interpretation is, in fact, always present in the League's public communications, but has not been dominant during its ascendancy. If this had occurred, a different reading of the conflict would have developed, and the chances of mobilization would have been less certain. An ethno-nationalist frame would, in fact, have precluded the League from winning electoral and active support from the substantial population of southern origin living in the north, in contrast with what has actually happened (Diani 1996).

The opponents of the Northern League have attempted to deny the existence of the 'southern question' – for example, by stigmatizing the criticism which the League has made of the clientelistic use of public funds in the south as evidence of anti-southern racism and lack of solidarity. They have attributed the crisis of the state machine and the economic differences between north and south to political patronage mechanisms and the block forces which have until now governed the country. Thus they have attempted to reframe the north–south question as a left–right division, by which they have developed, and continue to define, their own political identities. The aim – which they have largely failed to achieve – was to prevent diverse groups, such as small business people fed up with a suffocating bureaucracy, or those dissatisfied with the quality of public services, or sectors of the population biased against southerners from identifying themselves with a view of the conflict which hinged on the north–south divide.

The action of interpreting the world goes beyond identifying problems, however. It involves seeking solutions, hypothesizing new social patterns, new ways of regulating relationships between groups, new articulations of consensus and of the exercise of power. There is often a strong Utopian dimension present in this endeavour. The symbolic elaboration of a movement is thus not necessarily limited to the selection, on the basis of the parameters of instrumental rationality, of 'practical' goals, in a given social and cultural context. Rather, it opens new spaces and new prospects for action, making it possible to think of aims and objectives which the dominant culture tends instead to exclude from the outset. In this sense, it is possible to conceive of movements as media through which concepts and perspectives which might otherwise have remained marginal, are disseminated in society.[16]

The anti-nuclear movements mobilized around issues of great emotional impact, and for this reason, mobilization might seem relatively easy to achieve. Even in this case, however, an act of symbolic re-elaboration was required, in order to avoid reducing the whole question to the problem of the physical risk to those who might be involved in nuclear accidents. In other words, it was necessary to produce interpretative frames which outlined a broader vision of a denuclearized society or which identified the social (not just the physical) risks connected to the nuclear option, thus neutralizing the charge of anti-modernism or irrationality levelled at them by the supporters of atomic energy (Touraine et al. 1983a; Diani 1994).

Analogous considerations can be applied to the Lombard League. Introducing the prospect of federalism, the League identified a new route by which to escape the state of political and social crisis which a growing number of people were finding intolerable. It is of little importance whether or not this was a realistic prospect, or seriously promoted (Diamanti 1994): what counted was the fact that through a highly symbolic message of federalist reform for the country the League turned the elimination of a system controlled by traditional parties under a constitutional aegis, into an achievable goal. At the same time, the advent of the League enabled people to voice views and orientations which previously had been relegated to the sphere of private feelings and excluded from contemporary political debate – such as an aversion for southerners or blacks;[17] thus a new way of defining the world, one which had previously been denied, emerged.

On another level, symbolic elaboration is essential in order to produce the motivation and the incentives needed for action. The unknowable outcomes and the costs associated with collective action can be overcome only if the actors are convinced (intuitively even before rationally) of the opportunity for mobilizing and of the practicability and the legitimacy of the action. It is therefore important that frames do not address only the level of social groups and of collective actors but link the individual sphere with that of collective experience. At the same time, they must generalize a certain problem or controversy, showing the connections with other events or with the condition of other social groups; and also demonstrate the relevance of a given problem to the life experience of the individual (Gerhards 1995). Along with the critique of dominant representations of order and of social patterns, interpretative frames must therefore produce new definitions of the foundations of collective solidarity, to transform actors' identity of the actors in a way which favours action.[18]

In the case of the League, the northern question in Italy has been represented in such a way as to emphasize the link with supranational cultural tendencies and currents: for example in the positive performances of countries with a federal structure, such as Germany; in the more general aspirations to territorial decentralization and self-government; in tendencies towards the reduction of fiscal pressure and the deregulation of the economy, brought about by the neo-liberal governments of the principal western nations. At the same time, the inefficiency of the state and its corrupt system of patronage, or the risks deriving from the crisis in state finances were explicitly linked to the individual's perspective on life. For example, the way in which the supposed control held by southerners over the political class, and the resulting patronage politics, limited access to public positions for those not originally from the south, was highlighted. So was the consequent damage to professional opportunities for northern voters (Todesco 1992).

It is important to stress the strong connection between action in the symbolic sphere and action directed towards the control of material and organisational resources. The goals of action can, on occasion, relate principally to economic resources or those of power; at other times, to a modification in lifestyles and dominant cultural codes. However, in both cases, an adequate representation of their own situation will make it possible for social actors to evaluate the material and organizational resources at their disposal. These are, in fact, largely neutralized if the cultural perspective which actors adopt prevents them from forming alliances, from sending an easily understood message to the rest of society, or from mobilizing their supporters to take action. Often the actors who have the greatest success are not those with the greatest resources but 'those whose actions are coherent with the ideological dynamic. It is not simply that ideology contributes to the resources of certain groups vis-a-vis others, but rather the resources themselves are constituted through discourse' (Moaddel 1992: 375).

3.2.3 Frame alignment

An important condition determining the success of attempts at mobilization is that a frame alignment occurs between movement activists and the populations they intend to mobilize.[19] In other words, what is necessary is a 'linkage of individual and SMO interpretative orientations, such that some set of individual interests, values and beliefs and SMO activities, goals and ideology are congruent and complementary' (Snow et al. 1986: 464).[20] Collective action thus becomes possible at the point at which mobilizing messages are integrated with some cultural component from the population to which they are addressed.

Frame alignment can take various forms. First, messages sent out by movement organizers can incorporate elements shared with interpretations of reality which are produced by sectors of public opinion which might otherwise remain separated from each other (*frame bridging*, in the language of Snow and his collaborators). Furthermore, through *frame amplification* move-ment activists can articulate and further define an interpretation of the world which could otherwise remain confused and vague. *Frame extension* allows the specific concerns of the movement's potential base to relate to more general goals, in contexts where the connection might not be at all evident. Finally, *frame transfor-mation* of the messages of a movement renders them more coher-ent with the values and the dominant codes of interpretation of reality found in public opinion.

Frame alignment thus presupposes a dynamic relationship between the development of a movement and the cultural herit-age of both the country in which it operates, and of its institu-tions.[21] First, movements make reference to cultural currents which, while well rooted in a given country, were, at that time, overshadowed (Alberoni 1984). The new right in the USA has drawn inspiration largely from the authoritarian, communitarian, illiberal traditions of American society. While *liberal* culture was, in the 1960s and the early 1970s, able to limit the impact of the new right on public discourse, these currents have remained alive in broad sections of public opinion (Wallis and Bruce 1986; Bruce 1988; Oberschall 1993: ch. 13).

Second, emerging movements draw on their own traditional heritage and on that of the broader oppositional movements in a given country, presenting them, however, from a new perspect-ive. Western ethno-national movements of the 1960s and 1970s were often successful in linking traditional themes of peripheral nationalism, such as territory or language, which were previ-ously perceived to be predominantly a conservative issue, with radical, anti-establishment perspectives typical of movements of that period. The defence of local culture thus came to be associ-ated with youth counterculture, in a common reaction to mass culture. At the same time, the defence of territory took on new meanings in the light of the anti-militarist and anti-nuclear strug-gles of the period, to which was added the aspiration to reduce the control which the politico-military elites of centralized states had of peripheral territories. The critique of the distortion of capitalist development provided a common base for challenges to the economic subordination of 'internal colonies' and for solid-arity with third world anti-colonialist movements (Touraine et al. 1981, 1983a; Beer 1980; Melucci and Diani 1992; Tejerina Mon-tana 1992; Connor 1994).

Symbolic production also often occurs in the course of events, demonstrations, celebrations, which form part of the institutionalized culture of a given people, as in religious ceremonies. The celebrations of the orthodox church provided the context for the production and spread of nationalist interpretative frames in the Baltic republics at the time of their involuntary association with the Soviet Union. The Catalan and Basque churches played a similar role during the Francoist period in Spain (Johnston 1991a, 1991b, 1994). The legitimation of religious rituals creates opportunities for collective gatherings, and therefore for the strengthening and the diffusion of alternative messages, in repressive regimes. The funeral of the Abbot of Montserrat monastery, a well-known Catalan nationalist and opponent of the Franco regime, in 1968, represented an opportunity for different sectors of Catalan opposition to get together and reinforce their collective solidarity (Johnston 1991b: 156–8). Likewise, religious functions in Reza Pahlevi's Iran not only supported the emergence of opposition cultures in that country, but also ensured that these cultures developed a marked theocratic character, paving the way for the advent of the ayatollahs' regime (Moaddel 1992).

Finally, it is possible for movements to re-elaborate codes and symbols which not only form part of the mainstream culture of a particular society but which are also explicitly associated with its dominant groups. In contrast with other leaders of the Afro-American civil rights movement in the 1960s, Martin Luther King was careful, in his speeches, not to emphasize the differences between blacks and whites. In fact, he tended to avoid the construction of 'polemic identities'. Instead, he used references to the themes and the values of the heritage of the white American elites of that period, such as the relationship between individual liberty and a sense of responsibility towards the community (McAdam 1994: 38). It was precisely these values, rather than antagonistic values, which provided him with a base from which to argue the full legitimacy of the demands of the civil rights movement (McAdam 1994; Eyerman and Jamison 1991: 166–174).

In different ways, these examples of symbolic re-elaboration remind us that collective action is both a creative manipulation of symbols and a re-affirmation of tradition. The insurgence of a new wave of mobilization does not, in fact, represent simply a signal of innovation and change, in relation to the culture and the principles prevalent in a given period. It is, rather, a confirmation of fundamental continuity values and historic memories which have, in recent times, been neglected or forgotten.

Reference to the past can operate both as an obstacle and as an opportunity for action. It can represent an obstacle in that long-established ways of thinking and values systems can noticeably reduce the range of options available to the actor (Lofland 1995; Johnston and Klandermans 1995). Too strong an identification with tradition, or, in the same way, an excessive distance between the culture of the activists and sympathizers in a movement, and the rest of society, can, in certain cases, reduce the efficiency of symbolic re-elaboration (Swidler 1986). It can, in particular, make the processes of realignment of interpretative frames very difficult; and, as we have seen, these are crucial for the success of mobilization. On the other hand, the ability to refer to one's cultural heritage puts the cognitive and value-related resources at the disposal of actors. On the basis of these resources, it is possible to found alternative projects and an alternative political identity. In the absence of references to one's own history and to the particular nature of one's roots, an appeal to something new risks seeming inconsistent and, in the end, lacking in legitimacy.

3.2.4 Dominant interpretative frames

The fact that movements and conflicts do not develop in isolation but tend rather to be concentrated in particular political and historical periods (Tilly et al. 1975; Tarrow 1989a, 1994), is also reflected at the level of symbolic elaboration. The discourse of a single movement (or the organization of a movement) must then be placed in relation to the general orientations of a given period. If it is possible to identify conjunctions which are particularly favorable to the development of collective action, the dominant visions of the world in that period will inform – or at least influence – the representations produced by the movements taken together.[22] Thus a restricted number of dominant interpretative frames (or *master frames*: Snow and Benford 1989, 1992) will emerge, to which the specific elaborations of the various organizations or movements can be reduced, more or less directly.

In the early 1970s in Italy, the dominant vision of the conflict which the movements made their own was that of the class struggle. At that time, various types of conflict were interpreted and classified in the light of the Marxist model. The women's movement was seen, first, from the perspective of emancipation and conquest of equal opportunities rather than as an affirmation of gender differences. In the same way, representations of youth movements often connected their response with their social position and their precarious status. At a more directly political level, the rapid transformation of the student movement into little groups organized to resemble – or to caricature – the Leninist party can also be considered proof of Marxism's cultural domination. Models of counterculture and political proposals such as that of the environmentalists, which had little in common with representations of a classist nature, were accorded little space in the development of the movements, although they were also present (Diani 1984; Lodi and Grazioli 1984).

In contrast, in the USA, interpretative frames linked to the role of the individual, to his or her rights and aspirations for personal and civic growth, acquired considerable weight. For this reason, a cultural climate more favourable to the spread of movements which were profoundly different from those which developed in Italy was created. At a more directly political level, movements aimed at the protection of the freedom of expression (such as the Free Speech Movement), the granting of full citizenship to African Americans, or protest against American involvement in Vietnam, prospered (McAdam 1988; Eyerman and Jamison 1991: ch. 5). The presence of alternative and countercultural movements was also more evident. These were not limited to strictly communitarian and other world-rejecting forms, typical of the hippy movement and various religious currents of neo-orientalist derivation. They also showed some overlap with broader attempts to support practices designed to encourage inner growth and individual realization, as in the case of the human potential movement.[23]

3.3   Types of Interpretative Frames

Analyses of collective action centred on the concept of the interpretative frame – just as those which focus on the role of organizational resources or of political opportunities – are not exempt from ad hoc explanations. At any moment it is, in fact, possible to uncover the existence, within a given society, of a multiplicity of cultural models. It is not, therefore, difficult, for those studying any movement enjoying a certain success, to identify the cultural elements with which the specific interpretative frame of the movement is aligned. This poses the problem of formulating systematic hypotheses concerning the relationship between symbolic production activities and the success of attempts at mobilization set up by the organizations of the movement. It is therefore necessary to link the properties of different modes of categorization of reality to the specific nature of the movements and the conflicts which these represent. But it is essential to identify, as a preliminary step, classification criteria for interpretative frames.

One possible route consists of proposing typologies of interpretative frames, which relate the representations produced by specific movements with more general forms of symbolic production. Inspired by the concept of 'knowledge interest' developed by Jürgen Habermas (1978), Eyerman and Jamison (1991: 68ff) have identified three principal levels of symbolic elaboration ('cosmological, technological and organisational knowledge interests'). The first, 'cosmological' level relates to the elaboration of fundamental principles and the ultimate goals of the movement. The second, 'technological' level refers to the technical-practical dimension of action, the type of perception which the movements develop of dominant forms of knowledge in a given society, and of the alternatives which the movements represent. Finally, elaboration at the organizational level refers to social forms through which the movements produce and disseminate their own vision of the world. In Eyerman and Jamison's analysis, categories which for Habermas are ahistorical and indifferent to context, can assume particular concrete contents, which vary as they pass from one movement to another.[24]

Eyerman and Jamison recognize that the properties of the context in which movements act condition both the possibility of an action developing on cognitive terrain and the consolidation of the movements as autonomous social actors. Where representations produced by the movements (that is to say, the knowledge interests) are rapidly incorporated into the discourse of institutionalized actors, space for the existence of the movements is notably reduced. Among the explanations offered for the notable failure of a strong ecology movement to develop in Sweden, independently of traditional political organizations and of state agencies, is the speed with which these bodies moved to include in their political discourse the themes and references peculiar to the environmentalist culture (Jamison et al. 1990).

Another classification of interpretative frames explicitly links the symbolic production of the movements to the more general representations of the political context (Diani 1996).[25] It is not enough to look for links – though these, as we have already noted, are easy to find – between the interpretative frames of movements and any other representation of the world which is commonly found in a given society. Rather, it is necessary to concentrate on the relationship between the activists' frames and those specific representations of the political context, which are dominant in the population which the former intend to mobilize. The chances of success of a particular interpretative frame developed by movement activists are, all things being equal, greater when the specific mobilizing message is in alignment with the dominant master frame in that period – or, at least, with one of the dominant master frames, given that there are frequently sectors of public opinion which are deeply divided in terms of global perceptions of the opportunities offered by the political system.

Any hypothesis on which to base the classification of interpretative schemes needs to be based on the most general level, constituted by dominant interpretative schemes.[26] A useful starting point for analysis may be the way in which people represent, in general terms, the political opportunities offered by a given system. In this context, one may adopt two basic classification criteria, drawing on the dimensions identified by Sidney Tarrow (1994). The first refers to the stability, or instability of ideological divisions which traditionally structure a political system. The more these emerge as incapable of capturing and interpreting new interests and concerns and therefore lacking consolidated representation, the greater are the opportunities, for emerging movements, of introducing new political identities. The second criteria, on the other hand, refers to the possibilities for autonomous action within the system, offered to new political actors who have not been institutionalized by a given political regime. These depend on the configuration of institutional channels for dealing with demands, on the presence or absence of potential allies in the political system, and on the importance of internal divisions to the elites.

Four fundamental representations of the political environment can be established by categorizing different perceptions of opportunities within the system:[27] *antisystem frames, realignment frames, inclusion frames* and *revitalization frames. Antisystem frames* 'challenge both fundamental traits of a political system: on the one hand, its dominant cleavages and identities, and on the other, its capacity to accommodate heterogeneous and often conflicting interests and orientations within the political process. Antisystem frames therefore advocate a radical transformation of the polity' (Diani 1996: 1057). In the Italian situation, the success of the

League seems to have been supported by the greater congruence of its regional-populist frame with a dominant interpretation, in which distrust of the possibility that the system could guarantee sufficient space for collective action was combined with a reduced identification with traditional ideological divisions.

A *realignment frame* combines the perception of good opportunities for independent action with the decreasing capacity of traditional alignments to support collective identities and structure political action. It emphasizes the need to restructure political systems on the basis of new collective identities, without entailing a global delegitimation of the established members and procedures of the polity. The insurgence in Italy in the early 1980s of environmentalist movements profited from the presence of representations of the political system relating generally to realignment.[28] While they invoked the overcoming of classist or religious definitions of the political struggle, they had faith, even though critical, in the opportunities for independent action offered by the political system.

Inclusion frames are rhetorical devices, emphasizing the need for new political actors to be recognized as legitimate members of a polity, where definitions of the major cleavages are not challenged. Political innovation following the inclusion of new actors thus affects the composition of the political system rather than its structure. In this perspective, the limited success of the non-parliamentary left in the 1970s could be attributed to their reticence in elaborating inclusion frames. They focused instead, in rhetorical terms, on the radical subversion of the political system and therefore on antisystem frames. This was in spite of the fact that the classic version of the right–left axis, hinging on the clash between Christian Democrats and the Italian Communist Party, still represented for most Italians a solid principle articulating political identities.

Finally, *revitalization frames* are perceptions of the political environment according to which cleavages are stable, and opportunities for independent action limited. In such a context, the most reasonable option open to challengers is that of entering established political organizations in order to redirect their goals and revitalize their structures from within. The rise of Catholic dissent in the 1960s was prepared for by mobilization within the church of energies seeking the renewal of ecclesiastical practices. These had largely based their action on revitalization frames.

This classification of dominant frames has the advantage of placing the discussion on the role of rhetorical abilities in mobilization processes, in a more realistic perspective. When organizational resources and communicative capacities are equal, the success of a particular frame is much more likely when its basic elements are coherent with the representations of the political system dominant among its potential base during a given phase.

3.4   Summary

There are at least two ways of looking at the relationship between collective action and culture. The first stresses above all the values component of culture. Action is thus seen to ensue from the identification of the actor with a certain set of principles and concerns. Interpretations of movements in recent decades which have adopted this perspective have insisted in particular on the shift from materialist values to postmaterialist values. The second approach which we have dealt with here sees rather a cognitive praxis in culture, a way of giving meaning to the actor's experience. In this context, mobilization does not depend so much on values as on the process of interpretation of reality which makes collective action appear to be an adequate and feasible response to a condition which is perceived to be unjust. Action is facilitated by processes of 'interpretative frame alignment' or, in other words, by the convergence of models of interpretation of reality adopted by movement leaders and those of the population which they intend to mobilize. Movements' cultural production implies a relationship which involves both conquering and revitalizing aspects (or at least some aspects) of a given population's traditions. This is both an impediment and a resource for action. Explanations of collective action which are centred on the concept of the 'interpretative frame' nevertheless often carry the risk of ad hoc explanations. One way out of this difficulty lies in linking various types of interpretative frames developed by actors with certain perceptions of the political opportunities provided by the environment. In the next chapter, which looks at mechanisms for production of identity, we shall see how the cultural and symbolic dimension is linked to the subjective experience of the individual.

4
Collective Action and Identity

I think it's made me stronger. I think it's made me really clear about who I am . . . I almost feel my life has a theme. It's not just like I'm this little ant out there living and working with all the other ants on the anthill. There are things that I care really, really deeply about, and that sort of infuses my whole life with meaning. And I've retained that, and I think I always will.

> Radical feminist activist, Columbus, Ohio, USA,
> quoted in Whittier 1995: 95

Until two years ago, I was a woman who belonged to a man. Then I met the women of the collective, and slowly I have acquired the ability to develop new and different relationships with people. Today, I feel myself to be equal in my relationship with this man and in my relationships with the women of the collective.

> Martina, member of a women's collective, Milan, Italy,
> quoted in Bianchi and Mormino 1984: 160

After Greenham I realized how in fact I was putting myself down on occasions. Simply because there were men around I wasn't verbalizing my thoughts enough. I wasn't coming forward . . . the men were dominating, and I was allowing them to dominate me.

> Carola Addington, Greenham Common camper, UK,
> quoted in Roseneil 1995: 146

If someone asks me, 'Who are you?' I'm a radical feminist . . . And I see radical feminism as my life's work, even though I'm spending most of my days, most of my weeks, most of my years, doing something else.

> Employee of a public interest organization, Columbus,
> Ohio, USA, quoted in Whittier 1995: 95

For me, being part of a women's group is an essential influence not only on my way of life but also on my thinking. It is important to know yourself. The collective has died and been reborn many times over, along with my own aspirations. Wherever I go, I will always find a women's group.

> Irma, Member of a women's collective, Milan, Italy,
> quoted in Bianchi and Mormino 1984: 159

There was the miners' strike and a lot of miners' wives used to come down . . . And there was the American Indian from the Indian reservation . . . And there were delegations from South Africa. And we were just dead ordinary working class women from the inner cities and we were talking to people who were directly involved in struggles from all over the world.

> Trisha, Greenham Common camper, UK,
> quoted in Roseneil 1995: 149

Irma and Martina were part of the Ticinese Collective, a group of women active in Milan around the end of the 1970s and the beginning of the 1980s (Bianchi and Mormino 1984). Trisha and Carola were among the women who took part in the occupation of the Greenham Common area, site to Cruise missiles in Britain between 1983 and 1991 (Roseneil 1995). The two anonymous quotes[1] belong to women who were involved in the radical feminist movement in the American city of Columbus, Ohio, between the 1970s and the early 1990s (Whittier 1995, 1997). The characteristics of these movements were different, and so was the political and cultural context in which they developed. And yet, for all the differences, these quotations reveal more than random commonalities. They all appear representative, in their own ways, of the relationship between collective and individual experience in social movements. In particular, they tell us about the intersection of collective involvement and personal engagement which characterizes so much of collective action (Melucci 1982, 1989, 1995; Rupp and Taylor 1987; Calhoun 1994a).

On the one hand, these stories are about personal change: they testify to the new sense of empowerment, and to the strengthening of the self, which originate from collective action. For

Carola, fighting the Cruise missiles in the context of a 'women only' campaign meant the awareness of how much she had undervalued her potential in the past, especially in situations with a strong male presence. For Trisha, being at Greenham Common opened up spaces for contacts and experiences that her working-class origins would have denied her otherwise. For Martina, joining a self-awareness group signified transforming her private life, without developing a strong commitment to public engagement. Even in her case, however, it was the nature of collective experience which enabled her to achieve personal growth. On the other hand, these stories are about the sense of continuity to one's life that a strong sense of collective belongingness provides. For Irma as well as for the Columbus women, being a feminist provided a linkage between different life stages and different types of experiences. The linkage is not necessarily between different points in time; it is also – as Trisha's story suggests – between people acting in different localities and on different specific issues, still united by a common set of values and aspirations.

These stories are, in other terms, about identity: in particular, about the relationship between identity and collective action (Pizzorno 1978; Cohen 1985; Melucci 1989; Calhoun 1991; Mach 1993). In speaking of identity we are not referring to an autonomous object, nor to a property of social actors; we mean, rather, the process by which social actors recognize themselves – and are recognized by other actors – as part of broader groupings. On the basis of such allegiances, they give meaning to their own experiences and to their development over time.[2] It is worth noting the complexity of the relationship between the individual dimension and the collective dimension in processes which define identity. On the one hand, through the production, maintenance and revitalization of identities, individuals define and redefine individual projects, and possibilities for action open and close. The stories just reported show us precisely that 'identities are often personal and political projects in which we participate' (Calhoun 1994a: 28). On the other hand, the construction of identity cannot be reduced simply to psychological mechanisms; it is a social process. The rediscovery of oneself becomes possible as a result of collective processes.

In the following pages, we are concerned, then, with identity construction and will discuss some of its characteristics. We will show, first, that identity production is an essential component of collective action, through the identification of actors involved in conflict, the activation of trusting relationships among them and the establishment of connections linking events from different periods. Subsequently, we will confront some of the paradoxes which a concept as fleeting as that of identity inevitably creates. The first of these is linked to the simultaneously static and dynamic nature of social identification. On the one hand, reference to identity evokes the continuity and the solidity of allegiances over time. On the other, one cannot ignore the fact that identity is open to constant redefinitions. Links postulated by social actors with certain historical experiences and with certain groups, appear, in fact, always to be contingent. They are the fruit of symbolic reinterpretations of the world which are inevitably selective and partial. As a result, in spite of their relative stability, even feelings of identification can be – and in fact are – subject to recurring modifications.

A second paradox is represented by the presence of multiple identities, or, in other words, individuals' feelings of belonging to several different collectives. From a certain point of view, identity operates as an organizing principle in relation to individual and collective experience: for example, it helps actors to identify their allies and their adversaries. At the same time, however, the definition of lines of solidarity and of opposition is often anything but clear: the rise of feminist movements has created, for example, new lines of identification which have often revealed themselves to be in contrast with those which preceded them (for example, those of class). Rather than uprooting these older lines of identity, new identities co-exist with them, generating tensions among actors' different self-representations,[3] or between activists who identify with the same movement yet belong to different generations (Whittier 1995, 1997).

The third and last paradox which we shall discuss relates to the role of identity within the framework of rational interpretations of collective action. As the definition of identity comes into contact with components relating to the emotions or to values, its relationship with models of rational action, concerned with the calculation of costs and benefits, can seem extremely weak. However, many scholars have made reference to the notion of identity precisely to explain collective action in rational terms (for example, Pizzorno 1978). It is therefore necessary to be aware of this duplicity in the use of the concept and in the debate which has developed.

4.1 Identity and Collective Action

Identity construction should not be regarded simply as a precondition for collective action. It is certainly true that social actors' identities in a given period guide their subsequent conduct. Action occurs, in fact, when actors develop the ability to define themselves, other social actors and the content of the relationships which link them (Touraine 1981). At the same time, however, identity is not an immutable characteristic, pre-existing action. On the contrary, it is through action that certain feelings of belonging come to be either reinforced or weakened. In other words, the evolution of collective action produces and encourages continuous redefinitions of identity (Hirsch 1990; Fantasia 1988). It is therefore possible to hold that the processes of construction of collective identity are an integral component of collective action (Melucci 1995).

Let us look more closely at the mechanisms by which action 'constitutes' identity. This happens, first, through the definition of boundaries between actors engaged in a conflict. In contrast to macro-structural approaches to the analysis of social conflicts, the sociology of action has drawn attention to the problematic nature of the structure–action nexus, and has particularly emphasized the way in which conflict cannot be explained exclusively in the light of structural relationships and of contrasting interests which these have determined. It originates, rather, in the interaction between structural tensions and the emergence of a collective subject which can see itself as the bearer of certain values and interests, and define its adversaries on the basis of these (Touraine 1981). Collective action cannot occur in the absence of a 'we' characterized by common traits and a specific solidarity. Equally indispensable is the identification of the 'other' to which can be attributed the responsibility for the actor's condition and against which the mobilization is called (Gamson 1992b). The construction of identity therefore implies both a positive definition of those participating in a certain group, and a negative identification of those who are not only excluded but actively opposed. It also includes a relationship with those who find themselves in a neutral position, as far as the conflict is concerned. It is with reference to these three components[4] that movement identities are formed and come to life.

In the second place, the production of identities corresponds to the emergence of new networks of relationships of trust among movement actors, operating within complex social environments.[5] The existence of widespread relationships of trust guarantees movements a range of opportunities (see ch. 5). They are the basis for the development of informal communication networks, for interaction and, when necessary, for mutual support. They seem to be an essential replacement for the scarcity of organizational resources; furthermore, information circulates rapidly via interpersonal networks, compensating at least in part for limited access to the media; trust between those who identify with the same political and cultural endeavour enables those concerned to face with greater efficacy the costs and the risks linked to repression; finally, identifying themselves – and being identified – as part of a movement means also to be able to count on help and solidarity from its militants (Gerlach and Hine 1970; Gerlach 1971).

The risks and uncertainties related to collective action would prevent people's involvement in the absence of strong feelings of identity and of collective solidarity. In the case of the workers' movement, the activation and the reproduction of these feelings was facilitated by the close proximity of workplaces and living spaces (see chapter 2). In post-industrial society, however, direct social relationships founded on territorial proximity have become weaker. While this has not necessarily meant the disappearance of community relations, on the whole, systems of social relations are more distantly connected than they were in the past to a defined territorial space (Wellman et al. 1988; Martinotti 1993). Their borders extend now to encompass entire national and supranational communities (Giddens 1990). As a result, collective actors are now less likely than in the past to identify themselves in terms of a strongly rooted territorial base. Collective identity is less dependent on direct, face-to-face interactions which develop in the local community and in everyday spaces. Phenomena of this type had already signalled the shift from pre-modernity to modernity, and the emergence of public opinion integrated via the printed word (Anderson 1983; Tarrow 1994). But they have undergone a further acceleration with the expansion of the media system and the telematics revolution (Calhoun 1992; Wasko and Mosco 1992).

To identify with a movement also means to have feelings of solidarity towards people with whom one is not, in most cases, linked by direct personal contacts,[6] but with whom one shares, however, aspirations and values. Activists and movement sympathizers are aware of participating in realities which are much vaster and more complex than those of which they have direct experience. It is in reference to this wider community that the actor draws motivation and encouragement to action, even when the field of concrete opportunities seems limited and there is a strong sense of isolation.

Third, collective identity guarantees continuity to experiences of collective action over time. Movements characteristically alternate between 'visible' and 'latent' phases (Melucci 1984a). In the former, the public dimension of action prevails, in the form of demonstrations, public initiatives, media interventions and so on, with high levels of cooperation and interaction among the various mobilized actors. In the latter, action within the organizations and cultural production dominate. Contacts between organizations and militant groups are, on the whole, limited to interpersonal, informal relationships, or to interorganizational relationships which do not generally produce the capacity for mass mobilization. In these cases, collective solidarity and the sense of belonging to a cause are not as obvious as they are in periods of intense mobilization. Identity is nurtured by the hidden actions of a limited number of actors. And it is precisely the ability of this group to reproduce certain representations and models of solidarity over time which creates the conditions for the revival of collective action and allows those concerned to trace the origins of new waves of public action to preceding mobilizations (Melucci 1984a; Rupp and Taylor 1987; Johnston 1991b; Mueller 1994).

This linking function of identity does not operate only on the plane of collective representations and socially widespread perceptions of certain social phenomena. It relates the latter to individual experience. In constructing their own identity, individuals attribute coherence and meaning to the various phases of their own public and private history. This often reflects in their life stories. It is true that any wave of mobilization attracts to social movements people with no previous experience of collective action – at least for biographical reasons. Still, continuity in militancy – the fact that those who have already participated in the past are more likely to become active once again than those who have never done so – has been confirmed by a large number of studies, devoted to both contemporary (McAdam 1988; Diani 1995a; Whittier 1995 and 1997; Klandermans 1997; ch. 4) and 'historic' examples of collective action (Thompson 1963; Gould 1995).

Speaking of continuity over time does not necessarily mean assuming that identity persists, let alone that it is fixed. Reference to the past is, in fact, always selective. 'Continuity' in this case means rather the active re-elaboration of elements of one's own biography and their reorganization in a new context. In this way, it becomes possible to keep together personal and collective occurrences which might otherwise appear to be incompatible and contradictory. As an example, let us look at a case of radical collective action, which would seem to presuppose a drastic personal transformation at the moment of mobilization – that of terrorism. Biographies of Italian terrorists of the 1970s (della Porta 1990) show that they had, in many cases, moved from militancy in Catholic organizations to armed struggle. In this case, there was clearly a marked caesura in forms of action and political programmes. Nevertheless, there were also elements of coherence in these histories which seem, on the surface, to be so lacking in continuity. One of these was the aspiration to construct social relationships which went beyond the inequalities and the distortions of the present. Also common to both phases was a conception of collective action as being concerned with the proclamation of absolute truths and with the concrete testimony of one's own ideal (and ideological) principles, no matter how distorted.

On the other hand, the outset of each new experience of collective action inevitably means also breaking with the past, to some degree. In some cases, the decision to move to collective action or to belong to an organization or to a project whose characteristics are clearly different from the previous experience of those concerned, results in a radical transformation of the individual. In these cases, people experience genuine conversions, which often means breaking with their previous social bonds. The transformation of identity can be much more profound in these cases. It will relate not only to the political leanings of the individual and his or her level of involvement in collective action, but also global life choices and even the organization of everyday life.

The same phenomena are often found among those who join religious movements (Robbins 1988: ch. 3; Snow et al. 1980; Wilson 1982; Wallis and Bruce 1986).[7] Furthermore the history of conflicts typical of the industrial society documents the force of 'traditional' political identities and the often exclusive and sectarian nature of collective action. In the century of great ideologies, abandoning political and/or class positions – that is, giving up a certain system of social relationships and of affective identifications in order to adopt another – has always been costly. A good example of this is provided in the segmentation along religious lines of Northern Ireland. Religious identities have provided a criteria for the organization of social relations at all level, including community and family linkages. Ties cutting across sectarian barriers are infrequent and people involved in them regularly meet with ostracism from their own communities (Bew et al. 1979; McAllister 1983; O'Sullivan See 1986; Maguire 1993). Political life in Italy in this century has also been shaped – although in less dramatic forms – by two great political subcultures – the Catholic and the socialist (Ginsborg 1990). They formed the basis for the definition of fundamental political identities, making reference to the church and to the parties of the left. Feelings of loyalty and of identification with other organizations (trade unions, cultural associations, cooperatives and so on) played a subordinate role, in that context, in relation to the principal ideological positions. Subcultures, at least up until the 1970s, were largely impenetrable. The two worlds – the Catholic and the socialist – rarely communicated with each other. Movement from one to the other often meant overturning a whole series of personal relationships, including family ties, at times. The decision to change political allegiance was equated to betrayal, and was usually a traumatic experience, representing a drastic cut-off from one's past.[8]

4.2 Identity as a Social Process

4.2.1 Self- and hetero-definitions of identity

If identity is a social process rather than a property of social actors, it follows that feelings of belonging and of solidarity in relation to the members of a certain group, the recognition of elements of continuity and discontinuity in the history of individuals and the identification of one's own adversaries, may all be subject to recurring re-elaboration. Identity is that which emerges from the individual's process of self-identification and external recognition. The notions which actors develop of themselves are, in fact, continuously confronted with images which other social actors (institutions, sympathetic and hostile social groups, public opinion, the media) produce of them.

The construction of identity at the same time contains an aspiration to differentiate oneself from the rest of the world and to be recognized by it (Melucci 1982; Calhoun 1994a). A collective actor cannot exist without reference to experiences, symbols and myths which can form the basis of its individuality. At the same time, however, symbolic production cannot count solely on self-legitimacy. It is necessary for certain representations of self to find recognition in the image which other actors have of the subject. In other words, the definition which the group has produced of itself must be taken account of by other actors when they elaborate their own world view. It is only in the context of mutual recognition among actors that conflict and, more generally, social relationships, can exist (Simmel 1955; Touraine 1981). Without this, self-affirmed identity on the part of a group will, inevitably, lead to its marginalization and reduction to a deviant phenomenon.

The story of movements is therefore also the story of the ability of their members to impose certain images of themselves, and to counter attempts by dominant groups to denigrate their aspirations to be recognized as different. An example would be conflicts whose origins can be traced back to the construction of the nation state. The development of vast, highly centralized political units led to an emphasis on cultural homogenization, through the affirmation of one 'national' language and one 'national' culture. Assimilationist policies often followed from this, in view of the multicultural nature of the territories coming under the dominion of new state formations. Cultural traditions which differed from those of the social groups which were protagonists in the construction of new nation states were stigmatized as relics of the past. For example, the construction of the French national identity led to the marginalization of the Provençal and Breton cultures. These became mere residues of a backward, pre-modern society, whose survival would represent an undeserved obstacle to the spread of the positive values of progress, of which the French state made itself the bearer (Beer 1977, 1980; Safran 1989; Canciani and De La Pierre 1993).

The ability to impose negative and stigmatized definitions of the identity of other groups constitutes, effectively, a fundamental mechanism of social domination. If a group is perceived by the rest of society to be the bearer of values and of experiences which, if not deviant, are certainly backward, dysfunctional and potentially harmful to the common good, and if its members are not able to spread alternative representations successfully, then members' capacity for collective action will be extremely limited. Indeed, they will even find it difficult to conceive of themselves as subjects, legitimately able to claim civic rights on a par with those which other social groups enjoy. The negative impact of others' definitions of identity contributes, for example, to explaining the low capacity for collective action, often found among residents of urban ghettos. Solidarity and interaction networks and various forms of group life are to be found within groups formed in this context, but the fact that external observers describe these areas primarily in terms of deprivation and of social disintegration often hinders their inhabitants from grasping and valuing possibilities for self-organization, even when these are present within the group (Wacquant 1994). Stigmatization from outside therefore ends up blocking the development of a strong autonomous identity and limiting the possibilities for collective actions. Similar conclusions can be drawn from the fact that women are often represented as paying little attention to the public and political dimensions of social life. The emphasis placed on the presumed inclination of women towards the private sphere, and on their presumed lack of rational abilities, which are held to be essential in order to act in the public sphere, eventually put a break on the direct involvement of women in collective action. At the centre of feminist movements' action, alongside the creation of practical opportunities to facilitate women's participation, has been the overturning of images and of traditional stereotypes (Zincone 1992; Taylor and Whittier 1995).

4.2.2   Identity as 'rediscovery' or as 'creation'

The identity of a movement almost inevitably ends up being described by its militants as 'natural'. Through collective action, individuals rediscover their 'natural' affinity with other, like-minded people, which had, for too long, been hidden. To feel oneself to be part of a common project is the 'natural' response to a shared condition of deprivation. For a militant Scottish nationalist, for example, being politically active is the obvious consequence of the solidity of the historic cultural link. In comparison, being a 'British subject' appears to be only an administrative condition, in this context. For those who work in the women's movement, collective action reflects the unfolding of a solidarity which, in most cases, had been denied in the past.

On the other hand, if the emphasis on the authenticity of the origins and the 'naturalness' of the group functions as a way of legitimizing its aspirations, it is equally crucial for a movement not to present itself as an actor focused purely on its own origins and traditions. It is also necessary to reveal the elements of 'newness' which a new movement or a new phase of collective action presents, in relation to the past. Various waves of women's mobilizations have borne witness to the constant attempt of militants to recreate the link with earlier experiences, but at the same time to draw a line under these (Bianchi and Mormino 1984; Rupp and Taylor 1987; Whittier 1995, 1997). Identity construction always entails both continuity and a change in direction, whether individual or collective.

In this symbolic conflict, movement adversaries adopt very similar strategies. On the one hand, they do not miss the opportunity to show the constructed, arbitrary, 'unnatural' side of the images which movements create of themselves. In the Scottish situation, once again, critics observe that historical experience challenges, rather than confirms, to deep-rooted solidarity and shared interests across the various strata of Scottish society which are postulated by the nationalists. Or, in the case of the women's movement, in contrast to the view that feminine solidarity is natural it is claimed that the traditional model of relationships between the sexes is the natural one, as it has been reproduced with minor variations over the centuries.

Conflicts relating either to the affirmation or to the negation of the natural foundations of certain self-images determined by social actors therefore cover a wide range. From this observation there emerges an important question for students of collective action: whether the production of identity is to be understood primarily as the rediscovery of permanent traits, rooted in the personality and/or in actors' collective memory but previously hidden by a certain dominant system, or whether identity constitutes a creative process, based on a constant action of symbolic reproduction is still open to debate.

In discussing the nature of contemporary nationalism, many have identified the deep roots of national identities in historical experiences over a long period of time, and in cultural models which were formed in the pre-modern era. Although nationalism has taken a distinctive and accomplished form in the last two centuries, national identities draw upon events, institutions, myths and narrations, which precede by a long period of time the existence of the nation state (Smith 1981, 1986). Others have pointed out the constructed nature of much of modern national identities, whether institutionalized or in the course of formation, as in the case of many recent ethno-national movements. A large part of the myths on which these are based do not have any historical foundation (Anderson 1983; Hobsbawm 1991). In reality, it would be legitimate, in such cases, to talk of the 'invention of tradition' (Hobsbawm and Ranger 1984).

Similar considerations apply also to identities of an ethnic but non-territorial nature: it has been observed that in societies which are characterized by multiple cultures and traditions, as in the USA, conditions exist for the development of forms of 'symbolic ethnicity' (Gans 1979). These are forms of identification which have no foundation in the historic and cultural heritage of a given group, but mix together symbols and references deriving from diverse social groups to form a new synthesis. For example, collective identities such as Rastafarianism are founded only partly on specific cultural models and religious allegiances. They are also the product of choices made by individuals who come from a range of backgrounds but derive feelings of belonging and incentives for action through reference to a particular culture. It is therefore possible to be a 'Rasta' without having historical roots in this group.

The spread, in recent times, of constructivist perspectives in the social sciences (Agger 1991; Swidler and Arditi 1994) has made the vision of identity as creation increasingly popular among scholars of collective action (Melucci 1989, 1991; Calhoun 1994a; Hunt 1992). Even where identity appeals to the history of the group and to its territorial and cultural roots, symbolic re-elaboration is always present. Studies of collective memory have shown that actors reappropriate social awareness and history, manipulating them and transforming them creatively, forging new myths and new institutions (Swidler and Arditi 1994: 308–10).

The question to be resolved is, perhaps, to what extent the margins of freedom in symbolic creation processes can be increased (Mennell 1994). It is not, in fact, necessary to be able to attribute 'objective' foundations to identity in order to recognize its continuity over time. A national sense of belonging, for example, is not reproduced only at times of great patriotic fervour. On the contrary, its revitalization over time also depends – perhaps most importantly of all – on preconscious practices and on the persistence of mental forms and consolidated lifestyles (Billig 1995).

4.2.3   Political opportunities and identity

The construction of identity is often conditioned by variables of a strictly political nature. The criteria by which social groups

identify themselves and are identified externally echo characteristics of the political system and of the political culture of a
given country. It seems that the development of collective identity can be explained by reference to a reformulated version of
the well-known argument that forms of policy-making direct
forms of political action, and not vice versa (Lowi 1971). Social
actors, in fact, tend to recognize themselves in certain characteristics, but not in others, in a way which is coherent with particular policy networks or the issues which inspire certain public
policies (Bartholomew and Mayer 1992; Jenson 1995).

The emergence of a specific identity for Asian–Americans does
not, for example, seem to be explainable exclusively by reference to an independent development of this by social actors. It
has, instead, been put down to the fact that, in crucial areas such
as those of immigration policy and the rights of minority groups,
public agencies tended to treat ethnic groups as homogeneous,
even although they saw themselves as profoundly different, such
as the Vietnamese or the Koreans. In this case, it is held that the
adoption of a certain political/administrative criterion produced
interests and identities which facilitate the overcoming of marked
historical and cultural differences (Omi and Winant 1986). Similarly, the homogeneity of Scotland as a nation is more easily
recognized in an institutional context in which the government
is located in London. Nevertheless, there are numerous demands
that the specific identities of parts of the population living in
particular areas, such as the Hebrides or Shetland, be recognized
(Kinnear 1990). Their visibility and salience might increase if the
country became independent or, as a minimum, once important
functions of government are transferred to Edinburgh.

On another level, actors' identities are defined also in the context of dominant political divisions in a given society. Movements
develop in political systems which already have a structure: they
modify this and activate processes of political realignment (Tilly
1978; Dalton et al. 1984). To this end, they have to produce identities which are sufficiently specific to provide the foundations
for the diversity of the movement, in relation to its adversaries;
but at the same time, sufficiently close to traditional collective
identities in order to make it possible for movement actors to
communicate with those who continue to recognize themselves
in consolidated identities. The importance of elements of contact
between institutionalized and antagonistic identities become even
stronger, the more the former maintain elements of vitality, and
vice versa.

The emphasis placed by the regional Leagues in northern Italy, in recent years, on territorial identities, with a strong populist and separatist dimension cannot be explained primarily by the presence of strong native cultural traditions. What appears to have been most influential is, rather, the purely political necessity of differentiating themselves clearly from the main collective identities, based on class or religion, which dominated the country. The introduction of further specific elements in relation to 'moderate' versions of regionalism which were already in existence, even though weak, in the practice of the left, has similarly been influential. As it was in power in some important regions, though not in the centre, the left had an interest in emphasizing the autonomy of regional institutions. However, it was not prepared to go as far as advocating a separatist perspective. It would not, therefore, have been sensible for the League to construct an identity which combined territorial and class allegiances, based on the model of 'internal colonialism' (Hechter 1975); nor would it have been sufficient to construct the regionalist actor on the basis of the notion of the citizen as protagonist, without further qualifications in a battle for administrative decentralization. Both definitions were already present in the practice of the left, and this made it necessary to develop a specific territorial identity. Furthermore, the importance of the crisis of traditional political identities made it less urgent to develop identities which could identify elements of convergence, in addition to those of differentiation, with other political actors (Biorcio 1992; Diani 1996).

4.2.4   Production of identity and identification rituals

If we accept a process view of the identity of a movement, it then becomes important to look to the ways in which this can be developed and sustained. These go beyond intellectual and doctrinal development. It would be dangerous to hazard a complete classification, but it is, nevertheless, possible to identify some basic manifestations.[9] The identity of a movement is, first, reinforced by reference to *models of behaviour* which define in various ways the specificity of its activists in relation to 'ordinary people' or their adversaries. In adopting certain styles of clothing, differentiating clearly their own appearance and/or their own behaviour, movement militants directly express their difference. They also refer to a series of *objects*, associated in various ways with their experience. Among these are a series of *identifiers* which enable supporters of a particular cause to be instantly recognizable

(such as the smiling sun of anti-nuclear protesters or the Pales-
tinian keffiyeh); *characters* who have played an important role in
the action of a movement or in the development of its ideology;
artifacts, including books or visual documents which help people
to reconstruct the history of the movement and its origins in
time, or to identify its stakes; and *events or places* of a particular
symbolic significance. An additional level is created by *stories*
which circulate among members of a movement, reflecting their
vision of the world and reinforcing solidarity. Sometimes these
are expressed in a particular language, which is virtually or completely unintelligible to those outside the group.

Models of behaviour, objects and narratives are often found to
be combined in specific ritual forms. The ritual component fulfils an important role in movement practice, and above all in the
production of identities. In general, rituals represent forms of
symbolic expression by which communications concerning social
relationships are passed on, in stylized and dramatized ways
(Whutnow 1987). These consist, in particular, of procedures which
are more or less codified, through which a vision of the world
is communicated, a basic historical experience is reproduced, a
symbolic code overthrown (Sassoon 1984a, 1984b). They contribute to the reinforcement of identity and of collective feelings of
belonging; and at the same time, they enable movement actors
to give free rein to their emotions.

Recurrences of particularly significant events in the history of
opposition movements or their constituency are often marked
by ritual practices. By demonstrating on 1 May or the 8 March,
workers' and women's movements remind themselves and society at large of their roots, thus revitalizing their identity. On a
more modest scale, protest movements across the world have
promoted demonstrations on the anniversaries of crucial events
in their development, from the assassinations of black American
leaders Martin Luther King and Malcolm X, to the Chernobyl
nuclear accident, to the Milan bombings which, in 1969, marked
the beginning of a particularly dramatic period in Italy's life.
Rituals remain important even in those cases where movements
have succeeded in gaining power. The French revolutionary
government celebrated the advent of 'new man' in ceremonies
at the Champs de Mars; the Italian Fascist regime, for its part,
stressed its continuity with the glorious past by celebrating the
anniversary of the foundation of Rome.

Ritual practices cannot, however, be reduced simply to public demonstrations of a celebratory nature. All protest events

promoted by movements have a ritual dimension which often assumes a powerfully dramatic and spectacular quality. The forms which demonstrations take, the type of slogans shouted, the banners or placards waved, even the conduct of marshal bodies, are all elements which, potentially, render the practice of a movement distinctive. Opponents of nuclear energy have often acted out, in the course of their demonstrations, the catastrophic consequences of an atomic explosion. Similarly, women's, ethno-nationalist, and youth movements have included theatrical-type performances in their repertoire of collective action, alongside political demonstrations. Through rituals, traditional symbolic codes are overturned and the rules which habitually determine appropriate social behaviour are denied. For example, by recounting in public their experiences of sexual abuse, many American women have transformed episodes which might otherwise have produced only feelings of shame and personal isolation into a source of pride (Taylor and Whittier 1995).

Rituals which relate to the internal life of a group and are not in public view should not be forgotten. Procedures signalling the admission of new members into movement organizations often take on the form of genuine 'rites of passage' (van Gennep 1983; Sassoon 1984a, 1984b). The fact that membership entails – to a degree, at least – the death and rebirth of one's personality, is of particular relevance in the case of neo-religious movements (Berger and Luckmann 1966). Furthermore, procedures which signal some form of transformation of the position of militants, at times when their involvement seems to have increased, are found in virtually every type of organization. In radical extra-parliamentary groups, becoming a member of marshal bodies was usually preceded by other forms of militancy which were less demanding and less risky, such as distributing leaflets. These duties also fulfilled the task of determining the trustworthiness and firmness of the political passion of the new militant (della Porta 1990). In many feminist groups behavioural rituals support the action of consciousness-raising and personal transformation (Taylor and Whittier 1995).

4.3 Multiple Identities

In modern society, social movements are often represented as 'characters' with a strategic capacity for action and bearing a specific cultural role. For these reasons, they are also seen as having a homogeneous and integrated identity. Little attention has been given to the systems of relationships in which actors are involved, and this has prevented the multiplicity of identities and allegiances among militants and movement groups from being recognized. It has, rather, favoured the tendency to see identity as the mirror of an underlying objective reality.[10]

In fact, however, collective identification is rarely expressed through the integrated and homogeneous identities which these visions of movements presuppose.[11] As identity is, first, a social process and not a static property, feelings of belonging among groups and collectives which originated from these are, to a certain extent, fluid. A less rigid approach to the question of identity leads us to recognize that it does not always presuppose a strong 'collective we' (Lemert 1994; Billig 1995). Identifying with a movement does not necessarily mean sharing a systematic and coherent vision of the world; nor does it prevent similar feelings being directed to other groups and movements as well. Forms of allegiance which are not particularly intense or exclusive can, in certain contexts, guarantee continuity of collective action (Melucci 1984a; Diani 1995a). In reality, it is rare that a dominant identity is able to integrate all the others. More usually, identities have a polycentric rather than a hierarchical structure.[12] But excessive insistence on the role of identity as a source of coherence often leads to the neglect of the importance of forms of multiple identity (Calhoun 1994a).

Tensions among various types of identification have to do, first, with the relationship between individual adherents to a movement organization and its 'official' image – that which is expressed by the leaders of the group. The motivations and the expectations which lie behind the individual's participation in a movement are, in fact, richer than representations of the movement, produced by its most influential activists, recognize. All members take part in the life of their movement organizations, and seek from them answers to their own aspirations and concerns. The Milanese women studied by Melucci and his collaborators in the early 1980s, for example, saw their participation in many different ways. Some gave pride of place to personal reflection, others gave greater relevance to external intervention. Some valued group action, above all solidarity and affective elements while others insisted on the importance of developing new forms of interpreting the world (Bianchi and Mormino 1984). Even the identity of a single group can therefore be seen as a meeting point for histories, needs and heterogeneous representations.

Similar – or, in some cases, more exaggerated – mechanisms are to be found, in the relationship between single organizations and movements, in the broad sense. On the one hand, organizations aim to affirm their own specific formulation of their collective identity as the global identity of the movement. On the other hand, the reinforcement of an organizational identity allows, at the same time, for differentiation in relation to the rest of the movement (Taylor 1989). One identifies with an organization, therefore not only to feel oneself part of a wider collective effort but in order to be a particular, autonomous component. In this way, it becomes possible to anchor identity to organizational forms which are more structured and solid than those constituted by networks of informal relationships among the various components of a movement. What is cursorily termed 'movement identity' is, in reality, largely a contingent product of negotiations between collective images produced by various actors and various organizations. Moreover, even small groups can experience the multiple orientations which characterize the identity of a movement in its entirety (Melucci 1984a).

In Milan, for example, analysis of the experience of the Ticinese Collective facilitated the identification of two basic tensions in the way in which feminist practice was perceived (Bianchi and Mormino 1984). The first distinguished between action aimed at society beyond the movement and that which was inwardly directed, towards small groups; the second between action which was purely affective and solidaristic and that which aimed to value women's competences and professional qualities. The same dichotomies offered a useful key to reading the dynamics which related to the definition of the identity of the movement as a whole. There were, in fact, consciousness-raising groups or lesbian groups which were virtually unconcerned with the outside world and concentrated on the affective-solidaristic side of action. On the other hand, writers' groups and those concerned with reflection on intellectual issues from a women's perspective associated a low level of external intervention with their goal of calling attention to women's intellectual and professional capacities. Among the groups concerned with external intervention, some placed a high value on the solidaristic element, such as feminist collectives in squatter communes; others were concerned with consolidating women's social presence, both on the economic level, and on that of cultural production (Bianchi and Mormino 1984: 147).

It must be remembered that movement identities can be shared by individuals, detached from every organizational allegiance.

In fact, it is possible to feel oneself to be part of a movement without having similar expectations of specific organizations and, indeed, expressing what is at times explicit dissent towards the notion of organization in general. In particularly effervescent conditions, simply to participate in meetings and demonstrations gives the sensation of being able to count on the definition of strategies and on goals, even without having passed through the filter of specific organizations. More generally, as we have noted earlier, to be in a movement means precisely to feel part of a collective effort of broad concern. On the other hand, when identification mechanisms tend to shift mainly towards specific organized actors, the dissolution of movements is facilitated. One of the characteristic traits of the wave of working-class protest which crossed Italy between 1968 and 1972 was the modification of the relationship between militancy in specific trade union organizations and militancy in the workers' movement in its broad sense (Pizzorno et al. 1978). New forms of representation were introduced in factories (factory councils). They offered ample opportunities for participation even to those who were not enrolled in any of the traditional unions. The push towards trade union unity and to overcome pre-existing group allegiances was also strong in those years. Group allegiances came to dominate once more only when mobilization was in decline and movement identity was weak. Analysis of grassroots working-class action in the USA also supports this claim: phases of rising conflict tend to strengthen broader collective solidarities rather than identification with specific unions (Fantasia 1988).

In some cases, certain collective identities expressed by various movements or by various movement organizations can be incompatible with certain fundamental principles. The rise of feminism has revealed the persistent subordination of women within workers' movement organizations or in many of the 'new movements' themselves. In this way, they have shown the deep contradictions in actors' identities which, nevertheless, can generally be explained with reference to the same area of 'progressive' movements. From another point of view, the salience which identities of a religious or ethno-nationalist type has recently acquired has often left actors facing dramatic dilemmas, in view of the difficulty of integrating these and other sources of identification. For example, allegiance to a radical nationalist ideology such as that of the Serbs, or to a religious movement such as Algerian fundamentalism, places considerable difficulties in the path of those women who want both to maintain and affirm their gender identity (Calhoun 1994a; see also Fantasia and Hirsch 1995).

4.4   Identity, Collective Action and Free Riding

4.4.1   Identity and 'rational' action

Reference to identity is essential, even if, as we shall see, controversial, in order to understand the mechanisms underlying individuals' decisions to become involved in collective action. The debate has lasted for some thirty years now, having started in the 1960s with the provocatory thesis put forward by Mancur Olson (1963), on the irrationality of collective action. Olson's argument is well known and can therefore be reviewed in a few sentences. The starting point for his reflection is the concept of collective action as concerned with the production of collective goods. These derive their nature from the fact that, once obtained, they may be enjoyed by any member of a social group, regardless of his/her contribution to the cause. Sometimes, the 'social group' consists of people living in a given territory. For example, once a local environmental coalition has had stricter controls on car emissions implemented in its community, the collective good 'cleaner air' is accessible to all the residents, no matter whether they supported the campaign or not. At other times, the 'social group' may consist of a collectivity defined by specific characteristics. For example, once voting rights were extended to women, any woman was entitled to them, again irrespective of her contribution to the suffrage movement. Or, if a regional business association successfully pressurizes the government to launch a plan of massive investement in public communications in the area, all single-business operators will profit from it, including those who are not members of the association. The properties of collective goods determine the fundamental irrationality of collective action, if valued on the basis of criteria of instrumental rationality. It would not be at all rational for an individual actor to invest resources in an undertaking – the production of a collective good – if the actor would have to bear all the costs of failure but could enjoy all the fruits of success without having contributed directly to the production of the good.

In order for there to be collective action, it is necessary for organizations to be able either to coerce their members or to distribute selective incentives – to enable participants in collective action to receive greater benefits than those who do not participate. This problem applies above all to large groups – or, in other words, to those groups in which no individual contribution is so relevant as to affect the final result of a collective undertaking. Two factors increase the difficulties of mobilization for large groups: first, their great size implies high coordination costs, which render collective action difficult; second, certain social incentives – prestige, respect or friendship – which can work with small groups are all the more difficult to activate as the dimensions of the group increase.

Reactions to Olson's proposal have been, not surprisingly, very different.[13] Some scholars have extended the notion of selective incentives in such a way as to include rewards of a solidaristic and normative type. These can, in their turn, be divided into at least two categories. External selective incentives consist of expectations which individuals have of the group to which they refer; these are seen, more generally, as rewards and as sanctions which this group and other social actors can make use of, when facing a decision or else a refusal to become involved collectively. Internal selective incentives cover the internal mechanisms which bring individuals to attribute to collective action a certain normative value, or else to derive from this an intrinsic pleasure or to experience a cathartic transformation (Opp 1989: 58–9). According to numerous pieces of research on individual participation, among the 'selective incentives' it is references to the values and the solidarities of the group, rather than motivations of a material kind, which have been shown to be the best predictors of collective action (Marwell and Ames 1979; Walsh and Warland 1983; Oliver 1984; Opp 1988, 1989).

The incorporation of normative and symbolic elements into selective incentives does not, however, resolve one of the main problems raised by the Olsonian model, which is its lack of attention to the diachronic dimension. The micro-economic rationality on which Olson's argument is based unravels itself in a short period of time. In contrast, collective action is a process which develops over time, in particular, when considering the achievement of goals. It is difficult, if not impossible, to determine costs and benefits appropriately, therefore. On the one hand, there is the certainty of engagement and of the acceptance of risk in the short term; on the other, the unknown territory of results which are not only difficult to calculate, from the point of view of the individual but whose achievement also seems a distant prospect. The existence of a collective identity enables these difficulties to be overcome. Feeling part of a shared endeavour and identifying one's own interests not only at an individual level but also at the collective level makes costs and risks more acceptable than they would otherwise have been, if considered from the point of view of the maximization of individual utility over a short period (Pizzorno 1978, 1983, 1986).

On the other hand, as we have just seen, the intensity and, above all, the exclusiveness of collective identity in defining actors' limits, can vary. A key question is therefore whether various identity traits influence decisions to move to action, and, if so, how. Some have hypothesized a link, in inverse proportion, between the level of inclusiveness and openness of a particular definition of identity and the capacity for mobilization: 'Some groups attempt to mobilize their constituents with an all-inclusive we . . . Such an aggregate frame turns the "we" into a pool of individuals rather than a potential collective actor . . . Collective action frames, in contrast, are adversarial' (Gamson 1992b: 85).

The problem is therefore how to reach a satisfactory balance between the number of people that a particular definition of identity can include, and the ability to talk to provide with appropriate incentives that section of the potential base of a movement which would in any case be the most willing to take action.[14] An inclusive and flexible identity will not determine rigidly the criteria for belonging to a group. In other words, it will not associate the movement with a particular social group, a specific ideology, lifestyle or symbolic code. In this way, it will facilitate communication among movement activists and the outside world, as well as their capacity to speak to different cultural and political contexts. On the other hand, an exclusive identity which defines the profile of a particular movement with some force, will tend to stress isolation, in relation to the outside world: but will probably be able to provide more notable (selective) incentives for action to its base, making the definition of both the actor and of its adversaries more precise in the process (Friedman and McAdam 1992).

One should be aware, though, that how to combine these two contradictory demands effectively is only partially under actors' control. Collective identity is surely affected by actors' deliberate attempts to craft and manipulate identifying symbols. It is, in other words, partly a result of strategic action. But it also depends – and in all likelihood, much more heavily – on mental attitudes and collective memories, consolidated over time, over which movement activists have little control. Not to mention the fact that other social actors (for example, the media: Gitlin 1980; Gamson and Wolfsfeld 1993; van Zoonen 1996) may be capable of intervening (with varying degrees of manipulativeness) in the image which a particular collective has of itself.

Furthermore, it is important to distinguish, in this regard, between the mobilization of people, and the mobilization of other resources, for example organizational or financial (Oliver and Marwell 1992). Exclusive identities which can define adversaries precisely as well as what is at stake in the conflict, appear to be more effective in motivating direct participation. Inclusive identities, however, seem more favourable, in principle, to the mobilization of the second type of resource (Diani and Donati 1996). Attempts to mobilize resources on the part of movement organizations are increasingly conducted by traditional marketing techniques and strategies like direct mail (McFarland 1984; Donati 1996; Jordan and Maloney 1997). Although messages of this type are often carefully tailored to specific sectors of the public and specific market niches, still their contents tend to be far more inclusive and all embracing than those passed by movement activists through their personal networks (Snow et al. 1980). Access to the general public is therefore globally easier for movement actors who are bearers of an inclusive identity. Conversely, organizations with a more clear-cut cultural and political identity will have easy access only to the most sympathetic sectors of public opinion.

4.4.2   Identity and 'non-rational' action

While they recognize both the limits of a strictly economic reading of collective action, and the opportunity to take into account non-material incentives, the positions we have just presented are compatible with a rationalist paradigm. Other movement scholars have, however, expressed serious reservations about the opportunity to apply to the analysis of collective action concepts which were originally developed with reference to individual action of a utilitarian type (Fireman and Gamson 1979; Marx Ferree 1992; Melucci 1989). There are a number of reasons why it would be improper to speak of non-material incentives, or to look at identity as a criterion which enables costs and benefits of action to be calculated over time. They include all the basic presuppositions underlying approaches derived from micro-economics, such as the idea of the rational actor, acting as an isolated individual, able to choose from a range of options on the basis of personal preferences and of cost–benefit analysis.

First, the assumption that social actors always move on the basis of rational principles is debatable. The relevance of non-rational elements, such as emotions, affections and feelings, as some of the factors which direct action, is upheld by a number of scholars (Melucci 1989; Flam 1990; Marx Ferree 1992; Taylor and Whittier 1995; Scheff 1994a, 1994b; Jasper and Paulsen 1995; Jasper 1997). Those supporting this position recognize that the recent predominance of rationalist perspectives has arisen for reasons which are historically contingent. Stress on the rational component of action has certainly contributed – particularly in the 1960s – to criticism of functionalist readings which reduced movements to a show of irrationality, the mere product of gaps in socialization processes (Taylor and Whittier: 179–80). However, this does not authorize support for the notion that emotions and reason are irreconcilable (Turner and Killian 1987).

Critics also charge the rationalist approach with overlooking the fact that social actors act and make choices within a system of interdependence with other actors. The decision to participate in action is, in reality, conditioned by the actor's expectations of those to which it is linked. The actor's capacity for autonomous choice varies according to the social class to which it belongs, and is limited by asymmetries in the distribution of power and social resources (Marx Ferree 1992). From the moment in which one comes to recognize that, increasingly, even economic action is governed by networks of relationships and of norms which bind actors (for example, White 1988; DiMaggio and Powell 1991; Granovetter 1985), recourse to the concept of rational actor for the analysis of collective phenomena seems to critics to be ever more debatable.

A further problem derives from the fact that the goods among which the actor has to choose would naturally be different from those to which models of economic derivation normally refer (Fireman and Gamson 1979: 23–7). The legitimacy of the analogies between individual interests and collective interests should not be discounted. Many of the 'goods' concerning which movements mobilize owe their existence – not just the fact of being controlled by one social group rather than another – to collective action. For example, the reinforcement of identity and transformations in private and public life, which many women have achieved as a result of militancy in feminist movements did not exist prior to their action. These are goods produced in the course of action, goods which would be inconceivable if action had not occurred. The dilemma of whether or not to contribute to the achievement of these kinds of goods must be seen in terms which differ substantially from those postulated by an Olson-style model and by his definition of public good.

Finally, even the last presupposition of rationalist paradigms – that of the stability of the structures of preference on which individual decisions to act are based – seems very unlikely in the case of collective action. The matter would be broadly plausible if the problem of collective action were one of decisions limited to a single moment, such as those relating to whether or not to participate in a particular demonstration. However, collective action is often a process which develops over time, in which the motivation which leads to action, and the concerns which underlie it are modified through relationships with other actors, and where the decision to remain involved is continually renewed. In particular, it has been held that many participants in collective action do not mobilize on the basis of a solid pre-existing identity, but that this may well develop in the course of action (Hirsch 1990; Fantasia 1988): this makes it difficult to support the idea that a structure of preferences exists.

To summarize, from the model of the rational actor emerges a vision of action which, according to its critics, is fairly unrealistic and fails to take account either of the dynamic nature of action or of the importance of processes of identity creation. Furthermore, the adoption of a rational choice perspective, paradoxically, ends up by obscuring the same role of interests: actors are not considered to be bearers of specific concerns or demands, in whose support they mobilize. They tend, rather to become involved in those forms of collective action for which the greatest incentives are available. Finally, the extension of the model to incentives of a normative and solidaristic type would bring about a broadening of the concept of incentive to the point of tautology (Fireman and Gamson 1979).

As this is a controversy which covers the whole gamut of the social sciences, it would be completely unrealistic to think that it is possible to arrive at an appropriate synthesis of the two perspectives which we have reviewed here, in the context of a study of collective action (Cohen 1985). Supporters of rational-choice approaches have attempted to confront criticism directed at them by those upholding the identity paradigm. In particular, they have tried to analyse the location of actors in complex interdependent relationships, developing a vision of action which is more realistic and further away from the original hypothesis of the independent actor (Marwell and Oliver 1993; Gould 1993; Opp and Gern 1993; Oberschall and Kim 1996; Heckathorn 1996).

4.5   Summary

The construction of identity is an essential component in collective action. This enables actors engaged in conflict to see themselves as people linked by interests, values, common histories – or else as divided by these same factors. Identity develops and is renegotiated via various processes. These include conflicts between auto- and hetero- definitions of reality; the tension between a vision of identity as 'rediscovered' in characteristics which were always present in the actors' experience, and a vision of identity as symbolic 'creation'; the rituals which support it. It is important, furthermore, to bear in mind public conditions which can influence definitions of identity.

Feelings of belonging do not always have an exclusive element to them. On the contrary, actors frequently identify with heterogeneous collectives who are not always compatible among themselves on fundamental issues. To reconstruct the tensions through the different versions of identity of a movement represents, according to some scholars, a central problem for the analysis of collective action. Finally, identity plays an important role in the explanation of collective action even for those who see in collective action a peculiar form of rational behaviour. Those who perceive in collective identity certain criteria for evaluating, in the medium and long term, the costs and benefits of action, are numerous. Those who hold that this use of the concept of identity cannot be proposed are equally numerous, however. Because of its strongly emotive and affective components, as well as its controversial and constructed nature, it is difficult to associate identity with behaviour of a strategic type.

5
Movement Networks

Nationalist and regionalist movements have played a major political role in contemporary Spain. Earlier, they were among the chief opponents to Francisco Franco's regime; later, they have been among the protagonists of the democratization process in the country, fostering, in particular, the reform of the Spanish state in the direction of greater decentralization and regional autonomy (Johnston 1991a, 1991b, 1995b; Heiberg 1989; Zirakzadeh 1991; Diez Medrano 1995; Tejerina Montana 1992; Keating 1988). Even in the 1980s, protest activities promoted by regional and nationalist movements in the country were far more important than similar actions in other west European countries, both in terms of numbers of events and of size of participation (Koopmans 1996b: 38–39).

Since the end of the civil war in 1939, nationalist forces in non-Castilian-speaking regions like Catalonia and the Basque country operated in an extremely closed political environment: not only were political activities forbidden, but even the use of local languages and specific cultural practices were banned as the regime proved determined to eradicate any potential source of differentiation from the state centre, and therefore any potential for the development of oppositional identities. Under such unfavourable conditions, resistance to the regime often took a submerged, and largely cultural shape. On the one hand, it relied upon forms of association which could not be forbidden, such as those related to the local churches. These played a key role in both Catalonia and the Basque country (Johnston 1991b: 125–6). On the other hand, the defence of specific cultures and national identities was also largely organized through the informal, everyday-life relationships which linked members of the local communities to each other.

When the regime started to crumble, opposition took an increasingly distinctive political guise. In both Catalonia and Euzkadi a broad spectrum of organizations were either revitalized or created anew, ranging from moderate parties such as the Basque National Party (Partido Nacionalista Vasco-PNV), or the Catalan Convergence and Union coalition (Convergencia i Unio-CiU) to more radical groups such as Herri Batasuna in the Basque country or the Republican Left of Catalonia (Esquerra Republicana de Catalunya). However, the patterns of alliance and coalition between these groups, as well as the overall form that national politics took in the two regions, have been rather different: moderate and with substantial unity between the different branches of the movement in Catalonia, polarized and with a strong radical and violent component in Euzkadi (Johnston 1995b). No Catalan counterpart can be found for an organization like ETA, and even well into the 1990s Catalan political life is immeasurably more peaceful than that of the Basques.

How did nationalist identities and organizations manage to survive during the dictatorship? And why did they take such different political and organizational forms, despite operating in an institutional context which was largely the same? While we should be wary of monocausal explanations, it seems plausible to argue that social networks were crucial in both cases. Nationalist ideals and organizations successfully resisted fierce repression (also) because their supporters were embedded in systems of relationships (based on kin, friendship, religious and/or communitarian activities and so on) which exceeded by far the sphere of overt political action. As such, they were largely impermeable to state repression.

At the same time, though, the two movements evolved differently because the configuration of their networks was different. For several reasons, social networks in Catalonia were more interconnected than those in Euzkadi. There were more linkages cutting across localities, clans, generations, and thus capable of bridging ideological and social barriers. In contrast, in the Basque country ties were mostly within other types of groups

– however defined. Growing on a social basis which was already heavily fragmented, the different components of the Basque movement had less opportunity to reconcile their original ideological or political differences, and to strengthen feelings of mutual trust – all outcomes that crosscutting personal linkages would have facilitated. In contrast, they rather tended to develop in isolation and sometimes in explicit conflict against each other (Johnston 1995b).

The case of national movements in Spain reminds us of the importance of the complex web of relationships, allowing movement groups and organizations which might individually be relatively weak and isolated to play a significant political role. We can identify at least three types of networks, on which social movements depend for their existence and efficacy: those which link the various movement organizations either in times of mobilization, or through more or less permanent consultation mechanisms; those which connect the same organizations by means of activists which they have in common; and, finally, those which enable activists to be recruited, and which are often based on preceding forms of participation. In this chapter, we will be concerned with these networks, with the contribution which they make to movement action and with the logic which informs their activation. We will be looking in detail, in other words, at those systems of relationships which connect the sphere of the actor (whether an individual or an organization) to that of broader social dynamics, and which, in the process, enable new interpretations of reality to develop, new solidarities to emerge and new potential for conflict to be transformed into collective action.

We start by analysing interpersonal links among militants (potential and actual) and supporters of the movements, stressing their role as facilitators of individual participation. We then go on to consider another important relationship: that which bridges different organizations, thanks to their activists' multiple membershisps. The rest of the chapter is dedicated to the analysis of interorganizational relationships. We outline, first, a typology of these, and then identify certain factors which can guide movement organizations' choice of allies.

5.1 Social Networks and Individual Participation

At least until the 1960s, many scholars saw collective action primarily as a consequence of a breakdown of the mechanisms of social integration (Kornhauser 1959). In accordance with this perspective, those most likely to join movements or religious sects were considered to be people who were integrated only at a low level in associations, and, more generally, in social links of various types; precisely for this reason, they were considered more likely to be attracted to 'total' experiences, largely segregated from the rest of society.

This position has been challenged subsequently by those who interpreted collective action as a product of integration rather than of social disintegration (among others: Gusfield 1962; Tilly 1978; Useem 1980; Walsh and Warland 1983; Oberschall 1993). We have already noted that the social composition of those forming the core group within a movement includes a high percentage of people from a mid or high social position, people whose control of resources such as education does not permit us to attribute to them a marginal social position (see chapter 2). Furthermore, contrary to the expectations of those who stressed the anomic nature of protest movements, their militants and supporters have been recognized as the bearers of solid value orientations and specific solidarities (see chapters 3 and 4). Finally – and this is the point which we are concerned to explore in greater depth here – people involved in movements have demonstrated extremely high levels of integration in social networks of various types.

An impressive body of research relating to collective action, on different issues and in different countries, has confirmed how important networks are for the recruitment of activists and the mobilization of supporters. In their comparison of recruitment mechanisms among several American religious sects and denominations, Snow et al. (1980) found that the percentage of people recruited through social networks regularly exceeded 75 per cent, with the only exception being adherents to Hare Krishna. In the case of a sample of university students involved in political activities, they found that two-thirds of them had been recruited through some type of social networks. Their finding is very close to what Diani (1995a: 71–2) discovered in his analysis of environmental activists in Milan, of whom 72 per cent had joined their current organization via social networks.[1]

Just as with conventional political participation, people seem more likely to join a protest movement if they are connected to others who are highly sensitive to particular causes, or prone to become involved in collective action generally. It is through these links that potential activists develop a certain vision of the world, acquire information and the minimum competences necessary for collective action, and learn from the example of those already involved, receiving both stimuli and opportunities. In many cases, these relationships, which are based on shared experiences of solidarity, and which developed through earlier experiences of militancy and/or of associated lifestyles, facilitate new forms of involvement. In its more inclusive formulation, this argument posits that the larger the number of organizations – particularly those of an explicitly political nature – to which individuals have belonged in the past (and, therefore, the higher the probability of having developed or maintained personal relationships in those contexts), the higher their chances of becoming involved again in collective action of some kind; likewise, the more numerous the contacts one has with others engaged in a particular cause, the greater the probability of joining them (see, for example, Walsh and Warland 1983; McAdam 1986). Even links of a strictly private nature (among relatives, friends, colleagues at work, neighbours) can in certain circumstances encourage individual participation in an equally significant way (see, for example, Snow et al. 1980; Diani 1995a: ch. 4; Ohlemacher 1996).

Scholars with different theoretical perspectives attach different qualifications to this point. Rational choice theorists argue that 'potential participants in any collective action are rational actors embedded in networks . . . integration into networks makes it more likely that the individual will value the identity of "activist" and choose to act in accordance with it' (Friedman and McAdam 1992: 161 and 170). For critics of utilitarian theories of action, social networks represent, rather, the context in which symbolic production takes place and in which the affective dimension of primary and communitarian relations are connected to political mobilization (Melucci 1984a, 1989; Taylor and Whittier 1992). Thus the relationship between social networks, the elaboration of cognitive and value models and the production of motivations – and not of 'incentives' – for action, comes to light. Despite differences, both perspectives converge in considering the extent of integration in certain networks as an important conditioning factor in relation to the formation of individual orientations. The denser the links within certain social environments, the greater the probability that their members derive their inspiration from each other in the development of their own convictions and points of view (Erickson 1982: 164).

The idea that social roots must facilitate mobilization has not been accepted uncritically, however. First, it has been observed that the people most prone to action are those from age groups which are biographically available and able to sustain the costs (and, in particular, the risks) which action involves: in other words, young people, whose earlier links have been weakened or broken; and who are not conditioned in their choice of new family or professional ties, still in the process of being formed (Piven and Cloward 1992: 308–9; see also McAdam and Paulsen 1993: 660–1). The greater propensity of unmarried people to married to take part in protest action, according to some research (Opp 1989: 187–9) bears out this point. It has also been noted that movements' recruitment messages do not necessarily address people who are already connected through networks to current participants; they are often broadcast to strangers, and still manage to be successful. As Jasper and Poulsen's (1995) study of animal rights activism suggests, supporting networks need not be there when rhetorical images and messages are strong enough to induce 'moral shocks' among prospective participants.

Finally, it is argued that the fact that participants are integrated in some form of social network, linked to their private lives or to their public activities, is not particularly significant: given that, in reality, each one of us is involved in some kind of link, however fragile, it will always be possible to identify social networks capable of providing the opportunities needed to involve individuals in protest. The role of networks in fostering participation should therefore not lead analysts to expect any sort of integration in the community to be similarly conducive to collective action. For example, in her analysis of participation in neighborhood associations in Detroit, Pamela Oliver (1984) found that while activists had more close ties than non-activists, in global terms they identified less with their neighborhoods. This led her to conclude that 'current activism arises not from a generalized collective neighborhood spirit, but rather from particularistic ties [to other participation-prone individuals]' (Oliver 1984: 607). Some critics have gone much further, and suggested that the concept of social networks is actually incapable of explaining collective action in any way: 'lateral integration, however fragile, is ubiquitous, thus making opportunities for protest ubiquitous' (Piven and Cloward 1992: 311).

Awareness of the fact that participants are not isolated individuals is not therefore enough for an adequate understanding of the relationship between social networks and individual participation. One needs rather to stress differences between various types of social networks and to ask what the contribution of each of these can bring to explanations of various types of collective action.[2] One attempt to specify more clearly the relationship between social networks and individual rectruitment has focused on the intensity of ties and the costs and risks attached to collective action. All the rest being equal, the intensity of the personal links necessary to become involved in action has been expected to increase in parallel with the costs associated with the action itself. The level of practical and emotional investment, and the extent of the personal transformation required of those who decided to join a particular movement or a particular campaign can, in fact, vary noticeably. When participation appears to be particularly costly, the strength of relationships which link potential activists to each other and to those already committed can be the key factor in determining who will mobilize and who will not. Furthermore, it is not only the extent and the intensity of integration in certain organizations which counts; the overlap of various types of link is also important.

Analysing mobilization among Italian terrorist groups of the 1970s, Donatella della Porta (1990) has shown that allegiance to a clandestine group was greatly facilitated by the overlap of organizational ties and strong affective links – often, indeed links via relatives – among potential militants. They were more likely to become involved in high-risk activities if the recruitment came through people with whom they shared not only militancy in 'visible' movement organizations, but longer lasting and more intimate relationships. To take a historical example, Roger Gould (1991) has shown how the capacity for collective action among the Paris communards in the National Guard of 1870 depended on the overlap of neighbourhood and organizational links: the territorial recruitment system of members of the Guards led to a situation in which people already united by pre-existing social links were to be found in the same battalions.[3]

In order to determine the cost of action we may focus not on the risks run by the individual but rather on the extent of the personal transformation to which the decision to participate leads. This is often the case in membership of religious sects. Here, evidence is more uncertain. The existence of strong personal links (often via relatives) with leaders and influential activists has sometimes been regarded as essential in explaining why people join and remain members of sectarian groups (for example, Stark and Bainbridge 1980). In general, these factors, rather than difficult personal circumstances, are the ones which attract some people rather than others to a sect.[4]

However, other findings suggest that, when membership of a specific group is exclusive, and presupposes the severing of previous social ties, then social networks may play a very limited role. In their comparison of the role of social networks in explaining recruitment to Nichiren Shoshu and Hare Krishna, Snow et al. (1980) found that the former recruited mainly through networks (82 per cent of their adherents had been contacted in that way), while the latter, far more exclusive, recruited largely in public places (96 per cent). Given the depth of the transformation implied by membership of Hare Krishna, people involved in some type of social ties might well have met not only with encouragement and support, but also with opposition to so radical a choice. In sum, if any relationship between social networks and intensity of personal transformation exists at all, it seems to be of a curvilinear type, with networks playing a greater role when the transformation is deep enough to entail some costs, and thus to require support, yet not deep enough to imply a total rejection of individuals' previous life experiences.

What is, then, the relationship between networks, community and movement participation? The generic integration of individual networks into voluntary associations or, more generally, into the community, should not be regarded as an automatic factor in participation (Snow et al. 1980; Opp 1989; McAdam and Paulsen 1993). On the contrary, associative involvement leads to action only if the culture of the community is globally conducive to collective action. If the cultural perspective of a movement is regarded as relatively legitimate and acceptable in the community where it operates, mobilization and recruitment can take place through non-specific channels, typical of everyday life, such as acquaintances or work colleagues. In relation to decisions to participate in action, purely individual choices – those which have not developed within a network – will also be more significant (Opp 1989).

Consistently, McAdam and Paulsen (1993) found that neither organizational affiliations nor personal ties to people already active are capable of generating individual mobilization per se. Social ties actually matter only in as much as they develop in organizational milieux which are broadly perceived as close to the specific cause which people are expected to identify with. What matters is in other words 'a strong subjective identification with a particular identity, reinforced by organizational or individual ties, that is especially likely to encourage participation' (McAdam and Paulsen 1993: 659).

If the perspective of a movement is not viewed entirely favourably by its community, or strong alternative milieux are missing, then adhesion to the movement is usually facilitated by more specific relationships, which originate in the individual's membership of certain political organizations. Let us think, for example, of those American students who in 1964 had to decide whether or not to join the *Freedom Summer* campaign (McAdam 1988) and spend the summer in the southern states, trying to persuade Afro-American citizens to register to vote. It was not an easy decision. The risks connected to a political campaign of this type were, in fact, extremely high: in the event, three activists were killed and many others wounded by racist extremists or the local police forces. For those students who lived on campuses where, on the whole, movements had little influence or legitimacy, the chances of them joining the movement were markedly increased if they had already belonged to political organizations; the importance of this factor was much reduced, in contrast, in places where a movement counterculture was solidly established. In these cases, the decision was influenced principally by friendships amongst potential activists (McAdam and Fernandez 1990).

Non-dissimilar conclusions can be drawn when considering less demanding or risky forms of action, such as subscribing to a petition. A study of the Popular Petition against Cruise missiles, organized in the Netherlands in 1985 (Kriesi 1988b), showed that involvement in the various local initiatives supporting the petition was facilitated, in situations where pre-existing countercultural networks were weak or barely integrated, by earlier political experiences; while friendship, rather than organizational connections, prevailed as a facilitating mechanism in contexts characterized by a strong counterculture.[5]

5.2 Individuals and Organizations

The importance of social networks for collective action in movements is not limited to the phase in which individual militants are recruited. On the contrary, by participating in the life of a movement and, in particular, in that of its various organizations, activists create new channels of communication among different organizations, and increase the scope for promoting common campaigns. Links founded on multiple allegiances are therefore an important element connecting movement areas internally, as well as supporting communications between movements and their environment. There are of course, exclusive allegiances, in which a single organization monopolizes the commitment and the affective investment of individual members; but the inclusive model is more usual.

5.2.1   Exclusive affiliations

In some cases these are exclusive relationships, precluding, for that reason, membership of other organizations. The typical organizational context is that of a self-referential community or sect whose main characteristics are closure in the face of the outside world, a totalitarian structure, incompatibility with other forms of collective engagement and the view – among themselves – that adherents are the repositories of truth (Wallis 1977). Though not necessarily residential communities, the lifestyle of these groups is markedly separate. Interaction with other groups is usually limited, while the tendency to concentrate on activities internal to the group is very strong. Organizations active in neo-religious or neo-communitarian movements often fall easily into this category; but political fundamentalists, such as certain radical elements among the environmental movements, or terrorist organizations, are similar.

In these cases, the single adherent/activist inhabits a world in which relationships and norms are highly structured: this leads to a radical personality transformation (see chapter 4). The prevalence of sectarian organizations within a movement area produces networks of relationships which are highly, if not completely, fragmented. The only significant level of relationship is among adherents to a specific organization. In some cases (for example, those sects which can count on numerous local groups, such as the Jehovah's Witnesses, but also political organisations with a strong territorial presence) these contacts can also develop over a wide geographical area. However, contacts rarely extend beyond the confines of the single organization. The 'movement network' consists therefore of a series of cliques,[6] that is to say groups of actors – members of a given organization – who are strongly linked to each other and barely or not at all with adherents to other groups.

5.2.2   Multiple affiliations

Nevertheless, participation in movements is not necessarily restricted to individual organizations. We have already presented, at the beginning of this chapter, data relating to the involvement of Milanese environmental activists in the life of the movement. This is not an atypical example. Research conducted in other European countries has revealed comparable levels of participation (Kitschelt and Hellemans 1990) or even higher (Kriesi and van Praag 1987).

Multiple affiliations have an important role to play in integrating different areas of a movement. Of particular note is a dual dimension to the dynamics of individual–organisation relationships. On the one hand, individuals (not only leaders, but also, more frequently, simple activists) come into contact with each other through membership of organisations. To belong to the same movement organizations (just as, more generally, to organizations of other types) facilitates personal contact and the development of informal networks which, in their turn, encourage individual participation and the mobilization of resources. In other words, the movement organization represents in this case a link between individuals. On the other hand, the existence of multiple affiliations and personal contacts among exponents of different organizations facilitates interaction between the latter. Through their multiple affiliations, activists create bridges between organizations, making it easier for information and resources to circulate.[7]

To regard organizational affiliations as opportunities for connections among individuals reflects a concept of movement networks as specific subcultural forms. Taking part in the life of several organizations and coming into contact with their activists and supporters, individuals construct, in fact, a series of unique social relationships. In these, the political dimension of action intersects and overlaps the private dimension. It is not by chance that these links are referred to as the foundations of a specific form of subculture. The separation of movement areas, understood as sites of countercultural production and internal change, from the strictly sectarian dimension referred to above, has been one of the major achievements of research in the last decades. A model of movement networks which stresses flexibility and inclusiveness has been developed: in this model, it is the freedom of individuals to enter into relationships of different types with a range of groups which prevails, rather than their submission in the face of a single, omnipotent, possibly sectarian organization (Melucci 1984a).

In a movement network, in fact, individuals pursue their goals – which are concerned both with political ends and with personal self-realization – interacting with other individuals and with multiple organizations. They do this in various ways and with varying degrees of intensity. In most cases, organisational affiliations are not exclusive but rather compatible. Participants in the movement come together from time to time for specific initiatives and activities organized by cultural operators, service structures, and so on. Affiliation to a particular movement area can therefore be seen as a strictly personal choice, which brings with it a low level of identification with movement organizations. Similarly, the adoption by movement activists of alternative symbolic codes does not automatically create a homogeneous identity, nor does it provide the legitimation for rigid organizational structures. A shared identity certainly characterizes a movement understood in its entirety, but this is then articulated with extreme variability and flexibility by different actors.

Personal contacts are also instrumental in linking organizations with other groups. As happens in economic organizations (Stokman et al. 1985; Mizruchi and Schwartz 1987), political organizations are often connected by the fact that they share certain activists (or rather certain leaders); or else by personal relationships and friendships among activists or leaders. Carroll and Ratner's (1996) study of movement activism in the Greater Vancouver area well exemplifies these processes.[8] By looking at the joint affiliations of over 200 activists in seven social movements (labour, urban/antipoverty, gay/lesbian, feminism, environmentalism, peace, aboriginal) they have been able to document not only the extent of overlapping memberships, but their patterning. Among Vancouver activists, only 27 per cent were active in one single organization, whereas 28 per cent collaborated to multiple organizations within the same movement, and 45 per cent to multiple organizations in several movements (Carroll and Ratner 1996: 605). Activists of peace and urban/antipoverty movements were the most inclined towards multiple memberships (67 per cent and 71 per cent were involved in multiple organizations in multiple movements), while gay/lesbian, feminist, environmentalist, and aboriginal activists seemed to be the least so (34, 32, 39 and 42 per cent of them were actually committed to a single organization). Overlapping memberships constituted a core bloc of labour, peace, and urban/antipoverty organizations. Feminist and environmental organizations were linked to this bloc through their connections to labour and peace movements (1996: 605–6). While the specific pattern of linkages discovered by Carroll and Ratner need not be taken as the norm, and it may well vary substantially in different periods and localities, still the Vancouver study shows the potentiality of a network approach to the study of movement sectors.

Overlapping memberships contribute to social movement activity in a variety of ways. First, they facilitate the circulation of information and therefore the speed of the decision-making process. This is essential, inasmuch as the speed of mobilization compensates at least in part for the lack of organizational resources over which movements have control. In the absence of formal coordination among organizations, mobilization becomes possible through informal links among leaders (Killian 1984; Knoke and Wisely 1990). Activists working across organizations also facilitate the development of a shared representation of conflicts. Among Vancouver activists different ways of framing the conflicts could be found, one based on a political-economy perspective, another based on an identity perspective, and a third based on a liberal perspective. The distribution of these frames varied depending on activists' commitment to overlapping memberships: those who acted as linkages between different movements and organizations were disproportionately close to a political-economy frame, whereas adopters of an identity frame were more inclined to concentrate on individual organizations (Carroll and Ratner 1996: 611).

Another important function of multiple memberships lies in their contribution to the growth of feelings of mutual trust. Whether it is a question of economic activities or of political mobilization, committing resources to a joint initiative involving other actors is always, to some extent, risky. In each case, the route to mobilization requires a kind of 'investigative process' (Diani 1995a: ch. 1), or exploration, on the part of the organization, of their own environment in search of trustworthy allies. This process is made much simpler if there are ongoing links between the central activists of the various organizations concerned. This does not mean that other alliances are not possible – and sometimes they are even more common. But the relative cost of forging these other alliances will usually be higher, in as much as contacts between the different groups are not 'routinized'.

The hypothesis that cooperation among organizations is more likely where personal contacts exist among their leaders has been supported by a few studies, dedicated both to movements and to political organizations in the wider sense. In both cases it has become clear that the leaders of organizations who work or campaign together tend to be linked by shared experiences which precede the formation of the coalition itself (Galaskiewicz 1985: 293; Turk 1977; Diani 1990). The denser the relationships among the leaders and the activists of various movement organizations, the higher the chances of cooperation among them (Zald and McCarthy 1980). There is no reason to think that the impact of networks which pre-date the emergence of a particular movement is limited to individual decisions to participate; rather, they also influence opportunities for cooperation among organizations.[9]

Finally, looking at the multiple affiliations of activists can constitute a useful way of comparing the structure of particular movements in different periods, and of reconstructing modifications over time. In their pioneering study of the organizational affiliations of 202 key figures in the women's movements of the state of New York between 1840 and 1914, Naomi Rosenthal and her collaborators reconstructed the structure of the interorganizational networks in three different historical phases, identifying the central organizations in each phase (Rosenthal et al. 1985; Rosenthal et al. 1997). A phase of powerful activism between 1840 and the end of the 1860s saw numerous overlaps between participation in women's organizations and in anti-slavery or temperance organizations. The following phase, until the end of 1880 saw a reduction in conflict, and was, in contrast to the previous phase, characterized by the disappearance of many organizations and by the difficulty of revitalizing organizations of national importance. Between 1880 and 1914, there was a revival of activism and a new intensification of multiple affiliations, corresponding to campaigns for universal suffrage. The configuration of networks seems to have depended significantly on the characteristics of the environment in which the movements were operating and on the availability of resources for mobilization. In local networks, where resources were usually limited, the integration and density of relationships were higher. In fact, it was essential to use the available resources to best effect. In contrast, organizations whose structures were on a national scale and who could therefore count on greater organizational resources, could find that this accentuated rivalries and ideological distinctions. As a result, relationship networks were more fragmented and consisted of different subgroups (or cliques) which were barely connected to each other.

Multiple affiliations and personal contacts among leaders and core activists in movement organizations also represent an important channel of communication and of interaction between a movement and its social environment. In the 1980s, more than a quarter of the Milanese environmentalist activists were involved in political organizations other than those of the movement, or else in non-political associations (Diani 1995a: ch. 4). This observation is even more valid if applied solely to those who occupy leadership positions. For example, the German peace movement of the 1980s had strong relations to significant sectors of the establishment – including churches, trade unions, universities and media – through the overlapping memberships of its core activists (Schmitt 1989: 592).

Links between movement leaders and other organizations do not only expand opportunities for activating alliances or obtaining access to information and other relevant resources, over which institutionalized organizations have greater control. They serve also to guarantee and to reinforce the legitimacy of movement organizations. It has, in fact, been noted that in general it is easier to achieve legitimization of organizations if they are associated with symbols and figures of power which are already legitimized in their environment. This can happen, for instance, when movement exponents participate in the management of institutionalized organizations rich in prestige and legitimacy. In the case of the environmentalist movement, such organizations might, for example, be scientific foundations. Furthermore, the stronger the personal involvement of leaders in group networks and in the management of community issues, the greater the influence of a particular organization in that field (Perrucci and Pilisuk 1970; Galaskiewicz 1979; Knoke and Wood 1981; Knoke 1983).

5.3   Interorganizational Networks

It is rare for an organization to be able to monopolize the representation of a certain complex of interests and values. Normally, it is essential to coordinate action and joint campaigns in order to achieve widespread protest, place certain themes on the political agenda and disseminate new interpretations of political and social conflict. Movement organizations need systematic forms of coordination in order to respond to the problems or emergencies which they face from time to time. The existence of a significant number of allies increases the chances of success for groups promoting protest.[10]

Interorganizational relationships can vary markedly in terms both of content and of intensity. They can involve the exchange

		Cooperation	
		Yes	No
Competition	No	Non-competitive cooperation	Neutrality
	Yes	Competitive cooperation	Factionalism

Figure 5.1 *Types of interaction between movement organizations*

of information, and the pooling of resources for specific projects. They can then maintain continuity at a relatively high level over time, until eventually they adopt stable relationships and information exchange mechanisms and establish a permanent level of cooperation on joint projects, or even the promotion of permanent joint organizations (Diani 1995a; Zald and McCarthy 1980: 10ff).

Opportunities for alliances among movement organizations are, however, severely limited by the quantity of resources (in terms of time, personal energy, willingness to mediate) necessary for their activation and their maintenance over time. In reality, cooperation is relatively rare. Furthermore, interaction between movement organisations tends to vary according to whether or not they are in competition for the acknowledgment and support of the same social base; if, that is, they are trying to acquire essential resources for action by tapping the same (limited) mobilization potential. By combining these two criteria (presence/absence of cooperation and presence/absence of competition), we can elaborate (figure 5.1) a typology of forms of interorganizational relationships, which recognizes their plurality.[11]

Where cooperation and competition co-exist, situations which we will define as *competitive cooperation* occur. In such cases, two (or more) movement organizations concerned with the same issues are keen to develop joint initiatives, based on compatible definitions of the issues and some degree of identity; but at the same time, they find themselves facing stiff mutual competition for the same support base, and for similar sectors of public opinion whose interests they wish to represent. A model of interaction characterized by a degree of interorganizational polemic emerges, but does not lead to a severe breakdown of channels of communication. The new left groups which in the 1970s competed for control of youth radical movements in Italy provide a fitting example of this model (Tarrow 1989a; della Porta 1995);

so do the relationships between women's organizations supporting abortion rights in the USA (Staggenborg 1991).

In contrast, there are also situations in which an absence of
cooperation corresponds to an absence of competition. This may
be defined as *neutrality*. Such situations occur with organizations whose definitions of issues and whose own concerns make
explicit cooperation difficult. At the same time, however, they
do not need to compete with other organizations not only because they represent and mobilize relatively diverse sectors of
opinion, but also because they lack shared networks which would
allow them to activate contacts and, when appropriate, to overcome the differences which make it hard to initiate cooperative
endeavours. The environmentalist movement of the 1970s in Italy
was close to this model. Its components were ideologically far
enough apart to make it difficult for them to cooperate with
each other. This did not lead to conflict, however, as both conservation and political ecology organizations were somewhat
eccentric in relation to the principal, class-based conflicts in that
period (Diani 1995a). Similar remarks may apply to environmentalism in a country with a far lower salience of the left–right divide
like Britain. There, a political-ecology sector hardly developed
at all in the 1970s, as new left groups were strictly focusing
on traditional class issues and hardly paying any attention to
environmental problems (Lowe and Goyder 1983).

High levels of competition and low levels of cooperation among
movement organizations are characterized as *factional* relationships. In such cases, the fight to represent the same social
constituency reaches a level which leads to fragmentation and
sectarian-type divisions. Cooperation among movement organizations whose reference to cultural models and styles of action
which are largely compatible, is thus hindered. Donatella della
Porta (1990) and Sidney Tarrow (1989a) have shown how the
competitive dynamics within Italian movements eventually produced outcomes of this type at the end of the 1970s. The Italian situation was characterized at that time by transition from
models which were predominantly cooperative, although also
competitive, to models where cooperation was absent. The reduction of the potential to mobilize played a crucial role in this context. This brought various organizations into open competition
with each other, emphasizing their ideological differences; and
the potential for conflict within movement areas grew.

Finally, a high degree of cooperation and a low degree of
competition is defined as *non-competitive cooperation*. Movement

organizations are not in competition for the same political market but have, at the same time, sufficient interests and motives for convergence to activate joint mobilizations. Cooperation is, moreover, limited, to the extent that it neither presupposes nor requires the development of a homogeneous perspective or of a 'strong' and (semi) exclusive notion of collective identity. Relationships between central organizations with diverse concerns in the Italian environmentalist field in the 1980s were close to this model: political ecology groups such as Legambiente cooperated with conservationist groups such as Italia Nostra without coming into competition, inasmuch as the areas from which they could draw their support differed substantially (Diani 1995a: ch. 5).

5.4   Social Movement Networks as Constraints and as Products of Action[12]

When speaking of the connection between networks and individual choice in relation to mobilisation, or of the continuity of cooperation among movement organisations, we emphasise above all the role of networks as pre-conditions for action. From this perspective, their configuration – or the density of relationships among the various actors and their internal articulation – will direct the way in which essential resources for action circulate within a movement. At the same time, it will determine both actors' opportunities and the limits to their action.[13] This view coincides with one of the dominant themes of structural analysis, focusing above all on the capacity to condition behaviour which structures exert over individuals (see, for example, Wellman 1988).

Other than as preconditions for action, however, movement networks can be read in another way. They can also be analysed as *products* of action: in other words, as the result of a series of acts through which groups and individuals engaged in a movement choose their own interlocutors and/or allies, in the case of an organisation; or else their own multiple memberships, in the case of individual activists.[14] The resulting networks condition in their turn successive developments in collective action. To reconstruct the logic according to which movement networks are constituted means looking at interactions between conditioning factors and the actor's margins of autonomy.[15]

To speak of choice does not mean, however, to hypothesize that networks are, necessarily, the product of a conscious strategy.

Their particular form is not, in fact, the result of deliberate planning but rather of provisional or contingent choices (Padgett and Ansell 1993). To speak of 'choices' when referring to the behaviour of movement actors is particularly appropriate, inasmuch as their capacity to activate and maintain relationships is severely handicapped by the scarcity of resources under their control. 'Networking', in fact, is an expensive activity, in terms both of time and of personal commitment (Wellman 1988; Marwell and Oliver 1993). Movement organisations must therefore choose between a number – often a relatively high number – of potential partners.[16] In other words, they need some criteria by which they may reduce the complexity of their organisational environment. Below we refer to some of these elementary criteria, derived from major theoretical approaches in the field.

5.4.1   Coalitions as the product of instrumental choices

Movement actors can choose their interlocutors on the basis of purely instrumental considerations. It is, in other words, possible to see interorganisational relationships from a perspective close to that of the theory of resource mobilization (Zald and McCarthy 1987) which underlines the tactical-strategic element of mobilization processes. According to this reading, the types of relationship in which diverse movement organizations find themselves engaged depend on their organizational characteristics. Large organizations with a relatively well-articulated internal structure usually face different problems from those which are typical of informally structured grassroots groups. For example, they tend to take on the role of representing the whole of the movement, for the purposes of public opinion, and of making contacts with the media and with institutions, more frequently than is the case with grassroots groups (Dalton 1994; Diani 1988; Rucht 1989). In contrast, mobilizations promoted by informal groups tend to have more limited and more specific objectives.

From the structural point of view, symmetric relationships will tend to prevail amongst groups with the same organizational properties, while asymmetric relationships will be more likely among organizations which differ on this point. The most influential associations tend to enliven dense interactive networks, founded on predominantly egalitarian terms. For example, regular patterns of consultation and coalition may be detected among the most important environmental organizations in different countries. In Britain as in Italy or in Germany, groups like Friends of Earth, Greenpeace and WWF have increasingly got involved in systematic cooperation, while retaining their independence (Rucht 1989; Donati 1996; Szerszinski 1995). Informal groups do the same thing, clustering on a territorial or thematic basis. In the Milan environmental movement analysed by Diani, systematic cooperation was not restricted to the local branches of the most important national associations. Active clusters of cooperation could be detected among neighborhood associations – one consisting of groups active in the northern periphery, the other of those located in the south-west periphery – as well as among conservation associations of local, rather than national, relevance (Diani 1995a: ch. 5). In defining symmetric relationships, what counts is not a balanced exchange of resources but rather the quality of the relationship: in particular, the fact that, in principle, all actors engaged in exchanges recognize each other as suitable and equally respected partners. The same cannot be said for exchanges between large associations and grassroots groups (Lawson 1983; Farro 1991; Diani 1995a: ch. 5; Oberschall 1993: ch. 3). The former provide the latter mainly with cognitive resources, orientation or advice; the latter provide the former principally with militancy resources. The differences in their organisational profiles will hinder the development of contacts through which actors might enjoy comparable status and influence (Diani 1988: ch. 4).[17]

The decision to cooperate can therefore be affected by a shared interest in particular problems. This observation is less banal than it might appear at first reading. In fact, when certain organisations develop a strong identification with a given movement, they can be encouraged to mobilise on issues which were not high in their own original agenda. Interaction between the various groups and associations engaged in a movement leads to progressive adaptations and transformations of their original strategies and priorities. In the case of Italian environmentalism there are several examples of organizations which set out from a political ecology position, implying a strong interest in urban ecology, but finished up by including in their agenda concern for animal rights. There are, on the other hand, cases of animal rights associations which have, over time, increased their activities in the cause of urban ecology, such as noise or atmospheric pollution.[18] Speaking of instrumental criteria in choosing allies therefore means hypothesizing that each organization will initiate exchanges and cooperative relationships only with groups and associations which share its peculiar interests and goals. Conversely, there will be no instrumental exchange when one of the organizations involved moves away from its original concerns to cover a broader set of issues and goals.

The existence of some division of labour among movement organizations with different characteristics is important for the maintenance of different coalitions. On the one hand, the tendency of various organizations to cooperate with relatively similar groups seems linked to the fact that, when one of the components of the coalition is much stronger than the others, fears about its excessive influence on the alliance emerge, and the stability of the alliance is therefore weakened (Staggenborg 1986). On the other hand, it seems equally important that within a coalition there are consolidated organizations capable of providing organizational infrastructures, facilitating contact, and, if necessary, coordinating lobby action which would be too expensive to take on in isolation (Staggenborg 1986). From an instrumental perspective, a model of the kind described seems opportune, as it puts groups of equal dimensions and influence in contact with each other, via more intense relationships. At the same time, it links, in more flexible and limited relationships, groups which differ according to the resources which they control. It is necessary, moreover, to consider that in all of these cases a reduction of the resources at their disposal – for example, of the willingness of supporters to contribute actively to the cause – could accelerate competitive dynamics between movement organizations with similar characteristics, with potentially dangerous results for the solidarity of the coalition itself.

5.4.2   Movement networks and conflicts

In reality, a structure inspired by strictly instrumental criteria represents only one among several possible configurations of relationships. First of all, the same perception of instrumental interests – not to mention, more generally, the same identification of relevant social problems – is the product of a social construction process (Hilgartner and Bosk 1988; Best 1989). For example it seems difficult to maintain that the stress placed by former militants of new left groups on urban ecological issues is independent of a more general attention to social conflict which is present in their 'interpretative frames'. Similarly, differences in organizational forms can be linked to differences of an ideological nature. Above all, in phases characterized by a high level of radicality in conflicts, the political culture of actors is not unrelated to the choice of certain organizational forms.[19] One of the recurring themes in protest movements since the 1970s has been criticism of the bureaucratization of associative forms, which are therefore considerably less open to grassroots participation (Kitschelt 1990; Poguntke 1993).

In order to understand the structure of movement networks, it is therefore advisable to take into account the nature of the social conflicts in which the movements are actors, and the characteristics of the belief systems and the identities which these develop. The structure of social movements may be shaped by the characteristics of the different social groups that mobilize within them. It has been repeatedly noted how the development of broad alliances on environmental, gender, or citizens' rights issues may be hampered by the strength of cultural differences – in turn based on race, class, or again gender – running within the communities that movements are supposed to mobilize (Lichterman 1995b; Croteau 1995). The anti-nuclear movements saw, for example, the convergence of local populations, mainly from traditional middle classes, and of activists from ecological groups of a more radical orientation, closer to the new middle classes (Rüdig 1990; Flam 1994d). The question in this case is whether the structure of choice can be conditioned by similarities and differences in social composition and in levels of education, noticeable among various movement actors: do relationships between movement organizations cut across main class – or other fundamental – divides? Or do they rather reflect those fundamental differences?

The decision to develop or not to develop relationships can also be affected by the possible presence of solidarity links which have already been activated among participants. In this case it can be useful to differentiate among various types of experiences of mobilization and to evaluate the relative incidence of these. It is thus necessary to go beyond the observation that experiences of political engagement in the past which have permitted the acquisition of specific competences and sensibilities, represent in general terms a strong predictor of subsequent participation.[20] It is necessary to ask whether differences in past experiences of collective action determine variable forms of collective identity which are, in their turn, capable of influencing later choices.

The ways in which movement actors represent themselves, their adversaries and what is at stake in the conflict in which they are involved, can also have multiple effects on the selection of potential allies. Difficulties in cooperation between movement organizations and other voluntary organizations or public agencies all engaged with the same concerns can derive from incompatibilities in relation to their respective representations of the issue. On the other hand, indifference and hostility can develop not so much from dissent in the perception of a specific problem but rather from diverse ideological positionings. In a political phase strongly characterized by certain representations of the conflict, possibilities for interaction among groups which take up opposing positions in relation to the principal cleavage, may be limited, despite their shared concern for specific problems.

By these observations we do not intend to suggest that interaction within movement networks is always inspired by evaluations of ideological and political affinity. In fact, cooperation among actors espousing different points of view is a permanent feature of movements. At the same time, however, neither alliances among organizations nor multiple allegiances can develop if actors see themselves as differing on points which they hold to be non-negotiable during a particular political phase. In Italy during the 1970s, the persistent force of the right–left division certainly hindered the start of consistent and long-lasting collaborations among moderates and radicals in environmental organizations of the period. Representing the conflict in class terms was, in fact, a priority in comparison with alternative conceptions (Diani 1988: ch. 3). Even in contexts where the identities related to major political divisions are far less strong, as in the United States, ideological disputes within movements may radicalize to the point of preventing possibilities for alliances even in those cases when cooperation would seem an obvious option (Benford 1993; Gamson 1995; Lichterman 1995b).

The restriction of alliances to actors who are ideologically and culturally most similar may also be fostered by other reasons. As we have seen, in movement organizations, symbolic and value incentives often play a central role in promoting and subsequently maintaining the mobilization of supporters (for a discussion: Opp 1989, ch. 1). However, any decision to activate alliances with actors who do not entirely share their world vision means that groups risk limiting their own capacity to provide the stimulation and motivation for action to their own bases. In certain phases of the conflict, the construction of alliances which suggest excessive concessions on points of principle could, in fact, seem to militants to be further signs of the prevalence of an unacceptable tendency towards compromise. If the conviction that goals have been betrayed by the leadership becomes widespread, this could provoke dangerous tendencies to demobilize. For similar reasons, one can expect that the development of relationships based on personal friendships, or on forms of multiple militancy tends to diminish in inverse relation to the ideological distance between the organizations to which those interested in interaction make reference.

5.4.3 Movement networks and political processes

Theories of movements as actors in specific conflicts lead us to consider three categories of factors which have the potential to influence decisions relating to cooperation and individual allegiances. These are the social position of the activists; the solidarity links which derive from their past experiences in 'old' and 'new' conflicts; and the symbolic systems adopted by actors. The likelihood that these factors will influence the structure of movement networks – in the same way as organizational and interest variables – varies, however. Certainly, one cannot ignore the relative stability of solidarity links based on previous shared experiences or on adhesion to certain visions of the world. But neither can one forget that the intensity of such sentiments can vary cyclically over time (Fantasia 1988). At times these factors have the effect of segmenting a movement network (Diani 1988: ch. 2; Rucht 1989; Lichterman 1995b). They can erect barriers to others who may adopt a different kind of identity, thus precluding systematic interaction between them. At other times, however, their impact may appear to be fairly low.

How can we explain the fact that particular differences among movement actors can lead to fragmentation in certain phases but not in others? To answer this question it is necessary to take the political conditions in which movements operate into account. We shall return systematically in the following chapters to the relevance of political variables. The reference to these in the present context is important, inasmuch as they influence movement actors' perceptions of operating in an environment which is open or closed to their own concerns and demands. In general, when a movement does not succeed in obtaining recognition and legitimacy, and/or concrete results in terms of policy, moves towards demobilization become stronger.[21] As a result, movement organizations tend to use symbolic and solidaristic resources *en masse*, in order to keep their mobilizing capacity at a high level. They place ever greater emphasis on the uniqueness of their perspective, of their political origins, and of the interests they sustain (Tarrow 1990; della Porta 1995). In parallel with this, the weight of competitive cooperation in interorganizational relations increases. This in turn creates ever greater divisions within movement areas, proportional to the emphasis placed on the elements which divide as opposed to those which support convergence. All other conditions being equal, this leads to a greater segmentation across all movement networks; and in some cases, this phenomenon can assume the form of explicit conflict among organizations.

The picture seems very different in contexts characterized by positive political opportunities. The perception that the possibility of developing effective action exists, leads actors to stress the pursuit of specific goals rather than the possibility of global change. Furthermore, attempts are made to develop forms of communication which can reach public opinion at its widest, rather than those limited sectors which are already felt to be very close to the movement. In both cases, recourse to ideology as an instrument of mobilization is reduced, as are references to specific identities and solidarities. Competition rarely goes beyond sectarian divisions and conflicts. Instead, non-competitive forms of cooperation tend to increase. Overall, the criteria by which movement actors select their allies are more inclusive than they are when opportunities for the movements seem more limited (Diani 1995a, 1995b).

To sum up, it seems plausible to hypothesize that political and cultural differences among movement actors are particularly salient, and have a direct influence on the construction of alliances, in periods in which the perception that there are few opportunities for action leads individual actors to value their uniqueness, as a way of increasing their mobilizing capacities. In contrast, the perception that there are abundant opportunities facilitates, all things being equal, models of interaction inspired principally by pragmatic and instrumental criteria.

Although available evidence about movement networks is still too scattered to allow for a conclusive validation of these hypotheses, it still appears largely consistent with them. In his comparison of the German and French environmental movements in the 1980s, Dieter Rucht (1989) identified two different types of network structures. In both cases the movements actually consisted of three subnetworks, linking organizations which were close respectively to a conservationist, an environmentalist and a political ecology perspective. However, the relationship between these sectors was different. In the German case, characterized by a favourable opportunity structure, regular exchanges and consultations between the different movement sectors had developed both at the national and the local level (Rucht 1989: 74–9). In the French case, where opportunities were globally more limited, no evidence was found of systematic linkages among the political ecology and the other two sectors (1989: 82–5).

Although Rucht refers to political opportunities in order to account for movements' global success or failure, yet his line of reasoning may be extended to the shape of interorganizational networks. The less favourable opportunities offered by the French political system seem to have forced groups in the different traditions to stick to their own peculiarities and to be less open to mediation and compromise with perspectives different from their own: the moderatism of conservation groups was instrumental in granting them (limited) access to state support, a strategy which could not be jeopardized by the development of stronger linkages to radical political ecologists; conversely, the centralization of the French state and its closure towards challengers encouraged political ecologists to emphasize some traits – for example, their opposition to formal organizational structures – which also proved an obstacle to the establishing of stronger cooperation across sectors. Mario Diani's study of Italian environmentalism supports similar conclusions (1988, 1995a): exchanges across different sectors of the environmental movement became more intense during the 1980s, when opportunities for autonomous environmental action grew in correspondence with the weakening of the left–right divide which had mainly shaped patterns of alliance and opposition in the previous decade.

5.5   Summary

Social movements are based on free-flowing interaction among organisations and among individuals. Personal links play, firstly, an important part in facilitating individual participation in action. Their role can be crucial, depending on the characteristics of collective action: specifically, on the investment in personal energy and time which this entails, the risks implied and the radical nature of the objectives. In particular, we can distinguish between social links of a private nature and contacts which originated in other collective experiences. Activists' personal contacts are, nevertheless, an important component in movements' structures in another sense. Their multiple allegiances represent a bridge linking the various movement organisations to each other, as well as to their environment.

It is, moreover, essential to examine the relationships – of co-operation and of exchange of information – which link movement organizations. First, it is notable that the absence of contacts among movement organizations is an equally interesting phenomenon – and a much more frequent one – than the existence of interaction. It is therefore important to distinguish between various forms of interorganizational relationships, on the basis of the presence or absence of cooperation between two organizations, and of the presence or absence of competition between them for the support of the same potential base. The criteria on which various movement actors can base their choice of alliance (or, in the case of individuals, their multiple alliances) are wide ranging. Among these, the following seem to have theoretical relevance: instrumental considerations, divisions of a structural or ideological nature, and the varying degrees of salience which such distinctions can assume – or not – in various political contexts.

6

Social Movements and Organizational Form

In many western democracies the student movement of the late 1960s was among the first to criticize the traditional left's bureaucratic structures and to seek new models of organization. In the early stages of mobilization students in both Italy and Germany (as well as in many other countries) organized assemblies, study groups, 'alternative' courses and faculty or institutional-level collectives.[1] Decisions were taken in open assembly; the movement's leaders were simply those individuals who had most time and effort to devote to collective action, and numerous ideological tendencies coexisted without dramatic tension. Until 1969 students in both countries theorized direct democracy, self-organization, grassroots participation and permanent control. The movement's organizations were initially inclusive and the boundaries between them flexible. Adherence was more a matter of shared sentiment than official membership and the feeling was of being part of the movement as a whole rather than any particular organisation. Participation in more than one organization was not simply permitted but encouraged.

In both countries, however, the most innovative of these organizational principles proved difficult to apply to the reality of mobilization. Bernd Rabehl, a German student leader, later confessed: 'Yes, assemblies were public, but a small group would sit down in a café and decide in half an hour what had not been decided there in five hours. It was necessary. We could not do otherwise. We could not leave everything to spontaneity' (in Bauss 1977: 334). The need to go beyond the movement's initial 'spontaneity' intensified, particularly as mobilization spread and a plethora of organizations became active in different geographical areas and spheres of activity. Activists in both Italy and Germany sought a model of organization which would help to coordinate protest. At the highpoint of student protest in Germany the movement was led by the SDS (Sozialistischer Deutscher Studentenbund), a decentralized but well organized group, traditionally attentive to ideological debate (though also accustomed to negotiation) and entirely composed of students. In Italy the local nuclei from the universities merged with the workers groups active in the factories to form the organizations of the new left. These organizations were characterized by an initially informal structure, were highly ideological and their attention was largely turned outside the universities themselves.

Organizational changes took place after the decline in student mobilization. Many groups disappeared, while others attempted to 'export' protest to other social strata. Activists in both countries either swelled the ranks of other political and trade union organizations, dispersed into small local groups or re-aggregated in more structured forms. A number of the organizations which survived the disintegration of the student movement underwent a process of 'institutionalization'. Organizational boundaries became clearer, though there were a few exceptions. Participation in one organization began to preclude that in others and militants increasingly identified themselves with their own organization rather than the movement as a whole. When protest spread to other sectors, re-forming (in a decentralized way) around particular collectives and committees, however, the groups which had originated in the student movement demonstrated different levels of influence in the two countries. In Italy, new left groups provided organizational resources for later movements, occupying an important place in many grassroots committees and promoting radical ideology and practice within them. In Germany, on the other hand, the (communist) K-Gruppen and the small counterculture groupings had little influence on the pragmatically organized Bürgeriniziativen, dedicated to non-violent civil disobedience and with a decentralized, flexible structure for coordinating the rare national campaigns undertaken.

The choice of an organizational model to adopt was an important strategic decision for other movements and in other countries just as it had been for the student movements in Italy and Germany. It is no accident that the question of organization has received close attention from (and been fiercely debated by) both activists and students of social movements. A first and central question in the present study regards the relevance of organizational structure itself. As noted in chapter 1, absence (or weakness) of organization is an important element in the *collective behaviour approach* definition of a social movement, which classifies them, like crowds or fashion, as 'spontaneous'. From the late 1960s the *resource mobilization approach* began to criticize the dominant theories which assimilated social movements to other spontaneous, and partly irrational, forms of behaviour and focused attention on social movement organizations (or SMOs), defined as rational organizations capable of gathering resources from their surrounding environment and allocating them with the aim of bringing about political transformation.

Although it is generally accepted that social movements and the organizations involved in them are not the same thing, an understanding of the latter's functions is central to any study of collective mobilization. And indeed, studies focusing on this argument became more common from the 1970s, particularly among American sociologists. Such studies have concentrated on a number of crucial questions and these will be analysed in the present chapter, using the student movement in Italy and Germany for illustration. First, the search for characteristics 'typical' of social movement organisations has produced very different organisational typologies (6.1). Regarding organisational evolution, research has similarly led to discussion of differing paths of development rather than a single model of organizational evolution (6.2). A further important question for the study of social movement organization therefore concerns the internal and external variables which lead to the choice of one organizational model rather than another. As with any organization, strategic options are influenced above all by the presence or absence of given resources in the surrounding environment (6.3). It should be added, however, that the number of such options is limited. In other words, they form a repertoire of organizational forms which tends to survive over time (6.4). If the choice of a particular model of organization is constrained by the characteristics of a movement and its surroundings, the consequences of adopting a given organizational model also need to be considered (6.5).

6.1. Do Typical Forms of Social Movement Organization Exist?

According to one well-known definition, an SMO is a complex organization whose goals coincide with the preferences of a social movement and which tries to realize those goals (McCarthy and Zald 1977: 1,218). In general, each organization must fulfil a number of functions contemporaneously: inducing participants to offer their services; defining organizational aims; managing and coordinating contributions; collecting resources from their environment, and selecting, training and replacing members (Scott 1981: 9). Social movement organizations must mobilize resources from the surrounding environment, whether directly in the form of money or through voluntary work by its adherents; they must neutralize opponents and increase support from both the general public and the elite (for example, McCarthy and Zald 1987b [1977]: 19).[2] Social movement organizations, like any other, are composed of *social structures* (patterned or regular relationships within the organization); *participants* (individuals contributing to the organisation); *goals* (definitions of the organization's aims), and *technologies* (machinery and technical skills) (Scott 1981). In other words, they possess the means and organizational mechanisms to mobilize resources for protest in order to further the movement's objectives (Rucht 1996).

When the sociology of social movements became a field of study in its own right, it was generally agreed that such movements were characterized by a weak and informal organizational structure. Research has continued to emphasize certain organizational peculiarities.

First, as was noted in the preceding chapter, social movements have been described as *decentralized* in structure. Adopting Gerlach's much-used categories, social movements are: (1) *segmented*, with numerous different groups or cells in continual rise and decline; (2) *policephalous*, having many leaders each commanding a limited following only; and (3) *reticular*, with multiple links between autonomous cells forming an indistinctly-bounded network (Gerlach 1976). Social movements have been identified with *loosely structured collective conflict*, in which 'hundreds of groups and organisations – many of them short-lived, spatially scattered, and lacking direct communication, a single organisation and a common leadership – episodically take part in many different kinds of local collective action' (Oberschall 1980: 45–6). Coordination of the movement is assured by different organizations in different phases: journals, newspapers and other publications sympathetic to the movement's aims will 'launch' discussion of a particular theme; committees set up for the purpose (but with no formal authority) elaborate proposals during periods of mobilization; the alternative press circulates information among peripheral groups of sympathizers. No single group tends to (or should) be recognized as representing the movement's wider interest (Diani and Donati 1984).

Second, social movements – or at least those libertarian left movements with which the majority of sociological studies are concerned – are characterized by their emphasis on *participation*. In favour of direct democracy, they distribute power widely among individuals, allow only limited delegation of power and privilege consensual decision-making. It has been noted that in the student movements of the 1960s 'the distance between leaders and participants, between national officers and membership, was vigorously solved by eliminating leaders, office functions, the division of labour, centralised decision making, formal democracy' (Breines 1989: 51). Democratic participation, anti-bureaucratic politics, community versus organization and the demand for a 'way of life that called for equal and caring relationships' (Breines 1989: 48) were all catchphrases of new left ideology. Subsequent movements have also invoked the general principle of direct democracy, characterized as a decision-making process in which 'a large number of movement participants gather together in a single place and undertake an interchange of ideas about the immediate or ultimate direction of the movement. The process (explicitly or implicitly) involves consideration of alternative actions, and is sometimes concluded by the group as a whole making a collective decision, either through consensus or a formal vote' (Rosenthal and Schwartz 1989: 46).

A decentralized and participatory structure also tends to favour the third characteristic of social movement organizations: powerful *internal solidarity*. Having only limited access to material resources, unlike political parties or pressure groups, social movements substitute for this with symbolic resources. For the most part building incentives to solidarity,[3] social movement organizations give particular importance to internal relations, transforming the very costs of collective action into benefits through the intrinsic rewards of participation itself. As well as formal organizations, small groups held together by personal relations survive during periods of latency, providing important bases for the revival of movement activities. In particular, a small group of activists 'uses naturally occurring social relationships and meets a variety of organisational and individual needs for emotional support, integration, sharing of sacrifice, and expression of shared identities' (Gamson 1990: 175). Within cohesive groups the conditions for the development of alternative value systems are constituted and 'communal associations become free spaces, breeding grounds for democratic change' (Evans and Boyte 1992: 187). In these 'free spaces' a 'sense of a common good' develops alongside the construction of 'direct, face-to-face, and egalitarian relationships' (1990: 190–1). Thus an all-embracing participation tends to permeate every aspect of the day-to-day life of activists. 'In the climate of the late sixties', it has be noted of the student movement, 'commitment to revolution had implications for carrying out virtually every detail of daily life: to be a revolutionary was to dress, eat, make love, and speak in certain ways and not others' (Whalen and Flacks 1989: 249). Where politics 'marks every moment of the day' fellow militants become a 'family', as it is sometimes put on the extreme left in Italy (in della Porta 1990: 149–50). So much so that, in their values system and lifestyle, 'those who participated in the youth revolt continue to be affected by it' (Whalen and Flacks 1989: 247).

Finally, social movements have a particular type of *leadership*. Studies of social movements have insisted on defining leadership legitimation as neither traditional nor rational-legal. Rather, it is charismatic in the Weberian sense, dependent above all on the ability of leaders to embody the movement as a whole, contributing to the creation of a collective identity (see, for example, Alberoni 1984). Manipulation of ideological resources has in the past been considered as an important basis for charismatic leadership. More recently it has been noted that experts have replaced ideologists in contemporary movements. Involved as they are in technological issues, contemporary movements assign a very important role to natural scientists and engineers: 'challenging sophisticated technologies . . . such organised protests are dependent on recognised experts to interpret the issues and achieve public credibility' (Walsh 1988: 182). Because it is dependent on possession of constantly changing resources, leadership in social movements is *ad hoc*, short lived, relates to specific objectives and is concentrated in limited area of the movements themselves (Diani and Donati 1984).

While many studies have emphasized the distinctiveness of the organizational structure of social movements compared with other complex organizations, others have played down the differences. Rather than putting forward a single alternative model (constructed primarily by looking at the early growth phase of the movements which have emerged since the 1970s) the latest research has identified a number of organizational models. More specifically, a number of classifications can be constructed from degree of organization, distribution of power and levels of participation.

Degree of organization is central to any analysis of both political and non-political groupings.[4] The sociological literature on political parties singles out variables such as structural articulation, intensity (as indicated by the number of grassroots units, for example), dimension (the number of members in each area of activity), pervasiveness (the number of parallel units), frequency of local and national meetings and the presence of written records (Janda 1970: 104–12).[5] As far as SMOs are concerned, Hanspeter Kriesi (1996) has described their *internal structuration* as deriving from: (1) formalization (with the introduction of formal membership criteria, written rules, fixed procedures, formal leadership and a fixed structure of offices or bureaux); (2) professionalization (understood as the presence of paid staff who pursue a career inside the organization); (3) internal differentiation (involving a functional division of labour and the creation of territorial units); and (4) integration (through mechanisms of horizontal and/or vertical coordination).[6]

The *distribution of power* within an organization also needs to be considered. Power can be more or less centralized, as the literature on political parties in particular has revealed. National structures can have greater or less weight; there can be greater or lesser participation in decisions concerning resource allocation, goal definition, candidacies or disciplinary procedures; and there can be greater or lesser centralization of leadership (Janda 1970: 104–12). Concerning social movement organizations more specifically, McCarthy and Zald distinguished between federated and non-federated structures. In a federated structure (with either branch building or the aggregation of pre-existing organizations as its basis) members are organized in small, local units. Non-federated SMOs, on the other hand, do not have branches, dealing directly with adherents by mail or through travelling staff. Members do not usually interact on a face-to-face basis in such an organisation (McCarthy and Zald 1977 [1987b]: 29). James

Q. Wilson (1973), on the other hand, distinguishes between caucus organizations, in which a large but inactive base finances a small number of active leaders, and primary organizations, where there is a high degree of member participation. In general, social movement leaders have differing resources as well as degrees of power.[7]

Finally, social movements vary in the degree of *commitment* they demand from participants, some being inclusive others exclusive. Inclusive organizations allow membership overlap with other political organizations and have frequent dealings with the outside world, exclusive ones do not (Curtis and Zurcher 1974).[8] Unlike inclusive organizations, exclusive ones demand a long novitiate, rigid discipline and a high level of commitment, intruding upon every aspect of their members' lives (Zald and Ash 1966). In general, the greater the degree to which an organization is founded on symbolic incentives – either ideological or solidaristic – the more exclusive it will be.

A glance at the panorama of social movement research reveals different kinds of organization ensuring a movement's survival at particular moments in time. First, there are a series of organizations whose principal task is mobilization for protest action. At the most decentralised level are *local nuclei*, relatively unstructured, inclusive and predominantly based on symbolic incentives (see Rosenthal and Schwartz 1989: 44–5, for a similar definition). The faculty collectives of the student movement provide an example of such a form of organization.

In certain phases various local nuclei may create an *umbrella organization* to coordinate, on an ad hoc basis, pursuit of specific objectives. Within a movement, the various organizations build coalitions for mobilizing protest, collecting money, lobbying or forming political parties. Specialized organizations of an inclusive nature usually cooperate through the construction of movement networks, the exchange of services and resources and so on.[9] In this kind of organization a more formal and action-oriented structure exists and the incentives to participation are predominantly instrumental.

There are other, more structured organizations for mobilization, however, with a legal constitution, internal power hierarchies, leadership elections, set methods of fundraising and membership and supporter lists (Rosenthal and Schwarz 1989: 44–5). Some of these organizations more closely resemble political parties,[10] others pressure groups (Rucht 1994: 313–14). Again taking our examples from student movements, with their centralized structure and exclusion of participation in other organizations the communist K-Gruppen in Germany and the new left groupings in Italy were closer to the *party model*. However, the party model itself has been changed with the emergence of the greens, formed (for the most part) during the 1980s campaigns on environmental issues, and nuclear energy in particular (although they have never been the official political representatives of the environmentalist movement) (Rootes 1994). In seeking to defend nature, these parties also sought to apply the 'think globally, act locally' principle to their organizations. The greens rejected, initially at least, any structured organizational power, just as they rejected centralizing technologies. The model of open assemblies and ad hoc revocable delegates did not survive long, however. Particularly after they entered first regional and then national parliaments, the greens began to create a stable organizational structure, with membership cards, representative rather than direct democracy within the party and a stable leadership. Public funding of the parties created a constant and generous flow of finance which was used to develop a professional political class, set up newspapers and open flanking institutions. The green parties' structure thus became formal and centralised. Participation moved towards excluding membership of other organizations, and ideological incentives began to predominate.

The *public interest group* model, on the other hand, although similarly formal and centralised, does not exclude participation in other organisations and indeed there may be material incentives to do so. A *professional social movement organization* would belong to this category, having '(1) a leadership that devotes full time to the movement, with a large proportion of resources originating outside the aggrieved group that the movement claims to represent; (2) a very small or non-existent membership base or a paper membership (membership implies little more than allowing a name to be used upon membership rolls); (3) attempts to impart the image of "speaking for a constituency", and (4) attempts to influence policy toward that same constituency' (McCarthy and Zald 1987a [1973]: 375).[11] However, professional SMOs do not necessarily address themselves to those whose interests they wish to promote, as a normal pressure group would. Rather, they have a 'conscience constituency' composed of those who believe in the cause they support. Their leaders are entrepreneurs whose 'movements' impact results from their skills at manipulating images of relevance and support through the communication media' (McCarthy and Zald 1987a [1973]: 374).[12] Ordinary members have little power and 'have no serious role in organisational policy-making short of withholding membership dues. The professional staff largely determines the positions the organisation takes upon issues' (McCarthy and Zald 1987a [1973]: 378).

Not all social movement organizations are directly concerned with resource mobilization, however. Some of them, described recently as *movement associations*, are formed to meet specific needs among the movement's constituency (Kriesi 1996). Communes, therapy groups and rape crisis centres were formed through the feminist movement, for example (see, for instance, Ryan 1992: 135–44). As far as the student movement is concerned, used-book stalls and advice centres of various kinds offered logistical support to sympathizers, allowing protest action in favour of the right to education to be combined with concrete activity aimed at 'putting the end into practice', while at the same time they helped widen support. Movement associations, too, are diverse in terms of levels of organization, internal power distribution and degree of participation. Self-help groups, for example, tend to be informal, decentralized and are frequently totalizing, while associations offering services to a wider public may adopt a more formal structure, a hierarchical distribution of power and fuse symbolic and instrumental incentives.

Besides groups involved in political mobilization and movement associations, both predominantly inward-looking, *supportive organizations* (Kriesi 1996) are also part of social movement organizational structure. Service organizations such as newspapers, recreation centres, educational institutions or friendly printing firms, which contribute to a movement's aims while at the same time working on the open market, fall into this category. The film clubs, theatres, photocopying shops and publishing houses created within the student movement in order to further collective mobilization increasingly became market-oriented, commercial enterprises with audited accounts, salaried staff and a competitive market ethos. The spread of this kind of structure contributes to the creation of movement countercultures in which political engagement permeates the whole of life.[13] These organizations tend, with a few exceptions, to be formal (though decentralized) and participation is inclusive and instrumentally motivated for both members and clients.

6.2 Organizational Evolution

Just as the organizational characteristics of social movements vary, there is no predetermined model for the evolution of particular groups within them, as the present section will seek to demonstrate. A Weberian approach, focusing attention primarily on the process of bureaucratization, initially dominated in the sociology of social movements as in other areas. Michels' 'iron law of oligarchy', which states that in order to survive as an organization a political party gives diminishing importance to external goals and an increasing amount of its energies to adjusting to the environment,[14] was also held valid for social movements.

As far as social movement organizations are concerned, institutionalization used to be considered a natural evolution. Recurrent lifecycles were identified in the histories of a number of movements. Herbert Blumer (1951: 203), for example, distinguished four stages in the typical social movement lifecycle. The first, or 'social ferment', stage is characterized by unorganized, unfocused agitation during which great attention is paid to the propaganda of 'agitators'. In the second phase, of 'popular excitement', the underlying causes of discontent and the objectives of action are more clearly defined. In the third phase, of 'formalization', disciplined participation and coordination of strategies for achieving the movement's aims are achieved by creating a formal organization. Finally, in the 'institutionalization' stage the movement becomes an organic part of society and crystallizes into a professional structure.

Other authors have cast doubt on the 'necessity' of such an evolution, however. Even organizational sociologists point out that adaptation is only one evolutionary possibility among many. In fact, an organization need not react by moderating its aims when conflict with the surrounding environment arises. It can also become more radical, hoping that a small but powerful nucleus of dissent will form in this way (Jackson and Morgan 1978). Moreover, rather than adapt to external demands it may simply reduce contacts with the outside world (Meyer and Rowan 1983). Although he referred to the Michels hypothesis (and emphasized that 'there are organisational characteristics that dictate organisation maintenance over every other possible goal'), Ted Lowi (1971: 31) noted that 'the phenomenon has little to do with goal displacement. Rather, the goals of an organisation have become outwon with the need of maintaining the organisation'.

As far as SMOs are concerned, institutionalization rarely occurs. In the first place, few of them actually survive. Some dissolve because their aims have been achieved. Organizations formed to coordinate specific campaigns, for example, tend to disappear as soon as that campaign is over (Zurcher and Curtis 1973).[15] Leadership splits during downturns in mobilization and the resultant processes of disintegration and realignment cause others to disappear. In the case of social movement organizations whose life expectancy is short and aims limited, an interest in the organization's continuing existence may not even develop. In other words, their members' first loyalty continues to be to the movement and the organization is simply seen as a temporary instrument for intervention. Indeed, recent research has revealed a pattern of multiple adherence, with simultaneous participation in a range of organizations belonging to different social movements. This has led to the idea that there are social movements 'families'; clusters of movements which have different specific objectives but share a similar world view, overlap in membership and frequently work together in protest campaigns (della Porta and Rucht 1995).

Moreover, the organizations which *do* survive do not not always develop in the same directions. Some organizations indeed become *bureaucratized*, resembling ever more closely a political party or pressure group. They develop internal organization, become more moderate, adopt a more institutional repertoire of action and integrate into the system of interest representation. The parties of the new left developed out of the student movement in this way, gradually finding a niche in parliament and (occasionally) in local government, while learning to use more conventional tactics. Moreover, student unions with formal regulations and procedures often re-emerged to represent students on school and university governing bodies after the movement itself had subsided.

Moderation of an organization's aims is not, of course, the only possible development. Other social movement organizations become *more radical*. Their aims become more ambitious, the forms of action adopted *less* conventional and they become increasingly isolated from the outside world. One outcome of 1968, although certainly not the only or the most important, was the formation of clandestine organizations which adopted increasingly radical forms of action, to the point of murdering political opponents. The clandestine organizations which grew

6.3   Structure and Strategy: Movement Goals and Organizational Form

In an article on the evolution of SMOs Mayer Zald and Roberta Ash (1966) suggested that the 'iron law of oligarchy' was only valid for certain kinds of organization and environment. In particular, the process of goal moderation can be obstructed by certain organizational characteristics (such as the prevalence of solidaristic-type incentives which reduce pressure to accommodate to the external environment, the diffusion of organizational exclusivity increasing an organization's power over its members or the presence of fundamentalist ideologies challenging the bases of authority itself) and by certain conditions in the surrounding environment (such as the presence of radical preferences or sentiments in society).

The question of organizational evolution carries with it a number of problems concerning the determinants of organizational form itself. Form is, in fact, a part of strategy and what determines organizational strategy is one of the chief questions in organizational sociology. The two main approaches have offered somewhat different answers to the problem. The 'closed system' approach claims that organizations are in a position to control all relevant variables and thus choose the optimal strategy for achieving their goals. The 'natural system' approach, on the other hand, maintains that there are limitations on an organization's capacity for information gathering and that, as a result, they look for the most 'satisfactory' rather than optimal strategy (for a review, see Thompson 1967; Scott 1981; Hall 1982). Moreover, organizations attempt to fulfill their *operational* goals (those aims which appear in operative policy) rather than their official ones (those set out in their charter or in public statements) (Perrow 1961).

Both approaches can be found in the sociology of social movements. Applying a number of hypotheses developed by the 'resource dependence' approach in the field of organizational studies, the 'resource mobilization' approach has suggested that the growth of a social movement depends on the activities of social movement 'entrepreneurs' who stimulate protest and mobilize resources (McCarthy and Zald 1987b [1977]: 17–18). Organizational form can therefore be considered as a strategic choice made by leaders on the basis of the organization's goals. In organizational sociology Chandler has suggested that 'structure follows strategy' (in Bontadini 1978). Regarding social movements, a number of scholars have considered their degree of centralization to be dependent on goal orientation, expressive movements preferring decentralized forms and institutional change movements opting for centralized ones (for a review see Jenkins 1983; also Freeman 1983a and Rucht 1984: 611).[18] Along with goal orientation, membership conditions (and in particular the degree of exclusivity/inclusivity) have also been considered as important in determining four organizational characteristics: incentive type (solidaristic or instrumental); the nature of contacts with the wider environment (highly specific, moderately specific or broad); style of leadership (directive, mixed or persuasive); and type of membership (homogeneous, moderately homogeneous or heterogeneous) (Curtis and Zurcher 1974: 358). However, strategic choices must take into account resources. In fact, organizational structure can be understood as a strategic option determined by the presence of *mobilizable resources* but constrained by the *limits to their rational use* such as values, previous experience, reference groups, expectations and relationship to target groups (Freeman 1979). In the rest of this section we will consider, first, mobilizable resources and, second, restraints on elaborating organizational strategies for their exploitation.

6.3.1   Modernization and organizational form

First, technological development may change the amount of available external resources. In his well-known study, Charles Tilly (1978) suggested that the past four centuries have seen a shift from decentralized and informally coordinated movements to centralized and formally coordinated ones; from short-term, reactive action by small-scale, informal solidarity groups or communities to long-term proactive action by large, special-purpose associations (see chapter 7). Technological change has influenced the organizational structure of social movements as well as the tactics they adopt. The expansion of both printed and electronic means of communication has permitted an 'externalization' of certain costs (Tarrow 1994: 143–5). If highly structured organizations were previously required to get a message across, today a lightweight one which can gain media attention is sufficient. The diffusion of cheap global means of communication (such as faxes and electronic mail, for example) reduces the cost of coordination, though the level of professionalization required for mobilization increases.

The expansion of education and the proportionate growth of the middle classes increases the propensity to organization because 'more people are in a position to join and contribute money' (McCarthy and Zald 1987a [1973]). As has been noted, '(1) the growth of mass higher education creates a large pool of students whose discretionary time can be allocated to social movement activities; (2) as the relative size of the social service, administrative, and academic professions increases, more and more professionals can arrange their time schedules to allow participation in activities related to social movements; and (3) a relative increase in discretion over work-time allocation permits the emergence of transitory teams to engage in sociopolitical activities' (McCarthy and Zald 1987a [1973]: 355). Moreover, belief in one's ability to influence the wider world, and therefore the motivation for collective action, generally increases along with education. Associationism facilitates the growth of social movements, which are usually in a position to benefit from the chance to recruit ready-formed activists.

In general terms, economic progress may also have a beneficial effect on the organizing capacity of social movements since 'as the amount of discretionary resources of mass and elite public increase, the absolute and relative amount of resources available to the SMS [Social Movement Sector] increases' (McCarthy and Zald 1987b [1977]: 25). These resources include time and money, but also political freedom, means of communication, transportation etc. With this growth the amount of resources available for new organizations and movements would also increase. Economic development, and the economic and time resources it creates should lead to a growth in professionalized, formal groupings: 'The larger the income flow to an SMO, the more likely that cadre and staff are professional and the larger these groups are' (McCarthy and Zald 1987b [1977]: 35).

6.3.2   Organizational structure and institutional resources

Part of the resources available to social movement organizations are channelled through institutional actors. The latter may therefore influence the nature of mobilization. The effects of institutional characteristics on social movement organizations are not very clear, however. Social movements tend to imitate powerful opponents by creating similarly formal structures for themselves. Thus, a repressive, centralized state may well produce well-organized movements (Rootes 1997), sometimes with radical repertoires of action (della Porta 1995).[19] An 'accessible', decentralized state, on the other hand, would appear to favour the development of a similar organizational structure on the part of social movements. The decentralized structure of the American anti-nuclear movement, for example, has been explained by the decentralized structure of that country's electricity industry (Rucht 1990b: 209). Returning to our initial example, by allying itself with the old left the Italian student movement found itself involved in an extremely polarized political conflict. The political system's closure and frequent physical clashes with neo-fascists and police favoured the development of the centralized and bureaucratic organizations of the new left. In Germany, on the other hand, institutional openness (particularly during the period Social-Democrat Willy Brandt was Chancellor) favoured the proliferation of decentralized movement organizations, such as the Bürgeriniziativen (della Porta 1995, ch. 4).

It is not always the case, however, that head-on confrontation generates centralized organizations, nor that a willingness to negotiate on the part of the authorities always favours decentralization. First, rather than imitating their adversaries, a movement may demonstrate its opposition to existing institutions in its choice of organizational form as well as in other ways. Thus, 'French environmental movement organisations – *presumably as a negative reaction to political and administrative centralisation* – tend towards a loose and decentralized structure' (Rucht 1989: 85, emphasis added). Moreover, the openness of the political system as regards access to decision-makers may also favour the development of formal organizations (Rucht 1994). Proportional representation, for example, can promote the formation of movement parties, as happened when the various organizations of the new left in Italy stood lists at administrative and political elections in the 1970s.[20]

Similarly, in an open institutional system the availability of public or semi-public resources facilitates the creation of powerful lobbies with links to social movements themselves. Research on the civil rights movement in the United States, for example, has shown the way that funds from federal and local government agencies and programmes such as the Community Action Programs or Volunteers in Service to America stimulated the creation of movement organizations at the same time as the Peace Corps and alternative military service provided paid positions for activists. The conditions governing access to public and private

funding, tax exemption or advantageous postage rates influence
the organizational structure of groups who wish to benefit from
these possibilities. Thus the terms 'funded' (McCarthy and Zald
1987a: 358ff.) or 'registered' (McCarthy, Britt and Wolfson 1991:
68) social movement organizations have been used. Remaining
in the United States, organizations wishing access to a series of
material resources must respect, first and foremostly in their
organizational structure, a long list of laws and regulations including 'federal tax laws and policies and their enforcement by
the Internal Revenue Service, the actions of formal coalitions of
fundraising groups, United States Postal Service Regulations and
their consequences for access to the mails, the rules and actions
of private organizations monitoring groups, the dynamics of
combined charity appeals, and state and local level fundraising
regulations and their enforcement' (McCarthy et al. 1991: 46). In
particular, 'not-for-profit' or 'non-partisan' organization status,
usually necessary for access to the above-mentioned resources,
involves adhesion to the models considered legitimate for such
organizations (the presence of a governing body and annual
audit, for example) (1991: 61). From this point of view, certainly,
increased availability of institutional resources accentuates the
presence of formal, centralized organisations, as American public-
interest groups (such as Common Cause) with thousands of contributors and hundreds of local branches demonstrate (McFarland
1984: 61–92).

6.3.3   Organizational structure and the presence of allies

Social movements may also receive resources from institutional
allies. As is also the case with other characteristics (see ch. 8), the
organizational choices made by social movements are influenced
by the presence or otherwise of institutional allies. It can be
suggested, first, that there is a tendency for a division of labour
to be created. The presence of powerful institutional allies makes
available organizational resources, and social movements will
not therefore need to develop formal structures of their own (see
also Rucht 1996). Given the tendency to meet internal competition through image differentiation,[21] it is possible (in an alliance
with a political party, for instance) that a social movement
organization will emphasize its structural differences, paving
the way for a kind of division of labour. A comparison of Italy
and Germany indicates that where strong links exist between

social movements and the old left the former are able to rely on their more powerful allies to provide the infrastructures necessary for mobilization. As a result social movement infrastructure tends to be relatively weak and in periods of latency many movement activists join old left organizations. Where there is competition with the old left, on the other hand, social movements must build their own infrastructures and this helps to explain the existence of a denser and more widespread network of 'alternative' initiatives (ranging from self-help groups to commercial ventures) in Germany than in Italy.

At the same time, however, it can be assumed that social movement organizations will also have a tendency to imitate powerful allies. As remarked in chapter 3, they must 'bridge' the gap between their own frame of reference and that of a wider constituency. This refers to the creation of 'linkages of individuals and social movement orientations, so that individual interests, values and beliefs and social movement organisations' activities, goals and ideology are congruent and complementary' (Snow et al. 1986: 465). Organizational form must be added to activities, goals and ideology. Social movements must therefore take into account what forms of organization are acceptable to that wider constituency. A strong alliance with a political party may push a social movement organization to greater structuration. Returning to our illustrative case, the organizations involved in both the Italian and German student movements imitated the organizational characteristics of their allies to some extent. The Italian new left adopted forms of organization reflecting old left traditions: 'In a country in which the strongest party in the institutional left had obtained its hegemony by stressing the idea that it represented many social forces allied to the working class, those who wanted to create a political space to its left had to structure their demands in a meaningful way for the traditional political culture of the left' (Tarrow 1989b: 51). Born within the SPD, the SDS in Germany also embraced the organizational model predominant in the old left, at least in part. As already noted, the student movement's evolution in the two countries was at least partially different, a more decentralized organizational structure emerging in Germany, a more centralized one in Italy. This may, then, be explained by differences in the organizational characteristics of the old left. The German SPD was no longer a centralized class party and there was therefore more room for *innerparteiliche* Opposition. In Italy, on the other hand, the PCI (Partito Comunista Italiano) remained a working-class party in both ideology and strategy. It was centralist in orientation and allowed little in the way of internal dissent, driving the smaller groupings to its left towards a sort of compulsive imitation of its organizational model.

6.4 The Repertoires of Organizational Form

So far the adaptive capacity of organizational structure has been stressed. However, it must be remembered that constraints exist as well as resources. Just as we may speak of repertoires of forms of protest (chapter 7), we may do so for forms of organization (Clemens 1996). In any given country and at any given time, that repertoire is restricted. Although it can be expanded by borrowing from other countries or domains, such transformations are slow. Thus the *organizational resources* already present within the social movement sector tend to influence the evolution of single organizations and, more generally, the forms of protest adopted. The dominant organizations in any given phase tend to contribute organizational resources to later mobilizations, thus contributing also to the definition of their strategies. Adopting the terminology of the resource mobilization approach, the SMOs created during a particular phase of mobilization 'manufacture' resources for succeeding phases, influencing, or at least attempting to influence, their character.

Organizational choices, therefore, are influenced by the pre-existing structures within which movements form, inheriting ideas, constraints and facilitations as well as allies and opponents. Thus earlier historical movements or 'early riser' movements help produce their 'spin-offs'. During periods of mobilization there is an assimilation of inputs from existing movements, often involving joint campaigns with coordination between organizations and overlapping memberships from within the same subculture. The student movement provided the organizational resources for the formation of groups with objectives as diverse as defending the rights of the poor (Delgado 1986) and those of animals (Jasper and Nelkin 1992). Similarly, the women's movement, formed within its student predecessor, would later transmit ideological frameworks, tactical innovations, organizational structures and leadership to the peace movement (Meyer and Whittier 1994). Over time, then, a sort of collective memory on organizational possibilities is passed down from one generation of militants to the next or from one movement to another: 'one movement can influence subsequent movements both from outside and from within: by altering political and cultural conditions it confronts in the external environments, and by changing the individuals, groups and norms within the movement itself' (Meyer and Whittier 1994: 282). For this reason it can be very difficult to change certain initial organizational decisions, as they come to form a kind of genetic patrimony for movement organizations (see, among others, Panebianco 1982).

Returning to the example under analysis here, it can be noted that the organizational repertoires available to the student movement influenced not only the choices made by that movement itself but also those of later movements. In Italy and Germany the early organizational resources for the student movement came from the small cliques present within the organs of student self-government in the universities and from Marxist groups whose activities were prevalently theoretical. In both countries protest was guided by organizations with a left-wing ideology, furnishing the student movement with a utopian vision of large-scale social and political transformation. Moreover, the initial resources for mobilization in both countries were provided by intellectual circles who elaborated an ideological critique 'from the left' of the traditional left's organizations. A number of differences between the two countries can be noted, however. In particular, the German student movement was part of the so-called Ausserparlamentarische Opposition (APO), the extra-parliamentary opposition, which consisted in a network of loosely-structured campaigns such as the Kampagne fuer Abruestung (KfA) and the campaign against the Notstandsgesetzgebung (Otto 1989: 41). The APO had a campaign-oriented organizational structure and was extremely decentralized and inclusive (Otto 1989: 13). The Italian new left, on the other hand, looked to the centralized, Leninist model of organization, as well as developing a propensity for semi-clandestinity, the latter legitimized by reference to the wartime Resistance. In short, the organizational repertoires present in the two countries were slightly different. This influenced the choices made by the two movements and this in turn had long-term consequences for subsequent movements. Thus, later movements in Italy adhered to the centralized model of the Leninist parties while those in Germany adopted the decentralized forms which had characterized postwar movements in that country.

The evolution of organizational models would therefore seem to be determined by a complex amalgam of continuity and change. Continuity with the past can be explained by the tendency for organizational models to survive over time. If, however, social movements must decide on forms of organization from within the restricted number of repertoires present in their environment, each new wave of mobilization increases both the number of repertoires and the overall quantity of resources available to social movements.

It should be added that particular groups tend to have particular organizational repertoires because these are determined by levels of exposure to a whole series of experiences. Thus the adoption of a particular organizational model becomes more likely 'to the extent that the proposed model of organisation is believed to work, involves practices and organisational relations that are already familiar, and is consonant with the organisation of the rest of those individuals' social worlds' (Clemens 1996: 211). In fact, in order to understand an SMO's organizational strategy we must consider which sectors of the population it attempts to mobilize. In his analysis of the micro-processes of mobilization, Klandermans (1988) defined *mobilization potential* as the people within a society who, because they sympathize with the means as well as the ends of a social movement, can in theory be mobilized.[22] The activities of a social movement are designed to win support from those who constitute its recruitment reservoir, or mobilization potential. From this derives the hypothesis that choice of organizational form is linked to the organizational repertoires typical of the social groups which a movement is seeking to mobilize. Returning to the German and Italian student movements, differences in mobilization potential influenced the forms of organization adopted by the two movements after mobilization in the schools and universities had declined. Both movements attempted to mobilize a variety of social groups: workers, marginal youth, soldiers, prison inmates, migrants and so on, but while in Italy there was a 'meeting' of student and working-class activists, this did not take place in Germany. This meeting produced in Italy what Luigi Manconi has described as a shift from a 'student' to a 'workerist' model of organization. The former was characterized by an 'accordion-like structure' which 'expanded for direct action . . . and shrank in periods of preparation'. Its typical organizational space was 'the (informal but consolidated) small group meeting' (Manconi 1990: 68). The 'workerist' model, on the other hand, was constituted by 'social location, physical proximity, organisational stability, community of values and teleological projection' (Manconi

1990: 61). For historical and practical reasons protest in the large factories took centralized and tendentially exclusive forms.

6.5   Functionality and Problems of Social Movement Organizational Form

Having analysed the determinants of organizational form, it remains to consider the question of the effects of choosing a particular type. Are the organizational forms chosen by social movements effective or otherwise in achieving their ends? A flexible and decentralized organizational structure (considered typical of social movements by some) has often been regarded particularly effective in achieving the aims of protest. The characteristics of social movement structure – segmented, multi-cephalous and reticular – should allow rapid development. In fact, they should: (1) avert the danger of suppression by opponents; (2) allow inter-penetration; (3) maximize adaptability; (4) produce a solid system; (5) allow the escalation of action by distributing the effects of one group's activities to all of them; (6) promote innovation; and (7) reduce the negative effect of failures (Gerlach 1976). The alternation of periods of visibility and latency should also have positive effects because while visibility allows political bargaining with the authorities, latency produces affective solidarities and eases the development of 'new codes' (Melucci 1984a). Echoing Michels' analysis of the bureaucratization of socialist parties, Piven and Cloward (1977) considered the development of formal organizations as hampering goal attainment in protest movements of the poor. Investment in building a permanent, mass organization was seen as a waste of scarce resources. Moreover, such organizations tended to reduce the only resource available to the poor: mass defiance. By taming protest they would lead to defeat (Piven and Cloward 1977).

On the other hand, the advantages of more traditional forms of organization have also been highlighted. In his comparative analysis of American social movements, Gamson (1990: 1990) found that 'challengers' are more likely to win when they possess a well-structured organization. Formal organizations would appear better placed to mobilize 'because they facilitate mass participation, tactical innovations, and rapid decision-making' (Morris 1984: 285). Structured organizations are also more likely to survive beyond a wave of protest to favour mobilization in succeeding waves (McCarthy and Zald 1987b [1977]). Professional organizers often spread mass defiance rather than dampening it and 'professionalisation of leadership and the formalisation of movement organisations are not necessarily incompatible with grass-roots protest' (Staggenborg 1991: 154–5; also Jenkins 1985). Moreover, long-term survival is favoured by the presence of motives for and methods of action which are already legitimated (Minkoff 1993, 1995).

It should be added that concrete realization of the organizational principles of grassroots democracy has never been a simple matter. Indeed, many activists have complained of the de facto oligarchies which tend to form and impose their will when collective decision-making becomes difficult. An organized minority can win out in an assembly by wearing down the majority, and forcing them to give up and leave after hours of strenuous discussion. In a few, extreme cases physical force has been used by some groups to occupy important decision-making positions such as the chair of meetings. Every campaign of mobilization since 1968 has taken the 'organizational question' as central, seeking solutions to the problem of oligarchic manipulation implicit in direct democracy, the difficulty of coming to a decision where there is no delegation of authority and the dangers of isolation from the external world. It has been observed of the student movement that 'it was no easy task to build new relationships and a community when mailing had to be gotten out, the newspaper written and printed, new membership processed, leadership provided, decisions of all sorts made' (Breines 1989: 49).

As with repertoires of action (see chapter 7), however, the simultaneous presence of many differing objectives makes the identification of an optimal organizational model extremely difficult. Choosing a particular model of organization means choosing between a number of different dilemmas. In general, conflict arises between respect for democratic rules and bureaucratic structures (Knoke 1990). Internal and external objectives cannot always be reconciled easily. More structured organizations have a greater capacity for decision-making but more spontaneous ones are generally more successful in maintaining internal solidarity. Ideological incentives are an important surrogate for a lack of material resources, but their use increases the rigidity of the organizational model because transformations have to be incorporated into the normative order of the group (Zald 1970). Moreover, organizations employing symbolic incentives will run a greater risk of internal conflict (McCarthy and Zald 1987b [1977]: 33). While professional organizations can generate a constant flow of funding they are bound by the wishes of their benefactors. 'The growth and maintenance of organisations whose formal goals are aimed at helping one population but who depend on a different population for funding are ultimately more dependent upon the latter than the former' (McCarthy and Zald 1987b [1973]: 371). Closure to the external world helps form identity but also reduces the capacity to handle reality and identify reasons for failure.[23] Patrons provide important resources but they are usually available only for groups with low-level claims and consensual legitimation (the handicapped rather than the unemployed, say) (Walker 1991). Coalitions increase the resources available to social movement organizations but also the danger of internal conflict: 'coalitions do allow member groups to expand their influence through joint action and to conserve resources by dividing labour and sharing overhead costs. On the other hand, coalitions tend to produce organisational and ideological conflicts' (Kleidman 1993: 39–40). Affinity groups seek to solve the problem of maintaining members' loyalty in a non-bureaucratic way but their low level of coordination makes decision-making difficult (Gamson 1990). A broad dispersal of power within an organization lessens the risks of oligarchic domination but also introduces sources of power which are very difficult to control. The experts who legitimate social movement organizations, for example, are not subject to democratic election. Even an increase of resources can lead to contradictory results:

> The establishment of a working relation with the authorities also has ambivalent implications for the development of the SMO: On the one hand, public recognition, access to decision making procedures and public subsidies may provide crucial resources and represent important successes for the SMO; on the other hand, the integration into the established system of interest intermediation may impose limits on the mobilisation capacity of the SMO and alienate important parts of its constituency, with the consequence of weakening it in the long run. (Kriesi 1996: 155–6)

The need to balance differing objectives and dissatisfaction with existing forms of organization has pushed social movements towards continual searching and innovation. To overcome what were seen as its errors, movements subsequent to the student movement have sought to perfect a ritual of direct democracy by introducing consensual decision-making, rotation of chairmanships and so on. These rules, however, have reduced the decision-making efficiency of assemblies and often lead to very long periods of confusion and incertitude. In such situations more formal, efficient but less participatory organizations have been formed to pursue ad hoc objectives. Social movement structure would therefore seem to have become increasingly pluralistic without, however, abandoning the search for a form of organization which can combine the needs of participation with those of efficiency.

6.6 Summary

Social movements, or at least those which have been the object of most research in the late twentieth century, declare that they wish to construct a new model of democracy, and the organizations involved in them have been described as being permeated with a participatory and decentralized conception of it. However, research has shown that, in reality, a plurality of organizational models coexist within any social movement. The various organisations have different degrees of structuration, centralisation of power and grassroots participation. Neither is the evolution of social movement organizations unidirectional: some organizations become institutionalized, turning themselves into political parties or interest groups; others become more radical and turn to violent forms of action; some turn commercial and involve themselves in the market; yet others turn inward, becoming similar to religious sects. While it is not possible to identify any 'iron laws', there are certain similarities in the organizational evolution of social movements since the 1970s. Organizational goals tend to be different in different phases of mobilization. During the phase of primary accumulation, pre-existing communication networks with their social background and value systems need to be co-opted for spontaneous activity to emerge. In fact, social movements frequently emerge within host institutions, taking their initial resources from the very organizations they then attack. In the high-mobilization phase one of the most typical organizational needs is coordination. Different sections of the movement with different ideologies, geographical or structural areas of activity and tasks must be coordinated. Finally, in the phase of declining mobilization the problem to be faced is the survival of movement identities and further changes in forms of organization take place.

The chosen model of organization, and its evolution over time, are the product of complex processes of adaptation to the environment, attempts to change it, conscious strategic choices and acceptance of tradition. In general, the models of organization adopted by social movements are continually transformed in a process of 'adopting, adapting, and inventing' (McCarthy 1996). First, it should be noted that, to a certain extent, 'structures follow strategy'. In other words, social movement organizations tend to adapt their structure to their objectives and the characteristics of the social groups they seek to mobilize. However, these choices are influenced by the resources and constraints present both within movements themselves – their initial cultural resources and model of organization – and in their environment. Technological change, economic development, increasing levels of education and more free time all produce more resources for social movement organizations, making their construction and structuration easier. Resource availability, however, also brings constraints. Resources channelled by institutional actors through 'non-profit organization' legislation or anti-poverty campaigns, for example (subsidies, contracts, tax deductions and so on), produce pressure for the creation of 'registered' social movement organizations, complete with formal structures, membership books and audited accounts.

Alliances with institutional actors can also push in the opposite direction, however. By leaving certain tasks to their better organized allies, social movement organizations can maintain a more informal and decentralized structure. Nevertheless, processes of imitation also need to be considered alongside this division of labour. Along with the other actors in social movements, institutional allies contribute to defining the repertoire of organizational forms considered as legitimate and the available repertoire restricts the choices open to social movements. Every 'early riser' tends to transmit such organizational traditions to its 'spin-off' movements and change in this respect is gradual. However, continual tensions between different, and sometimes contradictory, requirements pushes in the direction of experimentation with various forms of organization contemporaneously. While this may not achieve the utopian ambition of 'grassroots' democracy, it does amplify the spectrum of organizational forms available to social movements.

7
Forms, Repertoires and Cycles of Protest

Only weeks after being elected President of France, Jacques Chirac, announced the decision, in July 1995, to begin a series of nuclear tests on the Pacific atoll of Mururoa the following September. A matter of days later and the *Rainbow Warrior II*, a ship belonging to the international environmentalist organization, Greenpeace, was in the area. Greenpeace, which had successfully prevented Shell from dumping the Brent Spar oil platform at sea shortly before, had already taken action against nuclear testing in the past. In 1972 the organization's then President, David McTaggart, had sailed into the waters around Mururoa to protest against an earlier series of French tests. In the mid-1980s the French secret services sank another Greenpeace ship, the *Rainbow Warrior*, killing the Portuguese journalist aboard at the time. Nor would the French Navy have hesitated to ram *Rainbow Warrior II* in 1995, forcing her to leave Mururoa. While the crew of *Rainbow Warrior II* were being given a hero's welcome on Papeete, three Greenpeace 'pirates' remained hidden on Mururoa in defiance of the French Foreign Legion. Protest against the French nuclear tests spread rapidly. The anniversary of the French Revolution on 14 July was the occasion of protest throughout the world. In Seoul, Manila, Tokyo, Toronto, Santiago and Paris protest marches were accompanied by symbolic acts of provocation. The German newspaper *Die Tageszeitung* carried the title 'Kreativ gegen Radioaktive' (Creative against Radio-active'). The demonstrators carried placards with slogans such as: 'Ban the Frogs from Sydney Olympic Games'; 'Pres. Chirac: We, the Children of the World, Deserve to Live'; 'El Angel de la Muerte Vuelve a Mururoa' (The Angel of Death Returns to Mururoa'); 'Non à la Bombe in Polynesie' ('No to the Bomb in Polynesy'); 'Ein Schande fuer Europa: Frankreich verseucht die Suedsee' ('A Shame for Europe: France Contaminates the South Sea'). Fireworks in the form of a nuclear mushroom cloud were let off in front of the French consulate in Hamburg. In Madrid a wooden mushroom cloud was erected in the French consul's garden. In Santiago, Chile, environmentalists declared 14 July 'Day of Nuclear Terror'. In Rome, the popular rock singer Gianna Nannini improvised a concert for peace dangling from the façade of the French Embassy and some guests at a reception in the Embassy displayed a placard condemning the French tests from the balcony. Six demonstrators occupied the French Embassy in Canberra, displaying a banner 'SOS Mururoa' from the roof. A 'peace flotilla', composed of dozens of private yachts and launches, proposed a peaceful occupation of the territorial waters around Mururoa in order to prevent the tests, and forty parliamentarians, from Australia, New Zealand, Indonesia and Hong Kong, announced their willingness to participate. The New Zealand President, Jim Bolger, promised at least one navy vessel to protect the 'flotilla'.

Representatives from other institutions and political parties also became involved. Members of the Green and socialist groups in the European Parliament displayed placards opposing the French tests. The government of New Zealand boycotted an official French Embassy reception to mark the founding of the Republic and threatened to cite France before the International Court of Justice. The French Socialists demanded a referendum on the tests. The Mayor of Brisbane ended the city's twinning with Nice. Oscar Luigi Scalfaro, President of Italy, having been presented with a petition of 30,000 signatures opposing the tests by a Greenpeace delegation, appealed to Chirac to abandon his plans and described the planned explosions in the Pacific as 'odious for the concept of peace'. A number of national parliaments discussed measures to oppose Chirac's testing plans.

This was not all. A boycott of French goods was promoted by a number of organizations, particularly in Japan and Australia. Despite opposition from the Greens and from Greenpeace itself, spontaneous boycotts also developed in Germany, Norway and

Sweden, gradually spreading to other European countries as well. Australia and New Zealand went as far as considering an embargo on French goods. In Italy Vincenzo Onorato, owner of a shipping company sailing to and from Elba, Sardinia and Corsica, had his ships fly the Greenpeace flag. Advertising firms, banks and entrepreneurs in Sydney organized a subscription to fund a publicity campaign in French newspapers. Norwegian actress Liv Ullmann threatened to return a prestigious French award. A Munich restaurant proprietor declared his premises a 'Champagne and Cognac-free Zone'.

Leaving aside the actual results obtained by the above actions, it should be noted that the decision of the French government to resume nuclear testing resulted in a huge international protest campaign. Demonstrators from many countries challenged the legitimacy of the decision and sought to hinder the French plans. They did not do so through normal diplomatic channels or through elections. Rather, they sought to influence public opinion. In fact, as we shall see in section 7.1, a characteristic of protest is its the capacity to mobilize public opinion through unorthodox forms of action and so put pressure on decision-makers. The brief outline given above of the beginnings of protest against French nuclear testing on Mururoa describes a series of different actions which, taken together, form what we will define in section 7.2 as a repertoire of collective action. In section 7.3 the peace movement[1] will be used to illustrate that tactics very different in terms of their radicalism and the 'logic' driving them coexist within such a repertoire. For social movement organizations choices concerning the forms of action to adopt are an important but difficult strategic decision. In fact, as we shall see in section 7.4, the necessity to simultaneously address different types of public creates a number of tactical dilemmas. In addition, such choices are influenced both by internal variables and by interaction with other actors (section 7.5). The mutable character of these decisions leads, in section 7.6, to an analysis of the cyclical dynamics of protest and the nature of change over time.

7.1 Protest: A Definition

In protest against the French decision to resume nuclear testing in the Pacific Ocean, anti-nuclear groups arranged blockades and the occupation of French embassies. Demonstrations took place all over the world. Pop singers staged concerts; actors threatened to return prizes they had been awarded. Prominent politicians and anonymous entrepreneurs promoted boycotts of champagne and Camembert. What, then, do all these actions have in common?

In the first place, they are unconventional methods of intervening in a government's political decision-making. In fact, 'social movements employ methods of persuasion and coercion which are, more often than not, novel, unorthodox, dramatic, and of questionable legitimacy' (Wilson 1973: 227). According to the principles of representative democracy, the decisions of a government can be challenged immediately by the parliamentary opposition or punished subsequently by the voting choices of citizens in elections. Aside from military intervention, the channels for exerting pressure on a foreign government include bilateral diplomacy or negotiations in one of the many International Government Organizations (IGOs). However, increasing numbers of citizens have come to affirm the legitimacy of other forms of pressure on government, particularly since the 1970s. When faced with laws or decisions considered to be unjust these citizens adopt forms of action which lie outside earlier norms. Especially from the 1960s on, a 'new set of political activities has been added to the citizen's political repertoire' (Barnes et al. 1979: 149).[2] According to the research just cited, a long list of new and unconventional forms of political participation, including signing petitions, lawful demonstration, boycotts, withholding of rent or tax, occupations, sit-ins, blocking traffic and wildcat strikes, have been added to the more traditional ones such as following politics in the newspapers, discussing politics with others, working for political parties or their candidates, attending political meetings, contacting public officials or persuading friends and acquaintances to vote in particular ways. These newer forms have become increasingly legitimised. 'In advanced industrial societies direct political action techniques do not in fact bear the stigma of deviancy. Nor are they seen as antisystem-directed orientation' (1979: 157). This expansion of the repertoire of political participation appears to be a 'lasting characteristic of democratic mass publics' (1979: 524).

A second important characteristic of protest is that it uses indirect channels to influence decision-makers. As Michael Lipsky noted (1965), protest is a political resource of the powerless. The events which shook the United States in the 1960s, from the 'Freedom Summer' campaign to register black voters in the Southern states, launched by civil rights activists in 1964, to the 'March on Washington' in support of ethnic minority civil rights, all

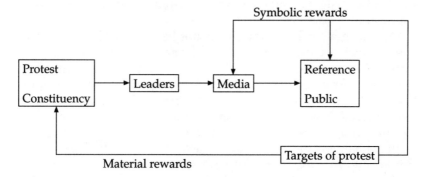

Figure 7.1   *The communication process of protest*
Source: Adapted from Lipsky (1965: 163–82)

had something in common: 'They were engaged in by relatively powerless groups; and they depended for success not upon direct utilization of power, but upon activating other groups to enter the political arena. Because protest is successful to the extent that other parties are activated to political involvement, it is one of the few strategies in which even politically impoverished groups can aspire to engage' (Lipsky 1965: 1).

Protest, then, sets in motion a process of indirect persuasion mediated by the mass media and by more powerful actors. As figure 7.1 suggests, for those without power to have policies in their favour approved they must mobilize the support of more powerful groups. In fact, protest mobilizes a variety of actors. Those directly interested by political decisions comprise a protest constituency. From this constituency a leadership emerges to direct action and maintain external relations. The mass media spreads the message, a message directed in the first instance at the reference audience of the decision-makers. The latter are the true targets of protest. In order to succeed protest must produce positive stimuli, winning the sympathies of those who have more resources to invest in the arenas where decisions are taken. While collective action by groups who already possess power can be aimed directly at decision-makers, the powerless must seek to involve those who have the possibility of influencing them. In addition, the influence exerted by social movements can be either positive, creating sympathy for their cause, or negative, threatening (for example) to create disorder. In the latter case, the reference audience becomes the object of protest, as in the case of protest which appears directed at faculty councils or a school principal whereas the target is really a government minister.

Social movements certainly do not have a monopoly on protest. Other actors, such as political parties or pressure groups, also make use of protest action and occasionally make alliances with social movements for particular campaigns. However, protest (particularly at its most innovative and radical) has been considered as a form of action typical of social movements because, unlike political parties and pressure groups, they have fewer channels through which to access decision makers. Forms of action are particularly important since social movements are 'often remembered more for the methods of persuasion adopted by them than for their objectives' (Wilson 1973: 226).

7.2   Repertoires of Action

The marches, boycotts, occupations and other forms of action used in the campaign against French nuclear testing have something else in common. They are all part of a modern repertoire of collective action, the 'whole set of means [a group] has for making claims of different types on different individuals' (Tilly 1986: 2). Charles Tilly has made an important contribution to the study of collective action by identifying the differences in types of contentious action[3] in particular historical periods. Protest was certainly not unheard of prior to the formation of the nation state: peasants burnt down mills in protest against increases in the price of bread; subjects dressed up in order to mock their superiors; funerals could be turned into the occasion for denunciations of injustice.[4] The tactics adopted by protestors varied in extremity from the utilization of irreverent symbols and music (as in charivari) to field invasions and grain seizures. However, they all had two characteristics in common. 'Broadly speaking, the repertoire of the mid-seventeenth to the mid-nineteenth century had a *parochial* scope: it addressed local actors or the local representatives of national actors. It also relied heavily on *patronage* – appealing to immediately available powerholders to convey grievances or settle disputes, temporarily acting in the place of unworthy or inactive powerholders only to abandon power after the action' (Tilly 1986: 391–2, emphasis in the original).

The forms taken by collective action began to change in the nineteenth century. The old parochial and patronage-dependent

repertoire was replaced by one which was national and autonomous, involving actions such as strikes, electoral rallies, public
meetings, petitions, marches, insurrection and the invasion of
legislative bodies.

> The repertoire that crystallised in the nineteenth century and prevails
> today is, in general, more *national* in scope: though available for local
> issues and enemies, it lends itself easily to coordination among many
> localities. Compared with the older repertoire, its actions are *auto-*
> *nomous*: instead of staying in the shadow of existing powerholders
> and adapting routines sanctioned by them, people using the new
> repertoire tend to initiate their own statements of grievances and
> demands. Strikes, demonstrations, electoral rallies, and similar actions
> build, in general on much more deliberately constructed organisation
> than used to be the case. (Tilly 1986: 391–2)

Whereas the older repertoire tended to use the same forms of
action as the authorities, either in the form of caricature or temporary substitution, the new one invented autonomous forms;
people participated in the traditional repertoire of collective action
as members of pre-constituted communities, whereas they do so
as representatives of particular interests in the modern repertoire.
The old repertoire took advantage of official celebrations or occasions; the new involves the deliberate organisation of assemblies
and occasions for action. In the past, assemblies converged on
the private residences of the crowd's enemies, whereas today
the preferred targets are the seats and symbols of public power
(Tilly 1986: 392–3).

This transformation in the form of protest followed from the
creation of the nation state, the development of capitalism and
the emergence of modern means of communication. As Tilly
puts it:

> As capitalism advanced, national states became more powerful and
> centralised local affairs and nearby patrons mattered less to the
> fates of ordinary people. Increasingly, holders of large capitals and
> national power made the decisions that affected them. As a result
> seizure of grain, collective invasions of fields and the like became
> ineffective, irrelevant, obsolete. In response to the shifts of power
> and capital, ordinary people invented and adopted new forms of
> action, creating the electoral campaign, the public meeting, the social
> movement, and the other elements of the newer repertoire. (Tilly
> 1986: 395–6)

The new repertoire responded to a new situation in which politics was increasingly national in character, the role of communities diminished and organized association spread, particularly among the labouring classes (Tilly 1984: 309).

There is another characteristic typical of the modern repertoire besides its national scale and autonomous character and that is its *modular* quality. In other words, it can be used by a variety of actors to achieve a variety of objectives:

> Implicit in the concept of a repertoire is that it is more or less general. But the old and the new repertoires are not *equally* general. The forms of action used in attacks on millers and grain merchants, *charivaris* and religious conflicts from the sixteenth to the eighteenth centuries were not as widely used against others as the strikes, demonstrations and insurrections of the next two centuries. Herein lies a key to the nature of the modern repertoire. For it was precisely the *lack* of generality of the older forms of collective action that impeded the rise of the national social movement; and it was the general nature of the new ones that gave movements a common cultural and behavioural foundation. (Tarrow 1994: 33–4, emphasis in the original)

In traditional societies the repertoire was specific, direct and rigid: 'In a society divided into orders, isolated by poor communication and lack of literacy and organized into corporate and communal groups, it was rare to find forms of collective action distinct from the conflicts that gave rise to them' (Tarrow 1994: 35). The consolidation of the nation state, the expansion of the means of communication (whether roads or newspapers) and the growth of private associations favoured the development of a new, general, flexible and indirect repertoire. This in its turn facilitated the diffusion of protest and the mobilization of new and diverse groups within the population.

According to Tilly and Tarrow, the modern repertoire which emerged with the French Revolution has changed little since. Boycotts, barricades, petitions and demonstrations are all still present (and indeed probably dominant) in the panorama of protest. However, if we look back at the example which opened the chapter, a number of new elements can be identified; elements which can be explained by transformations in the very characteristics held to be essential for the emergence of the modern repertoire. While the nation state has certainly not disappeared, it is now flanked by sub- and supra-national entities which possess increasing, though not enormous, powers (see chapters 2 and 9). In addition, media such as television, fax and the Internet have transformed the ambitions and capacity for intervention of social movements.[5] Returning to the example of French nuclear testing, protests against President Chirac's decision took place mainly outside France, and it was not limited to western Europe. Demonstrators in the various countries involved coordinated their actions and used a common language. A further element must be considered as well: the modern repertoire of collective action has tended to adopt forms of action which reflect a particular political logic. The attempt to influence decision-makers rested on a demonstration of strength, either in numbers (mass demonstrations, petitions and so on) or, to use a military analogy, by inflicting maximum damage on the enemy for minimum losses (strikes, barricades). This type of political logic had not been abandoned in the repertoire used to oppose the French nuclear tests in the Pacific, but another, more symbolic logic was also employed, the logic of bearing witness, designed to convince rather than to win.

7.3 The Logic and Form of Protest

The citizens and organizations opposing nuclear testing by France and others did so in a variety of ways. First, the forms of action presented at the beginning of the chapter were more or less extreme in nature, ranging from more conventional petitioning to more conflictual occupations, and including a number of episodes of violence. Opinion poll research has suggested that a number of levels exist in relation to the extremity of action:

> The various unconventional forms of participation are ordered along a single continuum from least to most extreme. This continuum is marked by several thresholds. The first threshold indicates the transition from conventional to unconventional politics. Signing petitions and participating in lawful demonstrations are unorthodox political activities but still within the bounds of accepted democratic norms. The second threshold represents the shift to direct-action techniques, such as boycotts. A third level of political activities involves illegal, but nonviolent, acts. Unofficial strikes or a peaceful occupation of a building typify this step. Finally, a fourth threshold includes violent activities such as personal injury or physical damage. (Dalton 1988: 65)

Second, although the forms of actions adopted concentrated to a large extent on the political system, it should be noted that movements also made use (to differing degrees) of cultural strategies aimed at changing value systems. While political strategies seek, above all, to change external realities, cultural strategies seek an interior transformation. As already noted, some social movements are directed primarily to value systems, while others concentrate on the political system (for example, Rucht 1994). Moreover, movements themselves alternate between phases of greater 'politicization' and retreat into countercultural activity (Melucci 1984a; on Italy, della Porta 1996a). In addition, both cultural and political strategies are also characterized by varying degrees of extremeness, ranging from moderate subcultural evolution to radical countercultural challenge in the first case and from negotiation to confrontation in the second (Rucht 1990a).

However, as we shall seek to demonstrate more fully in what follows, forms of action can also be distinguished according to the 'logic', or *modus operandi*, which the activists assign them.

7.3.1 The logic of numbers

The logic of numbers, to which James DeNardo referred in *Power in Numbers* (1985), underlies numerous forms of protest. Since 'there always seems to be power in numbers' (1985: 35), a movement's destiny depends to a great extent on the number of its supporters. As DeNardo notes, the 'size of the dissidents' demonstrations affects the regime both directly and indirectly. Naturally the disruption of daily routines increases with numbers, and the regime's ability to control crowds inevitably suffers as they grow larger. In addition to the immediate disruption they cause, demonstrations (by their size) also give the regime an indication of how much support the dissidents enjoy' (1985: 36). Just as political parties attempt to increase the number of electors who support them and pressure groups seek to maximize the number of their adherents, social movements should seek to mobilize the greatest number of demonstrators possible. From this point of view, protest stands in for elections. The logic behind it is the same as that behind representative democracy: implementation of the majority's decisions. Protest serves to draw the attention of elected representatives to the fact that, at least on certain issues, the majority in the country is not the same as the majority in parliament. Thus, the fear of losing electoral support should push the people's representatives into changing their position, realigning themselves with the country 'at large'.

Marches are one of the main tactics designed to demonstrate the numerical strength behind protest. The protest against French nuclear testing on Mururoa was just one in a long series of attempts by the peace movement to influence parliaments and governments through mass demonstrations. In December 1979 NATO's decision to modernize its intermediate nuclear forces by deploying 572 Cruise and Pershing II missiles in the German Federal Republic, Italy, Belgium, the United Kingdom and the Netherlands caused waves of protest on a scale rarely seen in Europe. After a first, 100,000-strong, march in Brussels, 200,000 took part in demonstrations in London, Brussels and Bonn, and half a million in Italy and France, in the of autumn 1981. American President Ronald Reagan's visit to Europe in June 1982 witnessed demonstrations of over 200,000 in Rome, London, Bonn and Berlin. The various marches and demonstrations in European cities in October 1983 involved three million people: more than a million in a single day in Germany; over 400,000 (about 4 per cent of the Dutch population) in Amsterdam; half a million in Brussels and in Rome; 300,000 in London (Rochon 1988: 3–6).

Petitions and referendums are also used to demonstrate the numerical strength of support for movements. Petitions and demands for referendums were presented in all of the countries affected by the deployment of Cruise and Pershing missiles. Millions of signatures were collected in Italy, the Netherlands, Germany and the United States. In 1984 and 1985 pacifist groups in a number of European countries suggested that voters demand guarantees on peace issues from the electoral candidates of all parties.

The logic underlying such actions is totally coherent with the principles of representative democracy: an attempt is made to influence public opinion, the final repository of political power. Given that demonstrators are also voters, it is assumed that their representatives will change their position rather than risk not being re-elected. However, the campaign against Cruise missile deployment demonstrated that this logic does not always work. Despite opinion polls in most of the countries involved demonstrating that a majority opposed the deployment of Cruise missiles, the governments of these countries stood their ground.

The 'logic of numbers', then, does not always function as it should, and indeed it would be naïve to assume that the opinions of elected representatives simply follow those of the general public on every occasion. First, voting is structured by a whole series of questions and depends on a balance between different motivations. It is far from certain that an individual will abandon their traditional political party simply because it does not adopt a social movement's position on a particular issue, even when the individual agrees with the movement on that issue.[6] Second, protest campaigns have a limited duration and, as a result, their political influence is less direct. Indeed, 'the problem with all movement alliances, but especially those with the parties, is how to keep commitment firm once the persuasive sounds of the marching thousands have become a distant echo' (Rochon 1988: 174). However, as the numerous defeats in social movement-inspired referendums demonstrate, a further and perhaps more decisive factor counts against the logic of numbers: protesters (sometimes referred to as 'active minorities') do not always reflect the opinions of a majority of the public (Kriesi and Wisler 1994). Thus, it would be extremely dangerous for social movements to depend solely on such a logic; a logic which does not in any case fully reflect their own concept of democracy.

7.3.2   The logic of material damage

The logic of inflicting material damage, in a modus operandi analogous to war, must be considered alongside the logic of numbers. This logic lies behind the industrial strike, a form of action which continues to be widespread. By striking, workers halt production and inflict damage on their employer; this economic cost should lead a rational employer to reach agreement with the workforce. More extreme forms of action such as wildcat or rolling strikes and industrial sabotage can be used to increase pressure on the employer by exacerbating the economic cost. These forms of action reflect a view of politics as a power struggle in which participation in civil society is not confined to the act of voting in elections.

In the political system this logic is reflected, in its most extreme form, by political violence. In violence against property the costs are still largely economic, but the logic becomes increasingly 'military' in violence against persons. Remaining with the peace movement, a wave of attacks (the chief targets of which were NATO bases) were carried out in the mid-1980s by what would become known as 'Euroterrorists': the remnants of the Red Brigades in Italy, the Red Army Faction in Germany, the Cellules Communistes Combattents in Belgium and Action Directe in France. In a campaign 'for the construction of an anti-imperialist front', the terrorists destroyed military equipment

and killed individuals they held to be responsible for the 'impe-
rialist plan' (della Porta 1996b).

Leaving aside cases of this nature, however, a certain amount
of material disruption is present in many forms of protest. The
action taken by social movements is often inherently disruptive
in the sense that it obstructs the normal course of events by
threatening disorder (Tarrow 1994: 103). Their challenge to the
elites accentuates uncertainty and by so doing produces tangible,
and on occasion material, losses. The use of boycotts during the
protests against nuclear testing has already been mentioned. By
hitting French goods, the boycotts aimed to 'disturb' the French
government in two ways: directly in the first instance, by hitting
the profits of state enterprises such as Air France; and, second,
by alienating support for the government among others directly
affected in agriculture and industry (including the workforce)
and so on.

The logic of material damage, present in all forms of public
demonstration (a march through the streets blocks the traffic; a
train strike inconveniences passengers), also has its limitations
and constraints. In the first place, violent action may cause an
escalation in repression and alienate sympathizers. Violence pol-
arizes the conflict, transforming 'relations between challengers
and authorities from a confused, many-sided game into a bipo-
lar one in which people are forced to choose sides, allies defect,
bystanders retreat and the state's repressive apparatus swings
into action' (Tarrow 1994: 104). Although it is true that a lack of
resources may encourage the use of more extreme tactics, 'this
impulse is constrained . . . by the erosion of support occasioned
by repression and moral backlash. The crucial question, therefore, is whether the government's additional responsiveness to
violent protest will provide sufficient compensation for the movement's smaller size' (DeNardo 1985: 219). While direct action
has on occasion been associated with substantive successes by
social movements, it has also been noted that extreme action
often leads to an escalation in conflict.[7] In a democratic regime
the state holds a monopoly on the legitimate use of force and
most challenges to that monopoly are doomed to fail, transforming political conflict into a military confrontation in which the
state has by far the greater firepower (della Porta 1995).

However, the logic which underlies the industrial strike is
equally difficult to translate into forms of action less extreme
than those just considered. The opposing party is less easily
identified and 'disruption' tends to work through the trouble it

causes to third parties not directly responsible for public decisions and who may turn against the protesters as a result. Thus, one of the principal dilemmas of protest lies in the often contradictory requirements of threatening disorder on the one hand, while on the other seeking to avoid mobilizing the public against the very cause which, in most cases, it is hoped they will be persuaded to support. Indeed, unions in the service industries are themselves becoming more cautious about using the strike weapon, knowing that they risk losing public support rather than undermining the legitimacy of government decisions. It is also significant that debate has arisen within social movements over the acceptable degree of 'disruptiveness' of other forms of direct action. If violence, including violence against property, is almost unanimously condemned by social movements today (or at least by those which have close relations with the left), other tactics which may harm an 'innocent' public also causes increasing perplexity within movement ranks. The boycott of French goods in protest over Chirac's nuclear test decision, for example, encountered opposition from many environmentalist organizations such as the German greens and Greenpeace, worried that it would alienate the social groups directly affected by such action.

7.3.3   The logic of bearing witness

Forms of protest which might be defined as based on a logic of bearing witness have developed alongside those based on the logic of numbers or the logic of inflicting damage, particularly since the 1970s. Such action is not designed to convince the public or decision-makers that the protesters constitute a majority or a threat. Rather, it seeks to demonstrate a strong commitment to an objective deemed vital for humanity's future. This logic is perhaps most in accord with the concept of participatory democracy widespread among social movement activists.[8] The right to influence decision-making processes comes from neither formal investiture nor intrinsic power but from force of commitment. Actions of this kind tend to reinforce the moral message being conveyed by a movement because activists are willing to run personal risks to demonstrate their convictions.

Bearing witness is expressed, in the first instance, through participation in actions which involve serious personal risks or cost. Civil disobedience, knowingly breaking what are considered to be unjust laws, rests on this logic. Thus, numerous examples of civil disobedience can be found during the campaign

against Cruise missiles: restitution of military discharge certific-
ates, hunger strikes by armament industry workers or refusal
to pay taxes devoted to military expenditure. Non-violent direct
action follows a similar logic, designed to make a direct impres-
sion on the object of protest while avoiding violent escalation.
The obstruction of missile base entrances by protesters belongs
in this category.[9] The emphasis on individual sacrifice emerges
from a reconstruction of the protest action against General
Dynamics' Electric Boat Division in Groton, Connecticut, where
Trident submarines were built:

> Protesters regularly attempted to invade the site by land and sea in
> order to damage new Trident submarines with hammers and their
> own blood; they were often surprisingly successful with guerilla-
> style attacks. While Feminists Against Trident spraypainted 'Trident-
> Omnicide' on Electric Boat's engineering building, four members of
> the Trident Nein groups were able to reach the USS Florida by canoe
> and paint *USS Auschwitz* on the submarine in ten places. In the 45
> minutes on the vessel before they were apprehended, they also poured
> their own blood down the missile hatches. Another group of five
> simultaneously invaded by land, banging on two sonar bubbles and
> hanging a banner, '*USS Auschwitz*: An Oven without Walls' over
> the damaged bubbles. The last group spent some three hours on the
> site before being arrested by the Groton police. (Meyer 1990: 202,
> emphasis in the original)

The physical risk of arrest and the symbolic sacrifice of blood
were designed to convey the activist's commitment to the cause.
The peaceful invasion of the exclusion area around Mururoa
carried out by Greenpeace (and projected by the 'peace fleet')
carried the risk of attack by the French navy or even of contam-
ination by radiation. They thus testified to the conviction that
something had to be done about a decision considered profoundly
unjust, even if this involved running very serious risks indeed.

A further characteristic of action based on the logic of bearing
witness is its sensitivity to values and culture. Conferences, journals, concerts and documentaries have the job of educating the
public to accept a different understanding of the world. Although
in the majority of cases contemporary social movements seek to
bring about political transformations they share the conviction
that reform cannot come from above. Changes in individual consciousness must accompany the transformation of political structures. Thus cultural as well as political strategies must be adopted.
The peace movement actively engaged in organizing exchange

programmes between citizens of the east and west: cultural and scientific exchanges during international conferences, direct contacts between individual citizens, twinning of towns, meetings between local administrators from the two 'blocs' and so on. All of these forms of action had as their objective the fostering of tolerance through reciprocal knowledge: 'Hundreds of schools, churches, athletic leagues, community groups, and business organisations sponsored their counterparts from the Eastern bloc, enabling Americans to get to know 'the enemy' on a face-to-face level' (Meyer and Marullo 1992: 123). The research and conferences organized by pacifist groups and institutes for peace studies sought to elaborate alternative defence models and security strategies, thus conveying to the public the idea that change was possible. The emphasis placed on the participation of professional groups such as doctors and scientists demonstrates the attention paid to knowledge as the foundation for a new consciousness.[10]

The logic of bearing witness also leads to an accentuation of the emotional intensity of participation. The peace movement has borrowed from and adapted the old repertoire of public demonstration in precisely this direction. Inspired by Catholic tradition (and, in particular, the model of pilgrimage), pacifists organized numerous long-distance marches, as well as masses, vigils, torchlight processions, communal prayers and the Stations of the Cross on Good Friday. Human chains connected places of symbolic importance, meetings of the world's leaders were symbolically besieged and street demonstrations were turned into theatrical 'happenings', acting out the consequences of nuclear war.

The capacity to directly transmit their message is a further characteristic of forms of action which rely most heavily on the logic of bearing witness. Because they oppose the idea that the ends justify the means, contemporary social movements have sought forms of action which reflect the objective to obtained as closely as possible.

> The forms of symbolic activity within the peace movement are as wide as the imagination of the activists. The West German group Women for Peace demonstrated outside NATO headquarters in Bonn during a meeting of the Nuclear Planning group by spreading sand on the ground and saying 'We don't want sand in our eyes.' CND held a demonstration in central London during the economic summit of western industrialised nations in June 1984, at which many activists carried models of Cruise missiles marked 'Return to sender'. In London, a woman dressed as a waitress offered passing businessmen

a platter with a Cruise missile on it, asking each if he had ordered it. Activists in Germany baked waffles in the shape of tanks and passed them out during the 1981 peace week, saying 'Waffles instead of weapons!' The Greenham Common campers have encircled the missile base to lock in militarism, held up mirrors to reflect its evil back onto itself, and thrown seeds over the fence to bring life to death. (Rochon 1988: 120)

The attention paid to the immediate impact of symbols seeks to facilitate the diffusion of the social movement message in a situation where the media tends to report superficially: 'If the message is embedded in the activity, then a report of the activity makes people think about the issue as well' (ibid.).

7.4   Strategic Options and Protest

Forms of protest, then, are extreme to different degrees and, most importantly, follow different types of logic. How and why is one form of protest chosen rather than another? A first answer can be sought in the complexity and multiplicity of the object-ives protest is meant to achieve. Returning to figure 7.1, we can note that 'protest leaders must nurture and sustain *an organization* comprised of people with whom they may or may not share common values. They must *articulate goals and choose strategies* so as to maximize their *public exposure* through communications media. They must *maximize the impact of third parties* in the political conflict. Finally, they must try to *maximize chances of success among those capable of granting goals*' (Lipsky 1965: 163, emphasis in the original). As Rochon (1988: 109) observes in connection with the peace movement, 'the ideal movement strategy is one that is convincing with respect to political authorities, legitimate with respect to potential supporters, rewarding with respect to those already active in the movement, and novel in the eyes of the mass media. These are not entirely compatible demands'.

First, given that every action has an attached cost but can also be a benefit in and of itself (Hirschman 1982), it is important for social movements to find tactics which are also suitable for realizing internal aims. In fact, protest action has an important internal function: creating that sense of collective identity which is a condition for action towards a common goal (Pizzorno 1993). For the labour movement strikes had more than a simply in-strumental function, attacking their opponents (Fantasia 1988), and this is also true of occupations for the student movement

(Ortoleva 1988). They reinforced a sense of identity as well. Solidarity is born out of shared risks on the barricades: 'As they faced off against hostile troops or national guardsmen, the defenders of a barricade came to know each other as comrades, developed a division of labour of fighters, builders and suppliers, and formed social networks that would bring their survivors together in future confrontations' (Tarrow 1994: 44). The peace camps which spread throughout Europe in the wake of the First European Convention on Peace and Disarmament in Brussels in 1981 similarly played an important role in the elaboration of a pacifist identity. Over the logn term, pickets set up outside a number of nuclear bases activists from different countries met each other and friendships were formed. Non-violent direct action strengthened the feeling of belonging; 'a community that is formed in the process of struggle is a very precious thing, and fulfills a lot of needs that are not met in daily life' (Epstein 1991: 8).

However, the fact that actions which strengthen internal solidarity rarely serve to create support outside the movement constitutes a problem. Looking at Figure 7.1 it can be remarked that, if leaders of protest often must favour more radical action in order to maintain rank-and-file support, these are precisely the kinds of action which risk alienating potential allies. Protest leaders must avoid action which is too extreme if they are to win over their target groups within the public. But in doing so they run the risk of losing the confidence of their protest constituency.[11] Opinion polls have shown that the more peaceful and institutional a course of unconventional political action is (petitioning, for example) the greater the level of public approval. Approval falls where the action taken is direct but non-violent and is minimal where violent action is concerned (Barnes et al. 1979).[12] Returning to the peace movement, the number of those in Great Britain who supported the movement's ideas outnumbered those who approved of its tactics. Thus, the movement needed to find a way 'to convey to the public its ideas about nuclear weapons without having those ideas associated with protest tactics of which the public [did] not approve' (Rochon 1988: 105).

Leaders face similar problems in their relations with the media. The latter play an important role in determining the resonance given to, and therefore the effectiveness of, protest. The success of protest action is undoubtedly related to the amount of media attention it receives, and this also affects the character of social movement organizations (Gitlin 1980). As careful research on protest coverage has demonstrated (McCarthy, McPhail and Smith 1996), action must involve a great many people, utilize radical tactics or be particularly innovative in order to obtain media coverage. It should be remembered that it is the content of the message transmitted as well as the quantity of publicity received which is important for a social movement. Journalists can be particularly demanding as concerns protest: on the one hand they demand 'news', and therefore novelty; on the other, they tend to conform to accepted standards of 'good taste'. Thus, 'Conformity to standards of news worthiness in political style, and knowledge of the prejudices and desires of the individuals who determine media coverage in political skills, represent crucial determinants of leadership effectiveness' (Lipsky 1965: 170). Though their obligation to the wider community may lead many journalists to sympathize with certain demands, they will, nonetheless, condemn extreme forms of action. On the other hand, more moderate action, although it might garner greater support, is rarely 'newsworthy'.[13]

> One difficulty for political movements is that the media generally present images of their protest without any elaboration of the substantive issues involved. Demonstrations are described as large or small, well-behaved or unruly, a cross section of the populace or composed of fringe elements. But the issues that brought the protesters together are presented in terms of one-line slogans, if at all. The problem is not so much one of political bias as it is a matter of the exacting criteria used by the media to determine what is newsworthy. Size, novelty, and militancy are newsworthy. Critical policy perspectives are not. (Rochon 1988: 102)

In conclusion, for the most part social movements use forms of action which can be described as disruptive, seeking to influence elites through a demonstration of both force of numbers and activists' determination to succeed. At the same time, however, protest is concerned with building support. It must be innovative or newsworthy enough to echo in the mass media and, consequently, in the wider public which social movements (as 'active minorities') are seeking to convince of the justice of their cause. Forms of protest, therefore, must adapt as occasion requires to the needs of potentially conflicting objectives such as threatening elites and winning over the public (through the intervention of a third actor, the media, which has an agenda of its own).

7.5 Factors Influencing Repertoire Choice

The leaders of social movement organizations find themselves faced with a series of strategic dilemmas in choosing the form that protest should take. Any form of actions needs to cover a plurality of sometimes contradictory objectives. In addition, strategic options are limited by a series of factors internal and external to protest itself.

First, the repertoire of action is finite, constrained in both time and space. The 'technology' of protest evolves slowly, limited by the traditions handed down from one generation of activists to the next, and crystallized in institutions. The public march is a good example and it was still one of the principal forms of protest in the campaign against French nuclear testing in the Pacific. Having developed out of the practice of electoral banqueting, the technique was slowly perfected and institutionalized by the elaboration of rituals and structures such as the closing rally and the stewarding of marches (Favre 1990).

Thus, repertoires are handed down, reproduced over time, because they are what people know how to do when they want to protest. The forms of action used in one protest campaign tend to be recycled in subsequent ones. The anti-Vietnam war movement in the United States adopted tactics which had earlier been used by civil rights campaigners. The youth movement in mid-1970s Italy 'inherited' (in a radicalized form) the modes of protest used by the student movement of the late 1960s (della Porta 1995). In addition, the adaptation of older forms of action legitimizes protest by referring to myths and heroes of the past:

> the use of standard protest forms also evokes past political movements whose struggles have long since been vindicated as just. Nuclear freeze activists in the United States sang 'We Shall Overcome'. The Dutch People's Petition against the Cruise missiles recalls the great petition of the last century to gain public funds for religious schools, as well as the petition in 1923 that gathered over a million signatures, brought repeal of a planned expansion of the Dutch fleet, and toppled the government of the day. Marchers to Greenham Common chained themselves to the perimeter fence to evoke earlier actions of the suffragettes. (Rochon 1988: 110)

It should be borne in mind, however, that such references to the past are a constraint on social movements as well as a resource.[14] In any given period, knowledge concerning 'what is to be done' to protest against a decision by those holding power is limited, and this limits collective action: 'The existing repertoire constrains collective action; far from the image we sometimes hold of mindless crowds, people tend to act within known limits, to innovate at the margins of the existing forms, and to miss many opportunities available to them in principle' (Tilly 1986: 390). Rooted in the shared subculture of the activists, repertoires contain the options considered practicable, while excluding others:

> Any population has a limited repertoire of collective action: alternative means of acting together on shared interests . . . These varieties of action constitute a repertoire in something like the theatrical or musical sense of the word; but the repertoire in question resembles that of *commedia dell'arte* or jazz more than that of a strictly classical ensemble: people know the general rules of performance more or less well and vary the performance to meet the purpose at hand. (Tilly 1986: 390)

These limitations on the range of protest forms are only part of the story: although some forms of action can be adapted to more than one situation, many others cannot. They divide, above all, along social-group lines: prisoners climb onto the roofs of jails; soldiers refuse rations; students organize 'alternative' courses. One of the most common forms of collective action taken today, the strike, was until recently considered as a tactic adapted almost exclusively to the working class. In fact, repertoires depend to a great extent on the cultural and material resources available to particular groups. The most militant styles of action will be most widespread among those groups which face particular difficulty in obtaining material rewards and for whom symbolic gratification acts as a substitute. Moreover, the particular subcultures to which movements refer contributes to the creation of distinctive repertoires. Religious organizations, for example, employ and modify rituals typical of their faith. The peace movement is nonviolent because the use of violence is too close a reminder of the militarism they wish to condemn. Finally, repertoires change from state to state. It is more common to build barricades in France than in Switzerland; on the other hand, direct democracy is resorted to more frequently in Switzerland than in France.

While the weight of tradition must be acknowledged, there is also innovation in protest as in other forms of action: 'contenders experiment constantly with new forms in the search for tactical advantage, but do so in small ways, at the edge of well-established actions. Few innovations endure beyond a single cluster of events; they endure chiefly when associated with a substantial new advantage for one or more actors' (Tilly 1986: 7). Forms of action initially restricted to particular actors (and condemned by others) become generalized: white-collar workers go on strike, shopkeepers block the streets. New tactics are constantly being created in order to meet media criteria of 'newsworthiness'. Particularly in phases of rising collective action, given forms of action spread from one social group to another, and often from one country to another. Non-violent direct action was imported to Martin Luther King's America from Ghandi's India. The student movement brought sit-ins across the ocean to Europe. In the wake of a massive wave of labour mobilization in Italy in the late 1960s the use of the strike quickly became widespread among many different sections of the population. In the peace movement dozens of camps sprang up around nuclear missile bases after the initial example of Greenham Common. The peace movement also adopted a series of protest forms which had originated in other traditions: vigils from religious groups, civil disobedience from the women's movement and so on.

It should be added that socialization in protest tactics is not a matter of blind reflex but a critical learning process. Thus, not all forms of action carry over from one period to the next, one social group to another, or from one country to another. It is, above all, those considered as successful, or particularly well adapted to a movement's context or culture which are most easily imported. During the campaign against France's nuclear testing in the Pacific, the rapid spread of boycott tactics may be explained by the success obtained only a few weeks earlier when an international boycott convinced Shell to give up its plans to ditch the Brent Spar oil platform at sea. Protest forms which have proved unsuccessful have far less probability of surviving. In Italy, for example, the movement against Cruise missiles marked a major change in tactics by left-libertarian movements. While the late 1970s had been characterized by violent escalation, the peace movement emphasized non-violence with the specific objective of marking its discontinuity with the past and contributing to dissociate the 1980s protest from the bloody memory of the preceding decade in the collective imagination (della Porta 1996a).

Repertoires also emerge, and are transformed, in the course of physical and symbolic interaction. Changes take place in encounters with the authorities, in a series of reciprocal adjustments. Political violence, for example, is rarely adopted overnight or consciously. Rather, repeated clashes with police and political adversaries gradually, and almost imperceptibly, heighten extremism, leading to a justification for ever more violent forms of action. In Italy during the 1970s extremist tactics emerged in the course of an escalation of the use of force during marches and demonstrations (della Porta 1995). The interventions of the police and *carabinieri* became increasingly determined while extreme left and right groups clashed with ever more lethal weapons: stones, molotov cocktails, spanners and eventually guns. Radicalization develops in a spiral of negative and unforeseen feedback. Those involved (particularly the police and demonstrators) interact, causing escalation through a series of self-sustaining vicious circles.[15] In these situations participants react according to their own world view, gambling that the outcome will be as they expected. Their choices, however, are based on erroneous calculations. This circle of action and reaction becomes a routine until a more or less casual event produces a qualitative leap in the level of violence (Neidhardt 1981).

Protest does not always develop towards violence, however. The peace movement, frequently used as an example so far in this chapter, has adopted almost entirely non-violent repertoires. A learning process on the part of both movement activists and the police defused the forms of conflict which had characterized the 1970s. Despite moments of (sometimes severe) tension, particularly during direct action such as the blocking of gates at military bases, activists and police were experienced in avoiding escalation into violence:

> Demonstrations are carefully choreographed in advance. Similarly, activists who expect to participate in actions of civil disobedience, such as blockades, are usually required to undergo training in passive resistance and nonviolence. The police they face have been trained in crowd control and in dealing with nonviolent protest. The image so frequently broadcast of police carrying a demonstrator off to jail looks like an image of conflict. It is. But it is also an instance of two sets of professionals carrying out their jobs with precision. (Rochon 1988: 186–7)

There is a further variable (to be dealt with at greater length in the next chapter) which affects the strategic choices made by social movements. Lipsky noted that the forms taken by protest must be in a position to mobilize potential allies and influences elites. It is normal that the greater the possibility of widening their range of alliances the greater the attention social movements will pay to the preferences of potential supporters. The peace movement, for example, has counted powerful allies in its various campaigns. In the Netherlands and Italy the parties of the left and (a minority) of religious groups opposed the installation of nuclear missiles and local government bodies and official agencies lent their support to the protest in a variety of ways. The peace movement received both material and cultural resources, as well as channels of access to the public decision-making process, from these sources: alliance with the parties of the left increased the strength of mobilization for pacifist demonstrations; religious groups introduced a series of intensely emotive forms of action; local government bodies offered resources for a range of actions from peace education to the proclamation of nuclear free zones. Groups of scientists, doctors, lawyers, teachers, and even military officers, furnished technical expertise. The support of prominent individuals both attracted media attention and discouraged coercive intervention on the part of the police. The support of these institutional groups undoubtedly contributed to the peace movement choosing moderate strategies.

7.6   Cycles of Protest

The strategic choices made by social movements evolve over time and are the result of interaction between a number of different actors. In fact, a final concept, particularly useful for analysing evolution over time, must be introduced to conclude the analysis of forms of collective action: the protest cycle. Though varying in dimension and duration, protest cycles have had a number of common characteristics in recent history: they coincide with 'a phase of heightened conflict and contention across the social system that includes: a rapid diffusion of collective action from more mobilized to less mobilized sectors; a quickened pace of innovation in the forms of contention; new or transformed collective action frames; a combination of organised and unorganised participation; and sequences of intensified interactions between challengers and authorities which can end in reform, repression and sometimes revolution' (Tarrow 1994: 153). Repeatedly in the history of countries:

> Early claims grew out of concrete conflicts of interest. But as the protests spread, coalitions of challengers formed organisations and broadened their claims, often radicalising them into a general challenge to authority. The breadth of these movements and their rapid diffusion seemed to threaten the established order, giving rise to

countermovements, demands for law and order, and sometimes to reform. In the end, what began as conflicts over claims became interlaced with struggles for power . . . Viewed from a distance, each wave of collective action described a parabola; from institutional conflict to enthusiastic peak to ultimate collapse. After gaining national attention and state response, they reached peaks of conflict that were marked by the presence of movement organisers who tried to diffuse the insurgencies to a broader public. As participation was channelled into organisations, the movements, or part of them, took a more political logic – engaging in implicit bargaining with authorities. In each case, as the cycle wound down, the initiative shifted to elites and parties. (Tarrow 1994: 168)

Protest cycles, then, correspond with moments of intensified collective action. As in culture and the economy,[16] there is a recurrent dynamic of ebb and flow in collective mobilization. In particular, by demonstrating the vulnerability of the authorities the first movements to emerge lower the cost of collective action for other actors. In addition, the victories they obtain undermine the previous order of things, provoking counter-mobilization.

This cyclical pattern has consequences on the repertoires of collective action. In the initial stages of protest the most disruptive tactics are often to the fore. New actors invent new tactics; the collective identities which are in the process of forming require radical action (Pizzorno 1978). As the cycle of protest extends, the reaction of the authorities produces simultaneous processes of radicalization and institutionalization.[17] Evolution in protest tactics, therefore, accompanies changes in the external environment:

When disruptive forms are first employed, they frighten antagonists with their potential cost, shock onlookers and worry elites concerned with public order. But newspapers gradually begin to give less and less space to protests that would have merited banner headlines when they first appeared on the streets. Repeating the same form of collective action over and over reduces uncertainty and is greeted with a smile or a yawn. Participants, at first enthused and invigorated by their solidarity and ability to challenge authorities, become jaded or disillusioned. Authorities, instead of calling out the troops or allowing the police to wade into a crowd, infiltrate dissenting groups and separate leaders from followers. Routinisation follows hard upon disruption. (Tarrow 1994: 112)

The analysis of protest cycles is particularly useful for an understanding of the development of political violence, frequently one (though not the only nor the most important) of protest's outcomes.[18] In fact, the forms of violence used tend to vary according to the stage of the cycle. At the outset of protest violent action is usually limited in its presence, small in scope and unplanned. Typically, violence in these phases is an unforeseen result of direct action such as sit-ins or occupations. As protest develops, violent forms of action initially spread more slowly than non-violent ones. They frequently take the form of clashes between demonstrators and police or counter-demonstrators. Starting out as occasional, such episodes, nonetheless, tend to be repeated and take on a ritual quality. During this process small groups begin to specialize in increasingly extreme tactics, build up an armoury for such action and occasionally go underground. The very presence of these groups accelerates the moderate exodus from the movement, contributing to a demobilization which only the most violent groups escape (at least temporarily). The final stages of the cycle thus see both a process of institutionalization and a growing number of violent actions.

A glance at the development of the anti-nuclear missile campaign would seem to confirm this broad pattern of protest cycle evolution.[19] The incubatory stages of mobilization had been characterized by activity which concentrated prevalently on providing information, with only a handful of symbolic demonstrations (such as Good Friday marches) carried out by small activist networks. The movement extended beyond its initial base during this phase, mobilizing groups involved in earlier movements (the women's movement, for example, and the environmentalist movement) or in political parties and religious associations. As noted above, each of these actors contributed particular forms of action to a common repertoire: the feminist groups brought the practices of civil disobedience they had honed in the campaign to legalize abortion; the religious associations brought with them the gospels; the environmentalists the practice of non-violent occupations they had previously used against nuclear power station sites; the parties of the left mobilized a mass following and offered channels of communication with public institutions. Although the heterogeneity of the various constituencies involved inevitably led to disagreements over what forms of action should be adopted, this diversity enriched rather than hindered the movement's capacity for mobilization during its expansionary phase.

After their initial indecision governments reacted by ordering police intervention, particularly to suppress direct action in front of military bases and break up the peace camps. While, on the whole, peace was maintained by both sides during these interventions, escalation did occur on some occasions, above all when police reacted in muscular fashion to attacks by fringe anarchist groups. The sporadic episodes of violence during the campaign coincided with the waning of mobilization. The movement declined after the massive demonstrations of autumn 1983. When governments confirmed their decision to go ahead with the installation of NATO's Cruise and Pershing missiles on their territories, many discouraged activists abandoned mass demonstrations and this decline accentuated conflict between the varied and heterogeneous organisations involved in the movement. It was at this stage that the remaining European terrorist groups focused their attention on NATO targets, hoping (without success) to recruit militants disillusioned by the failure of non-violence. Those who did not abandon the movement, in the meantime, prepared for a more continuous, if less visible, campaign: countercultural activity to strengthen pacifist consciousness and opposition to war among both governed and governors; legislative action to limit arms sales, facilitate conscientious objection to military service and the war industry. While remaining largely in a latent state, the peace movement remobilized for mass demonstrations on a number of occasions: against the Gulf War, for example, and in the action cited at the beginning of the present chapter against French nuclear testing in the Pacific.

At least two tendencies must be added to the cyclical evolution described so far. First, each cycle broadens the repertoire of collective action. This was as true of the Warsaw Pact countries in the years around 1989 as it had been of the waves of protest which swept Europe and the United States in the 1930s and the 1960s:

> At the peak of each wave, citizens developed particular forms of collective action. The factory occupations that marked the French 1936 strikes were similar to the sitdown strikes of Flint and Akron; while the university occupations of Berlin, Turin and Paris in 1968 linked students to their American homologues. As for Solidarity, its most striking feature would prove to be the roundtable discussions between Solidarity leaders and the government that foreshadowed the forms of negotiations that swept Eastern Europe in 1989. (Tarrow 1994: 167–8)

Second, the most radical forms of action declined, at least in western democracies. In the 1970s there had been a tendency to maintain media attention and 'threat potential' through an accentuation of extreme forms of action. Two new tendencies have also been identified: the spread of protest to institutional as well as non-institutional actors and a growing moderation in the repertoires of collective action adopted by social movements themselves (della Porta 1996a; also, Raschke 1988: 322–32).

7.7 Summary

The present chapter has been dedicated to the analysis of the principal forms of action adopted by social movements; in other words, to forms of protest. Protest has been defined as non-conventional action in which indirect channels of influence are opened through the activity of a series of collective actors. It has been said that the tactics used by social movements form repertoires with specific characteristics. In particular, a repertoire of national, autonomous and modular forms of protest have developed since the nineteenth century. More recent transformations in both the distribution of power at national and international level and in the structure of mass communications suggest that new repertoires will emerge. Distinguishing between the various forms of protest, the fact that different logics of action were simultaneously present in each repertoire was stressed: the logic of numbers, which seeks to display the strength of support for a movement; the logic of material damage, based on the capacity to interrupt everyday routine; and the logic of bearing witness, which seeks to demonstrate the emotional commitment of protesters. Social movement leaders face a series of strategic dilemmas in choosing one or another form of action because each sends messages to different publics with different demands: the movement rank and file who seek to reinforce internal solidarity; the media, in search of 'news'; potential allies, who prefer more moderate forms of action; and, finally, decision-makers, who seek partners whom they can trust. Moreover, historical traditions fostered through institutions and socialization limit the range of options which can be considered. A series of cyclical dynamics create a succession of waves and troughs in protest and radicalization and institutionalization in the forms of action adopted. Alongside these cyclical fluctuations, however, two more stable tendencies appear to apply, at least as far as western democracies are concerned, with a broadening of the repertoire of protest action and simultaneously a growing rejection of political violence.

8
The Political Context of Social Movements

On 26 April 1986 a nuclear reactor at Chernobyl in the Ukraine exploded. It was the worst disaster ever associated with the peaceful use of nuclear energy. The explosion of reactor No. 4 leaked 150,000 curies of radioactivity to into the atmosphere, one hundred times more than the bombs dropped on Hiroshima and Nagasaki. There were thirty-eight deaths in the area immediately affected and later the number of tumours and genetic deformities would rise dramatically. Some 130,000 sq. km. of territory in Russia, the Ukraine and Belarus were seriously contaminated. The explosion had wider consequences, however. Pushed by the wind, a rapidly expanding radioactive cloud moved across enormous distances and would eventually affect the whole of Europe. According to the OECD (Organization for Economic Cooperation and Development) Austria, Finland and Italy were the countries most seriously affected in the twelve months following the explosion, followed by Germany, Switzerland and Sweden and then France, the United Kingdom and the Netherlands (Rüdig 1990: 331). However, the radiation did not spread evenly and there were regions in less affected countries where radiation levels many hundreds of times higher than average were recorded.

Throughout Europe protest spread with the radioactive cloud. In the days following the disaster mass demonstrations took place in many European capitals demanding an end to the use of nuclear power. In a number of countries activists organized sit-ins and blockades at power stations in use or under construction. More institutionally minded organizations launched petitions and referendums. Smaller, more radical groups went the length of sabotaging electricity pylons leading to nuclear power stations. However, the characteristics of this wave of protest were very different from country to country. First, movements in different countries demonstrated differing capacities for mobilization. According to comparative research, based on newspaper reports, there were fifty protest actions recorded in Germany in the three months immediately following the explosion, ten in France and a handful each in Switzerland and the Netherlands (Kriesi et al. 1995, 149). The same research noted that participation in these demonstrations reached six per thousand inhabitants in Germany and four in Switzerland, but that in France and the Netherlands participation remained at levels appreciably less than one per thousand inhabitants (1995). Thus, while 'people demonstrated in Saarbrücken against the nuclear power station in French Cattenom, the same station remained unchallenged in France itself; and while the power station in North German Brockdorf – in an area only lightly affected by radiation – became the object of mass demonstrations, all was quiet round the two Dutch nuclear power stations' (1995: 150). The forms of action adopted were also different. To take only one example, between 1970 and 1992 protests linked to public hearings on nuclear questions accounted for 6.5 per cent of all anti-nuclear protest actions in Germany, but only 0.3 per cent in France; violence, on the other hand, was present in 24.3 per cent of protests in France compared with only 9.7 per cent in Germany (Rucht 1994: 461).

Government reaction to the Chernobyl disaster also varied from country to country. In Germany the local authorities issued strict prohibitions on the sale of contaminated agricultural products; products which could be freely bought and eaten in neighbouring France, on the other hand. In France the Socialist government continued to back that country's strongly developed nuclear power programme. The Dutch centre-right government put off indefinitely any decision on new power stations, as did the Swiss. Members of the governing CDU and FDP parties in Germany expressed doubts about their leaders' pro-nuclear stance. Finally, the majority of political parties in Italy adopted an anti-nuclear position in the referendums held in 1987. By 1988 France, Belgium and Japan had significantly surpassed the targets they had fixed for nuclear energy production in 1974. Italy, Norway, Austria, the Netherlands and Denmark, on the other hand, were well behind on their original programmes (Rüdig 1990). By the early 1990s opposition to nuclear power had been defeated in France but had achieved significant victories in the United States and Germany (Rucht 1990b). As far as left-wing political parties are concerned, the German SPD adopted a resolution on 'getting out of nuclear power' and the PCI in Italy (already under pressure from its youth wing) came out against nuclear energy (della Porta 1996a). The opinions which prevailed in the French left were very different. In 1987 anti-nuclear feeling grew throughout European public opinion with only two exceptions: France and Belgium. The size of the majority against nuclear power also varied from country to country. In Denmark those against outnumbered those in favour by 49 points, in Italy 46, in the Netherlands 27, in Germany 19 and in Switzerland 10 (Rüdig 1990, 346).

What accounts for these differences in the characteristics of mobilization and the responses to it? Naturally, the particular strategies of national movements can have an impact on the size and form of mobilization. As noted in earlier chapters, ideology, repertoires and structures constitute material and cultural resources for action which vary from country to country. Although they certainly have the capacity to interact with their environment in the attempt to transform it, social movements are nevertheless strongly dependent on external variables. Social structure, the degree of civic culture, economic development, technological diffusion and pluralism in the mass media have all been considered as important in defining the context of mobilization. Early democratic development, revolution and peasant revolts have, in the first instance, all been explained by social structure (Barrington Moore 1966; Skocpol 1979).

In attempting to select the most influential of the many determinants of collective action, quite a number of comparative analyses of social movements have concentrated on political variables. It has already been noted that the activities of social movements are in part expressive; in part instrumental; in part directed at their own members; in part designed to transform the external environment. In their protest activities social movements are eminently political: as such they are influenced by and influence first and foremost the political system. As was noted in the introductory chapter, the concept of political opportunity structure has become central to interpretations of interaction between institutional and non-institutional actors.

Taking illustrations principally from the anti-nuclear movement,[1] what follows will seek to identify the main variables of the political system and suggest some hypotheses on the way they influence particular characteristics of social movements. Beginning with an analysis of a number of 'stable' elements in the structure of opportunity we will identify the effects of institutions (8.1) and political cultures (8.2) on social movement repertoires. Thereafter attention will turn to the more dynamic elements of the system of political opportunities in order to discuss the strategies adopted by challengers' opponents (8.3) and their allies (8.4) and their effects on mobilization levels and the success of protest. Research on political opportunities has stimulated reflection, as we shall see in section 8.5, on the problems and possible solutions for comparative analysis of social movements and protest.

8.1 Political Institutions and Social Movements

Considering the characteristics of the political system which may affect social movements, political institutions immediately appear relevant. Comparative research has considered the degree of centralisation of the state apparatus, government control over market participation and the dependence of the judiciary on other arms of government (Kitschelt 1986: 61–4);[2] regime structure (Rucht 1994: 303–12); and territorial decentralization, the functional division of powers and direct democracy (Kriesi 1995).

Alexis de Tocqueville's famous contrast between 'weak' American government and 'strong' French government is usually an implicit or explicit starting point for analyses which link institutional factors and social movement development. Postulating an opposition between state and civil society, Tocqueville considered that a system in which the state was weak and civil society strong (the United States) would face a constant but peaceful flux of protest from below. Where the state was strong and civil society weak (France), on the other hand, episodic and violent revolt would result. In his most recent book on social movements Sidney Tarrow (1994: 62–5) has convincingly criticized this hypothesis, claiming that Tocqueville's analysis was partial even in respect of the historical situation to which the author referred. Not only does the American Civil War raise doubts about the capacity of a 'weak' state to integrate conflicting interests, but recent studies of the French Revolution have demonstrated the existence of a very robust civil society in that country. As Tarrow remarks, in both countries the state and the rights of its citizens grew in step: conscription mobilized citizens as soldiers, stimulating new demands; the unified fiscal system created a single target for protest; conflict within the elites pushed the various parties involved to appeal to public opinion, extending the franchise; the means of communication built by the state would also be used by challengers; new forms of aggregation and expression were legitimized by elections; the creation of new administrative units led to the creation of new collective identities.

If Tocqueville appears to have 'exaggerated' the characteristics of both France and the United States in order to construct a dichotomy between the 'good' and the 'bad' state, the idea that the strength or weakness of states influence social movement strategies remains central to the literature on collective action in general and on revolutions in particular. This approach, 'à la Tocqueville', has frequently been linked to a pluralist conception that a large number of points of access to the political system are an indication of 'openness'.

Many cases studies which use categories that refer to the 'power of the state' are really referring to the power of the central executive. In general, a system has been considered more open the more political decisions are dispersed. The prevalent belief is that the greater the number of actors who share in political power (the greater the checks and balances) the greater the chance that social movements can gain access to the system. However, while a weak executive may ease access to the decision-making process, it will have little hope of implementing policies to meet social movement demands. The hypotheses concerning the effects of institutional variables on the evolution of social movements cover three main areas: the territorial decentralization and functional dispersal of power, and the extent of power in the hands of the state.

A first set of hypotheses concern territorial decentralization. The basic suggestion is that the more power is distributed to the periphery (local or regional government, component states within a federal structure) the greater the possibility individual movements have of accessing the decision-making process. The 'nearer' an administrative unit is to ordinary citizens (in a conception of democracy very common in American social science, but also within social movements themselves) the easier it will be to gain access. Thus, all else being equal, the greater the degree of power passed from the national government to the regions, from the regions to the cities, from the cities to local neighbourhoods, the greater the openness of the political system to pressure from below. Following the same logic, federal states are considered more open than centralist ones (see, for example, Kitschelt 1986; Kriesi 1995; Giugni 1997).

As far as the functional separation of powers is concerned, the system can broadly be considered more open the greater the division of tasks between legislature, executive and judiciary. Moreover, looking at each of these powers separately, the greater the autonomy of individual actors the more numerous will be the channels of access to the system. In the first place, the parliamentary arena has been considered more open the greater the number of seats assigned by proportional representation, since the possibilities of access for a variety of actors will be higher (see, for example, Amenta and Young 1995). It also follows from the general proposition that 'a higher number of autonomous actors equals greater openness of the system' that, as far as the characteristics of the executive are concerned, the possibilities of access will be less in a presidential system than in a parliamentary one because there are fewer decision-makers. In the arena of government it can generally be expected that elite attitudes to challengers will depend on whether the government is homogeneous or a coalition. The more fragmented the government or the greater the differences between the parties which compose it the easier it will be to find allies, although the chances of actually implementing policies will be less. Cultural variables such as traditions of loyalty to the leadership or personalistic divisions within parties and the prevalence of individualistic or collective mediation of consensus, also influence government stability and compactness. The openness of the system to pressure from below should also increase the greater the power of elected organs.[3] As far as the characteristics of the bureaucracy are concerned, Kriesi et al. (1995: 31) note that 'The greater the amount of resources at its disposal, and the greater the degree of its coherence, internal coordination and professionalization, the stronger it will be. Lack of resources, structural fragmentation, lack of internal coordination and of professionalization, multiply the points of access and make the administration dependent on its private interlocutors in the system of interest-intermediation.' A further element of relevance for the functional distribution of power is the autonomy and powers of the judiciary. A strong judicial power can intervene in both legislative and executive functions, as when the Constitutional Court or the magistracy become involved in legal controversies between social movements and counter-movements or state institutions. The greater the independence of the judiciary the greater the possibility of access for social movements.

The last matter to be dealt with concerns the overall amount of power in the hands of the state as compared with other actors such as pressure groups, political parties, the media, ordinary citizens. For example, returning to public administration, the possibility of outside intervention varies a great deal from state to state. In general, where public administration is rooted in Roman Law, which rejects external contacts, there tends to be greater resistance to pressure from non-institutional actors (not simply social movements but political parties also). The Anglo-Saxon model of public administration, on the other hand, with more numerous channels of access for non-institutional actors, tends to be more open. In this respect the institutional structure of political opportunity will be more open (and the state weaker) where citizens maintain the possibility of intervening with the legislative and executive independently of mediation through political parties, interest groups or bureaucrats. The greater the degree of participation on the part of citizens, through referendums for the proposition or abrogation of particular measures and the procedures for appealing against the decisions of the public administration, the more open the system.

But what are the effects of all these institutional properties on the characteristics of social movements? In the first place, it is improbable – at a given level of democratic development – that they do much to explain the emergence of movements because they tend to be stable over the long term while social movements have a cyclical evolution.

Second, depending on the social movement alliance structure (whether or not it is possible to make allies within the central executive power), the openness of the institutional system would appear to have ambivalent effects on the possibilities of success for social movements. To begin with, it has frequently been observed that in decentralized states challengers can rely on a variety of actors to penetrate the system. Concerning the antinuclear movement Nelkin and Pollack (1981: 179) stated that the 'German decentralised decision-making context has provided ecologists with greater political opportunity, because they can play one administration against the other'. Unlike their counterparts in other countries, the German environmentalists were successful in using the judicial system. While the centralized system in France, for example, favoured political control by the government, in Germany the wide distribution of power 'allowed some courts to take a very powerful and independent role in nuclear disputes' (Nelkin and Pollack 1981: 159).

However, decentralisation of power does not always work in social movements' favour. Dispersal of power increases the chances of access not just for social movements but for *all* political actors, including counter-movements.[4] It can happen that a movement's allies find themselves in government at national level and take decisions favourable to that movement, only to find these decisions blocked by either decentralized bodies governed by other political forces or by other arms of the state such as the courts. Both of these things happened in Germany in the 1970s on the issues of abortion and nuclear power. Even the use of referendums can favour the opponents of social movements as well as the movements themselves.[5] Similarly, a weak bureaucracy can be influenced by political parties and pressure groups as well as by social movements; the mirror image of this is that a strong and independent bureaucracy increases the autonomous points of access to the decision-making process for social movements but also for other collective actors (Amenta and Young 1995). Thus, the early accommodating responses by institutionally open states to the anti-nuclear movement did not always have much effect on later developments in the conflict. In fact, it was precisely in more open states that powerful pro-nuclear interest groups could regroup and regain lost ground (Flam 1994b: 317, 321).

Institutional arrangements do not appear to have much weight in relation to levels of mobilization either. The research carried out by Hanspeter Kriesi and his collaborators, for instance, compared countries with varying degrees of central state power. Regarding geographical decentralization comparison was made between federal states (Germany and Switzerland) and unitary states (France and the Netherlands). Regarding the functional distribution of power – analysed in terms of parliament, the state administration and direct democracy – a weak state (Switzerland) was compared with two intermediate cases (Germany and the Netherlands) and one strong state (France).[6] According to this research, the effects of institutional closure or openness on levels of protest was far from unambiguous.[7] As table 8.1 shows, the highest number of occurrences of protest was registered in Germany (2,343 between 1975 and 1989), followed closely by France (2,132) and then the Netherlands (1,319) and Switzerland

Table 8.1   *Forms of protest in France, Germany, the Netherlands and Switzerland*

Distribution of unconventional events: 1975–1989 (%)				
	France	Germany	Netherlands	Switzerland
New social movements	36.1	73.2	65.4	61.0
Not new social movements	63.9	26.8	34.6	39.0
Total %	100.0	100.0	100.0	100.0
Number of events	2,132	2,343	1,319	1,215

Volume of participation in unconventional events in 1,000 per million inhabitants (1975–1989)				
	France	Germany	Netherlands	Switzerland
New social movements	43	168	143	101
Not new social movements	135	43	55	55
All mobilization	178	211	198	156
Number of events	2,076	2,229	1,264	1,027

Levels of mobilization in 1,000 per million inhabitants				
	France	Germany	Netherlands	Switzerland
SMOs membership	74	202	197	218
Direct democracy	—	4	—	195
Petitions	22	136	291	203
Festivals	36	18	3	83
Unconventional	178	211	198	156
Strikes	225	37	23	2
Total	535	608	712	857
% Unconventional	75	41	31	18

Source: Adapted from Kriesi et al. (1995: 20, 22, 45)

(1,215) (Kriesi et al. 1995: 20). Considering participation in unconventional actions per thousand inhabitants, Germany leads with 211 inhabitants per thousand involved, followed by the Netherlands (198), France (178), and Switzerland (158) (1995: 22). As far as new social movements are concerned, the highest level of mobilization was in the Netherlands, Switzerland following and then Germany and France. Mobilization by 'old' movements, on the other hand, was strongest in France, followed by Germany, Switzerland and the Netherlands. In short, no precise indications emerge concerning a correlation between institutional openness and levels of protest.

Institutional variables may have a stronger influence on the strategies adopted by social movements, however. Social movements tend to use the channels of access made available to them by 'weak' states. According to the research just cited, for example, the level of mobilization in unconventional forms of action was 18 per thousand in Switzerland and 31 in the Netherlands compared with 41 and 75 per thousand in Germany and France. On the other hand, according to the newspaper data used, in Switzerland 195 per thousand inhabitants were mobilized in forms of action involving the use of direct democracy compared with only 4 per thousand in Germany and none in the other two countries (Kriesi et al. 1995: 45). As will become clear in what follows, as far as the relative moderation of repertoires is concerned, institutional openness must be combined with traditional political culture (itself naturally codified, at least partly, in legislation).

8.2   Prevailing Strategies and Social Movements

A number of scholars have suggested that social movements are permeated by the political culture of the systems in which they develop. The strategies adopted by collective actors are influenced by the mutable and flexible spirit of the times – the *Zeitgeist* – which echoes developments within the economic cycle (Brand 1985) and also by certain relatively stable characteristics of national political cultures (Kitschelt 1985: 302–3). The more egalitarian, liberal, inclusive and individualistic the political culture, the less opposition should be antagonistic and confrontational. Taking further the analysis of those aspects of political culture relevant to interaction between social movements and institutions, Hanspeter Kriesi has emphasized the importance of prevailing strategies, which he defines, following Scharpf (1984: 260), as 'an overall understanding, among those who exercise effective power, of a set of precise premises integrating worldviews, goals and means'. Referring in particular to the procedures used by members of a system when dealing with 'challengers', he claims that 'national strategies set the informal and formal rules of the game for the conflict between new social movements and their adversaries' (1989a: 295). According to this hypothesis, countries with a strategy of exclusion (that is, repression of conflict) will tend to have an ideologically homogeneous governing coalition and polarization of conflict with opponents. Where there is a strategy of inclusion (co-option of emergent demands), on the other hand, governments will be ideologically heterogeneous and open towards external actors.

A country's democratic history may also influence its prevailing strategies. Past authoritarianism tends to re-emerge in times of turmoil. Young democracies tends to fear political protest, and also have police forces which remain steeped in the authoritarian values of the preceding regime (Flam 1994c: 348; on Italy, see Reiter 1998). In fact, it has been argued that in each country new social movements have 'inherited' consequences from the reactions reserved originally for the labour movement. In Mediterranean Europe, France and Germany, absolutism and the late introduction of universal suffrage led to a divided and radicalized labour movement. In the smaller, open-market countries, in Great Britain and in Scandinavia, on the other hand, where there was no experience of absolutism and universal suffrage was introduced early, inclusive strategies produced a united and moderate labour movement. As a comparative study of American, British and German unions shows:

> State repression of the rights of workers to combine in the labour market appears to have had three related consequences for unions. First and most obviously, repression politicised unions because it compelled them to try to change the rules of the game . . . A second consequence of repression is that, if sufficiently severe, it could reduce differences among workers originating in their contrasting capacity to form effective unions . . . Finally, . . . repression politicised unions in an additional and more subtle way, by giving the initiative within the labour movement to political parties. (Marks 1989: 14–15, passim)

These (self-reproducing) prevailing strategies influenced the way in which the conflict between labour and capital was confronted, leading to exclusion in certain cases and integration in others (Kriesi 1989). Initially elaborated in response to trade unionism, these strategies developed their own, self-perpetuating logic through political socialization and interaction:

> The duration and intensity of state repression of working-class organisations and the relative timing of the institutionalisation of unions and working-class political parties are crucial influences on the political orientation of the working classes in the nineteenth century. Once the relationship between the union and party-political wings of the labour movement had been moulded, it was difficult to break. (Marks 1989: 175)

The tendency of national strategies to live on beyond the conditions which gave rise to them would help to explain reaction to new social movements. Political systems characterized by inclusion would be open to these new challengers as they had been to the old; systems with excluding strategies, in contrast, would continue to be hostile to newly emerging claims. In fact, the difference in elite attitudes to challengers would appear to be linked to prevailing conceptions of relations with interest groups. The following has been said concerning the anti-nuclear movement:

> The speedy and substantial responses came in the nation-states whose political and bureaucratic state elites have either long ago (Sweden, Norway) or immediately after the Second World War, if not earlier (Austria, the Netherlands, West Germany) learnt to recognise as legitimate and even formalised interest groups representation and the influence that trade unions and employers exert over governmental decision making. (Flam 1994b: 309)

The elites in these countries tend to recognize the legitimacy of interests lying outside the party system, knowing that the movement of today may be the interest group of tomorrow; in other countries, France for example, an exclusionary attitude has been preferred. The size of a state also seems to have a bearing on the attitude of political parties to 'challengers': in small democracies, where two-way channels exists between interest groups and decision-makers and there is greater participation, political parties demonstrate greater sensitivity towards collective actors.

What, then, can be explained by this set of variables? First, it should be reiterated that an aspect which tends to remain constant cannot help explain the (cyclical) emergence of protest. In terms of its success, what was said concerning institutional openness also applies here, at least in part. While strategies of accommodation and inclusion may favour social movement access to the system, they will do the same for their opponents too. In an inclusive system, governments hostile to social movement claims can be forced to compromise; on the other hand, a government inclined to be friendly might also be constrained to follow a more moderate policy than they would otherwise.

The relative predominance of either a strategy of inclusion or a strategy of exclusion may also have contradictory effects on levels of mobilization. On the one hand, the anticipated costs of mobilization will be lower in traditionally inclusive countries, perhaps increasing willingness to use protest. On the other hand, the danger of being subjected to undesirable policies in the absence of mobilization will be more limited in a state which tends to integrate differing interests and the advantage to be expected from protest will thus be smaller. Cross-national comparison does not allow for strong hypotheses here either. Returning to table 8.1, for example, it will be noticed that overall levels of mobilization in Switzerland and the Netherlands, both traditionally inclusive countries,[8] are similar to those in France and Germany, countries with long traditions of repression. Added to that, according to opinion poll evidence the number of citizens who have taken part in direct action is particularly high in France; higher than in Great Britain, a traditionally inclusive country.[9] Moreover, the so-called 'old' movements, and the labour movement in particular, were more active in France and Germany than in the Netherlands and Switzerland. This would seem to confirm that neither the degree of repression nor the prospects for accommodation have an unequivocal effect on mobilization levels. Although repression heightens the costs of collective action, it also renders it in a certain way more necessary. The other side of the coin is that accommodatory strategies lessen the costs of action but also the costs of inaction.

The link between prevailing strategies and repertoires of action would appear clearer, however. In general, repertoires are more conventional in traditionally assimilative countries. In a comparison of political repression in nineteenth-century Europe, for example, it has been noted that 'those countries that were consistently the most repressive, brutal, and obstinate in dealing with the consequences of modernisation and developing working-class dissidence reaped the harvest by producing opposition that was just as rigid, brutal, and obstinate' (Goldstein 1983: 340). In fact, 'repression stimulated working-class radicalism; whilst political relaxation and a structure of free collective bargaining encourages reformism' (Geary 1981: 179). Returning to the antinuclear movement, in the United States a political culture traditionally hostile to the strong, centralized state created a climate favourable to assimilation, whereas in Germany, 'in a polarised political culture, the unresponsiveness of statist elites became mirrored in the antistatist disposition of the antinuclear movement' (Joppke 1993: 15).

Moreover, in the four countries analysed by Kriesi (1995: 50) the presence of violent episodes was highest in France (25.4 per cent) and Germany (9 per cent) and lowest in the Netherlands (6 per cent) and Switzerland (4.7 per cent). However, the differences in social movement strategies are less marked when episodes of limited violence are added to more extreme ones (11.1 per cent of cases in the Netherlands, 12.4 in Switzerland, 15.1 in Germany and 31.2 in France). Furthermore, concentrating on new social movements, we see that they chose violent strategies in 22.5 per cent of cases in France, 14.7 per cent in Switzerland, 15.1 per cent in Germany and 12.3 per cent in the Netherlands. The standings of the four countries change once again when confrontational action is considered: such action was more frequent in the Netherlands (35 per cent of cases) than in Germany (19.3 per cent) or in France (24.5 per cent). Individual participation in protest action, including the most extreme forms, on occasions turns out to be relatively high in traditionally inclusive countries and, vice versa, low in countries with a tradition of exclusion. For example, in a comparison of eight democracies,[10] the Dutch had the highest propensity to participate in direct action. They also had a greater disposition than citizens in many countries with exclusionary traditions, such as Germany, to participate in radical protest: wildcat strikes, writing graffiti, refusal to pay rent or taxes, damage to property and violence against the person.

While acknowledging a certain influence of political traditions on social movement strategies, it should be remembered that a country's 'traditions' are hardly set in stone. The nineteenth-century French elite, for example, were considered open to change, while their German counterparts were hostile to any and every reform:

> Where a national bourgeoisie is weak or tied to an existing and authoritarian state, as in Russia before the First World War, or countries in which the middle class increasingly abandons liberal values and comes to support a semi-authoritarian political system, as was to some extent the case in Imperial Germany and pre-war Spain, there the prospect of working-class liberalism appears to be weaker, while political radicalism on the part of labour becomes more marked. Conversely, the Republican traditions of at least some sections of the French bourgeoisie and the buoyant liberalism of the British middle class enabled a fair proportion of the workers to remain in the liberal camp. (Geary 1989: 2–3)

The picture changes in the second half of the twentieth century, however. In fact, after the Second World War, the collapse of Nazism and the Allied Occupation led to a rethinking of past repressive traditions in Germany and the adoption of inclusive strategies towards the labour movement. In France, on the other hand, the absence of such a historical rupture allowed strategies of exclusion to be maintained until at least the 1960s. It has also been noted that past elite behaviour is not enough to explain recourse to repressive strategies in relation to the anti-nuclear movement (Flam 1994c: 345).

In conclusion, while national strategies do have a certain influence on the repertoires of action adopted by social movements, they are not sufficient to explain the strategic choices they make. In the first place, they are not equally long-lived in every country. Second, they do not have the same effect on all movements. Third, they appear to affect some movement strategies and not others.

8.3 Repression and Social Movements' Opponents

So far, we considered relatively constant features of the system of political opportunities; both institutions and political cultures change slowly. For social movement activists these are givens. However, another, more dynamic set of variables – susceptible to change in the short term and the object of pressure from social movements – are also considered part of the political opportunity structure. Indeed, as already noted, among the first definitions of the political opportunity structure were those looking at changes which could cause sudden openings in the system. As Doug McAdam noted, '*any* event or broad social process that serves to undermine the calculations and assumptions on which the political establishment is structured occasions a shift in political opportunities' (McAdam 1982: 41, emphasis in the original). While McAdam was looking at war, industrialization, unemployment and migration primarily as causes of changes in power relations, others have considered their effects on the political system. Attention has therefore concentrated on aspects such as electoral instability or elite divisions (see, for example, Piven and Cloward 1977; Jenkins 1985; Tarrow 1983, 1989a).

Social movements move in an organizational forcefield, interacting with a variety of other actors. They find both allies and opponents within the public administration, the party system, interest groups and civil society. During the cycle of protest, social movement organizations, political parties, interest groups and voluntary associations frequently enter into relations of conflict or cooperation on both specific issues and the more general one of the right to protest. Many actors, including institutional actors, become involved in protest campaigns on particular demands such as peace or abortion, but coalitions also form on the issue of 'law and order', on the one side, and 'civil rights' on the other (della Porta 1998b).

In fact, institutional factors are mediated by two intervening sets of variables: the alliances structure and the opposition structure. Considering the field of action within which social movements move, alliance structure can be defined as those political actors who support them; the opposition structure as those political actors against them (Kriesi 1989a and 1991; Klandermans 1989b and 1990; della Porta and Rucht 1995). Alliances provide resources and political opportunities for challengers, opposition erodes them. Institutional actors (such as political parties and interest groups) and other social movements can be found on both sides. The 'configuration of power' – that is, the distribution of power among the various actors operating within the party or interest groups system – will determine the result of the conflict (Kriesi 1989a). While it is elections which determine whether the party allies or opponents of a social movement will be in power, the attitudes of the various actors mentioned above are influenced by other factors.

When looking at the opponents of social movements it must be stated at the outset that the state cannot be identified merely as an 'enemy' of social movements. Rather, the state is 'simultaneously target, sponsor, and antagonist for social movements as well as the organiser of the political system and the arbiter of victory' (Jenkins and Klandermans 1995: 3). State agencies may be either allies or opponents: 'Government agencies, the organised manifestations of the state, may be aligned with SM [Social Movements] or CM [Counter Movements] interests; SM-aligned agencies believe in movement goals; CM-aligned hold opposing beliefs' (Gale 1986: 205). Both can offer important resources to their respective sides. Not all public agencies are aligned, however, and, as the chapter which follows makes clear, many of them become arenas for transaction between different collective actors, social movements among them.

The state elaborates its responses to the various claims on it in the policy-making arena. Within this arena specific styles of conflict management develop. As Flam notes in relation to the anti-nuclear movement, it was 'not so much the formal (open or closed) state structures but rather movement-oriented counter-strategies and conflict-management styles displayed in the specific interactions between the state and the movement [that] would affect movement strategies' (1994a: 14). Thus it is the critical encounters between state and movement which define their relationship (1994a; see also della Porta 1995a: ch. 6). As will be seen in section 8.4, within this arena, the power of the various actors representing specific interests can influence the response of the state to social movements.

If, then, state institutions are on occasion allies of social movements and at the same time they are the arenas within which movements present their claims, there is also a sense in which the state is nonetheless an 'adversary' of protest. Possessing the monopoly of the legitimate use of force and as the guarantor of public order, the state uses the police to control protest, limiting the resources available for collective action. An important aspect of the state's response to protest, therefore, is the policing of protest, or, to use more neutral terms for what protesters usually refer to as 'repression' and the state as 'law and order', police handling of protest events (della Porta 1996c). Protest policing is a particularly relevant issue for understanding the relationship between social movements and the state. According to Lipsky (1970: 1) the 'study of the ways police interact with other citizens is of primary importance for anyone concerned with public policy and the just resolution of contemporary urban conflict. Police may be conceived as "street-level bureaucrats" who "represent" government to people. And at the same time as they represent government policies, police forces also help define the terms of urban conflict by their actions. The influence of police on political attitudes and developments is fundamental because of the unique role of law enforcement agencies in enforcing and reinforcing the norms of the system'. It can be added that, in their turn, protest waves have had important effects on police organization (see, for example, Morgan 1987; Reiner 1998).

In fact, the various styles of police intervention have received some attention in the sociological literature. Gary T. Marx (1979), working from a phenomenonological perspective, distinguished acts of repression according to their purpose: creating an unfavourable image of opponents; gathering information; restricting the flow of resources for movements; discouraging activists; fuelling internal conflicts within the leadership and between groups; sabotaging specific actions. Charles Tilly (1978: 106–15) classified political regimes according to the degree of repression or 'facilitation' they manifest towards different collective actors and actions. A comparative analysis of protest policing in Western Europe led to the development of a typology based on two factors: (1) *the range of prohibited behaviours and groups*, in order to distinguish between repressive and tolerant policing; and (2) *the dominant 'logic' of intervention*, to distinguish between reactive use of force and proactive use of intelligence information (della Porta 1995).

International comparative research since the 1960s has noted changes in protest policing. It has becoming increasingly tolerant, using coercion less frequently, although specialization between police branches has developed, and more sophisticated technology is used. In general, keeping the peace has prevailed over enforcement of the law. Violations of the law are tolerated if coercive intervention to prevent them or to arrest those responsible would risk the safety of peaceful protesters. Respect for democratic procedures has increased, less use being made of such devices as *agents provocateurs*. The reduction in coercion corresponds with an increased use of intelligence. More sophisticated techniques are used for information gathering and greater attention is paid to crime prevention. The development of structures for negotiation, as part of a 'policing by consent' strategy would also fall under a broad definition of prevention (della Porta 1998a; see also Waddington 1994; McPhail, Schweingruber and McCarthy 1998; Fillieule and Jobard 1998; Winter 1998).

International comparisons also indicate the presence of differing national styles of policing. Traditionally the Anglo-Saxon model of decentralized, unarmed policing has been considered the principal example of a style based on low levels of coercion and a well developed system of negotiation. In Germany the emphasis was on the police as firm but neutral upholders of the rule of law. In the Latin world, the police were understood to be the 'long arm of government', having discretionary powers and a political role (Wisler and Kriesi 1998). Different models of policing 'travelled' via colonialism, formal international networks and informal contacts, to different countries (McCarthy, McPhail and Crist 1998). The process of diffusion, however, has tended to reduce international differences (della Porta and Reiter 1998).

Changes in the repressive capabilities of regimes are an important factor in explaining the emergence of social movements. In France, Russia and China, social revolution broke out when political crisis weakened state control and repressive power (Skocpol 1979). Likewise, an inability to maintain social control facilitated the rise of the civil rights movement in the United States (McAdam 1982).[11] And in Italy, the protest cycle of the late 1960s first emerged as a more tolerant style of policing was developing (della Porta 1995).

As far as levels of mobilization are concerned, the harshest styles of protest policing ought to raise the cost of collective action and diminish the disposition of actors to take part. However, it should be added that many forms of repression, particularly when they are considered illegitimate, can create a sense of injustice which increases the perceived risk of inaction. It is not surprising therefore that these two divergent pressures produce contradictory results and empirical research indicates a radicalization of those groups most exposed to police violence in some cases and renunciation of unconventional forms of action in others (Wilson 1976). In fact, the relationship between the degree of violence in protest and coercive intervention by the authorities would appear to be curvilinear (Neidhardt 1989).

Institutional control strategies would appear primarily to influence protest strategies. First, they affect the models of organization adopted within movements. This was the case of French republicanism in the nineteenth century, where 'intensified repression typically reinforced the role of secret societies and informal centers of sociability like cafés, vintners, and cabarets' (Aminzade 1995: 42); on the other hand, 'the extension of universal male suffrage and civil liberties as well as a new geography of representation fostered the development of more formal organisation' (1995: 59). In more recent times, too, repression has led to a process of 'encapsulation' of social movement organisation, to the point of going underground in some cases (della Porta 1995a; Neidhardt 1981).

Strategies of repression also influence repertoires of action. A comparative study of Germany and Italy (della Porta 1995a), for instance, indicated that harsher policing techniques tended to discourage peaceful mass protest and at the same time encourage the more radical fringes of protest. Radicalization among social movements in Italy in the 1970s coincided with a period of harsher repression, the police killing a number of demonstrators during public marches. Moreover, the belief that the state was conducting a 'dirty war' poisoned relationships between its representatives and movement activists. In Germany, on the other hand, the reformist attitudes of the social democrat–liberal government and a tolerant, selective and 'soft' style of protest policing was reflected in a comparative low level of radicalization in the social movement sector. In both countries the high point of repression coincided with a shrinking of the movements' more political wing, a decline which indirectly aided the most extreme elements to prevail, particularly in Italy during the 1970s. The lower levels of violence involved in protest in the 1980s corresponded to an increasing tolerance of protest. Conflict management has also been considered a determining factor in the strategies adopted by the anti-nuclear movement (Diani and van der Heijden 1994).

The very aims of protest may be changed by police intervention, the focus of protest shifting from a single issue to the 'meta-issue' of protest itself. In his study of the Chicano movement in Los Angeles, Edward Escobar has stated that in 'a dialectical relationship, while the Los Angeles Police Department's tactics partially achieved the goal of undermining the Chicano movement, the police and their tactics became an issue around which Chicano activists organized the community and increased grass-roots participation in movement activity' (Escobar 1993: 1485). In conclusion, more tolerant and selective styles of protest policing have facilitated the integration of social movements within a complex structure of political bargaining. This has legitimated certain forms of protest and led to the stigmatization of violence, increasingly viewed as a form of deviancy (della Porta and Reiter 1998).

Finally, as far as movement success is concerned, Tilly (1978) has suggested an inverse relation between the possibility of access to the system and coercion. This relation does not always seem to hold true, however. Comparative openness to access from below does not always correspond to minor repression. This emerged from a comparative analysis of the anti-nuclear movement in Germany and France: 'The contrast in the government response to the anti-nuclear movement in France and Germany reveals some striking ironies. The French government uses less intimidation in its responses to radical forms of opposition but has few procedures through which critics can obtain information or influence decisions. The German government is more willing to enter into negotiation with ecologists and has a more open information policy but reacts more vigorously to radical dissent' (Nelkin and Pollack 1981: 181; also Wisler and Kriesi 1998).

So far, it is principally the role of the state that has been considered. However, it needs to be remembered that, just like their allies, the opponents of social movements too can be either institutional or non-institutional actors. In fact, the term counter-movement has been coined in relation to these actors. Counter-movements arise in reaction to the successes obtained by social movements and the two then develop in symbiotic dependence during the course of mobilization. In general, the relationship between movements and counter-movements is something that has been defined as loosely coupled conflict, in which the two sides rarely come to together face to face (Zald and Useem 1987; cf. also Lo 1982). To use Rapoport's typology (1960), conflict between social movements and counter-movements resembles a debate to the extent that it is based on an attempt to persuade opponents and the authorities, and a game to the extent that it is based on rational calculations of cost and benefit. Sometimes, however, as was the case in Italy in the 1970s, their interaction resembles far more a battle in which the objective is to annihilate the enemy. Interaction between movement and counter-movement leads to a strong sense of conflictuality and the prevalence of a manichean view of politics (Klandermans 1989b; della Porta 1995). Moreover, the two tend to imitate each other, reciprocally adapting particular tactics and the choice of arenas in which to act (see, for example, Rucht 1991c; Meyer and Staggenborg 1996; Bernstein 1995). The presence of non-violent counter-movements chiefly affects the chances of success for social movements; the presence of violent counter-movements, on the other hand, leads to radicalization of their repertoires of action.

8.4   Social Movements and Potential Allies

The greater the closure of the political opportunity structure, the more important the presence of institutional allies for gaining access to the decision-making process. Such allies come in a variety of forms. First, it has already been noted that social movements depend on the mass media to get their message across. The possibilities of access for challengers will be greater the more autonomous and pluralistic the media structure. General tendencies (journalistic preference for the visible and dramatic, for example, or reliance on authoritative sources of information) and specific characteristics of the media system (a greater or lesser degree of neutrality on the part of journalists, the amount of competition between the different media) both influence social movements (see, for example, Kielbowicz and Scherer 1986).

Second, as noted in chapter 6, the resource-mobilization approach has emphasized the role of 'reform professionals' (bureaucrats from certain public agencies, charities, religious organisations and so on) in helping some social movements. In the United States, for example, the churches, certain foundations and the agencies involved in federal anti-poverty programmes supported the civil rights movement (Morris 1984; McAdam 1982).

In addition, the trade unions have often been an important ally for emerging actors, such as the student movement or the women's movement, particularly in Europe. With a social base and very often privileged channels of access to institutional decision-makers (both directly through the public administration and indirectly through the political parties) the trade unions can increase the mobilization capacities and chances of success for social movements. It is probable that the weaker the institutional recognition of workers' representatives in the workplace and the decision-making process, the greater will be their propensity to assume a political role, allying themselves with social movements and taking part in public protest. The more influential interest groups are, the smaller will be the space for relatively unorganized movements because 'a well-resourced, coherently structured, and professionalized system of interest groups may also be able to prevent outside challengers from having access to the state. Moreover, highly institutionalized, encompassing arrangements of policy negotiations between the public administration and private interest associations will be both quite inaccessible to challengers and able to act' (Kriesi et al. 1995: 31). According to this point of view, neo-corporatism – with monopolistic, centralized interest representation (Schmitter 1974) and concerted decision making (Lehmbruch 1977) – should reduce the incidence of protest. Access to the institutional system of public decision-making would facilitate agreement between different social groups and the state without the need for non-institutional forms of collective action. Both control over the formation of social demand (Schmitter 1981) and the capacity to satisfy that demand (Nollert 1995) would have the effect of discouraging protest. However, if a neo-corporatist structure undoubtedly reduces strikes in industry,[12] its effect on protest in other sectors is far from clear. In fact, guaranteeing privileges to powerful interests could lead to rebellion by their weaker rivals and thus to the rise of powerful new movements (Brand 1985).[13] On the other hand, neo-corporatism could as easily create a tendency to incorporate emerging groups within the structure of concerted policy-making. A comparison between the American and German anti-nuclear movements revealed that the American system, with its multiple points of access and traditionally weak executive, favoured legal strategies and pragmatic movements. The initial closure of the German state (traditionally assertive of its supremacy over civil society) towards interests which cut across its corporatist outlook, on the other hand, favoured strategies of direct action (Joppke 1993). However, 'once new issues and interests pass the high hurdles of party and parliament, the German polity firmly institutionalises them' (Joppke 1993: 201).

Where social movement allies are concerned, however, it is on the *political parties*, particularly those of the left, that attention has mainly focused. Although the activities of social movements are rarely aimed directly at political parties, many new actors have seen the left as an ally. For example, while only 11 per cent of environmentalist groups claimed to have frequent contacts with political parties, both the greens and the old and new left were mentioned (by 21 per cent, 38 per cent and 29 per cent respectively of those interviewed) as tending to represent the movement's interests (only 2 per cent mentioned conservative parties in this context) (Dalton 1995: 308). In fact, the configuration of power on the left is particularly important for social movements (Kriesi 1989a: 296). More particularly, a whole series of potential exchanges develop between social movements and the parties of the left. As mediators between civil society and the state, the parties of the left need to mobilize public opinion and voters. For this reason they are far from indifferent to social movement pressure. Indeed, the programmes and membership of the institutional left, be it British Labour, German Social Democrats, French Socialists or Italian Communists, have all been altered by interaction with social movements (i.e., Maguize 1995; Duyrendak 1995; Koopmans 1995; Koelble 1991).

The strategy adopted by the left towards social movements has, however, not been unchanging over time and space. Hostility has sometimes prevailed, sometimes negotiation and sometimes co-option. Taking Kriesi's research (Kriesi et al. 1995: 61–7) as a point of departure once again, the position of the parties of the left has been a fluctuating one, particularly where the anti-nuclear movement is concerned. In France the Socialist Party (PS) sought to create a broad coalition, including the new movements, in the 1970s although its agreement with the French Communist Party (PCF) reduced its room for manoeuvre. Once in power, however, the Socialists abandoned certain movements, including the anti-nuclear one, while sponsoring others: the women's movement, the gay movement and, above all, the anti-racist movement. While in power in the 1970s, the German Social Democrats (SPD) had become more open to social movements but this changed when Helmut Schmidt took over as chancellor from Willy Brandt and as the economy began move in an unfavourable direction. Although the government did make a number of decisions compliant with new social movement demands (decisions blocked in certain cases by the *Bundesrat* or the Constitutional Court), conflict between the SPD and the social movement sector became more acute, particularly when protest came to focus on nuclear power stations. As the Green challenge mounted in the early 1980s, the SPD opened up once more to social movement issues and alliances became more frequent, particularly after the SPD returned to opposition in 1982. In the Netherlands the Social Democratic Party (PvDA) was already open to social movement influence in the early 1970s, to the extent that new left militants took control of the party, defining it as a 'party of action'. Between 1973 and 1977 the Social Democrats, part of a complex government coalition including liberal parties close to the social movement sector and more hostile Christian parties, followed a policy of protest prevention. In opposition again from 1977 their links with the movements became closer still, particularly on the issue of nuclear power. Although still in opposition, relations became more hostile after 1985 when the Social Democrats adopted a moderate strategy designed to allow a government coalition with the Christian Democrats (which eventually came about in 1989). In Switzerland the Social Democrats (SPS/PSS), in government continuously but always in a minority position, maintained an ambiguous attitude towards social movements. Although allied to social movements in the German-speaking cantons, the party maintained its distance in French-speaking cantons and it was here that the Green Party was born.

This brief description allows a number of the principal questions to emerge in the literature on the relationship between social movements and the parties of the left to be addressed. First, what explains the strategic choices made by the parties on the left? And second, what are the consequences of their attitudes for the emergence, strategy, mobilization capacity and chances for success of social movements?

What determines the attitudes of the old left to the new social movements? Attention has firstly been directed to ideological cleavages. While some have suggested that a rigid left–right division retards the development of new social movements (Brand

Table 8.2 *Protest and allies in France, Germany, the Netherlands and Switzerland*

Protest events supported by allies (%)

	France	Germany	Netherlands	Switzerland	Total
Old left	15.9	16.0	5.6	7.4	12.2
New left	5.7	11.0	3.9	5.8	7.6
Old and new left	17.9	20.2	6.4	9.8	15.0
Others	5.4	11.8	7.2	2.1	7.8
Total	21.2	24.9	10.9	11.5	18.8
Share of left	84.4	81.1	58.7	85.2	79.7
Number of events	775	1,770	863	772	4,180

Percentages of people mobilized in protest events supported by allies

	France	Germany	Netherlands	Switzerland	Total
Old left	70	41	56	11	37
New left	4	32	54	10	27
Old and new left	71	46	57	15	39
Others	4	29	26	1	16
Total	73	51	59	16	43
Share of left	97	90	97	94	91

Source: Adaptated from Kriesi et al. (1995: 68 and 69)

1985: 319), others have highlighted the stimulus provided by communist parties. Among the latter, Tarrow has argued that the parties of the left, in particular the Italian Communist Party (PCI), acted as 'offstage but creative prompters in the origins, the dynamics, and the ultimate institutionalisation of the new movements' (1990: 254). In general the old left appears more disposed to support social movements where exclusionary strategies have impeded the narrowing of the left–right divide. Returning to the data collected by Kriesi and his collaborators, table 8.2 shows that the activities of new social movements were supported more frequently by the traditional left in Germany and France than in the Netherlands and Switzerland: 21.3 per cent of protest actions were supported by external allies (the left in 84.4 per cent of cases) in France compared with an average of 18.8 per cent (the left in 80 per cent of cases), 24.9 per cent in Germany (the left in 81.1 per cent of cases), 10.9 per cent in the Netherlands and 11.5 per cent in Switzerland (Kriesi et al. 1995: 68).

Second, the existence of party divisions within the traditional left influences attitudes to social movements. Where class conflict is not institutionalized the left is frequently divided between a social-democratic (or socialist) and a communist party. Increasing the relevance of the working class vote, and therefore the use of class discourse and Marxist terminology, competition between social democrats and communists increases hostility to the middle classes, the social base of new movements, within the left (Kriesi 1991: 18). Conflict within the left leads social democrats to cultivate their links with the working class at the expense of new social movements and the latter's mainly middle-class core support. As the strategic turnaround of the German Social Democrats in the early 1980s shows, however, the presence of a substantial new left party such as the Greens will lead the traditional left to be more open towards social movements in an effort to reconquer those voters most sensitive to emerging issues.

In fact, electoral competition is an important variable in explaining the reaction of potential allies towards social movements. The propensity to support protest has been connected with electoral instability, which renders the winning of new votes particularly important. In fact, member–challenger coalitions are most probable in closely divided and competitive political situations (Tilly 1978: 213–14). Political instability favours protest movements: 'the political impact of institutional disruptions depends upon the electoral conditions. Even serious disruptions, such as industrial strikes, will force concessions only when the calculus of electoral instability favours the protesters' (Piven and Cloward 1977: 31–2). The success of the United Farm Workers in the United States, for example, has been explained by the electoral realignment which brought to power the liberal wing of the Democratic Party, particularly well disposed towards social movements (Jenkins 1985). From the 1950s on, the white, Protestant upper middle-class and the black electorate of the big cities began to abandon the Republicans and became increasingly volatile. As patronage politics became less and less effective, the traditional constituencies of New Deal politics, blue-collar workers, white ethnics, the Jewish community and Southerners were also moving towards the centre:

> The collapse of McCarthyism led to a leftward shift in electoral alignments and elite coalitions. In a series of closely divided elections, political elites found themselves competing for two new sets of restive voters: the newly urbanised blacks who were no longer wedded to the party of their grandfathers or their plantation masters, and the

new middle class that was increasingly non-partisan and interested in ideological visions. By the early 1960s, the Democratic Party had emerged as the victor, forging a loose coalition between these new contenders and the New Deal coalition. Democratic victories created new opportunities for insurgency, and after the 1964 electoral sweep, the Democrats were in a position to institutionalise a series of social reforms. (Jenkins 1985: 224)

It was above all electoral uncertainty which pushed the Democratic Party to work with social movements: 'In the context of a series of closely contested elections, in which the margin of victory was often less than one percent, the two swing voting blocs became increasingly decisive in the electoral calculations of political elites' (Jenkins 1985: 218). In fact, in such a situation 'parties court enfranchised voting blocs . . . Changes or instability in the partisan orientation of these voting blocs, especially those that promise the margin of victory, focus elite attention on the interest of these swing groups' (Jenkins 1985: 226).

Fourth, the position of the left towards social movements can be influenced by whether or not they are in government. Kriesi (1991: 19; see also, Kriesi 1989b: 296–7) has suggested that when in opposition social democrats take advantage of the push provided by social movements; in power, on the other hand, they are forced by budgetary and other constraints to limit their openness to emerging demands. To maximize their re-election chances they must privilege those economic questions which interest their hard-core vote. Out of power, the willingness of the left to support social movements grows with its needs to mobilize people around left-wing demands.

There is not always a correlation between participation in government and hostility towards social movements, however. In both Italy and Germany, for example, left-wing parties have been relatively sympathetic towards protest regardless of their 'proximity' to government (della Porta and Rucht 1995). Neither does the empirical research conducted by Kriesi provide unequivocal answers concerning the degree to which the left supported protest in or out of government. In fact, although in both Germany and the Netherlands the left facilitated protest action more frequently when in opposition than when in government (strongly and visibly in the first case, more weakly in the second), the exact opposite was true of France (Kriesi et al. 1995: 79). This ambiguity is particularly true as far as movements close to the traditional left, the pacifist movement or the movement against racism, are concerned.[14]

Rather than being in government or not, the attitudes of the parties of the left towards social movements are related to a fifth variable: their openness to reform politics. According to a comparative analysis of social movements in Italy and Germany, when both the PCI and the SPD were moving towards the centre between the 1970s and the 1990s, the movements of the libertarian left found fewer channels of access to the decision-making process (della Porta and Rucht 1995). Thus, the SPD–FDP coalition presided over by Willy Brandt in the early 1970s in Germany, which had a broad programme of reforms, was open to dialogue with social movements. Later on, the same coalition, now led by Helmut Schmidt, was driven to moderate its programme of reforms by an economic downturn and at the same time became 'cool' towards non-institutional actors.

It should be added that the actions of left-wing parties in government depend on their weight within the governing coalition. They are obviously freer to take decisions when governing alone. When in coalition with centre-right parties they will be forced to adopt policies less favourable towards the new social movements. When governing with other parties of the left, on the other hand, they will tend to adopt attitudes closer to these new collective actors. In France, for example, the early governments under François Mitterrand's presidency (coalitions with the Communist Party and with a majority in parliament) were more open to reform than later governments, involved in 'cohabitation' with a right-wing parliamentary majority. Many examples can also be found from the German *Länder*, where Red–Green coalitions have showed more willingness to accept social movement demands than coalitions of the SPD and FDP or, even worse in this respect, coalitions of the SPD and CDU.

However, leaving aside the question of their openness to influence by social movements, participation by left-wing parties in government would appear to have a negative effect on collective mobilization. In analysing data on Germany, France, Great Britain and the Netherlands between 1975 and 1989 and on Germany between 1950 and 1991, Koopmans and Rucht noted that right-wing protest increases under left-wing governments and vice versa. Since the right is generally less given to using protest, mobilization tends to be greater when there is a right-wing government than when there is a left-wing government (two times greater under Christian Democrat Chancellor Helmut Kohl than was the case under the Social Democrat Helmut Schmidt) (Koopmans and Rucht 1995). If the social movement literature has considered mobilization chiefly as a response to growing hopes for change (see, for example, Tarrow 1989a), these results suggest the importance of the potential risks of inaction. When faced with a government to which they feel closer, social movements (no longer 'powerless') tend to increase their use of direct pressure and reduce the use of protest. On the other hand, the risk of seeing their relative advantages attacked by a politically opposed government leads them to consider mobilization inevitable.

Turning to the second question, what consequences do the attitudes of potential allies have for social movements? It is widely held that the parties of the left play an important role, easing access to the decision making process and increasing social movements' capacity for mobilisation and chances of success. When the traditional left is hostile, on the other hand, social movements are politically emarginated.

The alliance with the traditional left has, first and foremost, reinforced social movements' capacity for mobilization. It has been noted that placing oneself on the left generally correlates positively with a willingness to use protest, particularly civil disobedience (Wallace and Jenkins 1995: 126). Because 'Leftism is consistently associated with left-party support' (1995), the position taken by left-wing parties tends to influence the levels of mobilisation of their social base. Indeed, left-wing activists are frequently involved in social movements as well as their own political party (see, for example, Kriesi and van Praag 1987). As can be seen from Table 8.2, the research of Kriesi et al. (1995: 69) showed that 43 per cent of participants in protest action were taking part in actions which had the support of allies (of the left in 90 per cent of cases). Some 71 per cent of people mobilized in France, 57 per cent in the Netherlands, 46 per cent in Germany and 15 per cent Switzerland were involved in events supported by left-wing allies. Looking at individual countries, it can be noted that mobilization increased in Germany in the 1980s, when the SPD abandoned a long period of hostility towards new social movements. In France, the Socialist Party's 'selective' approach killed off the anti-nuclear movement (thus hampering the emergence of the peace movement) but at the same time favoured the growth of the 'sponsored' anti-racist movement. Similarly, the weakening of support for social movements by the Dutch Social Democrats after 1985 led to a decline in mobilization.

The strategies of potential allies also affect the strategies of social movements themselves. First, the presence of powerful allies tends to have a moderating influence on social movement tactics. It is no accident that the moments of greatest political violence in Italy and Germany coincided with hostility on the part of the SPD and the PCI towards social movements in the second half of the 1970s (della Porta 1995; della Porta and Rucht 1995). Indeed, isolation and radicalization tend to be mutually reinforcing. The more isolated a social movement is, the greater the doubts that change can be realized in the short term will be, and the greater the need for ideological substitutes for missing material incentives. Thus, social movement strategies become more extreme. The wider the base of support, on the other hand, the more the risk of losing support acts as a restraint on the use of violence.[15] The more radical a movement, the greater will be the propensity of traditional left parties, scared by the risk of alienating their moderate voters, to assume a hostile attitude. It should be added that attempts at co-option tend to transform the whole organizational and ideological structure of social movement families. In Italy, for example, between the late 1960s and the early 1980s, a tendency towards co-option on the part of a powerful Communist Party caused an ideology and an organizational structure heavily influenced by the traditional left to prevail within the social movement sector (della Porta 1996a).

If, then, support from the parties of the left appears to influence levels of mobilization and the strategies adopted, the question relating to chances of success remains open. Despite the difficulties involved in evaluating the results obtained by social movements (to be dealt with in the next chapter), from everything said so far it is more than probable that a left-wing government would be more favourably disposed towards many of the demands put forward by the new social movements than a government of the right. In particular, memories of repression experienced in the past tend to make the left more liberal in matters of public order (della Porta 1998b). The left in power, moreover, tends to support demands which are moderate and on issues which are compatible with those of their traditional voters (Kriesi et al. 1995: 59).[16]

In conclusion, the presence of powerful allies is generally a factor facilitating social movement success. In many cases alliance with the left considerably enhance the mobilizing power of protest. However, the price of this is a kind of tutelage on the part of the left which can lead, particularly when the left is in power, to a diminution in protest.

8.5   The Political Opportunity Structure: Potential and Problems

The explanatory power of the concept of political opportunity structure has been amply demonstrated by the studies already cited. While research has concentrated on the contemporary western democracies, many of the hypotheses developed might profitably be applied to other historical periods and geo-political regions. Notwithstanding its actual and potential utility, however, a number of problems need to be considered.

First, there is a lack of consensus on the political opportunities which are relevant (McAdam 1996) and the result has been exponential growth in the concept's dimensions (della Porta 1996c). Early studies of political opportunities focused on a small number of variables. In the 1980s, however, a number of case studies and cross-national comparisons have referred to the political opportunity structure, frequently adding new variables to the original set (see, in particular, Brand 1985; Kitschelt 1986; Rucht 1989; Kriesi 1991). This has expanded the explanatory power of the concept, but reduced its specificity. The concept runs the risk of becoming a 'dustbin' for any and every variable relevant to the development of social movements. Most of the concept's problems arise from the way in which it has been developed, picking up variables from a variety of studies on a variety of movements. This accumulation of heterogeneous variables reflecting different authors' concerns and ideas has resulted in a concept which, to quote Sartori (1970; see also Sartori 1990), denotes much but connotes little. Particularly in international comparative studies it is impossible to handle the large number of variables and assess properly their explanatory power.

A further problem is represented by the fact that the distance between the variables indicated as part of the political opportunity structure and their assumed effects on social movements is so great that it is frequently difficult to show the logical connections between the two. Since movements do not react to abstract categories such as electoral volatility, but to a limited set of derivates (Koopmans 1990), the latter need to be properly identified.

A third problem arises when we wish to distinguish between 'objective' reality and its social construction (Berger and Luckmann 1966). Some changes in the political opportunity structure do not have any effect on a social movement unless they are perceived as being important by the movement itself. Structural availability must be filtered through a process of 'cognitive liberation' in order to unleash turmoil (McAdam 1986). For protest to emerge, activists must believe that an opportunity exists, that they have the power to bring about change and they must blame the system for the problem. Looking at structural opportunities without considering the cognitive processes which intervene between structure and action can be very misleading (Gamson and Meyer 1996). It is important, therefore, to analyse activists' understandings of available opportunities, the lenses through which they view potential opportunities for their movements (McAdam, McCarthy and Zald 1996). Perceptions of state response may be particularly influenced, for instance, by its more dramatic manifestations, such as repression, causing the less visible responses, such as negotiation, to be overlooked (della Porta 1996c).

Fourth, there is a lack of clarity concerning the explanandum. The political opportunity structure has been investigated in order to explain a growing number of dependent variables. Political opportunities have been used to explain social movement mobilization (Eisinger 1973), the emergence of the protest cycle (Tarrow 1983), the relationship between allies' attitudes and movement behaviour (della Porta and Rucht 1995) and the predominance of either confrontational or assimilative protest strategies (Kitschelt 1986: 67–8). And, indeed, from what has been said here it is clear that the character of institutions, prevailing strategies, choices on repression and alliance structure are all useful for explaining one or other of the characteristics of social movements. Few attempts have been made up until now, however, to address the question of which variables in the complex set, 'political opportunity structure', explain which (of the numerous) characteristics of social movements. If it cannot resolve these problems it is perhaps time that research and theoretical reflection at least took them up (in this context, see the essays collected in McAdam et al. (eds) 1996).

8.6 Summary

Among the many environmental variables which can influence social movement characteristics, the structure of political opportunity has received a great deal of attention. In particular, diachronic, cross-national comparative research has discussed the characteristics and effects of four groups of variables relating to: (1) political institutions; (2) political culture; (3) the behaviour of opponents of social movements; and (4) the behaviour of their allies.

The institutional variables most frequently discussed have related to the formal openness of the decision-making process. Starting from the hypothesis that the greater the number of points of access the more open the system, the relevance of the distribution of power and the availability of direct democracy have been discussed. Informal characteristics, and, in particular, traditional strategies of interaction with challengers, were considered as well as structural characteristics. Neither of these (tendentially stable) dimensions, however, are well adapted to explaining conjunctural events such as the rise and decline of protest or the mobilizing capacity of social movements. As far as the consequences of collective action are concerned, the formal or informal openness of the decision-making system does not automatically privilege emergent demands because institutions are also potentially open to social movements' opponents. Although the effects of the stable political opportunity structure in terms of social movement success thus appear ambiguous, the effects on the strategies adopted by movements seem less equivocal. The greater the opportunities of access to the decision-making system, the more social movements tend to adopt moderate strategies and institutional channels.

The conjunctural characteristics of conflict and alliances would appear to have a significant influence on the emergence of protest and on mobilization potential. Prevailing styles of protest policing, together with movement/counter-movement interaction, influence the rise of protest and movement strategies. Harsh and indiscriminate repression tends to lead to radicalization, whereas tolerant and selective control of protest produces growing rejection of more violent tactics. Alliances with the parties of the left and the trade unions provide important resources for social movements and increase their chance of success.

If the concept of political opportunity structure has assumed a central role in social movement research, its use has not been without problems: the number of elements considered relevant has constantly increased, the distance between the phenomena analysed and their presumed effects is often too great to allow the causal dynamics of protest to be understood; little attention has been paid to subjective perceptions of reality; the explanandum, the particular characteristic of a social movement influenced by the variables under examination, has not always been clearly identified. Recent research has begun to address these problems.

9
Social Movements: What Consequences?

The United Nations conference held in Beijing in the summer of 1995 once more recalled that the history of humanity has been one of continual discrimination against one half of the species: women. Gender, income, education and many other criteria, once the basis of legal discrimination, have continued to operate informally in modern, formally democratic societies (Zincone 1992: 187–9). The effects of the delayed acquisition of civil, political and social rights by women can still be seen in their subordination within the nuclear family, an institution which has long impeded their acquisition of rights as individuals. Family law has for a long time subordinated women to their husbands or fathers. Not only have strict prohibitions on contraception and abortion denied women the right to choice on child-bearing, but it was the father who was given authority over children once they were born. Discrimination against women in the field of civil rights can, in part, be explained by unequal access to political decision-making.[1] Research on voting patterns suggests that fewer women than men vote and that they participate less frequently in other conventional forms of political activity such as campaigning for political parties or membership of political organizations. Paradoxically, for a long time, women voted disproportionately for precisely those parties opposed to their emancipation. In the classic studies of participation women appeared less knowledgeable of, and less interested in, politics (see, for example, Verba et al. 1978). A consequence of the particular attitudes women have about politics has been that 'women's importance declines the nearer to the real locus of political power one goes' (Randall 1982: 69). In national parliaments and government women are consistently under-represented, and where they are represented they are usually confined to 'women's issues', such as welfare or family affairs.[2] The strong female presence in political parties and trade unions is not reflected at the level of office-holders. While women represent a growing majority of employees in the public administration, they rarely rise within the hierarchy, a scenario repeated in other labour markets. Women are also discriminated against socially. Traditionally, women have been the first to be expelled from the labour market in times of crisis. Female workers were openly discriminated against for a long time, receiving lower wages and less job protection. Women are still over-represented in lower-status jobs and in the least prestigious sectors of the labour market. Women are also expected to work for nothing in the reproductive sphere.

Since the 1960s, however, conditions for women have changed dramatically, at least in the 'First World'. Family law has been changed to give women equal rights within the family in most western democracies. Contraception and sex education are now freely available. Abortion is legal in the majority of western democracies, with certain exceptions and limitations on women's choice. In the political sphere research has indicated not only that gender differences in voting patterns are narrowing but also that women's participation in politics is selective and that they are more involved in decentralized political activities. Women are conspicuously present in less conventional political activities, particularly campaigns which focus on local and community issues.[3] The presence of women in local elected assemblies is also increasing, and a new, professional type of woman politician with greater experience is emerging. While equal social rights for women have certainly not yet been achieved, legal restraints at least have been abolished. Discrimination on the basis of gender is, in most cases, prohibited by law. Indeed, some states have introduced positive discrimination or even quotas for women. Looking at the young, women would appear to be at least as, if not better, educated than men.

Most of these transformations have followed the birth of the women's movement and its expansion on an international scale. Emerging from critiques of the 'male chauvinism' of new left organizations within the student movement, the feminist movement developed rapidly. Although it has been considered a movement more concerned with self-transformation than changing the world, subcultural rather than instrumental (Rucht 1994), the women's movement, nevertheless, achieved considerable institutional success as well.

At first sight, then, the women's movement appears to confirm the Chicago School's prediction that social movements are an important vector for change. Considering social movements as vehicles for social and political transformation, a number of authors have attempted to indicate in classifications and typologies the components of social movement success, frequently returning to the distinction made by one of the first scholars to work in this field, William Gamson, between new gains and levels of acceptance. The first refers to tangible changes in public policy on issues raised by protest, the second to changes movements bring about in the system of interest representation. Gamson (1975) combined these two variables into a typology of success distinguishing between: (1) full response, both gains and acceptance; (2) co-optation, recognition without gains; (3) preemption, gains without recognition; and (4) collapse, neither gains nor acceptance.[4]

In what follows we will use the women's movement to illustrate the potential and limitations of research on the outcomes produced by social movements. First, the difficulties movements face in identifying victorious strategies will be considered (9.1). Changes in policies (9.2) and in politics (9.3) will then be discussed. In section 9.4 one particular effect of social movements, the spread of protest beyond national boundaries, will be analysed. Considering also the 'wider reproduction of protest' *within* states (a process which has led to talk of a 'social movement society'), the fact that social and political modernization appears to have increased non-institutional actors' potential for intervention in the distribution of political power will also be discussed (9.5).

9.1   Social Movement Strategies and Their Effects

An analysis of the effects they produce is an integral part of the study of social movements as agents of social change. Different movements have achieved different degrees of success, and discussion concerning what determines the outcomes they achieve has been central to the debate on social movements. A number of social movement characteristics have been frequently cited as particularly influential in this respect. In general, research has concentrated on three questions: are movements which propose radical change more successful than those which propose moderate change or vice versa? Does violence work? Is a centralized and bureaucratic organization a help or a hindrance for social movements? In one of the first and most influential studies on the effects produced by the strategies social movements adopt, William Gamson (1990) identified the factors contributing to success as a minimalist strategy ('thinking small'), the adoption of direct action and a centralized and bureaucratic organization. This has not been unanimously accepted by other scholars of collective action, however. As already noted in relation to forms of action, violence has appeared a promising strategic choice at certain historical moments. Gamson himself has admitted (1990) that wider objectives reinforce internal solidarity and favour the creation of alliances. Finally, it has been pointed out that all organizations, including social movement organizations, tend to become bureaucratized and the desire for organizational survival comes to prevail over declared collective objectives. According to Francis Fox Piven and Richard Cloward (1977: xxi–xxii) the effort to build organizations is not only futile but damaging: 'by endeavoring to do what they cannot do, organizers fail to do what they can do. During those brief priods in which people are roused to indignation, when they are prepared to defy the authorities to whom they ordinarily defer . . . those who call themselves leaders do not usually escalate the momentum of the people's protest'. The search for material resources to ensure organizational survival leads inexorably towards the elites, who are happy to offer such resources precisely because they know it will serve to reduce the potential threat to the social order represented by its weaker members. However, it has been remarked that no particular strategic element can be evaluated in isolation and without taking into account the conditions within which social movements must operate (Burstein et al. 1995). And indeed, the identification of a 'strategy for success' is an arduous task both for activists and for scholars.

Consider the case of the women's movement. A number of studies have attributed the movement's success in the United States to its ability to create a strong pressure-group structure autonomous of both political parties and the state (Gelb 1989: 187). In the United States, unlike Great Britain or Sweden, avoiding confrontation combined with the use of protest action and securing a place in relevant policy networks allowed American feminists to achieve incremental success (Gelb and Palley 1982: see also, Boles 1991; Tarrow 1994: 184). But is this the 'winning' strategy, and, more importantly, can it be exported to other countries? Evaluating the success or failure of particular movements and their strategies presents a number of very difficult problems. First and most important, the attribution of particular interests to movements is not self-evident and it is often the case that movements which are judged successful from the outside are considered to have failed by the activists of the movements themselves. In fact, the demands made by social movements change. Frequently, the radical aims which predominated during the phase of constructing a collective identity give way to more moderate ones. Feelings of dissatisfaction have often been noted in relation to the women's movement, for instance, notwithstanding the important gains that were made (see, for example, Hellman 1987: 205). The simultaneous presence of a large number of objectives also makes it difficult to estimate what has been achieved on various fronts. Thus, policies for protecting women in the labour market and on social welfare appear better developed in Europe than in the United States, where the welfare state is weak.

The attribution of credit for obtaining substantive successes also faces a series of obstacles (Tarrow 1994; Rucht 1992; Giugni 1997; Diani 1997). The principal problem is one well known to social scientists: the existence of such close relationships between a set of variables that it becomes impossible to identify cause and effect. Urbanization and industrialization, for example, have facilitated organization by intensifying physical contacts. They have weakened certain sources of socialization and solidarity and favoured the development of others (for an overview, see Sztompka 1993; also chapter 2). Better educational provision has increased awareness of grievances and made defending one's own interests appear legitimate. An increasingly effective communications system spreads information on mass mobilizations throughout the world. Movements are born in the course of these transformations and contribute to them. In the case of the women's movement, too, social change and collective action are part of a single process: modernization. Social and economic development create the preconditions for gender equality: new technology reduces the domestic workload and (through birth control) the size of the family; mass education improves the resources available to women; secularization removes cultural obstacles to the integration of women in the labour market. And indeed women's participation in the labour force and in education has been found to foster feminist opinions (Banaszak and Plutzer 1993). The women's movement has grown alongside an increase in marital instability and a fall in fertility levels (Klein 1984). For its part, the women's movement has pushed forward economic, social and political emancipation.

Second, the presence of a plurality of actors makes it more difficult to attribute success or failure to one particular strategy (Diani 1997). Social movements are themselves complex actors, composed of many organizations pursuing profoundly different strategies. It is this interweaving of organizational models and diverse strategies which favours success. As noted concerning the protest cycle, every movement tends to utilize the gains made by other movements. Most importantly, movements are never the sole actors to intervene on an issue. Rather, they do so in alliance with political parties and, not infrequently, with public agencies. The policy choices of other social and political actors, for instance, are important in explaining the level of women's participation in politics. The preferences of the party or parties in government have a major impact on levels of women's pay and occupational segregation, as well as controversial positional issues such as reproductive rights and welfare (childcare facilities, for example) (Norris 1987: 73, 107). Furthermore, the left in power has created more political opportunities for women. As Norris remarks, it was 'Mitterrand who initiated the Ministry for Women's Rights in France, Papandreou, leader of Pasok, who created the Greek Council for Equal Rights, and the Labour Party which set up the Equal Opportunities Commission to monitor equal pay in Britain' (Norris 1987: 4; see also Katzenstein 1987: 6). In Southern Europe in particular, the principal institutional and cultural changes to affect women's conditions have been introduced by governments, either at local or national level, led by parties of the left (della Porta, Kousis and Valiente 1996). Thus, 'the outcome of bargaining is not the result of the characteristics of either party, but rather is the function of their resources relative to each other, their relationships with third parties, and other factors in the environment' (Burstein, Einwohner and Hollander 1995: 280). The results obtained by social movements have often been explained by environmental conditions, particularly the openness of the political opportunity system and the availability of allies. It is difficult nonetheless to identify which of the many actors involved in a given policy area are responsible for one reaction or another. If, as suggested earlier, the protest cycle is characterized by a large number of interactions, the results obtained will be the effect of that large number of interactions. Thus, it is always difficult to establish whether a given policy would have been enacted through other institutional actors anyway.

Thirdly, the difficulties created by a plurality of actors are added to by the difficulty of reconstructing the causal dynamics underlying particular public decisions. On the one hand, events are so intertwined that it is difficult to say which came first, particularly in moments of high mobilization. On the other, social movements demand long-term changes but the protest cycle stimulates immediate 'incremental' reforms. When social movements successfully place particular issues on the public agenda this 'does not happen directly or even in a linear fashion. In fact, as their ideas are vulgarised and domesticated, the early risers in a protest cycle often disappear from the scene. But a portion of their message is distilled into common frameworks of public or private culture while the rest is ignored' (Tarrow 1994: 185). This evolution is characterized by steps forward and steps back, moments in which public policy approaches the demands made by social movements and others in which the situation deteriorates.

Whether the results of protest should be judged in the short or in the long term represents a further problem. Social movements frequently obtain successes in the early phases of mobilization, but this triggers opposing interests and a backlash in public opinion is set in motion. Thus, while it is true that there is a broad consensus on many of the issues raised by social movements (peace, the defense of nature, improvements in the education system, equality), mobilization can nevertheless result in the polarization of public opinion. This normally produces a growth in movement support but very often there is also a growth in opposition. Furthermore, as noted in the preceding chapter, movement success on specific demands frequently leads to the creation of counter-movements. For instance, the victories of the women's movement on the abortion question has resulted in the formation of counter-movements which claim that the foetus is fully a person and defend the sanctity of life against the pro-choice position in many countries. Whether remaining in the shadow of powerful institutions such as the Catholic Church or taking to the streets to influence legislators and public opinion,

counter-movements have sometimes been successful in overturning the gains made by their movement opponents (Staggenborg
1991).

Particularly where comparison is being made between different movements or countries, the problems outlined above hinder
an evaluation of the relative effectiveness of particular movement strategies. There is also a problem, naturally, with the attribution of particular results to more institutionalised actors such
as political parties and pressure groups.[5] Factors particular to
social movements such as their distance from the levers of power,
lack of clarity in their objectives and organizational instability
further complicate matters. In what follows, therefore, we will
not attempt to identify winning strategies but rather to consider
some of the consequences of interaction between social movements and their environment.

9.2 Changes in Public Policy

A first area for measuring the effects produced by social movements is that of actual policy, as the example with which the
chapter opens showed. Generally, social movements are formed
to express dissatisfaction with existing policy in a given area.
Environmentalist groups have demanded intervention to protect the environment; pacifists have opposed the culture of war;
students have criticized selection and authoritarianism in education; the feminist movement has fought discrimination against
women. Although it is usual to make a distinction between political and cultural movements, the first following a more instrumental logic, the second more symbolic, all movements make
demands on the political system.

A particular demand frequently becomes the basis for a movement's identity and non-negotiable. In many countries, for example, the feminist movement has been constructed around the
non-negotiable right of women to 'choose' concerning childbirth;
the halting of the installation of NATO nuclear missiles fulfilled
a similar role for the peace movement. In the first case mobilization was pro-active, seeking to gain something new, the right to
free abortion. In the second it was reactive, seeking to block a
decision (to install Cruise missiles) which had already been taken.
In both cases, however, considerable changes in public policy
were being demanded. Characteristic of these non-negotiable objectives is their role in social movements' definitions of themselves

and of the external world (Pizzorno 1978). Demands whose symbolic value is very high, such as the Equal Rights Amendment in the case of the American feminist movement, remain central for a movement even when their potential effectiveness is questionable (Mansbridge 1986). The importance of such non-negotiable objectives is confirmed by the fact that although activists may be willing to negotiate on other demands, even partial victories on these issues, such as a woman's right to voluntarily interrupt pregnancy, are considered as defeats.

While non-negotiable demands are particularly important in the construction of collective identities, social movements rarely limit themselves to just these. Many others are usually added. In the case of the women's movement demands have emerged on a whole series of issues besides abortion, from changes in family law to censorship of pornography. In general new actors joining an expanding movement bring with them particular sensibilities which become concrete in a specific set of objectives. Taking the women's movement once more, alliance with trade unions focused attention on a series of questions related to protection in the labour market and the workplace; in the same way, the formation of lesbian groups opened up the question of civil rights for homosexuals. These additional demands are often so numerous, varied and durable that they come to form areas of public policy in their own right. Policy networks, the various individuals who collaborate for one reason or another in the formation of public policy in a particular sector, interact within the various policy arenas, the political spaces in which public policy is developed and implemented. If the women's movement is once more a pertinent example of this, it is far from the only one. A similar process is revealed on environmental and youth issues.

From the public-policy point of view, the changes brought about by social movements may be evaluated by looking at the various phases of the decision making process: the emergence of new issues; writing and applying new legislation; and analysis of the effects of public policies in alleviating the condition of those mobilized by collective action. Five levels of responsiveness to collective demands within the political system can be distinguished:

> The notion of 'access responsiveness' indicates the extent to which authorities are willing to hear the concerns of such a group . . . If the demand . . . is made into an issue and placed on the agenda of the political system, there has occurred a second type of responsiveness

which can here be labelled *'agenda responsiveness'* ... As the proposal ... is passed into law, a third type of responsiveness is attained; the notion of *'policy responsiveness'* indicates the degree to which those in the political system adopt legislation or policy congruent with the manifest demands of protest groups ... If measures are taken to ensure that the legislation is fully enforced, then a fourth type of responsiveness is attained: *'output responsiveness'* ... Only if the underlying grievance is alleviated would a fifth type of responsiveness be attained: *'impact responsiveness'*. (Schumaker 1975: 494–5, emphasis added)

The level at which analysis has concentrated in research on social movements has been the production of legislation. As a recent review of the literature noted, most 'studies focus on policy responsiveness, fewer on access responsiveness, and very few on the political agenda, outputs, policy impact, or structural change' (Burstein et al. 1995: 285). Having identified a series of areas in which movements intervene, quantitative and qualitative analyses attempt to measure the response of parliaments and governments. Returning to the example of the women's movement, a great deal of legislation has been produced since the 1970s on such matters as maternity rights, the legalization of contraception and divorce, family law, family planning centres, equal opportunities, abortion and violence against women.

An analysis of the concrete effects of social movements can begin, therefore, from the production of legislation. This is not enough, however. As noted in discussion of social movements and the political opportunity structure, different states have different capacities for implementing legislation and it is precisely from the implementation of legislation that concrete gains are achieved. In order to evaluate the results produced by a social movement, therefore, it is also necessary to analyse how the laws they helped bring about are actually applied. Implementation of laws on the voluntary interruption of pregnancy, for example, has varied a great deal from country to country. The same kind of formal condition allowing legal abortion (physical or psychological obstacles to continuing a pregnancy, for example) have been interpreted in restrictive ways in some countries, or even regions of the same country, and more permissively in others. The specific circumstances of individual public-health systems and the regulation of conscientious objection on the part of medical and paramedical staff has influenced the application of the right to voluntarily interrupt pregnancy. The situation in relation to equal opportunities is similar. Legislation in many countries has given women access to professions once considered the sole preserve of men, whether it be driving a bus or flying a 747. However, the capacity for removing obstacles to effective labour market equality, such as working hours or levels of physical exertion, have proved different from one country to another.

Real change, the effects produced by legislation however implemented, is even more difficult to judge. Laws which seek to meet certain of the demands of social movements may be limited in effect or even counterproductive, no matter how well implemented. Legislation on female unemployment and under-employment, considered by many a response to recurrent waves of protest, is a good example. Intervention in the labour market does not always produce the hoped-for encouragement of particular categories of workers because influence on the decisions of individual employers is limited. Thus, laws on protection in the workplace and on equal pay may simply discourage the hiring of women. Moreover, legislation in a particular area frequently fails to take account of changes in contiguous or related ones. In Italy, for example, new legislation in the 1990s obliged political parties to alternate a man and a woman in candidate lists. Yet women made up only 14 per cent of those elected to the following legislature, dropping further to 9 per cent in the next. In fact, the introduction of a semi-majoritarian system for parliamentary elections in the meantime had disadvantaged female candidates.

Alongside structural changes in the condition of those categories or social groups mobilized by collective action, cultural transformation is a further important element in achieving and consolidating new gains. Although it is true that all movements tend to request legislative change, it is also true that this is not their only, nor even perhaps their primary, objective. The effects of social movements are also connected with diffuse cultural change, the elaboration of 'new codes' (Melucci 1982; 1984a). While the capacity of social movements for 'thematization', the 'importation' of new issues into public debate, has been considered high, their capacity for 'realization' has been considered low. It is useful, therefore, to look at a movement's 'sensitizing impact', the 'possibility that a movement will provoke a sensitizing of some social actor in the political arena or the public arena, which goes in the direction of the goals of the movement' (Kriesi et al. 1995: 211). As has just been mentioned, a law on equal opportunities is unlikely to succeed in changing conditions for women unless it is accompanied by a legitimation of women's role outside the family and unless there is no general mistrust in women lawyers or doctors. Furthermore, social movements are more aware than some better-resourced actors of their need for public support. Since protest mobilization is short lived, social movements cannot content themselves with legislative reforms that can always be reversed later. They must ensure that support for their cause is so widely diffused as to discourage any attempt to roll them back.

It should be added that social movements aim not only to change public opinion. They also seek to win support among those responsible for implementing public policy, changing the values of political elites as well as those of the public. Although mass mobilization may temporarily convince political parties into passing a law, that law must also be applied. In this case also, social movements do not always have sufficient means of access to the less visible areas of policy implementation and their chances of success therefore depend on influencing the public agencies responsible for implementing the laws which concern them. From this point of view, the success of the women's movement has been linked to a growth in support in both elite and public opinion for women's participation in the professions and for equal pay, and growing opposition to sexual harassment in its various forms (Boles 1991).

9.3 Social Movements and Democracy

Social movements do not limit their interventions to single policies. They frequently influence the way in which the political system as a whole functions: institutional and formal procedures, elite recruitment, the informal configuration of power (Kitschelt 1986; Rucht 1992). Movements demand, and often obtain, decentralization of political power, consultation of interested citizens on particular decisions or appeals procedures against decisions of the public administration. They increasingly interact with the public administration, presenting themselves as institutions of 'democracy from below' (Roth 1994). As a comparative study of the anti-nuclear movement in eight countries noted:

> For reasons of this conflict relocation, collective protest at times assumes a mediated, representative form. New, 'protest' actors – playing the parts of 'movement representatives' – enter the stage: movement members, movement leaders, movement spokespersons, movement lobbyists and movement experts and so on, whether

Table 9.1 *Methods of political action of environmental organizations (% of organizations that use a certain form of action)*

	Often	Sometimes	Rarely	Never
Contacts with the media	86	13	2	–
Informal contacts with civil servants or ministers	53	34	11	1
Contacts with MPs/parliamentary committees	53	36	9	2
Contacts with local government authorities	45	38	14	3
Participation in the work of government commissions and advisory agencies	41	30	20	9
Formal meetings with civil servants or ministers	36	52	9	3
Contacts with the leaders of political parties	11	44	30	16
Direct actions	25	23	28	23
Legal recourse	20	19	30	31

Source: Adapted from Dalton (1994: 183)

(s)elected, appointed or self-proclaimed, hired or volunteer, take on the task of presenting the views and demands of a movement. (Flam 1994a: 18)

As table 9.1 shows, almost every Western European environmentalist group maintains contacts with bureaucrats, ministries, parliamentarians and parliamentary committees; many participate in governmental commissions; many also have informal contacts with government ministers and bureaucrats (Dalton 1994: 180).[6] Protest, only a small part of overall social movement activity, is undoubtedly considered important, but also ineffectual unless accompanied by more traditional lobbying activities. Although contacts with government ministries and the public bureaucracy may not be seen on their own as particularly effective in influencing policy, they are considered useful for information gathering and for countering the influence of anti-environmentalist pressure groups. As we shall see in what follows, social movements increase the possibilities of access to the political system, both through ad hoc channels relating to certain issues and through institutions which are open to all non-institutional actors.

First, as we have already noted, social movements contribute to the creation of new arenas for the development of public policy. These new loci of decision making vary in terms of their openness, duration and extent of power. They have two things in common, however: their legitimation is not based on the principles of representative democracy and they have greater visibility than institutional spheres of decision-making. In the first place, expert commissions are frequently formed on issues raised by protest and social movement representatives may be allowed to take part, possibly as observers. The 'President's Commission on Campus Unrest' which William Scranton presided over in the United States (in 1970) is one example. Others are the commission led by Lord Scarman into rioting in the United Kingdom in the 1980s and the commission of inquiry set up on 'Youth Protest in the Democratic State' in Germany (Willelms et al. 1993). Common to them all is a recognition that the problems they address are in some way 'extraordinary' and require extraordinary solutions. Although such expert commissions usually have a limited mandate and consultative power only, they enter a dialogue with public opinion through press contact and the publication of reports.

Besides commissions of enquiry, other channels of access are opened by the creation of consultative institutions on issues related to social movement demands. State ministries, local government bureaux and other competent bodies now exist on women's issues in many countries. For instance, under-secretariat on women's issues, commissions on family problems, women's advisory boards, equal opportunities committee were set up in most democratic countries. Such institutions, which are frequently set up on a permanent basis, have their own budgets and power to implement policies. They tend to have frequent contacts with representatives of the social movements involved in their areas, the movements taking on a consultancy role in many instances, and they sometimes develop common interests. The public administrators working in these institution mediate particular social movement demands through both formal and informal channels and frequently ally themselves with movement representatives in order to increase the amount of public resources available in the policy areas over which they have authority.

Third, in many countries direct democracy acts as a supplementary channel of access to those opened within representative democracy. On issues such as divorce or abortion, for example, the women's movement was in many cases able to appeal directly

to the people using either popularly initiated legislation or referenda for the abrogation of existing laws. Referenda have become
an increasingly important instrument of direct expression for
ordinary citizens, particularly on issues which are not directly
related to the social cleavages around which political parties
have formed. Referendum campaigns present social movements
with an opportunity to publicize the issues which concern them,
as well as the hope of being able to bypass the obstacle represented by a political system hostile to their demands. With the
exception of simply consultative referenda, this form of intervention, based on a direct expression of views by the electorate,
carries a great deal of power but is limited to single questions. In
fact, to a greater or lesser extent in different countries restric-
tions on calling referenda limit the range of application of direct
democracy, often concentrating attention on questions which are
not of central importance to social movements. In addition, the
duration of a campaign to mobilize public opinion is generally
short, concentrating on the period immediately preceding the
referendum itself.

From an institutional point of view, creating such channels for
intervention can represent an alternative to repression, which
becomes almost inevitable when conflict is primarily expressed
in the streets and public order is threatened. Information campaigns, expert-dominated decision-making or deliberations and
contest arenas have in common the capacity to 'socialize' the
issues raised by a social movement (Flam 1994b). The capacity
to develop such strategies of conflict socialisation seems particularly sensitive to democratic consolidation: the more consolidated
democracy is, the greater will be the willingness of elites to negotiate with emergent actors.

> Two different style of conflict management can be distinguished. A
> typical 'old pact' encounter trajectory in the nuclear conflict excluded
> the use of force in contrast with a typical 'new pact' encounter traject-
> ory. 'Old pact' elites tended not only to refrain from the use of force,
> but also tended to risk, sooner or later, the socialisation of conflict. In
> contrast, the 'new pact' elites avoided the risk of conflict socialisation
> and, if at all, engaged in very modest democratic experiments. They
> sooner or later opted for the use of force. (Flam 1994b: 348)

However, the two methods of conflict management – negotiation and repression – are frequently used either contemporaneously or sequentially. The creation of commissions of enquiry

normally follows the failure of repression, for example. As Willelms, Wolf and Eckert have pointed out, such commissions 'were themselves part of the process in which the problems were defined and the agenda set ... their very formation indicated that the routine praxis of the political system of decision making did not suffice, so that it was necessary to call for experts from the scientific institutions' (Willelms et al. 1993: 12). In this sense, they also demonstrated the limitations of the political parties as mediators in social conflict. However, in 'no win' situations the creation of other arenas parallel to parliament allows the parties to transfer the costs associated with decision-making to the public administration, the courts or to experts (Rochon and Mazmanian 1993).

But what exactly do these new arenas offer social movements? According to some authors the presence of such channels of access presents more risks than advantages. In the first place, movements are induced to accept the shifting of conflict from the streets to less congenial arenas where resources in which they are lacking, such as technical or scientific expertise, are particularly important. The organization of a commission may be nothing more than a symbolic elite gesture to their constituencies and a means of putting off a decision until quieter times prevail (Lipsky 1965). Indeed, the creation of new procedures and institutional arenas can be seen as a means of co-opting movement elites and demobilizing the grassroots (if they are naïve enough not to notice the deception) (Piven and Cloward 1977: 53). Moreover, ably manipulated experts can be used to legitimate as most 'scientifically appropriate' those solutions which suit government. Finally, referenda carry the risk that decisions will be made by the 'silent majority', uninterested in (and uninformed about) the issues and problems raised by social movements and therefore easily influenced by those with the most resources to devote to manipulating the consensus.

On the other hand, it needs to be said that social movements have frequently been able to profit (partly through alliances with experts and policy makers) from the switching of decision making to ad hoc commissions, certainly more open to public scrutiny than the normal arenas of policy implementation. New issues have been brought onto the public agenda through the work of such commissions: 'Commissions were themselves part of the process during which the problems were defined and the agenda set ... Their very creation indicated that the normal praxis of the political system to make decision was insufficient, and that it was therefore necessary to appeal to the experts belonging to the scientific institutions' (Willelms et al. 1993). Although social movements have not always been on the winning side in referenda, the latter have, nonetheless, contributed to putting new issues on the public agenda and to creating public sympathy for emergent actors. The ability to transform the rules of the political game, then, is a precondition for influencing public policy. In other words, procedural victories come (at least in part) before, and are indispensable for, successes on a more substantive level (Rochon and Mazmanian 1993).

Leaving aside the results obtained on particular demands, it must be added that the spread of new policy arenas has contributed to the realization of what has been considered one of the principal aims, if not the principal aim, of social movements: the creation of a new conception of democracy. In fact, it has been claimed that social movements do not limit themselves to developing special channels of access for themselves but that, more or less explicitly, they expound a fundamental critique of conventional politics, thus shifting their endeavours from politics itself to meta-politics (Offe 1985). From this point of view, social movements affirm the legitimacy (if not the primacy) of alternatives to parliamentary democracy, criticizing both liberal democracy and the 'organized democracy' of the political parties: 'The stakes and the struggle of the left and libertarian social movements thus invoke an ancient element of democratic theory that calls for an organisation of collective decision making referred to in varying ways as classical, populist, communitarian, strong, grassroots, or direct democracy against a democratic practice in contemporary democracies labelled as realist, liberal, elite, republican, or representative democracy' (Kitschelt 1993: 15). According to this interpretation, social movements assert that a system of direct democracy is closer to the interests of the people than liberal democracy, based on delegation to representatives who can be controlled only at the moment of election and who have total authority to decide between one election and another. Moreover, as bearers of a neo-communitarian conception of democracy, social movements criticize the 'organized' democratic model, based on the mediation by mass political parties and the structuring of 'strong' interests, and seek to switch decision making to more transparent and controllable sites. In the social movement conception of democracy the people themselves (who are naturally interested in politics) must assume direct responsibility for intervening in the political decision-making process.

It is certainly the case that the idea of democracy developed by social movements since the 1960s is founded on bases at least partly different to representative democracy. According to the representative democracy model, citizens elect their representatives and exercise control through the threat of their not being re-elected at subsequent elections. The direct democracy favoured by social movements rejects the principle of delegation, viewed as an instrument of oligarchic power, and asserts that representatives should be subject to recall at all times. Moreover, delegation is general in a representative democracy, representatives deciding on a whole range matters for citizens; delegation relates only to a particular issue in a system of direct democracy. It is up to citizen assemblies to define the objectives to be pursued as the occasion arises. Whereas representative democracy foresees the creation of a specialised body of representatives, direct democracy opts for continual turnover. Representative democracy is based on formal equality (one person, one vote); direct democracy is participatory, the right to decide being recognised only to those who demonstrate their commitment to the public cause. While representative democracy is often bureaucratic, with decision making concentrated at the top, direct democracy is decentralized and emphasizes that decisions should be taken as near as possible to ordinary people's lives.

In this sense, social movements are also a response to problems which have emerged in the system of interest representation, 'compensating' for the tendency of political parties to favour interests which pay off in electoral terms, and of interest groups to favour those social strata better endowed with resources while emarginating the rest. Direct democracy, on the other hand, should give a voice to those with neither material resources nor strength of numbers but who are committed to the just cause. While the principal instrument in the hands of citizens in representative democracy is the vote, direct democracy legitimates all those forms of bringing pressure to bear on the decision-making process that we have defined as protest repertoires.

In the late twentieth century social movements have indeed been able to introduce changes which move towards greater grassroots control. In many European countries administrative decentralization has taken place since the 1970s, with the creation of new channels of access to decision makers. Various forms of participation in decision making have been tried within social movement organizations. If the rise of mass political parties has been defined as a 'contagion from the left' and the democracy of the mass media as a 'contagion from the right', the new social movements have been acclaimed as a 'contagion from below' (Rohrschneider 1993a). Social movements have brought about a pluralisation of the ways in which political decisions are taken, pushed by cyclical dissatisfaction with a 'realist', centralized and bureaucratic representative democracy. In this sense, social movements have produced a change in political culture, in the whole set of norms and reference schemes which define the issues and means of action that are politically legitimate. Repertoires of collective action which were once condemned and dealt with simply as public order problems have slowly become acceptable (della Porta 1998b).

Can it be said, then, that social movements have contributed to the evolution of democracy? As Charles Tilly noted (1993–4: 1), there are two different conceptions of the role played by social movements in the process of democratization. According to the 'populist approach to democracy', emphasizing participation from below, 'social movements contribute to the creation of public space – social settings, separate both from governing institutions and from organisations devoted to production or reproduction, in which consequential deliberation over public affairs take place – as well as sometimes contributing to transfers of power over states. Public space and transfers of power then supposedly promote democracy, at least under some conditions'. To the 'populist' approach is counterposed an 'elitist' approach according to which democratisation must be a top–down process, while that an excess of mobilisation leads to new forms of authoritarianism. We can agree that social movements contribute to democratization only under certain conditions. In particular, only those movements which explicitly demand increased equality and protection for minorities promote democratic development. In fact, looking at the process of democratization it can be observed that collective mobilization has frequently created the conditions for a destabilization of authoritarian regimes, but it can also lead to an intensification of repression or the collapse of weak democratic regimes, particularly when social movements do not stick to democratic conceptions. While labour, student and ethnic movements brought about a crisis in the Franco regime in Spain in the 1960s and 1970s, the worker and peasant movements and the fascist movements which opposed them contributed to the failure of the process of democratization in Italy in the 1920s and 1930s (Tarrow 1995).

As far as the social movement critique of existing democracy is concerned, their search for an alternative cannot be considered concluded as yet. Not all students of social movement organizations agree that they have overcome the risk of producing oligarchies and charismatic leaders, the very problems at the centre of their critique of traditional politics. Although it maximizes institutional responsiveness, the direct democracy model has weaknesses as far as representation and efficiency are concerned (Kitschelt 1993). The problem of efficiency affects primarily the activities of movement organizations themselves. The problem of representation, on the other hand, is more important as concerns the legitimation of new forms of democracy. The refusal by social movements to accept the principles of representative democracy can undermine their image as democratic actors, particularly when they begin to take on official and semi-official functions within representative institutions, assuming the form of parties or public interest groups.[7] Moreover, looking beyond the movements themselves, the functioning of many new democratic institutions also presents a number of problems. Decentralized institutions are frequently too fragmented to have any real power or are just as bureaucratic and distant from ordinary people as national governments. Furthermore, if certain loci of power have become more transparent, others are progressively less so. Although it is true that certain repertoires of action have been legitimized, others (those involving violence, for example) are increasingly stigmatized and there is a danger that certain forms of protest will come to be seen simply as a public order problem (della Porta 1998a).

These limitations notwithstanding, it should be recognised that social movements have helped in opening new channels of access to the political system, contributing to the identification, if not the solution, of a number of representative democracy's problems.

9.4 The Cross-national Diffusion of Protest

Social movements act upon the environment around them, but their actions also have internal consequences. As noted in earlier chapters, social movements have effects on their own members. They also have effects on themselves as collective actors, on their organizational stability and on their ideology (Rucht 1992). New tactics are tried, ideologies are refined and organizational structures modified during the course of a protest campaign. Mobilization does not simply 'consume' movement resources, it also contributes to their reconstitution. This section will consider a particular kind of effect produced by social movements: the expansion of the social movement sector through a process of cross-national diffusion.

Like scientific or technological innovations, social movement ideas set in motion a process of diffusion:[8] 'Protest makers do not have to reinvent the wheel at each place and in each conflict . . . They often find inspiration elsewhere in the ideas and tactics espoused and practised by other activists' (McAdam and Rucht 1993: 58). Ideas concerning organizational structure, strategies of action or definitions of the world 'travel' from movement to movement, sector to sector, city to city, centre to periphery and, on occasions, periphery to centre. Diffusion can be either direct or indirect depending on whether they come about through unmediated contacts between movement members or are mediated by the mass media (Kriesi et al. 1995: 185). In the former case, they can also take the more formal shape of organisational exchanges (Kriesi et al. 1995, ch. 8). In addition, diffusion can come about through either unconscious or conscious imitation. In the past it has been claimed that collective behaviour spread through 'circular reactions', the responses of each individual reproducing the stimuli coming from his neighbour (Blumer 1951: 170). However, since the 1970s it has been recognized that the 'interpretative interaction' underlying more institutional forms of political participation are also present in protest. More rational processes such as identification and imitation are also present alongside more instinctive mechanisms such as suggestibility and circular reaction (Turner and Killian 1987). The greater awareness of the actors involved should favour, although it cannot automatically insure, the success of mobilization. As the next section will make clear, the diffusion of protest at both national and international level appears to have increased social movement strength, offering them an autonomous infrastructure. For the moment, however, we will concentrate on the effects social movements produce across national borders.

Comparative research has increasingly highlighted the existence of striking similarities between kindred movements in different countries (see, for example, della Porta and Rucht 1995). These similarities can be explained by both internal variables (the issues movements confront influence their strategies) and external factors (such as an increasing convergence of the environments in which movements must work). There is a further explanation, however: similarities are frequently deepened by interaction between movements in different countries. In fact, social movement ideas not only spread within national borders but also (in a process which is in part similar) beyond them. From this point of view, some movements produce effects on similar movements in other countries. The student movement in the 1960s, the feminist movement in the 1970s and the peace movement and the ecologic movement in the 1980s are all examples of what have been called 'global' movements, developing contemporaneously throughout the world and displaying significant similarities in different countries. Going further back in time, the revolutions of 1848 and the anti-slavery movement were collective phenomena which grew to cover more than one continent. However, while this may be considered a general tendency, it is also true that the process of diffusion does not involve all movements equally, nor is the exchange always symmetrical.

First, it is more likely that diffusion will take place between countries which are close together geographically. In fact, interaction will tend to be strongest between neighbouring countries. There are more links between the Scandinavian countries than between Denmark and Italy, for example. Geographical proximity is not always important, however. The past must also be taken into account. It is more likely that diffusion will take place between movements from countries with a history of past interaction; between movements in Italy and France, for example, rather than between movements in Italy and Ireland. Besides direct interaction itself, the 'cultural understanding that social entities belong to a common social category [also] constructs a tie between them' (Strand and Meyer 1993: 490). Similarities in social and political structure must also be taken into account. Thus, diffusion is more likely between Great Britain and the United States than it is between Great Britain and India, say, even if the latter is a part of the British Commonwealth. Finally, the status of the 'transmitting' country also has a certain importance. In fact, in the social movement sector as in others moving from centre to periphery, from the 'first' to the developing world, brings a reduction in influence.

All of the characteristics just mentioned influence both the direct diffusion through personal interaction emphasized by the traditional literature and the indirect diffusion by way of the media noted in more recent studies (Strand and Meyer 1993). As far as direct interaction is concerned, geographical proximity,

historical interaction and structural similarities all tend to produce language and laws which facilitates direct contacts between
the activists of parallel movements. Unmediated exchanges are
rendered more probable by the existence of cross-border associations, cultural exchange programmes, linguistic knowledge
or even a common language. To give a couple of examples, it is
not strange that the Italian women's movement imported certain elements from the French movement (particularly its psy-
choanalytic current) through contacts between Italian and French
feminists (Passerini 1988) or that some of the American student
movements strategies arrived in the Federal Republic along with
German students returning from study trips there (McAdam and
Rucht 1993).

The various levels of proximity discussed above also favour
the development of more formal contacts and organised channels
of communication. More particularly, relations will become more
formal after personal contacts have permitted initial exchanges to
take place and as the movements become increasingly structured.
Diffusion of ideas can then take place through the translation of
movement documents, the organization of international conferences, the creation of computer networks and so on. Mediated
forms of diffusion therefore take on increasing importance. It has
been noted that in the 1960s the process of diffusion between
student movements was initiated through personal contacts but
that 'once established, this identification enabled diffusion to take
place via a variety of nonrelational channels. These channels
included television, newspapers, and writings of both a schol-
arly and a radical nature' (McAdam and Rucht 1993: 71).

Geographical and cultural proximity is also important in producing functional equivalence, similarity in the situation of the
'transmitting' and 'adopting' movements, considered to be a factor in facilitating the process of diffusion. Furthermore, the same
elements facilitate the social construction of that similarity, the
definition of their situation as similar to that of the 'transmitter'
on the part of 'adopters' (Strand and Meyer 1993). Regardless of
actual similarities, the subjective perception of common circumstances leads to an idea being considered relevant and adopted.
The passage of ideas from the American student movement (the
'transmitter') to its German counterpart (the 'adopter') was facilitated by the existence of common elements in the two groups'
collective identities (McAdam and Rucht 1993). Similarly, the
theory of 'sisterhood' held by the women's movement favoured
the development of cross-national contacts.

The traditions of particular movements also help to explain a greater or less propensity to exchange information and to 'copy' each other at the international level. Despite appeals to internationalism, for example, the conviction that their destinies were more closely linked to those of capitalists in their own country than they were to workers in other countries appears to have prevailed in national labour movements. Environmentalist groups, on the other hand, have always been conscious of the difficulties in providing national solutions to environmental problems which spread from one country by way of polluted rivers and air. Thus, even today labour organizations appear to have more problems in acting within international bodies such as the European Union than do environmentalist groups (Marks and McAdam 1998).

If the degree of cross-national diffusion is influenced by the more or less cosmopolitan nature of movement identities, the latter bear the marks of the environment they faced as they emerged. Thus, if national labour movements are highly differentiated in their forms of organisation and action, this is also because they were aware, as they were in the process of forming, of marked differences between countries. The growing similarity of external conditions brought about by globalization, on the other hand, have facilitated the process of diffusion for new social movements. Contact between different movements has grown alongside the realization that certain problems can only be tackled at international level. This has resulted in the creation of a series of international organs (inter-governmental organizations, or IGOs) which may not be able to substitute for the nation-state but are capable of exercising some influence over agenda setting, the solutions adopted to particular problems and the formulation of recommendations to national governments. The creation of IGOs has in turn favoured the birth of transnational social movement organizations (TMSOs) specialized in supranational-level action.

The presence of these international organizations has also facilitated exchange between national movements. Movements with a particular dearth of resources, social movements under authoritarian regimes for example, have interacted with movements based in democratic countries or at supranational level in an attempt to improve their relative position. This cross-national mobilization has been aided by the fact that while formally the numerous IGOs have an extremely closed political opportunity structure (usually their members are not even elected), at an informal level they are more open because they possess an organizational culture which privileges compromise (della Porta and Kriesi 1998). On issues such as human rights or protection of the environment, social movements easily find allies within these institutions, exchanging technical information and legitimation to support their demands (Passy 1998; Smith 1998).

9.5 Social Movements and the Distribution of Power

In previous chapters the possible effects of both internal (organization) and external (political opportunities) characteristics of social movements were considered, beginning an analysis of the questions which have been more systematically dealt with in the present chapter. Having looked at the effects produced by social movements in terms of both policies and politics, and having drawn attention to their capacity for spreading protest, the present section will consider the consequences of collective mobilization on the distribution of power within society.

The question of social movements and power has chiefly emerged in local studies. Reference to the distribution of power, a central question for the social sciences, is implicitly made in many studies on social movements, and is made explicitly in the case of the much-cited work of Lipsky. According to the elitist conception, represented by Floyd Hunter (1953), for example, power is unequally distributed within the community. A leadership which is cohesive and not particularly visible (in the sense that its members do not always occupy public positions) concentrates power over various sectors, obstructing the entry of newcomers into the centres of decision-making. With power concentrating in restricted and largely invisible clubs, social movements would seem doomed to failure in most cases. A strong, cohesive and centralized power would be very difficult to dent in the absence of a temporary alliance with part of the elite. According to the influential work of Francis Fox Piven and Richard Cloward, for example, 'protesters win, if they win at all, what historical circumstances has already made ready to be conceded' (1977: 36). While the poor may obtain certain concessions in the early stages of protest through threatening insubordination, these very concessions will tame them and can then be withdrawn: 'when protest subsides, concessions may be withdrawn. Thus when the unemployed become docile, the relief rolls are cut . . . when the ghetto becomes quiescent, evictions are resumed' (1977: 34–5). Thus only those changes considered by the holders of power themselves as useful in bridling the insubordination of the masses will remain.

The pluralist conception of power whose principal exponents are Robert Dahl (1961) and his disciples has been counterposed to this elitist conception. According to the pluralist school, in the United States and more generally in advanced capitalist societies, elites are numerous, visible and institutionalized and their power is limited to specific arenas. Power resources are distributed among various groups which are frequently in conflict among themselves for control of particular decisions. Above all, the need to obtain the consensus of citizens (who therefore have a power of veto) places limits on the options available to decision makers. The result is an openness and responsiveness to new challengers. Given that no particular group has absolute power, emerging actors will easily find allies and therefore access to the political system. The impossibility of any one group obtaining its objectives without help from other groups will favour team playing: 'Because one center of power is set against another, power itself will be tamed, civilised, controlled and limited to decent human purposes' (Dahl 1967: 24). Since institutional channels of access to decision making are available, protest would be a strategic error (McAdam 1982: 6).

The so-called neo-elitists have criticised both these approaches, insisting that notable barriers exist for non-elite groups in gaining access to the decision making process. According to these authors, by 'mobilizing prejudice' in order to prevent awareness of problems from actually arising, a powerful elite can successfully stop certain issues dangerous for them from entering the public arena. In their analysis of the politics of poverty in Baltimore, for example, Peter Bachrach and Morton Baratz (1970: 63) found that despite undoubted improvements in their material conditions, Afro-Americans had not been able to gain access to the decision-making process. In his study of the New York rent strike, which proposed to 'assess the validity of the concept of American politics that viewed the system as responsive and open to the political demands of dispossessed groups' (1965: ix), Michael Lipsky reached similarly pessimistic conclusions. According to Lipsky, poor and marginal groups, having by definition little in the way of status or resources, are frequently kept out of decision-making arenas. Their chances of success depend chiefly on a variable internal to the government organizations they seek to influence: the need of government agencies to defend their budgets by manipulating their environment. If marginal groups manage to ally themselves with the constituencies of these government agencies they have some chance of receiving a response from them. These responses do not always go in the directions desired by marginal groups themselves, however. The authorities may in fact elaborate a complex series of responses which serve in substance to distribute symbolic satisfaction to their constituencies without affecting the material conditions of the poorer groups. Lipsky criticized the observations of the pluralists, concluding that it was highly unlikely that poorer groups could make themselves heard by policy-makers (1965: 201). Continual experience of frustration thus renders the apathetic and disinterested reaction of marginal groups to politics quite rational. The only solution would be to reinforce the organization of groups directly involved in protest, but this would be extremely difficult to achieve.

It should be added, however, that according to Lipsky's research certain conditions (which he himself considers exceptional) such as a particular sensitivity on the part of the public and certain public agencies to the issues involved in protest can lead to success. Moreover, both Piven and Cloward and Bachrach and Baratz admit that under certain circumstances challengers can put together a sufficient quantity of resources and alliances to overcome the barriers which defend the dominant value structure. Bachrach and Baratz in particular, borrowing hypotheses developed in other disciplines, propose a view of the decision making process as an incremental one. Once current prejudices have been transformed, new values are legitimized in a lasting manner (1970: 87).

Debate on the chances of social movements obtaining positive results has been more optimistic recently, although hardly to the point of suggesting that a pluralist position will return to favour in the sociology of social movements. Students of social movements have undoubtedly inherited the scepticism of elitists and neo-elitists concerning the openness of the decision-making process; social movements are, after all, the form of organization of the weakest groups in society. However, recent research has highlighted the fact that, as we saw in the present chapter, many groups once considered particularly deprived of organisational resources and identity (such as women) have improved their relative position, acquiring channels of access to the decision making system. In fact, from this research it would not appear possible to define protest, as Lipsky did, as a resource exclusively of the poor.

More particularly, two conditions considered as limiting social movement potential, at least as far as instrumental action is concerned, are in the process of changing: weak organizational structures and the absence of channels of access to the political system. In fact, mobilization would appear to be a resource replenished by use. Analyses of the evolution of left-libertarian movements concluded that different movements have developed in a similar direction, from the formation of a collective identity to its utilization in the political system (see, for example, della Porta 1996a). New movement organizations have emerged during this process and have, on occasions, survived the decline in mobilization. While public interest groups exploit the occasion offered by the creation of new channels of access, small counterculture nuclei keep alive and re-elaborate movement values within a structure of networks. This process has important effects on the social movement family. Most social movements survive the decline of mobilization, oscillating between visibility and latency (Melucci 1989: 70–3), within a larger family of movements, the organizational infrastructures and mobilization potential of which they help to increase. The 'force' of collective identities can vary, some stronger (the women's movement), others weaker (the youth movement); some relatively visible (the environmentalist movement), others less so (the peace movement); some have a stronger presence at national level (the anti-nuclear movement), others at local level (the urban movements); some are more political (federalist movements), others cultural (punks and skinheads). It rarely happens that a movement disappears leaving no cultural or organizational trace whatsoever.

Social movement resources increase over time, therefore, and movements become institutionalized, construct subcultural networks, create channels of access to policy makers and form alliances. This organizational continuity means that the experience of 'early riser' movements represent both resources and constraints for those which follow (Tarrow 1994; McAdam 1995). Processes of imitation and differentiation, of enforced repetition and of learning, take place contemporaneously. Movement activists inherit structures and models from their predecessors. At the same time, however, they learn from the errors of movements which have preceded them and seek to go beyond them. The greater the success achieved by 'early riser' movements and the greater the participation of ex-activists in subsequent mobilizations, the greater will be the continuity with the past.

The tendency towards the institutionalization of social movements and their diffusion as a form of organizing and mediating interests can be explained by the diffusion, with each wave of mobilization, of the capacities required for collective action. In fact, mobilization is facilitated by the presence of networks of activists willing to mobilise around new issues, where these are 'compatible' with their original identities, naturally. Moreover, the substantive gains made by one movement can have beneficial consequences for the demands of other movements and their success encourage further mobilizations. It can be concluded, therefore, that the importance of social movements tends to grow in as much as there is an ever-increasing amount of resources (both technical and structural) available for collective action.

9.6 Summary

Social movement mobilization has been followed by change in a variety of areas. As far as public policy is concerned, a great deal of legislation on issues raised during protest campaigns has been produced. Any evaluation of the significance of the changes introduced by these laws requires analysis of their implementation as well as of transformations in the value system and in the behaviour of both ordinary citizens and elites. Changes in public policy have been accompanied by the creation of new decision-making arenas, no longer legitimated by the model of representative democracy. Ad hoc commissions, new government ministries and local government committees constitute channels of access to the decision-making process frequently used by social movement organizations. Emerging elements which emphasize participation over representation thus enrich the concept of democracy. The process of cross-national diffusion has created stable organizational structures for social movements. Many of the transformations which have interacted with the development of social movements depend on a wider process of modernization of a complexity which hinders understanding of the causal dynamics which exist between particular phenomena. Although the variety of objectives, strategies and actors involved in this process renders it difficult to identify winning strategies for new collective actors, it can, nevertheless, be said that in recent decades the structure of power in liberal democracies appears to have been transformed in the direction of greater recognition for emerging interests.

Notes

1 The Study of Social Movements

1 In reality, the origins of the collective behaviour perspective are somewhat older, representing an evolution of symbolic interactionism and of the Chicago School; however, it acquired new vigour from the late 1950s onwards.

2 Eyerman and Jamison (1991). Christian Joppke (1993: 8) has emphasized this point in his comparative study of anti-nuclear movements in the United States and Germany.

3 This section is based largely on earlier work by Donatella della Porta (1996d).

4 There are, for example, differences which cannot be overlooked among scholars usually associated with the resource mobilization paradigm, such as Mayer Zald and John McCarthy (1987), on the one hand, and Anthony Oberschall (1993), on the other.

5 For example, in the work of William Gamson one can identify both interactionist influences (see, in particular, Gamson 1992a) and rationalist influences (see, in particular, Gamson 1990).

6 For example Alberto Melucci, one of the key figures in the development of the 'new social movements' perspective, has become increasingly detached from it. Conversely, theoreticians of resource mobilization such as John McCarthy (1994) are paying ever greater attention to the cultural production of movements.

7 Although this is not strictly a 'new' perspective, it forms the theoretical basis for the recent flowering of 'culturalist' approaches to the study of movements (Snow and Oliver 1995).

8   A number of prominent studies have made explicit reference to perspectives which we have not addressed here. Among many possible examples, see the re-evaluation of the Durkheimian approach proposed by Piven and Cloward (1992) or the redevelopment of the theory of relative deprivation undertaken by Rüdig (1990) in his study of anti-nuclear movements.

9   Theories of frustration and deprivation – to which we will make only fleeting reference in the course of this book – have decreased in importance from the 1970s onwards, and have become entirely marginal in the analysis of social movements in democratic societies. They have, however, maintained some relevance in comparative, large-scale analyses of social conflict (Gurr and Harff, 1994).

10   This is a much revised edition of a book originally published in 1957. In the new edition, Turner and Killian integrate some contributions of the resource mobilization school into their own model.

11   Attention to the link between collective behaviour and various indicators of social change (for example, the tendency towards large-scale organizations, population mobility, technological innovation, the growing relevance of the mass media, the fall of traditional cultural forms) connects this view to functionalist perspectives, but the interpretation provided is different. The processes of change reviewed are considered to be emerging conditions which encourage individuals to mobilize, not in order to re-establish an equilibrium which has been disturbed but, rather, to develop new ways of life and new types of social relationship.

12   Blumer comments, 'Sociology in general is interested in studying the social order and its constituents (customs, rule, institution, etc.) as they are. Collective behavior is concerned in studying the way in which the social order come to existence in the sense of the emergence and solidification of new forms of collective behavior' (Blumer 1951: 169).

13   See, for example, Gusfield's research (1963) into the prohibitionist movement, considered as an area of conflict between social systems, cultures and groups of different status.

14   This has led to a research programme whose continuity over time is demonstrated by the work of scholars such as Joe Gusfield (1963, 1981, 1994) and which has become particularly influential (Melucci 1989, 1996; Eyerman, Jamison 1991; McPhail 1991; Johnston and Klandermans 1995).

15   Charles Tilly (1978: 53) has spoken, in this context, of movements as 'challengers', contrasting them with members of a given polity.

16   See Scott (1990: particularly chapter 3) for an excellent synthesis of the main positions developed by this approach.

17   For several applications of this perspective in empirical researches on contemporary movements, see, for example, Touraine et al. (1981); Touraine et al. (1983a); Touraine et al. (1983b).

18   Many of the principal exponents of this approach have, however, modified their position. Offe (1990) has, for example, recognized the influence of traditional-style political action on the practices of the

movements. Melucci has come to concentrate on the mechanisms by which certain representations of the world and of individual and collective identities are produced and transformed over time (1989; on this point, see Bartholomew and Mayer 1992). Moreover, he has gone as far as to declare the debate of the 'newness' of contemporary movements to be outdated or irrelevant (see, for example, Melucci 1994).

19   This section is largely based on earlier work by Mario Diani (1992c).

20   Kriesi referred to the youth movements which developed in Zurich in the 1980s.

21   This makes it necessary to treat with some caution the results of surveys which claim to measure the extent of movement membership (Kriesi 1992).

22   It goes without saying that the real influence of the individual participant will depend largely on the personal resources (competence, prestige etc.) which he or she is able to control.

23   For an introduction and a definition, see Hinckley (1981: 4–6).

24   Here, we are clearly referring not to empirical phenomena defined conventionally as 'movements' but to the specific social dynamic whose characteristics we have attempted to delineate in this chapter.

25   They include, first, analyses dedicated to various types of collective behaviour: from religious movements (Wilson 1982; Robbins 1988) and counterculture (Yinger 1982) to voluntary action (Ranci 1992; Pearce 1994); from political violence and terrorism (della Porta 1990) to right-wing movements (Lo 1990; Ignazi 1994); not to mention analyses of the working-class action itself (for example, Pizzorno et al. 1978; Touraine 1985; Kimeldorf and Stepan-Norris 1992; Franzosi 1995). To these we must add research, conducted from a historical perspective, into phenomena ranging from nationalism (Smith 1981; Breuilly 1983; Hobsbawm 1991; Petrosino 1991) to revolutions (Skocpol 1979; Tilly 1993); from social conflict in the pre-modern age (Goldstone 1991; Somers 1993) to 'non-class' movements of the modern period (D'Anieri et al. 1990; Amenta and Zylan 1991; Calhoun 1993; D'Anjou 1996). See also the increasing body of work devoted to contemporary movements outside western democracies (Eckstein 1989; Escobar and Alvarez 1992; Shah 1990; Omvedt 1993; Joppke 1994; Foweraker 1995; Zirakzadeh 1997).

26   This would, moreover, be an arduous task, as other earlier attempts have shown (Rucht 1991a).

2   Social Movements and Structural Changes

1   We are not making any claim about the absolute or relative novelty of these phenomena (see later in this chapter). We are satisfied with noting that the rise of interest in environmental issues in the 1960s did not merely imply the revitalization of previous forms of civic involvement on these problems (Lowe and Goyder 1983; Dalton 1994). Also, the

view of the environmental movement presented here is entirely sche-
matic and selective. Its purpose is simply to illustrate possible differences between this type of conflict and conflicts with a socio-economic
base. In reality, the environmentalist world is, obviously, much more
heterogeneous (Dalton 1994; Diani 1995a; Jamison et al. 1990; Lowe
and Goyder 1983; Rohrschneider 1988, 1993b; Rucht 1989; Rüdig 1990;
Touraine et al. 1983a).

2 See Markoff (1996) for a broad historical account of the development
of social movements in contemporary society.

3 It would be impossible to try to synthesize an enormous body of literature such as that about recent transformations of industrial society.
Sparse – and admittedly, uneven – references to specific processes will
be found throughout the text. For a few syntheses: Lash and Urry
(1987); Crook et al. (1992); Kumar (1995); Castells (1996).

4 On the new middle class – or service class, as some refer to it – see
among many others Bell (1973); Gouldner (1979); Goldthorpe (1982);
Lash and Urry (1987); Esping-Andersen (1993); Brint (1994).

5 The experience of so-called 'industrial districts' – small areas characterized by specific industrial activities, which are based on densely
interwoven networks of social relationships (Piore and Sabel 1984;
Streeck 1992; Trigilia 1984) – seems to contradict the claim regarding
the de-localization of economy. However, the conditions for working-
class action do not appear to be favourable in those contexts, given
the density of ties between different social groups, and the resulting
increased opportunities of social control (Oberschall 1973).

6 See Giddens (1990) for a concise treatment of this point.

7 For different interpretations of globalization processes, see Featherstone
(1990); Waters (1995); Scott (1997). On changes in civil society see also
Keane (1988).

8 For example, in the Basque country or in Catalonia.

9 Examples are the phenomenon of squatting or, more recently, the invasion of abandoned industrial plants by alternative groups: from this
point of view, radical youth centres could be seen as no-go areas, or at
least as self-organized areas removed from institutionalized mechanisms of social control (Lyons 1988; Sanchez Jankowski 1991; von Dirke
1997).

10 For example, the effective political participation of women is limited
by persistent inequalities in the division of domestic responsibilities
(Lovenduski and Randall 1993; Siltanen and Stanworth 1984; Zincone
1992). On the role of women in modifying the boundaries between the
public and the private sphere, see also Showstack Sassoon (1987).

11 See Cartuyvels et al. (1997); Tondeur (1997); Rihoux and Walgrave
(1997). On that occasion, the parents of the murdered children were
the chief promoters of the protest activities.

12 Historically, the affirmation of the welfare state marks the passage
from a notion of (civil and political) rights understood, first, as 'against'
the state, to a notion of rights which presuppose cooperation 'with' the

state (Barbalet 1988). With the rise of multiculturalism, however, and, more generally, with the critique of the colonialization of the private sphere, the relationship with welfare and in general with state intervention becomes at the same time one of cooperation (in as much as one can identify positive elements in the expansion of welfare action) and of antagonism (in the need to limit the effects of standardization and control).

13   The most systematic treatment of the relationship between social movements and transformations in the private sphere is still that of Alberto Melucci, to which we refer readers (1989, 1996).

14   It should not be forgotten that we are dealing with the reinforcement of a process already set in motion in the industrial society. See among innumerable sources Featherstone (1995); Maffesoli (1995); Melucci (1996).

15   See, among others, Garofalo (1992); Redhead (1993); Jordan (1994); McKay (1996). Reference to recent countercultural or subcultural phenomena such as rap or rave should not hide the broader relationship which can be found between musical genres and different types of political protest (Eyerman and Jamison 1994, 1997).

16   In the course of his long intellectual career, Touraine has proposed a number of versions of his approach (1977, 1981, 1984, 1985, 1992). Here we are referring principally to the formulation put forward during the 1970s, which inspired the research programme 'Intervention Sociologique' (Touraine et al. 1983a; Touraine et al. 1983b). For a synthesizing but systematic presentation of Touraine's contribution see Rucht (1991b), as well as Touraine's response (1991).

17   Similar themes are found in the work of Habermas (1976); Melucci (1989); Giddens (1990), among others. For a critical synthesis, see Scott (1990).

18   See, in particular, Melucci (1989, 1994, 1996). For a critical but sympathetic discussion, see Bartholomew and Mayer (1992). It has to be said that later developments in Melucci's work seem to focus much more on the structural processes – in particular, the individualization process – which prevent the reproduction of traditional collective action, rather than on the structural preconditions for the development of new forms of collective action. The latter is, rather, explained in the light of the presence of interpersonal networks acting as facilitators, the relationship of which to structural dynamics is, however, somewhat underdeveloped.

19   While the rise of the new middle class has been a central theme of sociological debate since the 1970s, the empirical investigation of its relationship with political action has been a major, albeit not exclusive (e.g. Bechofer and Elliott 1985), interest of political scientists. See, among many others, Dalton (1988, 1994); Kitschelt (1989), Kitschelt and Hellemans (1990); Jennings et al. (1990), Poguntke (1993), Nas (1993), Rohrschneider (1988, 1993b), Inglehart (1990a) and Wallace and Jenkins (1995).

20 On the one hand, individuals who fulfil a supervisory function, rather than managers in a narrow sense, and, on the other, semi-professionals and highly qualified craft workers are included in the new middle class (1989b, 1993).

21 This definition includes human service professionals with other socio-cultural specialist figures which were previously treated in a different way (Brint 1984). See also Cotgrove and Duff (1980).

22 This is, in other words, the distinction drawn by Kriesi (1989b: 1,082) between 'technical specialists' (scientists, programmers, engineers etc.) and 'craft specialists' (highly qualified manual workers).

23 In particular, in a sample of 1,848 individuals, interviewed in 1987 (Kriesi 1993: 14).

24 With the partial exception of participation in liberal-bourgeois parties (Kriesi 1993: 105).

25 See Crompton (1993) for a summary of this traditional dilemma in class analysis, opposing notions of classes as aggregates to notions of classes as collective actors.

26 This uncertainty could also depend on the various operationalizations of the concept of new middle class adopted by the studies quoted here, not to mention the dependent variable selected. While Kriesi analysed the potential for mobilization in various types of new social movements, studies such as that of Wallace and Jenkins concentrate on a form of action – political protest – which, though particularly wide-spread among movements is certainly not limited to them. Extreme caution in the comparison of results obtained in different studies is required. See Kriesi (1992b) for a discussion of how different criteria for the operationalization of the potential for mobilization of the various social movements can influence the results of the analysis.

27 As Chris Rootes suggested (personal communication to the authors), this might well be due to the peculiar traits of the Dutch left, where both the small parties on the far left of the political spectrum and the more mainstream Labour Party have shown early attention to environmental, peace, and other new social movement issues.

28 Several of them have actually been mentioned in the previous pages. Additional references include Bruce (1988); Gallagher and Bull (1996); Wilcox (1996); Stefancic and Delgado (1996); Watts (1997).

29 See, for example, Pizzorno (1981) and Tarrow (1994). From a different perspective, see also Calhoun (1993) and D'Anieri et al. (1990).

3 The Symbolic Dimension of Collective Action

1 Among many others, see on Germany Watts (1997) and Koopmans (1997). On France: Orfali (1990); Ignazi and Ysmal (1992). On Italy: Gundle and Parker (1996); Diamanti (1993). For a comparative per-spective: Betz (1993, 1994); Kitschelt (1995); Koopmans (1996a).

2   It may seem odd to make reference to what is, ultimately, a political party, in order to introduce the question of the role of cultural production in movements. Nevertheless, as the League began to operate as a 'challenger' (Tilly 1978), destabilizing from the outside the structure of the Italian political system, it seems to us that it provides useful features for theoretical reflection on the study of movements and of collective action, in the broadest sense (see also Diani 1996).

3   The basic battery of items used to measure the level of materialism–postmaterialism consisted of four goals to place in a hierarchy: maintaining order in the nation, giving people more say in important government decisions, fighting rising prices, protecting freedom of speech (Dalton 1988: 75–95). In Europe, the surveys were conducted by opinion polls of European citizens, sponsored by the European Community and subsequently the European Union and known as Eurobarometer. There is data on values changes from 1970 onwards for six countries: France, Great Britain, Italy, West Germany, Belgium and the Netherlands (Inglehart 1990b). Surveys have gradually been extended to an ever-increasing number of countries, within and without the western world (Inglehart 1997).

4   See, apart from the texts by Inglehart already cited, Müller-Rommel (1985, 1989, 1990); Poguntke (1993); Rochon (1988); Rohrschneider (1988, 1993b); Dalton (1988, 1994); Opp (1990); Steel et al. (1992).

5   For an exchange of views on this point, see Boltken and Jagodzinski (1985) and Inglehart (1985).

6   On this point, see again Dalton (1988: 85, n. 2).

7   We use the term 'generation' here in the sense originally proposed by Karl Mannheim (1946), not as a specific age group but as a cohort of the population which has experienced and remains influenced by particular historical events. See also on this theme Braungart and Braungart (1992), Turner (1994), Pakulski (1995), Whittier (1995, 1997).

8   This aspect of Inglehart's analysis has also been criticized, precisely for neglecting analogies between the development of cultural change in the period following the Second World War and other periods over the last two centuries in which expressive orientations have led to change (K. W. Brand 1990; Inglehart 1990b).

9   According to two critics: 'Because [Inglehart's] index assumes that one cannot simultaneously embrace both postmaterialist and materialist values, the fundamental question of whether postmaterialist and materialist values necessarily exclude one another . . . is simply assumed' (Brooks and Manza 1994: 546).

10 For discussions directly related to the role of new politics, see, among others, Middendorp (1992) and Kriesi (1993).

11 On this point, among many others: Klandermans (1988); Melucci (1989, 1996); Gamson (1992a).

12 See Swidler and Arditi (1994) for a discussion of recent developments in the sociology of knowledge.

13 Benford and Hunt (1992: 38). See also Melucci (1984b, 1989); Sassoon (1984a, 1984b); Gusfield (1994).
14 On the concept of the schema of interpretation applied to the analysis of the movements, see also the large number of empirical and theoretical contributions from Hank Johnston (1991a, 1991b, 1995a).
15 What Snow and Benford (1988) define as the 'diagnostic, prognostic and motivational' dimension.
16 Michel Foucault (1977) noted, for example, that over time, not only what is thought but what can be thought or conceived of changes. This argument is valid for every phase of insurgency in collective action: it is, in fact, in these circumstances that spaces which were previously inconceivable, unexpectedly appear, enabling action to take place (Alberoni 1984; Melucci 1989, 1991).
17 See Diamanti (1993) for documentation of the existence – neither insignificant nor overwhelming – of xenophobia and racism among League voters.
18 Gamson (1992b) captures this multiplicity of dimensions when he identifies three central components of the collective construction of the terms: injustice, agency and identity frames. We will return to this point in more detail in the next chapter, when dealing with the role of identity.
19 One should obviously keep in mind that the distinction between 'activists' and 'population' is often quite vague.
20 See also on this topic Gamson (1988) and Gamson and Modigliani (1989).
21 See Tarrow (1994) for a broad analysis of the processes of production of interpretative schemata on the part of various movements in the nineteenth and twentieth centuries.
22 The inevitable reference here is to *Utopia*, used by Karl Mannheim (1946) to denote the complex of symbolic challenges presented in various historical periods to ideology as constituted at the time. Analogous themes have also been touched upon by Ralph Turner (1969, 1994), referring explicitly to *Ideology and Utopia*; and by Karl-Werner Brand (1990), who has associated cycles of insurgency in collective action with the *Zeitgeist* which characterizes the general climate of the time.
23 Derloshon and Potter (1982); Plumb (1993). This is not to forget the strong element of economic, redistributive and class conflict present in North American movements – especially in the Afro-American movements (Morris 1984) and generally in movements of the poor (Piven and Cloward 1977).
24 These are applied in particular to the ecology movement (Eyerman and Jamison 1991: ch. 3; Jamison et al. 1990).
25 See Koopmans and Duyvendak (1995) and Zuo and Benford (1994) for some attempts to integrate analyses of interpretative schemata and political opportunities.
26 See Billig (1995) for a discussion challenging the existence of global and relatively stable perceptions of political reality.

27 On the fact that political opportunities are to be considered perceptions and not objective reality, see Gamson and Meyer (1996). For a
systematic introduction to the concept of 'political opportunity structure' see chapter 8 in this book.

28 It should be noted that this judgement does not refer here to the full
range of public opinion but to the perceptions of sectors of public
opinion best disposed to change.

4 Collective Action and Identity

1 We have reported the sources of the various quotations as published in the original texts. This explains the discrepancy in the style
of referencing.

2 See, on this point, Pizzorno (1978) and Melucci (1989). If, in the text,
we speak at times of 'identity' rather than of 'processes of identity
construction' this stems purely from a desire to enhance readability. It
does not mean that identity is considered to be an objective property,
capable of affecting actors' behaviour by its presence or absence.

3 Roseneil (1995); see also Johnston (1991b: ch. 7), on the relationship
between nationalist and working-class identity in Catalonia.

4 Protagonists, antagonists and audiences, in the terms of Hunt, Benford
and Snow (1994).

5 See Seligman (1992) on the role of trust in the emergence of civil society (chapter 1).

6 Although these help with recruitment (see chapter 5).

7 This is not always true, however: the research project directed by
Alberto Melucci in Milan in the early 1980s showed how adherents to
local neo-Oriental groups had often been converted in less drastic ways
(Diani 1984, 1986).

8 Similar considerations can be made with reference to organizations
of the international communist movement. For a non-academic but
effective source – and a powerful narrative – see Koestler (1969).

9 This section is based partially on the analysis which John Lofland
(1995: 192ff) has suggested of the cultural forms of movements.

10 Craig Calhoun (1994a: 26) has spoken, on this point, of 'in-group
essentialism'.

11 For a now classic critique of this view: Touraine (1981); Melucci (1982,
1989, 1996).

12 See Stoecker (1995) for an interesting discussion of the relationship
between different levels of identity: individual, community, movement
and organizational.

13 See DeNardo (1985) and Chong (1991) for discussions of the rationality
of collective action. See also Hargreaves Heap et al. (1992) for an introduction to rational choice theories.

14 Marwell and Oliver (1993: 157–79) speak of *reach* and *selectivity* when
referring to these two dimensions.

5   Movement Networks

1   Syntheses of some of these discussions are to be found in Klandermans et al. (1988); Knoke and Wisely (1990); McAdam and Snow (1996: 120–71); For a few interesting case studies, Woliver (1993). However, there are also some exceptions. For example, in studying the Californian anti-abortion movement Luker (1984) discovered that only one-fifth of activists were recruited through personal networks (cited in Knoke and Wisely 1990: 69).

2   See Mullins (1987) for an analogous observation, referring to the relationship between integration in the local community and collective action. In our exploration we will adopt single individuals as our starting point, and examine the nature and form of the relationships in which they are engaged. In the language of network analysis, this approach is known as ego-networks (Burt 1980). For applications to the study of participation in networks, see McAdam and Fernandez (1990); Fernandez and McAdam (1989); Kriesi (1988b); Opp (1989). An alternative route consists of analysing the complex configuration of the links between components of a given population. Some scholars have analysed the probabilities of collective action within social groups characterized by different structures of internal relationships (Gould 1991; Marwell and Oliver 1993; Oberschall 1993). The complexity of many of these analyses has dissuaded us from dealing with them at any length in this volume.

3   See instead Ennis and Schreuer (1987) for an analysis of low-cost participation.

4   Stark and Bainbridge (1980). It is interesting to note how particularly intense relationships, such as those where relatives are involved, are distinguished from other forms of private contact, in explaining political action. McAllister (1983) shows, for example, that in situations where divisions are particularly sharply drawn, as in Northern Ireland, links between relatives are the only ones which join those who belong to different religious groups. Only those who have relatives of a different faith are prepared to discuss politics with those belonging to the other group. Discussions with friends, colleagues, neighbours etc., are limited to those who belong to the same religious group.

5   According to Kriesi (1988b: 52–3), a local counterculture can be considered strong when substantial numbers of people report that they know at least some of the activists in the movements. This distinction between strong and weak countercultures is compatible with our own which stresses the possibilities for alignment of frames between activists and the general public.

6   By the term cliques we are referring, in network analysis, to groups of actors characterized by a particularly high intensity of internal relationships: in the most extreme case, by the presence of direct contact among all the components of the group in question (Knoke and Kuklinski 1982: 56).

7   The central theoretical reference here is to individualization and to the construction of social space (Simmel 1955) and the application of this concept (Breiger 1988). Emirbayer and Goodwin (1994: 1,444–5) expand Simmel's notion of group affiliations in order to refer to identities which derive from the exposure of actors to a multiplicity of discourses, idioms and narratives. See also Curtis and Zurcher (1973); Knoke and Wisely (1990: 76ff); Diani (1988, 1995a).

8   We are grateful to Colin Barker for drawing Mario Diani's attention to this study.

9   For a systematic analysis of these relationships, see Diani (1995a: chs 5–6).

10 See Freeman (1983a); Rochon (1988); Gamson (1990 [1975]); Rucht (1989). This is the case both for alliances with other movement actors and for contacts with external actors. Jenkins (1983: 535) has noted, for example, how various movement organizations owe their success to their links with institutions which control considerable resources, and which are active in relation to the same issues. This is the case, for example, with movements for welfare rights, and farm workers' and women's movements in relation to foundations, public agencies etc.

11 Another typology (Rucht 1989) differentiates between relationships of neutrality, cooperation, competition and conflict: but these do not seem to us to be mutually exclusive.

12 This section elaborates on previous work by Mario Diani (1995a: ch. 1).

13 The constraining aspect of networks in relation to social action is the central focus of a revival of interest in structural approaches (Chiesi 1980; Marsden and Lin 1982; Burt and Minor 1983; Wellman and Berkowitz 1988). Stress has, for example, been placed on the influence of the network dimension on individuals' professional opportunities (e.g. Granovetter 1973), on the abilities of *corporate groups* to look after their own interests (e.g. Stokman et al. 1985), and on the formation of public policy (e.g. Laumann and Knoke 1987). In the field of movement studies, this view has largely influenced the analysis of recruitment processes, as we have seen.

14 This is a perspective which has rarely been explored. Partial exceptions are found in Friedman and McAdam (1992); Kaase (1990).

15 This line of analysis has been applied on a number of occasions. There have been several attempts to integrate network perspectives with approaches based on the concept of action. Whether close to an exchange theory perspective (e.g. Cook and Whitmeyer 1992) or to a vision more alert to the relationship between culture and action (e.g. Emirbayer and Goodwin 1994) these contributions have revealed a duality in social networks. That is, they have shown how, in most cases, the structure of a network depends, at least in part, on the choices made by actors participating in the network, with respect to those with whom they activate relationships of cooperation and interaction, or else of opposition and conflict (Berkowitz 1982: 60).

16   For example, in the Milanese ecology movement of the 1980s, each organization was involved, on average, in little more than three inter-organizational interactions, out of fifty-four recorded opportunities to forge alliances (Diani 1988: ch. 4). This is without taking into account opportunities for interactions with other types of organization, whether political or not, which were, obviously, much higher.

17   One might justifiably object that, in periods of strong polemic against bureaucratized organizations it would be right to expect the disappearance, or at least a drastic reshaping of asymmetrical relationships, and the development of independent networks for grassroots groups. We would find ourselves, however, in these cases faced with choices inspired by ideological or value considerations. We will return to this point in the next paragraph.

18   In the Italian environmental movement, Legambiente is an example of the first type of evolution. The LIPU (Italian League for the Protection of Birds) is an example of the second (Diani 1988, 1995a).

19   See chapters 6, 8 and 9.

20   Evidence on this point is most diverse and ranges from actual participation in both old and new movements (Thompson 1963; Pizzorno et al. 1978; Beer 1977, 1980; McAdam 1988; Diani 1995a) to a predisposition to protest behaviour (Barnes et al. 1979).

21   One could observe that demobilizations would also be encouraged by a full acceptance of the demands and perspectives of the movement, though this is unlikely to come about, in reality. On the other hand, in a situation of this kind, opportunities for action would, paradoxically, be as rare as in the context of total closure just described, although for completely different reasons. If only for reasons of survival, even in a case of this type, movement organizations could be induced to stress their specificity through recourse to ideological messages.

6   Social Movements and Organizational Form

1   On the organizational structure of the student movement in the German Federal Republic see Bock 1976: 242–3, Rolke 1987: 278; and Rabehl 1988: 225. For Italy, Ortoleva 1988; Manconi 1990; and della Porta 1996a: ch. 2.

2   The resources available to social movement organizations have been variously identified as: money, work, services and legitimation (McCarthy and Zald 1987b); work, land, capital and technology (Tilly 1978); financial resources, rank-and-file activists and legitimation (Rucht 1984).

3   On incentives, see chapter 4. A classification of incentives can be found in Zald and Jacobs 1978.

4   Although organizational sociology is rich in analyses of organizations on the basis of their organizational design, relations mechanisms, staff

and policy composition etc. (e.g. Jackson and Morgan 1978), most such variables have little relevance concerning political organizations.

5 Janda considers centralization of power, internal coherence and degree and type of involvement as well as degree of organization (Janda 1970: 104–12).

6 Methods of finance and membership size are also related here.

7 Different leadership styles have also been noted: agitator, prophet, administrator or statesman (Lang and Lang 1961); charismatic, administrator or intellectual (Killian 1964); charismatic, ideological or pragmatic (Wilson 1973); instrumental or affective (Downtown 1973).

8 On a scale of increasing commitment Lofland (1985b) identifies voluntary associations, offices, armies, communes (inhabited by members of a 'family'), workers' cooperatives and utopian communities.

9 While umbrella organizations and coalitions emerge particularly in periods of expanding resources, the creation of friendship ties and a sense of shared identity among their members may permit them to survive through periods of declining resources also (Hathaway and Mayer 1993–4).

10 Indeed, it has been suggested that, in certain situations, the party model represents an 'obscure object of desire' for social movements (Ibarra 1995).

11 McCarthy and Zald (1987b [1977] distinguish between potential beneficiaries, who directly gain from the movement's accomplishing its aims, and conscience adherents, who are part of a social movement but would not directly benefit from its success. On this basis they then differentiate between 'classical SMOs', which focus upon beneficiary adherents for resources, and 'professional SMOs', which appeal primarily to a conscience constituency and involve very few of their members in organizational work.

12 They rely more on their reputation for technical expertise on specific matters than on mass mobilization: 'Professional competence rather than broad citizens action characterises these organisations, with a heavy use of the media as a critical component of utilising this competence as a lever for social change' (McCarthy and Zald 1987a [1973]: 379).

13 Roth (1994) has analysed the role of such countercultures in the German *Alternativbewegung*. It should be noted, however, that the phenomenon is not peculiar to new social movements. In the labour movement, for example, 'the party, unions and cultural and service associations provided the physical and social space in which an alternative community could develop' (Nolan 1981: 301).

14 The institutionalization of political parties implies a passage from a system of rationality in which ideology dictates organizational goals, collective incentives predominate and control is exercised over the environment, to one of interests, in which the main goal is survival, incentives are selective and the environment is adapted to (Panebianco 1982).

15   On organizational dynamics during protest campaigns see Gerhards 1991 and 1993, and Gerhards and Rucht 1992.
16   These latter two directions of development have been described by Kriesi (1996) as, respectively, commercialization and involution.
17   It has been noted that transactions between voluntary organizations are initially hampered by a reciprocal lack of information, thus the importance of bodies concerned with coordination (White et al.1975).
18   A number of distinctions have been made in social movement goals: direct versus indirect (Gusfield 1968); public policy versus private change oriented (1968); general (uncoordinated efforts for general aims) versus specific (action by an organization for specific aims) (Blumer 1951); inward versus outward oriented; expressive versus institutional (for a typology of typologies see Lang and Lang 1961).
19   Strong external challenges can facilitate the formation of alliances between different organisations and movements (McCarthy and Zald 1987b).
20   The suggestion that proportional representation electoral systems favour the emergence of political parties linked to social movements (e.g. Brand 1985: 324) has been confirmed by comparative research on European Green parties. As Chris Rootes notes: 'In general, in countries with federal constitutions and proportional representation electoral systems, the institutional matrix is much more favourable for the development and success of Green parties . . . than it is in centralised unitary states with majoritarian electoral systems' (Rootes 1994: 6).
21   Similar organizations tend to differentiate themselves and define their recruitment base (or a niche in the surrounding environment where they can best compete) by emphasizing particular characteristics. As McCarthy and Zald note, 'where product differentiation is possible, sellers may attempt to divide the market into segments that they can "capture", to reduce competition and to establish more dependable and organisationally favourable relations' (Zald and McCarthy 1987 [1980]: 163).
22   Gamson (1990) uses similar concepts in distinguishing between: (1) targets of influence (policy-makers); (2) targets of mobilization (potential movement recruits); and (3) targets of benefit (beneficiaries of movement success). See also the definition by Barnes et al. (1979).
23   This has been noted of the evolution of extremist organizations (della Porta 1995) but also of other social movement organizations, particularly the most identity-oriented. On the United States women's movement, for example, see Mansbridge (1986: 191) and Krasniewicz (1992).

7   Forms, Repertoires and Cycles of Protest

1   For the peace movement in Italy see Battistelli 1990 and Lodi 1984; for France, Great Britain, Germany and the Netherland, Rochon 1988; the

United States, Meyer 1990; France, Netherland, Germany and Switzerland, Kriesi et al. 1995.

2 According to Barnes and Kaase (Barnes et al. 1979), 7 per cent of inhabitants in five countries mentioned protest as a legitimate reaction to unjust decisions in 1974. In Great Britain, the United States and the German Federal Republic the percentage of those who responded 'unconventional political action, like demonstration' to the question 'what can a citizen do about a local regulation considered unjust or harmful?' had been increasing. In Great Britain the percentage so responding had grown from 0.2 per cent in 1959–60 to 7.1 per cent in 1974 (+6.9); in the United States the figure had risen from 0.5 per cent to 6.9 (+6.4); and in the Federal Republic it had increased from 0.7 per cent to 7.8 (+7.1) (Barnes et al. 1979: 143). A similar trend existed in responses concerning unjust national legislation, with the percentage of those willing to consider unconventional action rising from 0 to 4.3 per cent in Great Britain, 0.3 to 3.6 per cent in the United States and 1.9 to 9.5 per cent in the Federal Republic (1979: 144).

3 Tilly defines contention as common action bearing directly on the interests of another acting group (Tilly 1986: 382).

4 Examples of the parochial and patronage-based repertoire include food riots, collective invasions of property, destruction of toll gates and other barriers, machine breaking, charivaris and serenades; physical expulsion of tax officers, foreign workers or other outsiders; tendentious holiday parades; battles between villages; the pulling down or sacking of private houses; forced illuminations; mock or popular trials and turnouts (Tilly 1986: 392–3).

5 In fact, Tilly has admitted that: 'Two features especially distinguish the actions of twentieth-century French social movements and quasi-movements from their nineteenth-century counterparts. The first is the increasing importance of seizing a space and using its possession both to symbolize a set of demands and to demand concessions . . . The second is the addressing of events that nominally involve two parties (such as workers and employers) to third parties, including the state and sympathetic members of the general public' (1988: 15).

6 An opinion poll conducted in Great Britain in 1981 showed that only 30 per cent of those interviewed would have switched their vote if they were not satisfied with their chosen party's policy on nuclear weapons.

7 In research on the political integration of ethnic minorities 'positive radical flank effects' have been mentioned: 'radical groups may bring about a greater level of responsiveness to the claims of moderates, either by making the latter appear more 'reasonable' or by creating a crisis which can be solved by the lesser concessions required by the moderates' (Haines 1988: 167; see also, Button 1978). These positive effects are associated with direct action rather than rioting (Haines 1988: 171). Gamson (1990) similarly noted that it was willingness to use non-institutional rather than violent means which favoured social movement victories.

8 For a more detailed analysis of social movement concepts of democracy see chapter 9.

9 The most famous example is Greenham Common in Britain, where women set up a camp, blocked entrances to the base, organized incursions into the base itself and occupied land owned by the Ministry of Defence (see Roseneil 1995).

10 On the role played by experts in new social movements see chapter 6. Cortright (1991: 56; also 1993) has emphasized the way in which the American peace movement became a principal source of information for the government on issues of war and peace through its use of the media.

11 In considering the widespread debate on "negro politics" of the time, Lipsky observed that the leaders of protest often face a choice between two equally risky paths: radicalism, which alienates external support, and moderation, which undermines the solidarity of their base. A radical leadership style, the aim of which is to win status through 'acting tough', will be effective in enhancing internal cohesion. A moderate leadership style which aims to broaden the welfare state through peaceful action will take greater account of external objectives.

12 While more moderate action has become increasingly legitimate, this is not true of more radical forms. From 1974 to 1981 support for petitioning had grown from 22 per cent to 63 per cent in Great Britain and support for legal demonstrations from 6 per cent to 10 per cent. The equivalent figures were 30 per cent to 46 per cent and 9 per cent to 14 per cent in Germany. Support for direct action such as occupations remained rooted at around 1 to 2 per cent (Dalton 1988: 65).

13 A further observation can be made. Until now, speaking about the strategic choices open to social movements, their leaders have been treated as a unitary group. In reality, social movements are composite actors: their organizations and networks interact, choosing at least partially different directions. As already noted, Greenpeace specializes in direct action while the Green grouping in the European parliament follows the logic of parliamentary democracy; some organizations called for a boycott of French goods while others considered such action counter-productive. This diversity of strategy may be positive since different organizations will be able to speak to different sectors of public opinion. However, it needs to be remembered that the single organizations within a movement compete with each other as well as cooperating. A particular organization's choice of strategy is also motivated, therefore, by the need to carve out a niche in the wider 'market' of the movement (McCarthy and Zald 1987b [1977]). These choices are not always beneficial to the movement as a whole, as the damaging effects of terrorist organizations on the less radical groups from which they sprang tragically testifies (della Porta 1995).

14 In relation to the anti-nuclear movement Christian Joppke notes that 'beliefs and ideologies are not only *facilitating* but also *constraining* devices that may prohibit flexible responses to shifting opportunities' (1993: 204, emphasis in the original).

15 For an example of such escalation see the very detailed description of student protest at Berkeley in 1964 by Max Heirich (1971).

16 Cyclical patterns have been observed in strike activity, for example, and their relationship with Kondratieff's economic cycles studied. Similarly, cycles of revolution have been linked to population growth and decline (Frank and Fuentes 1994).

17 This pattern has also been observed in the case of Germany (Koopmans 1995).

18 Cf. della Porta and Tarrow 1987; Tarrow 1989a; della Porta 1990 on the Italian protest cycle; Koopmans 1995 on Germany; and Kriesi et al. 1995 for comparative work on Germany, France, the Netherlands and Switzerland.

19 In the 1981 to 1986 protest wave in Germany and Holland, confrontational action such as blockades and occupations were concentrated in the initial stages. Gradually, as the authorities learned how to react to them and they became less novel, they declined in number. On the other hand, more moderate and demonstrative mass action such as legal marches, petitions and rallies increased, reaching their peak in 1983. The use of violence grew around 1985 (Kriesi et al. 1995: 129–34).

8 The Political Context of Social Movements

1 The most important cross-national and diachronic studies on collective movements will also be considered: Sidney Tarrow's study (1989a) of collective movements in Italy between 1965 and 1975; the study directed by Hanspeter Kriesi on new social movements in Germany, France, the Netherlands and Switzerland (Kriesi et al. 1995); and Dieter Rucht's study of Germany, France and the United States (1994). It should be mentioned that both Tarrow's and Kriesi's volumes focus especially on protest which, as mentioned, is one of the expressions of social movements, but not the only one. Moreover, as we also stated, social movements do not have a monopoly upon protest.

2 In his comparison of the French, German, Swedish and American antinuclear movements, Herbert Kitschelt (1986: 61–4) distinguished between the conditions which influence demands entering the political system and those influencing its output in terms of public policy. On the input side, a large number of political parties, the capacity of the legislature to develop and control policy independently of the executive, pluralist patterns of mediation between interest groups and the executive branch and the possibility of building policy coalitions (i.e., mechanisms for demand aggregation) are indicators of openness. On the output side, the capacity of the political system to implement policies is indicated by a centralized state apparatus, government control over the market and a low level of judicial independence from the other arms of the state.

3 In fact, in the United States Eisinger (1973) found a greater degree of openness in local government regimes where electors had more control over administrators.

4 Kriesi notes that while on the input side the degree of formal access to the state increases with territorial decentralization, the separation of executive, legislature and judiciary and low levels of coherence, internal coordination and professionalization in the public administration, in the presence of direct democratic procedures the same factors produce the opposite effects on the output side: 'Federal, fragmented and incoherent states with direct democratic institutions find it particularly difficult to arrive at decisions and to impose them on society' (Kriesi 1995: 172).

5 During the occupation of a community centre in Zurich, for example, the local authorities' decision to leave management of the facilities with the young people in occupation was twice overturned by a popular referendum (Kriesi 1984).

6 The German state was rated intermediate in relation to parliament, weak in the administrative arena and 'strong' in relation to direct democracy; the Netherlands was rated intermediate on the first two and 'strong' in relation to the latter (Kriesi 1984).

7 The research by Hanspeter Kriesi and his collaborators is based upon the collection of protest events from one daily newspaper per country. The reliability of these sources, in particular, for cross-national analysis, is problematic, since only a small percentage of protest events are covered by national newspapers, and, moreover, the selection bias is not systematic, since it may change in different countries, in different times and for different newspapers.

8 Both small countries, open to international markets, the Netherlands and Switzerland adopted a system of consensual democracy which has avoided the fragmentation of the state under the pressures of ethnic differences (religious in the Netherlands, linguistic in Switzerland). On consensual democracy, see Lijphart (1984); on the 'small' democracies, Katzenstein (1985).

9 According to a poll taken in 1981 comparing France and Great Britain, 26 per cent in the former and 10 per cent in the latter had taken part in legal demonstrations. There was also greater tolerance in France for non-violent illegal action such as unofficial strikes (10 and 7 per cent) and occupations (7 and 2 per cent) (Dalton 1988: 65).

10 See Wallace and Jenkins (1995: 102–3). The study is based on data from the earlier Political Action Project (Barnes et al. 1979), which compared the United States, Italy, Great Britain, the German Federal Republic, Switzerland, Finland, the Netherlands and Austria.

11 McAdam (1982) identified three important factors in the emergence and development of the movement: its alignment within the larger political context (political opportunity structure); the level of organization of the aggrieved population (organization potential); and its assessment of the chances of success (insurgent consciousness).

12 The number of days per 1,000 workers lost through strikes between 1965 and 1974 was a great deal higher in countries with a pluralist system (1,660 in Italy, 1,330 in the United States, 740 in Great Britain and 810 in Finland) than it was in countries with a neo-corporatist one (270 in the German Federal Republic, 70 in the Netherlands, 40 in Switzerland and 20 in Austria) (Wallace and Jenkins 1995: 106).

13 According to Frank L. Wilson (1990), however, the level of neo-corporatism has no influence on indicators of mobilization such as public attitudes towards a social movement, inclination to support a cause or willingness to use non-conventional protest tactics.

14 Moreover, changes in the attitudes of social democratic parties do not always coincide with entering or leaving office. They can be anticipated where a perception of electoral instability or conflict within elites open a 'window of opportunity' for social movements. On the other hand, a change in attitude may be delayed after leaving government, particularly where too much openness towards new movements is held responsible for electoral misfortune.

15 According to DeNardo, the effectiveness of violence is influenced by regime responsiveness and the distribution of preferences concerning dissidents' demands: 'When the bulk of the movement's potential support lies near its demands, however, the constraints on escalations are relaxed considerably' (DeNardo 1985: 223).

16 However, as the French case shows, a strong left-wing government faced by weak mobilization can undermine a social movement's organizational structure through a series of 'preventive' concessions, co-opting the leadership.

9   Social Movements: What Consequences?

1 For a good review of research on women and politics see Randall (1982).

2 Of 187 government ministers in the 10 EEC countries in 1984 only 10 were women and only 1 head of government was a women (Lovenduski 1986: 209).

3 According to the well-known research on attitudes towards political participation by Barnes and Kaase, in the 1970s women represented the majority of 'protesters', those who prefer direct action to conventional politics (Barnes et al. 1979: 184). They observed that the 'majority of women in the protesters category . . . undoubtedly reflects in part the domination of conventional politics by men' (1979: 534).

4 Similarly, Turner and Killian (1987) have spoken of realization of reforms and changes in power relations and Kitschelt (1986) of substantive and procedural impacts. Tarrow (1994) distinguished between effects on institutions and political structures and effects on political culture. Rucht (1992) added changes in attitudes, behaviour and public discourse to those in policy and power relations.

5 Although one speaks of the 'successes' obtained by a socialist party in government or by a trade union, the same problems identified concerning social movements are also likely to be met in such cases.

6 It is primarily 'older' movement organizations, with bigger budgets and paid staff, who maintain close links with the public bureaucracy (Dalton 1994).

7 As Rothenberg (1992) notes, the rules of democracy within many social movement organizations are merely for legitimation purposes and are not respected in practice.

8 The concept of 'diffusion' has been imported into social science from physics, more exactly from studies of the diffusion of certain kinds of wave from one system to another. In the social sciences it has been used to explain the transfer across time and space of particular cultural traits, information or ideas.

References

Abramson, Paul R. and Inglehart, Ronald 1992: Generational Replacement and Value Change in Eight West European Societies. *British Journal of Political Science*, 22, 183–228.

Agger, Ben 1991: Critical Theory, Poststructuralism, Postmodernism: Their Sociological Relevance. *Annual Review of Sociology*, 17, 105–31.

Alberoni, Francesco 1984: *Movement and Institution*. New York: Columbia University Press.

Amenta, Edwin and Zylan, Yvonne 1991: It Happened Here: Political Opportunity, the New Institutionalism, and the Townsend Movement. *American Sociological Review*, 56, 250–65.

Amenta, Edwin, and Young, M. P. 1995: Democratic States and Social Mobilization. Paper for the Annual Meeting of the American Political Science Association, Chicago.

Amin, Ash (ed.) 1994: *Post-Fordism. A Reader*. Oxford/Cambridge, MA: Blackwell.

Aminzade, Ronald 1995: Between Movements and Party: The Transformation of Mid-nineteenth-century French Republicanism. In J. C. Jenkins and B. Klandermans (eds), *The Politics of Social Protest. Comparative Perspectives on States and Social Movements*, Minneapolis: University of Minnesota Press, 39–62.

Anderson, Benedict 1983: *Imagined Communities*. London: Verso.

Bachrach, Peter and Baratz, Morton S. 1970: *Power and Poverty. Theory and Action*. New York: Oxford University Press.

Bagguley, Paul 1991: *From Protest to Acquiescence. Political Movements of the Unemployed*. London: Macmillan.

Bagguley, Paul 1992: Social Change, the Middle Class and the Emergence of 'New Social Movements': A Critical Analysis. *Sociological Review*, 40, 26–48.

Bagguley, Paul 1994: Prisoners of the Beveridge Dream? The Political Mobilization of the Poor against Contemporary Welfare Regimes. In R. Burrows and B. Loader (eds), *Towards a Post-Fordist State?*, London: Macmillan.

Bagguley, Paul 1995a: Middle Class Radicalism Revisited. In T. Butler and M. Savage (eds), *Social Change and the Middle Classes*, London: UCL Press.

Bagguley, Paul 1995b: Protest, Poverty and Power: A Case Study of the Anti-Poll Tax Movement. *Sociological Review*, 43, 693–719.

Banaszac, Lee A. and Plutzer, Eric 1993: The Social Bases of Feminism in the European Community. *Public Opinion Quarterly*, 57, 29–53.

Barbalet, Jack M. 1988: *Citizenship*. Milton Keynes: Open University Press.

Barcena, Inaki, Ibarra, Pedro and Zubiaga, Mario 1995: *Nacionalismo y Ecologia. Conflicto e Institucionalizacion en el Movimiento Ecologista Vasco.* Madrid: Libros de la Catarata.

Barnes, Barry and Edge, David (eds) 1982: *Science in Context*. Milton Keynes: Open University Press.

Barnes, Samuel H., Kaase, Max, Allerbeck, Klaus, Farah, Barbara, Heunks, Felix, Inglehart, Ronald, Jennings, M. Kent, Klingemann, Hans D., Marsh Alan and Rosenmayr, Leopold 1979: *Political Action*. London/Newbury Park, CA: Sage.

Bartholomew, Amy and Mayer, Margit 1992: Nomads of the Present: Melucci's Contribution to 'New Social Movement' Theory. *Theory, Culture and Society*, 9, 141–59.

Bartolini, Stefano and Mair, Peter 1990: *Identity, Competition and Electoral Availability. The Stabilization of European Electorates.* Cambridge: Cambridge University Press.

Battistelli, Fabrizio (ed.) 1990: *Rapporto di ricerca su: I movimenti pacifisti in Italia*. Gaeta: Rivista Militare.

Bauss, Gerhard 1977: *Die Studentenbewegung der sechziger Jahre*. Köln: Pahl-Rugenstein Verlag.

Bearman, Peter S. and Everett, Kevin D. 1993: The Structure of Social Protest, 1961–1983. *Social Networks*, 15, 171–200.

Bechofer, Frank and Elliott, Brian 1985: The Petite Bourgeoisie in Late Capitalism. *Annual Review Of Sociology*, 11, 181–207.

Beer, William R. 1977: The Social Class of Ethnic Activists in Contemporary France. In M. J. Esman (ed.), *Ethnic Conflict in the Western World*, Ithaca/London: Cornell University Press, 143–58.

Beer, William R. 1980: *The Unexpected Rebellion. Ethnic Activism in Contemporary France*. New York: Columbia University Press.

Bell, Daniel 1973: *The Coming of Post-Industrial Society*. New York: Basic Books.

Benford, Robert D. 1993: Frame Disputes within the Nuclear Disarmament Movement. *Social Forces*, 71, 677–701.

Benford, Robert D. and Hunt, Scott A. 1992: Dramaturgy and Social Movements: The Social Construction and Communication of Power. *Sociological Inquiry*, 62, 36–55.

Berger, Peter and Luckmann, Thomas 1966: *The Social Construction of Reality. A Treatise in the Sociology of Knowledge*. Garden City, NY: Anchor Books.

Berkowitz, Steve D. 1982: *An Introduction to Structural Analysis. The Network Approach to Social Research*. Toronto: Butterworths.

Bernstein, Mary 1995: Strategies, Goals, and Lesbian/Gay Policy Outcomes in the Face of Organized Opposition. Paper presented at the Annual Meeting of the American Sociological Association, Washington, DC, August.

Best, Joel (ed.) 1989: *Images of Issues. Typifying Contemporary Social Problems*. New York: de Gruyter.

Betz, Hans-Georg 1993: The New Politics of Resentment. Radical Right-wing Populist Parties in Western Europe. *Comparative Politics*, 25, 413–27.

Betz, Hans-Georg 1994: *Radical Right-wing Populism in Western Europe*. Basingstoke: Macmillan.

Bew, Paul, Gibbon, Peter and Patterson, Henry 1979: *The State in Northern Ireland, 1921–72: Political Forces and Social Classes*. Manchester: Manchester University Press.

Bianchi, Marina and Mormino, Maria 1984: Militanti di Se Stesse. Il Movimento delle Donne a Milano. In A. Melucci (ed.), *Altri Codici*, Bologna: il Mulino, 127–74.

Billig, Michael 1995: Rhetorical Psychology, Ideological Thinking, and Imagining Nationhood. In H. Johnston and B. Klandermans (eds), *Social Movements and Culture*, Minneapolis/London: University of Minnesota Press/UCL Press, 64–81.

Biorcio, Roberto 1991: La Lega Come Attore Politico: Dal Federalismo al Populismo Regionalista. In R. Mannheimer et al. *La Lega Lombarda*, Milan: Feltrinelli, 34–82.

Biorcio, Roberto 1992: The Rebirth of Populism in Italy and France. *Telos*, 90, 43–56.

Blumer, Herbert 1951: Social Movements. In A. McClung Lee (ed.), *Principles of Sociology*, New York: Barnes & Nobles, 199–220.

Blumer, Herbert 1971: Social Problems as Collective Behavior. *Social Problems*, 18, 298–306.

Bock, Hans-Manfred 1976: *Geschichte des linken Radikalismus in Deutschland. Ein Versuch*. Frankfurt am Main: Suhrkamp.

Boles, Janet K. 1991: Form Follows Function: The Evolution of Feminist Strategies. *The Annals of the American Academy of Political and Social Science*, 515, 38–49.

Boltken, Ferdinand and Jagodzinski, Wolfgang 1985: In an Environment of Insecurity. *Comparative Political Studies*, 17, 453–84.

Bonazzi, Tiziano and Dunne, Michael (eds) 1994: *Cittadinanza e Diritti nelle Società Multiculturali*. Bologna: il Mulino.

Bontadini, Paolo 1978: *Manuale di Organizzazione*. Milan: Isedi.

Bourdieu, Pierre 1977: *Outline of a Theory of Practice*. Cambridge/New York: Cambridge University Press.

Bourdieu, Pierre 1984: *Distinction*. Cambridge, MA: Harvard University Press.

Bourdieu, Pierre 1990: *The Logic of Practice*. Stanford: Stanford University Press.

Brand, Jack 1990: Scotland. In M. Watson (ed.), *Contemporary Minority Nationalism*, London/New York: Routledge & Kegan Paul, 24–37.

Brand, Karl-Werner 1985: Vergleichendes Resümee. In Karl-Werner Brand (ed.), *Neue soziale Bewegungen in Westeuropa und den USA. Ein internationaler Vergleich*, Frankfurt am Main: Campus, 306–34.

Brand, Karl-Werner 1990: Cyclical Aspects of New Social Movements: Waves of Cultural Criticism and Mobilization Cycles of New Middle-class Radicalism. In R. Dalton and M. Kuechler (eds), *Challenging the Political Order*, Cambridge: Polity Press, 23–42.

Braungart, Richard G. and Braungart, Margaret M. 1986: Life-course and Generational Politics. *Annual Review of Sociology*, 12, 205–31.

Braungart, Richard G. and Braungart, Margaret M. 1992: Historical Generations and Citizenship: 200 Years of Youth Movements. In P. C. Wasburn (ed.), *Research in Political Sociology*, vol. 6, Greenwich, CT: JAI Press, 139–74.

Brecher, Jeremy and Costello, Tim (eds) 1990: *Building Bridges; The Emerging Grassroots Coalition of Labor and Community*. New York: Monthly Review Press.

Breiger, Ronald L. 1988: The Duality of Persons and Groups. In B. Wellman and S. D. Berkowitz (eds), *Social Structures: A Network Approach*, Cambridge: Cambridge University Press, 83–98.

Breines, Wini 1989: *Community and Organization in the New Left. 1962–1968: The Great Refusal*. New Brunswick, NJ: Rutgers University Press.

Breuilly, John 1993: *Nationalism and the State*. Chicago: University of Chicago Press.

Brint, Steven 1984: 'New Class' and Cumulative Trend Explanations of the Liberal Political Attitudes of Professionals. *American Journal of Sociology*, 90, 30–71.

Brint, Steven 1994: *In an Age of Experts: The Changing Role of Professionals in Politics and Public Life*. Princeton: Princeton University Press.

Brissette, Martha B. 1988: Tax Protest and Tax Reform: A Chapter in The History of The American Political Process. *Journal of Law and Politics*, 5, 187–208.

Brooks, Clem and Manza, Jeff 1994: Do Changing Values Explain the New Politics? A Critical Assessment of the Postmaterialist Thesis. *Sociological Quarterly*, 35, 541–70.

Bruce, Steve 1988: *The Rise and Fall of the New Christian Right*. Oxford/New York: Oxford University Press.

Burstein, Paul, Einwohner, Rachel L. and Hollander, Jocelyn A. 1995: The Success of Political Movements: A Bargaining Perspective. In J. C. Jenkins and B. Klandermans (eds), *The Politics of Social Protest*, Minneapolis: The University of Minnesota Press, 275–295.

Burt, Ronald S. 1980: Models of Network Structure. *Annual Review of Sociology*, 6, 79–141.

Burt, Ronald S. and Minor, Michael J. (eds) 1983: *Applied Network Analysis. A Methodological Introduction*. Beverly Hills/London: Sage.

Button, James W. 1978: *Black Violence. Political Impacts of the 1960s Riots*. Princeton: Princeton University Press.

Calhoun Craig (ed.) 1992: *Habermas and the Public Sphere*, MIT Press: Cambridge, MA.

Calhoun, Craig 1982: *The Question of Class Struggle. Social Foundations of Popular Radicalism during the Industrial Revolution*. Oxford: Blackwell.

Calhoun, Craig 1991: The Problem of Identity in Collective Action. In J. Huber (ed.), *Macro-Micro Linkages in Sociology*, London/Beverly Hills, CA: Sage, 51–75.

Calhoun, Craig 1993: 'New Social Movements' of the Early 19th Century. *Social Science Journal*, 17, 385–427.

Calhoun, Craig (ed.) 1994a: *Social Theory and the Politics of Identity*. Oxford/Cambridge, MA: Blackwell.

Calhoun, Craig 1994b: Nationalism and Civil Society: Democracy, Diversity, and Self-determination. In C. Calhoun (ed.), *Social Theory and the Politics of Identity*, Oxford/Cambridge, MA: Blackwell, 304–35.

Canciani, Domenico and De La Pierre, Sergio 1993: *Le Ragioni di Babele. Le Etnie tra Vecchi Nazionalismi e Nuove Identità*. Milano: Angeli.

Carroll, William K. and Ratner, R. S. 1996: Master Framing and Cross-Movement Networking in Contemporary Social Movements. *Sociological Quarterly*, 37, 601–25.

Cartuyvels, Yves et al. 1997: *L'Affaire Dutroux*. Brussels: Editions Complexe.

Castells, Manuel 1977: *La Question Urbaine*. Paris: Maspero.

Castells, Manuel 1983: *The City and the Grass-Roots*. London: E. Arnold.

Castells, Manuel 1996: *The Information Age. Vol. I: The Rise Of The Network Society*. Oxford/Cambridge, MA: Blackwell.

Castells, Manuel 1997: *The Information Age. Vol. II: The Power of Identity*. Oxford/Cambridge, MA: Blackwell.

Cesarani, David and Fulbrick, Mary (eds) 1996: *Citizenship, Nationality and Migration in Europe*. London: Routledge.

Chatfield, Charles, Pagnucco, Ron, and Smith, Jackie (eds) 1996: *Solidarity Beyond the State: the Dynamics of Transnational Social Movements*. Syracuse, NY: Syracuse University Press.

Chesler, Mark 1991: Mobilizing Consumer Activism in Health Care: The Role of Self-help Groups. *Research in Social Movements, Conflicts and Change*, 13, 275–305.

Chiesi, Antonio M. 1980: L'Analisi dei Reticoli Sociali: Teoria e Metodi. *Rassegna Italiana di Sociologia*, 21, 291–310.

Chong, Dennis 1991: *Collective Action and the Civil Rights Movement*. Chicago: University of Chicago Press.

Clark, Martin 1984: *Modern Italy, 1871–1982*. London: Longman.

Clark, Robert 1989: Spanish Democracy and Regional Autonomy. In J. Rudolph and R. J. Thompson (eds), *Ethnoterritorial Politics, Policy, and the Western World*, Boulder, CO/London: Lynne Rienner, 15–44.

Clark, T. and Lipset, Seymour M. 1991: Are Social Classes Dying? *International Sociology*, 4, 397–410.

Clemens, Elisabeth S. 1996: Organizational Form as Frame: Collective Identity and Political Strategy in the American Labor Movement. In Doug McAdam, John McCarthy and Mayer N. Zald (eds), *Comparative Perspectives on Social Movements. Political Opportunities, Mobilizing Structures, and Cultural Framing*, Cambridge/New York: Cambridge University Press, 205–25.

Cohen, Jean L. 1985: Strategy and Identity: New Theoretical Paradigms and Contemporary Social Movements. *Social Research*, 52, 663–716.

Coleman, James 1990: *Foundations of Social Theory*. Cambridge, MA: Belknap.

Connor, Walker 1994: *Ethnonationalism. The Quest for Understanding*. Princeton, NJ: Princeton University Press.

Cook, Karen S. and Whitmeyer, J. M. 1992: Two Approaches to Social Structure: Exchange Theory and Network Analysis. *Annual Review of Sociology*, 18, 109–27.

Cortright, David 1991: Assessing Peace Movement Effectiveness in the 1980s. *Peace and Change*, 16, 46–63.

Cortright, David 1993: *Peace Works: The Citizen's Role in Ending the Cold War*. Boulder: Westview Press.

Cotgrove, Stephen and Duff, Andrew 1980: Environmentalism, Middle-class Radicalism and Politics. *Sociological Review*, 28, 333–51.

Cress, Daniel and Snow, David 1996: Mobilization at the Margins: Resources, Benefactors, and the Viability of Homeless Social Movement Organizations. *American Sociological Review*, 61, 1089–109.

Crompton, Rosemary 1993: *Class and Stratification. An Introduction to Current Debates*. Cambridge: Polity Press.

Crook, Stephen, Pakulski, Jan and Waters, Malcolm 1992: *Postmodernization. Change in Advanced Society*. London/Thousand Oaks: Sage.

Croteau, David 1995: *Politics and the Class Divide. Working People and the Middle Class Left*. Philadelphia: Temple University Press.

Cuminetti, Mario 1983: *Il Dissenso Cattolico in Italia*. Milan: Rizzoli.

Curtis, Russell L. and Zurcher, Louis A. 1973: Stable Resources of Protest Movements: The Multi-organizational Field. *Social Forces*, 52, 53–61.

Curtis, Russel L. and Zurcher, Louis A. 1974: Social Movements: An Analytical Exploration of Organizational Forms. *Social Problems*, 11, 356–70.

D'Anieri, Paul, Ernst, Claire and Kier, Elizabeth 1990: New Social Movements in Historical Perspective. *Comparative Politics*, 22, 445–58.

D'Anjou, Leo 1996: *Social Movements and Cultural Change. The First Abolition Campaign Revisited*. New York: Aldine de Gruyter.

Dahl, Robert 1961: *Who Governs? Democracy and Power in an American City*, New Haven: Yale University Press.

Dahl, Robert 1967: *Pluralist Democracy in the United States: Conflict and Consent*, Chicago: Rand McNally.

Dahrendorf, Ralf 1988: *The Modern Social Conflicts*. London: Weidenfeld & Nicolson.

dalla Chiesa, Nando 1987: *Il Giano Bifronte. Società Corta e Colletti Bianchi*. Milano: Etas Libri.

Dalton, Russell 1988: *Citizen Politics in Western Democracies*. Chatham, NJ: Chatham House.

Dalton, Russell (ed.) 1993: Citizens, Protest and Democracy. Special issue of *The Annals of the American Academy of Political and Social Sciences*, 528.

Dalton, Russell 1994: *The Green Rainbow: Environmental Groups in Western Europe*. New Haven: Yale University Press.

Dalton, Russell 1995: Strategies of Partisan Influence: West European Environmental Movements. In J. C. Jenkins and B. Klandermans (eds), *The Politics of Social Protest. Comparative Perspectives on States and Social Movements*, Minneapolis: The University of Minnesota Press, 296–323.

Dalton, Russell J. and Kuechler, Manfred (eds) 1990: *Challenging the Political Order: New Social and Political Movements in Western Democracies*. Cambridge: Polity Press.

Dalton, Russell J., Flanagan, Scott C. and Beck, Paul A. (eds) 1984: *Electoral Change in Advanced Industrial Democracies: Dealignment or Realignment?*. Princeton: Princeton University Press.

Davies, James 1969: The J-Curve of Rising and Declining Satisfactions as Cause of Some Great Revolutions and a Contained Rebellion. In H. D. Graham and T. Gurr (eds), *Violence in America*. New York: Praeger, 690–730.

Dawson, Jane 1996: *Eco-nationalism. Anti-nuclear Activism and National Identity in Russia, Lithuania, and Ukraina*. Durham/London: Duke University Press.

de Graaf, Nan Dirk and Evans, Geoffrey 1996: Why are the Young More Postmaterialist? A Cross-National Analysis of Individual and Contextual Influences on Postmaterial Values. *Comparative Political Studies*, 28, 608–35.

Delgado, Gary 1986: *Organizing the Movement: The Roots and Growth of ACORN*. Philadelphia: Temple University Press.

della Porta, Donatella 1988: Recruitment Processes in Clandestine Political Organizations: Italian Left-wing Terrorism. In B. Klandermans, H. Kriesi and S. Tarrow (eds), *International Social Movement Research*, Vol. 1, *From Structure to Action*, Greenwich, CT: JAI Press, 155–72.

della Porta, Donatella 1990: *Il Terrorismo di Sinistra*. Bologna: il Mulino.

della Porta, Donatella 1995: *Social Movements, Political Violence and the State*. Cambridge/New York: Cambridge University Press.

della Porta, Donatella 1996a: *Movimenti Collettivi e Sistema Politico in Italia, 1960–1995*. Bari: Laterza.

della Porta, Donatella 1996b: Il Terrorismo. In *Enciclopedia Treccani*. Rome: Treccani.

della Porta, Donatella 1996c: Social Movements and the State: Thoughts on the Policing of Protest. In D. McAdam, J. McCarthy and M. N. Zald (eds), *Comparative Perspectives on Social Movements. Political Opportunities, Mobilizing Structures, and Cultural Framing*, Cambridge/New York: Cambridge University Press, 62–92.

della Porta, Donatella 1996d: Movimenti Sociali. *Rassegna Italiana di Sociologia*, 37, 313–31.

della Porta, Donatella 1998a: Police Knowledge and the Public Order in Italy. In D. della Porta and H. Reiter (eds), *Policing Protest. The Control of Mass Demonstrations in Western Democracies*, Minneapolis: The University of Minnesota Press, 1–32.

della Porta, Donatella 1998b: The Political Discourse on Protest Policing. In M. Giugni, D. McAdam and C. Tilly (eds), *How Movements Matter*, Minneapolis: The University of Minnesota Press.

della Porta, Donatella and Kriesi, Hanspeter 1998: Social Movements in A Globalizing World: An Introduction. In D. della Porta, H. Kriesi and D. Rucht (eds), *Social Movements in a Globalizing World*, New York/London: Macmillan.

della Porta, Donatella and Reiter, Herbert 1998: The Policing of Protest in Contemporary Democracy: An Introduction. In D. della Porta and H. Reiter (eds), *Policing Protest. The Control of Mass Demonstrations in Western Democracies*, Minneapolis/London: University of Minnesota Press/UCL Press.

della Porta, Donatella and Rucht, Dieter 1995: Left-libertarian Movements in Context: Comparing Italy and West Germany, 1965–1990. In J. C. Jenkins and B. Klandermans (eds), *The Politics of Social Protest. Comparative Perspectives on States and Social Movements*, Minneapolis: University of Minnesota Press, 229–72.

della Porta, Donatella and Tarrow, Sidney 1987: Unwanted Children. Political Violence and the Cycle of Protest in Italy, 1966–1973. *European Journal of Political Research*, 14, 607–32.

della Porta, Donatella, Kousis, Maria and Valiente, Celia 1996: Women and Politics in Southern Europe. Paths to Women's Rights in Italy, Greece, Spain and Portugal. Paper presented at the SSRC Conference on Democratic Consolidation and Culture in Southern Europe, Palma de Mallorca, July.

DeNardo, James 1985: *Power in Numbers. The Political Strategy of Protest and Rebellion*. Princeton, NJ: Princeton University Press.

Derloshon, Gerald B. and Potter, James E. 1982: *The Success Merchants: A Guide to Major Influences and People in the Human Potential Movement*. Englewood Cliffs, NJ: Prentice-Hall.

Desario, Jack 1988: Consumers and Health Planning: Mobilization of Bias? In J. Desario, and S. Langton (eds), *Citizen Participation in Public Decision Making*, New York/Westport, CT/London: Greenwood Press, 133–51.

Diamanti, Ilvo 1993: *La Lega. Geografia, Storia e Sociologia di un Nuovo Soggetto Politico*. Roma: Donzelli.

Diamanti, Ilvo 1994: Geopolitica del Bluff Federalista. *Limes*, 4, 37–44.

Diamanti, Ilvo 1996: The Northern League: From Regional Party to Party of Government. In S. Gundle, and S. Parker (eds), *The New Italian Republic*, London/New York: Routledge, 113–29.

Diani, Mario 1984: L'area della 'Nuova Coscienza' tra Ricerca Individuale ed Impegno Civile. In A. Melucci (ed.), *Altri Codici*, Bologna: il Mulino, 223–66.

Diani, Mario 1986: Dimensione Simbolica e Dimensione Sociale nelle Esperienze di 'Nuova Coscienza'. Il Caso dell'Area Milanese. *Rassegna Italiana di Sociologia*, 27, 89–115.

Diani, Mario 1988: *Isole nell'arcipelago. Il Movimento Ecologista in Italia*. Bologna: il Mulino.

Diani, Mario 1990: The Network Structure of the Italian Ecology Movement. *Social Science Information*, 29, 5–31.

Diani, Mario 1992a: Analysing Social Movement Networks. In M. Diani and R. Eyerman (eds), *Studying Collective Action*, Newbury Park/London: Sage, 107–35.

Diani, Mario 1992b: Dalla Ritualita' delle Subculture alla Liberta' dei Reticoli Sociali. *Democrazia e Diritto*, 32, 199–221.

Diani, Mario 1992c: The Concept of Social Movement. *Sociological Review*, 40, 1–25.

Diani, Mario 1994: The Conflict over Nuclear Energy in Italy. In H. Flam (ed.), *States and Anti-nuclear Movements*, Edinburgh: Edinburgh University Press.

Diani, Mario 1995a: *Green Networks. A Structural Analysis of the Italian Environmental Movement*. Edinburgh: Edinburgh University Press.

Diani, Mario 1995b: Le Reti di Movimento: Prospettive di Analisi. *Rassegna Italiana di Sociologia*, 36, 341–372.

Diani, Mario 1996: Linking Mobilization Frames and Political Opportunities: Insights from Regional Populism in Italy. *American Sociological Review*, 61, 1053–1069.

Diani, Mario 1997: Social Movements and Social Capital: A Network Perspective on Movement Outcomes. *Mobilization*, 2, 129–47.

Diani, Mario and Donati, Paolo R. 1984: L'Oscuro Oggetto del Desiderio: Leadership e Potere nelle Aree del Movimento. In A. Melucci (ed), *Altri Codici. Aree di Movimento nella Metropoli*, Bologna: il Mulino, 315–44.

Diani, Mario and Donati, Paolo R. 1996: 'Rappresentare' l'Interesse Pubblico: La Comunicazione dei Gruppi di Pressione e dei Movimenti. *Quaderni di Scienza Politica*, 4, 1–42.

Diani, Mario and Eyerman, Ron (eds) 1992: *Studying Collective Action*. London/Beverly Hills: Sage.

Diani, Mario and van der Heijden, Hein-Anton 1994: Anti-nuclear Movements across Nations: Explaining Patterns of Development. In H. Flam (ed.), *States and Anti-nuclear Movements*, Edinburgh: Edinburgh University Press, 355–82.

Diez Medrano, Juan 1995: *Divided Nations: Class, Politics, and Nationalism in the Basque Country and Catalonia*. Ithaca: Cornell University Press.

DiMaggio, Paul J. and Powell, Walter W. 1991: Introduction. In W. W. Powell and P. J. DiMaggio (eds), *The New Institutionalism in Organizational Analysis*, Chicago, IL: University of Chicago Press, 1–38.

Dobson, Andrew 1990: *Green Political Thought*. London: Unwin Hyman.

Donati, Paolo R. 1989: Dalla Politica al Consumo. La Questione Ecologica e i Movimenti degli Anni Settanta. *Rassegna Italiana di Sociologia*, 30, 321–46.

Donati, Paolo R. 1992: Political Discourse Analysis. In M. Diani and R. Eyerman (eds), *Studying Collective Action*, Newbury Park/London: Sage, 136–67.

Donati, Paolo R. 1996: Building a Unified Movement: Resource Mobilization, Media Work, and Organizational Transformation in the Italian Environmentalist Movement. In L. Kriesberg (ed.), *Research in Social Movements, Conflict and Change*, vol. 19, Greenwich, CT: JAI Press, 125–57.

Donati, Paolo R. and Mormino, Maria 1984: Il Potere della Definizione: Le Forme Organizzative dell'Antagonismo Metropolitano. In A. Melucci (ed.), *Altri Codici. Aree di Movimento nella Metropoli*, Bologna: il Mulino, 349–84.

Donati, Pierpaolo 1993: *La Cittadinanza Societaria*. Roma-Bari: Laterza.

Downs, Anthony 1972: Up and Down with Ecology. The Issue Attention Cycle. *Public Interest*, 28, 38–50.

Downtown, James 1973: *Rebel Leadership. Commitment and Charisma in the Revolutionary Process*. New York: Free Press.

Duch, R. M. and Taylor, M. A. 1993: Postmaterialism and the Economic Condition. *American Journal of Political Science*, 37, 747–79.

Duffhues, Ton and Felling, Albert 1989: The Development, Change, and Decline of the Dutch Catholic Movement. In B. Klandermans (ed.), *International Social Movement Research*, Vol. 2, *Organizing for Change*, Greenwich, CT: JAI Press, 95–116.

Dunleavy, Patrick 1980: *Urban Political Analysis. The Politics of Collective Consumption*. London: Macmillan.

Duyvendak, Jan Willem 1995: *The Power of Politics. New Social Movements in an Old Polity. France 1965–1989*. Westview, Boulder.

Eckstein, Susan (ed.) 1989: *Power and Popular Protest. Latin American Social Movements*. Berkeley: University of California Press.

Eder, Klaus 1985: The 'New Social Movements': Moral Crusades, Political Pressure Groups, or Social Movements? *Social Research*, 52, 869–901.

Eder, Klaus 1993: *The New Politics of Class. Social Movements and Cultural Dynamics in Advanced Societies*. Newbury Park/London: Sage.

Eder Klaus 1995: Does Social Class Matter in the Study of Social Movements? A Theory of Middle Class Radicalism. In L. Maheu (ed.), *Social Movements and Social Classes*, London/Thousand Oaks: Sage, 21–54.

Eisinger, Peter K. 1973: The Conditions of Protest Behavior in American Cities. *American Political Science Review*, 67, 11–28.

Elkington, J. and Hailes, J. 1988: *The Green Consumer Guide*. London: Gollancz.

Emirbayer, Mustafa and Goodwin, Jeff 1994: Network Analysis, Culture, and the Problem of Agency. *American Journal of Sociology*, 99, 1411–54.

Ennis, James G. and Schreuer, Richard 1987: Mobilizing Weak Support for Social Movements: The Role of Grievance, Efficacy, and Cost. *Social Forces*, 66, 390–409.

Epstein, Barbara 1991: *Political Protest and Cultural Revolution. Nonviolent Direct Action in the 1970s and 1980s*, Berkeley, University of California.

Erickson, Bonnie 1982: Networks, Ideologies, and Belief Systems. In P. Marsden and N. Lin (eds), *Social Structure and Network Analysis*, Beverly Hills/London: Sage, 159–72.

Escobar, Arturo and Alvarez, Sonia (eds) 1992: *The Making of Social Movements in Latin America. Identity, Strategy, and Democracy*. Boulder/Oxford: Westview Press.

Escobar, Edward J. 1993: The Dialectic of Repression: The Los Angeles Police Department and the Chicano Movement, 1968–1971. *The Journal of American History*, March, 1483–1514.

Esping-Andersen, Gosta (ed) 1993: *Changing Classes: Stratification and Mobility in Postindustrial Societies*. Thousand Oaks/London: Sage.

Etzioni, Amitai 1985: Special Interest Groups versus Constituency Representation. In L. Kriesberg (ed.), *Research in Social Movements, Conflict and Change*, vol. 8, Greenwich, CT: JAI Press, 171–95.

Evans, Sara M. and Boyte, Harry C. 1986: *Free Spaces*. New York: Harper & Row.

Eyerman, Ron 1994: *Between Culture and Politics. Intellectuals and Modern Society*. Cambridge: Polity Press.

Eyerman, Ron and Jamison, Andrew 1991: *Social Movements: A Cognitive Approach*. Cambridge: Polity Press.

Eyerman, Ron and Jamison, Andrew 1994: Social Movements and Cultural Transformation: Popular Music in the 1960s. *Media, Culture And Society*, 17, 449–68.

Eyerman, Ron and Jamison, Andrew 1997: *Music and Social Movements*. Cambridge/New York: Cambridge University Press.

Fabbrini, Sergio 1986: *Neo-Conservatorismo e Politica Americana*. Bologna: il Mulino.

Fabbrini, Sergio 1988: *Politica e Mutamenti Sociali*. Bologna: il Mulino.

Fantasia, Rick 1988: *Cultures of Solidarity. Consciousness, Action, and Contemporary American Workers*. Berkeley, CA/London: University of California Press.

Fantasia, Rick and Hirsch, Eric 1995: Culture in Rebellion: The Appropriation and Transformation of the Veil in the Algerian Revolution. In H. Johnston and B. Klandermans (eds), *Social Movements and Culture*, Minneapolis/London: University of Minnesota Press/UCL Press, 144–159.

Farro, Antimo 1986: *Conflitti Sociali e Città*. Milano: Angeli.

Farro, Antimo 1991: *La Lente Verde*. Milan: Angeli.

Favre Pierre (ed.) 1990: *La Manifestation*, Paris: Presses de la Fondation Nationale des Sciences Politiques.

Feagin, Joe R. and Capek, Stella M. 1991: Grassroots Movements in a Class Perspective. In P. C. Wasburn (ed.), *Research in Political Sociology*, vol. 5, Greenwich, CT: JAI Press, 27–53.

Featherstone, Mike (ed) 1990: *Global Culture. Nationalism, Globalization and Modernity*. London: Sage.

Featherstone, Mike 1987: Lifestyle and Consumer Culture. *Theory, Culture and Society*, 4, 54–70.

Featherstone, Mike 1995: *Undoing Culture. Globalization, Postmodernism and Identity*. London/Thousand Oaks: Sage.

Fedel, Giorgio 1989: Cultura e Simboli Politici. In A. Panebianco (ed.), *L'Analisi della Politica*, Bologna: il Mulino, 365–90.

Fernandez, Roberto and McAdam, Doug 1989: Multiorganizational Fields and Recruitment to Social Movements. In B. Klandermans (ed.), *Organizing for Change*, Greenwich, CT: JAI Press, 315–44.

Fillieule, Olivier and Jobard, Fabien 1998: The Policing of Protest in France. Towards a Model of Protest Policing. In D. della Porta and H. Reiter (eds), *Policing Protest. The Control of Mass Demonstrations in Western Democracies*, Minneapolis: The University of Minnesota Press.

Fireman, Bruce and Gamson, William A. 1979: Utilitarian Logic in the Resource Mobilization Perspective. In J. D. McCarthy and M. N. Zald (eds), the *Dynamics of Social Movements*, Cambridge, MA: Winthrop, 8–44.

Fischer, Frank 1993: Citizen Participation and the Democratization of Policy Expertise: From Theoretical Inquiry to Practical Cases. *Policy Sciences*, 26, 165–87.

Flam, Helena 1990: Emotional 'Man': I. The Emotional 'Man' and the Problem of Collective Action. *International Sociology*, 5, 39–56.

Flam, Helena 1994a: A Theoretical Framework for the Study of Encounters between States and Anti-Nuclear Movements. In H. Flam (ed.), *States and Antinuclear Movements*, Edinburgh: Edinburgh University Press, 9–26.

Flam, Helena, 1994b: Political Responses to the Anti-Nuclear Challenge: I. Standard Deliberative and Decision-Making Settings. In H. Flam (ed.), *States and Antinuclear Movements*, Edinburgh: Edinburgh University Press, 299–328.

Flam, Helena 1994c: Political Responses to the Anti-Nuclear Challenge: II. Democratic Experiences and the Use of Force. In H. Flam (ed.), *States and Antinuclear Movements*, Edinburgh: Edinburgh University Press, 329–54.

Flam, Helena (ed.) 1994d: *States and Anti-Nuclear Movements*. Edinburgh: Edinburgh University Press.

Foot, John M. 1996: The 'Left Opposition' and the Crisis: Rifondazione Comunista and La Rete. In S. Gundle and S. Parker (eds), *The New Italian Republic*, London/New York: Routledge, 173–88.

Forbes, James D. 1985: Organizational and Political Dimensions of Consumer Pressure Groups. *Journal of Consumer Policy*, 8, 133–1.

Foucault, Michel 1977: *Discipline and Punish*. New York: Pantheon.

Foweraker, Joe 1995: *Theorizing Social Movements*. London: Pluto.

Frank, Andre Gunder and Fuentes, Maria 1994: On Studying Cycles in Social Movements. *Research in Social Movements, Conflict and Change*, 17, 173–96.

Franklin, Mark, Mackie, Tom, and Valen, Henry (eds) 1992: *Electoral Change*. Cambridge/New York: Cambridge University Press.

Franzosi, Roberto 1995: *The Puzzle of Strikes. Class and State Strategies in Postwar Italy.* Cambridge: Cambridge University Press.

Freeman, Jo 1979: Resource Mobilization and Strategy: A Model for Analyzing Social Movement Organizations. In M. N. Zald and J. D. McCarthy (eds), *The Dynamics of Social Movements. Resource Mobilization, Social Control, and Tactics,* Cambridge MA: Winthrop Publishing, 167–89.

Freeman, Jo 1983a: A Model for Analyzing the Strategic Options of Social Movement Organizations. In J. Freeman (ed.), *Social Movements of the Sixties and Seventies,* London: Longman, 193–210.

Freeman, Jo 1983b: On the Origins of Social Movements. In J. Freeman (ed.), *Social Movements of the Sixties and the Seventies,* New York: Longman, 8–30.

Freeman, Linton C. 1979: Centrality in Social Networks. I. Conceptual Clarifications. *Social Networks,* 1, 215–39.

Friedman, Debra and McAdam, Doug 1992: Collective Identity and Activism. In A. Morris and C. McClurg Mueller (eds), *Frontiers in Social Movement Theory,* New Haven: Yale University Press, 156–73.

Fuchs, Dieter and Rucht, Dieter 1994: Support for New Social Movements in Five Western European Countries. In C. Rootes and H. Davis (eds), *A New Europe? Social Change and Political Transformation,* London: UCL Press, 86–111.

Galaskiewicz, Joseph 1979: *Exchange Networks and Community Politics.* Beverly Hills/London: Sage.

Galaskiewicz, Joseph 1985: Interorganizational Relations. *Annual Review of Sociology,* 11, 281–304.

Gale, Richard P. 1986: Social Movements and the State. The Environmental Movement, Counter-movement, and Governmental Agencies. *Sociological Perspectives,* 29, 202–40.

Gallagher, John and Chris Bull 1996: *Perfect Enemies: The Religious Right, the Gay Movement, and the Politics of the 1990s.* New York: Crown Publishers.

Gallino, Luciano 1978a: Comportamento Collettivo. In *Dizionario di Sociologia.* Torino: UTET, 128–31.

Gallino, Luciano 1978b: Conflitto. In *Dizionario di Sociologia.* Torino: UTET, 156–61.

Gamson, Josh 1989: Silence, Death, and the Invisible Enemy: AIDS Activism and Social Movement 'Newness'. *Social Problems,* 36, 351–67.

Gamson, Josh 1995: Must Identity Movements Self-Destruct? A Queer Dilemma. *Social Problems,* 42, 390–407.

Gamson, William 1988: Political Discourse and Collective Action. In B. Klandermans, H. Kriesi and S. Tarrow (eds), *From Structure to Action,* Greenwich, CT: JAI Press, 219–46.

Gamson, William 1990: *The Strategy of Social Protest* (2nd edition). Belmont, CA: Wadsworth (original edition 1975).

Gamson, William 1992a: The Social Psychology of Collective Action. In A. Morris and C. McClurg Mueller (eds), *Frontiers in Social Movement Theory,* New Haven: Yale University Press, 53–76.

Gamson, William 1992b: *Talking Politics*. Cambridge/New York: Cambridge University Press.

Gamson, William and Meyer, David S. 1996: Framing Political Opportunity. In D. McAdam, J. D. McCarthy and M. N. Zald (eds), *Opportunities, Mobilizing Structures, and Framing*, New York/Cambridge: Cambridge University Press, 275–90.

Gamson, William and Modigliani, André 1989: Media Discourse and Public Opinion on Nuclear Power. *American Journal of Sociology*, 95, 1–37.

Gamson, William and Wolfsfeld, Gadi 1993: Movements and Media as Interacting Systems. *The Annals of the AAPSS*, 528, 114–25.

Gans, Herbert 1979: Symbolic Ethnicity: The Future of Ethnic Groups and Cultures in America. *Ethnic and Racial Studies*, 2, 1–20.

Garofalo, Reebee (ed.) 1992: *Rockin' the Boat: Mass Music and Mass Movements*. Boston: South End Press.

Geary, Dick 1981: *European Labour Protest 1848–1939*. New York: St Martin's Press.

Geary, Dick 1989: Introduction. In D. Geary (ed.), *Labour and Socialist Movements in Europe Before 1914*, Oxford/New York: Berg.

Gelb, Joyce 1989: *Feminism and Politics. A Comparative Perspective*. Berkeley: University of California Press.

Gelb, Joyce and Palley, Marian Lief (eds) 1982: *Women and Public Policies*. Princeton: Princeton University Press.

Gellner, Ernest 1993: *Ragione e Religione*. Milano: il Saggiatore (original edition *Postmodernism, Reason and Religion*, London: Routledge, 1992).

Gerhards, Jürgen 1991: Die Mobilisierung gegen die IWF- und Weltbanktagung in Berlin: Gruppen, Veranstaltungen, Diskurse. In Roland Roth and Dieter Rucht (eds), *Neue soziale Bewegungen in der Bundesrepublik Deutschland*. Bonn: Bundeszentrale für politische Bildung, 213–34.

Gerhards, Jürgen 1993: *Neue Konfliktlinie in der Mobilisierung öffentlicher Meinung. Warum die IWF Tagung in Berlin 1988 zu einem öffentlichen Streitthema würde*. Berlin: Sigma.

Gerhards, Jürgen 1995: Framing dimensions and framing strategies: contrasting ideal and real-type frames. *Social Science Information*, 34, 225–48.

Gerhards, Jürgen and Rucht, Dieter 1992: Mesomobilization Contexts: Organizing and Framing in Two Protest Campaigns in West Germany. *American Journal of Sociology*, 98, 555–96.

Gerlach, Luther 1971: Movements of Revolutionary Change. Some Structural Characteristics. *American Behavioral Scientist*, 43, 813–36.

Gerlach, Luther 1976: La Struttura dei Nuovi Movimenti di Rivolta. In Alberto Melucci (ed.), *Movimenti di Rivolta*, Milan: Etas, 218–32.

Gerlach, Luther and Hine, Virginia 1970: *People, Power and Change*. Indianapolis: The Bobbs-Merrill Company.

Giddens, Anthony 1983: La Società Europea negli Anni Ottanta: Divisioni di Classe, Conflitto di Classe e Diritti di Cittadinanza. In G. Pasquino (ed.), *Le Società Complesse*, Bologna: il Mulino, 153–200.

Giddens, Anthony 1990: *The Consequences of Modernity*. Cambridge/Stanford, CA: Polity Press/Stanford University Press.

Ginsborg, Paul 1990: *Italy since 1943*. London: Penguin.

Gitlin, Todd 1980: *The Whole World is Watching: Mass Media in the Making and Unmaking of the New Left*. Berkeley/Los Angeles, CA: University of California Press.

Giugni, Marco 1998: The Other Side of the Coin: Crossnational Similarities between Social Movements, *Mobilization*, 3, 89–105.

Goffman, Erving 1974: *Frame Analysis*. Cambridge, MA: Harvard University Press.

Goldstein, Robert J. 1983: *Political Repression in 19th Century Europe*. London: Croom Helm.

Goldstone, Jack A. 1991: *Revolution and Rebellion in the Early Modern World*. Berkeley/Los Angeles: University of California Press.

Goldthorpe, John H. 1982: On the Service Class, Its Formation and Future. In A. Giddens, and G. Mackenzie (eds), *Social Class and the Division of Labour*, Cambridge: Cambridge University Press.

Gould, Roger 1991: Multiple Networks and Mobilization in the Paris Commune 1871. *American Sociological Review*, 56, 716–29.

Gould, Roger 1993: Trade Cohesion, Class Unity, and Urban Insurrection. Artisanal Activism in the Paris Commune. *American Journal of Sociology*, 56, 721–54.

Gould, Roger 1995: *Insurgent Identities: Class, Community, and Protest in Paris from 1848 to the Commune*. Chicago/London: University of Chicago Press.

Gouldner, Alvin 1979: *The Future of Intellectuals and the Rise of the New Class*. New York: Continuum.

Granovetter, Mark 1973: The Strength of Weak Ties. *American Journal of Sociology*, 78, 1,360–80.

Granovetter, Mark 1985: Economic Action and Social Structure. The Problem of Embeddedness. *American Journal of Sociology*, 91, 481–510.

Grazioli, Marco and Lodi, Giovanni 1984: La Mobilitazione Collettiva negli Anni Ottanta: Tra Condizione e Convinzione. In A. Melucci (ed.), *Altri Codici*, Bologna: il Mulino, 267–313.

Gronmo, Sigmund 1987: The Strategic Position in the Information Society. *Journal of Consumer Policy*, 10, 43–67.

Gundle, Stephen and Parker, Simon (eds) 1996: *The New Italian Republic. From the Fall of the Berlin Wall to Berlusconi*. London/New York: Routledge.

Gurr, Ted R. 1970: *Why Men Rebel*, Princeton, NJ: Princeton University Press.

Gurr, Ted R. and Harff, Barbara 1994: *Ethnic Conflict in World Politics*. Boulder: Westview Press.

Gusfield, Joseph 1962: Mass Society and Extremist Politics, *American Sociological Review*, 27, 19–30.

Gusfield, Joseph 1963: *Symbolic Crusade*. Urbana, IL: University of Illinois.

Gusfield, Joseph 1968: The Study of Social Movements. In D. L. Sills (ed.), *International Encyclopedia of the Social Sciences*, New York: Collier & McMillan, 445–452.

Gusfield, Joseph 1981: Social Movements and Social Change: Perspectives of Linearity and Fluidity. In L. Kriesberg (ed.), *Research in Social Movements, Conflict and Change*, Vol. 4, Greenwich, CT: JAI Press, 317–39.

Gusfield, Joseph 1994: The Reflexivity of Social Movements: Collective Behavior and Mass Society Theory Revisited. In E. Larana, H. Johnston and J. Gusfield (eds), *New Social Movements. From Ideology to Identity*, Philadelphia: Temple University Press, 58–78.

Habermas, Jürgen 1976: *Legitimation Crisis*. London: Heinemann.

Habermas, Jürgen 1978: *Knowledge and Human Interests*. London: Heinemann.

Habermas, Jürgen 1987: *The Theory of Communicative Action*. Cambridge: Polity Press.

Habermas, Jürgen 1989: *The Structural Transformation of the Public Sphere*. Cambridge, MA: MIT Press.

Haines, Herbert H. 1988: *Black Radicals and the Civil Rights Mainstream, 1954– 1970*. Knoxville: University of Tennessee Press.

Hainsworth, Paul (ed) 1992: *The Extreme Right in Europe and the USA*. London: Pinter.

Hall, Richard 1982: *Organizations: Structure and Process*. Englewood Cliffs, NJ: Prentice Hall.

Hannigan, John 1995: *Environmental Sociology*. London/New York: Routledge.

Hargreaves Heap, Shaun, Hollis, Martin, Lyons, Bruce, Sugden, Robert, and Weale, Albert 1992: *The Theory of Choice. A Critical Guide*. Oxford/ Cambridge, MA: Blackwell.

Hathaway, Will and David S. Meyer 1993–4: Competition and Cooperation in Social Movement Coalitions: Lobbying for Peace in the 1980s. *Berkeley Journal of Sociology, A Critical Review*, 38, 157–83.

Heath Anthony, Jowell, Roger, Curtice, John, Evans, Geoffrey, Field, John, and Whiterspoon, S. 1991: *Understanding Political Change: The British Voter 1946–1987*, Oxford: Pergamon Press.

Hechter, Michael 1975: *Internal Colonialism: The Celtic Fringe in British National Development, 1536–1966*. London: Routledge & Kegan Paul.

Heckathorn, Douglas D. 1996: The Dynamics and Dilemmas of Collective Action. *American Sociological Review*, 61, 250–77.

Heiberg, Marianne. 1989. *The Making of the Basque Nation*. Cambridge/New York: Cambridge University Press.

Heirich, Max 1971: *The Spiral of Conflict: Berkeley 1964*. New York: Columbia University Press.

Hellman, Judith 1987: *Journeys among Women: Feminism in Five Italian Cities*. Oxford: Oxford University Press.

Hilgartner, Stephen and Bosk, Charles L. 1988: The Rise and Fall of Social Problems: A Public Arenas Model. *American Journal of Sociology*, 94, 53–78.

Hinckley, Barbara 1981: *Coalitions and Politics*. New York: Harcourt Brace Jovanovich.

Hirsch, Eric L. 1990: Sacrifice for the Cause: The Impact of Group Processes on Recruitment and Commitment in Protest Movements. *American Sociological Review*, 55, 243–54.

Hirsch, Joachim 1988: The Crisis of Fordism, Transformations of The 'Keynesian' Security State, and New Social Movements. *Research in Social Movements, Conflicts and Change*, 10, 43–55.

Hirschman, Albert O. 1982: *Shifting Involvements: Private Interests and Public Action*. Princeton, NJ: Princeton University Press.

Hobsbawm, Eric 1991: *Nazioni e Nazionalismo dal 1780. Programma, Mito, Realtà*. Turin: Einaudi. (Original edition *Nations and Nationalism since 1780*, Cambridge/New York: Cambridge University Press, 1993.)

Hobsbawm, Eric and Ranger, Terence (eds) 1983: *The Invention of Tradition*, Cambridge/New York: Cambridge University Press.

Hoffman, Lily M. 1989: *The Politics of Knowledge. Activist Movements in Medicine and Planning*. Albany, NY: SUNY Press.

Hunt, Lynn A. 1984: *Politics, Culture, and Class in the French Revolution*. Berkeley: University of California Press.

Hunt, Scott A. 1992: Critical Dramaturgy and Collective Rhetoric: Cognitive and Moral Order in the Communist Manifesto. *Perspectives on Social Problems*, 3, 1–18.

Hunt, Scott A. and Benford, Robert D. 1994: Identity Talk in the Peace and Justice Movement. *Journal of Contemporary Ethnography*, 22, 488–517.

Hunt, Scott A., Benford, Robert D. and Snow, David A. 1994: Identity Fields: Framing Processes and the Social Construction of Movement Identities. In E. Larana, H. Johnston and J. R. Gusfield (eds), *New Social Movements: From Ideology to Identity*, Philadelphia: Temple University Press, 185–208.

Hunter, Floyd 1953: *Community Power Structure. A Study of Decision Makers*, Chapel Hill: The University of North Carolina Press.

Ibarra, Pedro 1995: Nuevas Formas de Comportamiento Politico: Los Nuevos Movimientos Sociales. *Inuruak. Revista Vasca de Sociologia y Ciencias Politica*, vol. 13, 39–60.

Ignazi, Piero 1994: *L'Estrema Destra in Europa*. Bologna: il Mulino.

Ignazi, Piero and Ysmal, Colette 1992: New and Old Extreme Right-wing Parties. The French Front National and the Italian Movimento Sociale. *European Journal of Political Research*, 22, 101–20.

Inglehart, Ronald 1977: *The Silent Revolution. Changing Values and Political Styles among Western Publics*. Princeton: Princeton University Press.

Inglehart, Ronald 1985: New Perspectives on Value Change. *Comparative Political Studies*, 17, 485–532.

Inglehart, Ronald 1990a: *Culture Shift in Advanced Industrial Society*. Princeton, NJ: Princeton University Press.

Inglehart, Ronald 1990b: Values, Ideology, and Cognitive Mobilization in New Social Movements. In R. Dalton and M. Kuechler (eds), *Challenging the Political Order*, Cambridge: Polity Press, 43–66.

Inglehart, Ronald 1997: *Modernization and Postmodernization: Cultural, Economic, and Political Change in 43 Societies*. Princeton, NJ: Princeton University Press.

Inglehart, Ronald and Abramson, Paul R. 1994: Economic Security and Value Change. *American Political Science Review*, 88, 336–54.

Jackson, John Harold and Morgan, C. P. 1978: *Organizational Theory: A Macroperspective for Management*. Englewood Cliffs, NJ: Prentice-Hall.

Jamison, Andrew and Eyerman, Ron 1994: *Seeds of the Sixties*. Berkely/Los Angeles: University of California Press.

Jamison, Andrew, Eyerman, Ron and Cramer, Jacqueline 1990: *The Making of the New Environmental Consciousness. A Comparative Study of the Environmental Movements in Sweden, Denmark and the Netherlands*. Edinburgh: Edinburgh University Press.

Janda, Kenneth 1970: *A Conceptual Framework for the Comparative Analysis of Political Parties*. Beverly Hills, CA: Sage.

Jasper, James M. 1997: *The Art of Moral Protests*. Chicago, IL: University of Chicago Press.

Jasper, James M. and Nelkin, Dorothy 1992: *The Animal Rights Crusade: The Growth of a Moral Protest*. New York: Free Press.

Jasper, James M. and Poulsen, Jane 1995: Recruiting Strangers and Friends: Moral Shocks and Social Networks in Animal Right and Anti-Nuclear Protests. *Social Problems*, 42, 493–512.

Jenkins, J. Craig and Perrow, Charles 1977: Insurgency of the Powerless: The Farm Worker Movements 1946–1972. *American Sociological Review*, 42, 249–68.

Jenkins, J. Craig and Klandermans, Bert 1995: The Politics of Social Protest. In J. C. Jenkins and B. Klandermans (eds), *The Politics of Social Protest. Comparative Perspectives on States and Social Movements*, Minneapolis: The University of Minnesota Press, 3–13.

Jenkins, J. Craig 1983: Resource Mobilization Theory and the Study of Social Movements. *Annual Review of Sociology*, 9, 527–53.

Jenkins, J. Craig 1985: *The Politics of Insurgency: The Farm Worker Movement in the 1960s*. New York: Columbia University Press.

Jennings, M. Kent, van Deth, Jan, Barnes, Samuel, Fuchs, Dieter, Heunks, Felix, Inglehart, Ronald, Kaase, Max, Klingemann, Hans-Dieter and Thomassen, Jacques 1990: *Continuities in Political Action*. Berlin/New York: Walter de Gruyter.

Jenson, Jane 1995: What's in a Name? Nationalist Movements and Public Discourse. In H. Johnston and B. Klandermans (eds), *Social Movements and Culture*, Minneapolis/London: University of Minnesota/UCL Press, 107–26.

Johnston, Hank 1991a: Antecedents of Coalition: Frame Alignment and Utilitarian Unity in the Catalan Anti-Francoist Opposition. In L. Kriesberg (ed.), *Research in Social Movements, Conflict and Change*, vol. 13, Greenwich, CT: JAI Press, 241–59.

Johnston, Hank 1991b: *Tales of Nationalism: Catalonia, 1939–1979*. New Brunswick, NJ: Rutgers University Press.

Johnston, Hank 1994: New Social Movements and Old Regional Nationalisms. In E. Larana, H. Johnston and J. Gusfield (eds), *New Social Movements. From Ideology to Identity*, Philadelphia: Temple University Press, 267–186.

Johnston, Hank 1995a: A Methodology for Frame Analysis: From Discourse to Cognitive Schemata. In H. Johnston and B. Klandermans (eds), *Social Movements and Culture*, Minneapolis/London: University of Minnesota Press/UCL Press, 217–46.

Johnston, Hank 1995b: The Trajectory of Nationalist Movements: Catalan and Basque Comparisons. *Journal of Political and Military Sociology*, 23, 231–49.

Johnston, Hank and Klandermans, Bert (eds) 1995: *Social Movements and Culture*. Minneapolis/London: University of Minnesota Press/UCL Press.

Joppke, Christian 1993: *Mobilizing against Nuclear Energy. A Comparison of Germany and the United States*. Berkeley/Los Angeles: University of California Press.

Joppke, Christian 1994: Revisionisms, Dissidence, Nationalism: Opposition in Leninist Regimes. *British Journal of Sociology*, 45, 543–61.

Jordan, Grant and Maloney, William 1997: *The Protest Business*. Manchester: Manchester University Press.

Jordan, Tim 1994: *Reinventing Revolution: Value and Difference in New Social Movements and the Left*. Aldershot: Avebury.

Jünschke, Klaus 1988: *Spätlese. Texte zu Raf und Knast*. Frankfurt am Main: Neue Kritik.

Kaase, Max 1990: Social Movements and Political Innovation. In R. Dalton and M. Kuechler (eds), *Challenging the Political Order: New Social and Political Movements In Western Democracies*, Cambridge: Polity Press, 86–101.

Kanter, Rosabeth M. 1968: Commitment and Social Organization: A Study of Commitment Mechanisms in Utopian Communities. *American Sociological Review*, 33, 499–517.

Kanter, Rosabeth M. 1972: Commitment and the Internal Organization of Millennial Movements. *American Behavioral Scientist*, 16, 219–43.

Karstedt-Henke, Suzanne 1980: Theorien zur Erklärung terroristischer Bewegungen. In Erhard Blankenberg (ed.), *Politik der inneren Sicherheit*. Frankfurt am Main: Suhrkamp, 198–234.

Katz, Daniel and Lazarsfeld, Paul 1955: *Personal Influence*. Glencoe, IL: Free Press.

Katzenstein, Mary 1987: Comparing the Feminist Movements of the United States and Western Europe: An Overview. In Mary Katzenstein and Carol Mueller (eds), *The Women's Movements of the United States and Western Europe*. Philadelphia: Temple University Press, 3–20.

Katzenstein, Peter J. 1985: *Small States in the World Market*, Ithaca, NY: Cornell University Press.

Keane, John (ed.) 1988: *Democracy and Civil Society*. London: Verso.

Keating, Michael 1988: *State and Regional Nationalism. Territorial Politics and the European State*. London: Harvester-Wheatsheaf.

Kertzer, David 1988: *Rituals, Politics, and Power*. New Haven: Yale University Press.

Kielbowicz, Richard B. and Scherer, Clifford 1986: The Role of the Press in the Dynamics of Social Movements. *Research in Social Movements, Conflict and Change*, 9, 71–96.

Killian, Lewis 1964: Social Movements. In Robert E. Farris (ed.), *Handbook of Modern Sociology*, Chicago: Rand McNally, 426–45.

Killian, Lewis 1984: Organization, Rationality and Spontaneity in the Civil Rights Movement. *American Sociological Review*, 49, 770–83.

Kimeldorf, Howard and Stepan-Norris, Judith 1992: Historical Studies of Labor Movements in the United States. *Annual Review of Sociology*, 18, 495–517.

Kinnear, Ralph 1990: Visions of Europe. An Eco-Dynamic Approach to Ethno-Linguistic Conflict, Self-Organisation and the Role of the State. Unpublished paper. London School of Economics, London.

Kitschelt, Herbert 1985: New Social Movements in West Germany and the United States. *Political Power and Social Theory*, 5, 273–342.

Kitschelt, Herbert 1986: Political Opportunity Structures and Political Protest: Anti-Nuclear Movements in Four Democracies. *British Journal of Political Science*, 16, 57–85.

Kitschelt, Herbert 1989: *The Logics of Party Formation: Ecological Politics in Belgium and West Germany*. Ithaca NY: Cornell University Press.

Kitschelt, Herbert 1990: New Social Movements and the Decline of Party Organization. In R. J. Dalton and M. Kuechler (eds), *Challenging the Political Order*, Cambridge: Polity Press, 179–208.

Kitschelt, Herbert 1993: Social Movements, Political Parties, and Democratic Theory. *The Annals of the AAPSS*, 528, 13–29.

Kitschelt, Herbert 1995: *The Radical Right in Western Europe: A Comparative Analysis* (in collaboration with Anthony J. McGann). Ann Arbor: University of Michigan Press.

Kitschelt, Herbert and Hellemans, Staff 1990: *Beyond the European Left. Ideology and Political Action in the Belgian Ecology Parties*. Durham NC/ London: Duke University Press.

Klandermans, Bert 1988: The Formation and Mobilization of Consensus. In B. Klandermans, H. Kriesi and S. Tarrow (eds), *From Structure to Action*, Greenwich, CT: JAI Press, 173–96.

Klandermans, Bert (ed.) 1989: *Organizing For Change: Social Movement Organizations Across Cultures*. Greenwich, CT: JAI Press.

Klandermans, Bert 1989a: Grievance Interpretation and Success Expectations: The Social Construction of Protest. *Social Behavior*, 4, 113–25.

Klandermans, Bert 1989b: Introduction: Social Movement Organizations and the Study of Social Movements. In B. Klandermans (ed.), *Organizing for Change*, Greenwich, CT: JAI Press, 1–17.

Klandermans, Bert 1990: Linking the 'Old' and 'New': Movement Networks in the Netherlands. In R. Dalton and M. Kuechler (eds), *Challenging the Political Order: New Social and Political Movements in Western Democracies*, Cambridge: Polity Press, 122–36.

Klandermans, Bert 1997: *The Social Psychology Of Protest*. Oxford/Cambridge, MA: Blackwell.

Klandermans, Bert and Tarrow, Sidney 1988: Mobilization into Social Movements: Synthesizing European and American Approaches. In B. Klandermans, H. Kriesi and S. Tarrow (eds), *From Structure to Action*, Greenwich, CT: JAI Press, 1–40.

Klandermans, Bert, Kriesi, Hanspeter and Tarrow, Sidney (eds) 1988: *From Structure to Action. Comparing Social Movement Research across Cultures*. Greenwich, CT: JAI Press.

Kleidman, Robert 1993: *Organizing for Peace: Neutrality, the Test Ban, and the Freeze*. Syracuse, NY: Syracuse University Press.
Klein, Ethel 1984: *Gender Politics. From Consciousness to Mass Politics*. Cambridge: Harvard University Press.
Knoke, David 1983: Organization Sponsorship and Influence Reputation of Social Influence Associations. *Social Forces*, 61, 1,065–87.
Knoke, David 1990: *Organizing for Collective Action. The Political Economies of Associations*. New York: Aldine de Gruyter.
Knoke, David and Kuklinski, James H. 1982: *Network Analysis*. London/ Newbury Park, CA: Sage.
Knoke, David and Wisely, Nancy 1990: Social Movements. In D. Knoke, *Political Networks*, Cambridge/New York: Cambridge University Press, 57–84.
Knoke, David and Wood, James R. 1981: *Organized for Action. Commitment In Voluntary Associations*. New Brunswick, NJ: Rutgers University Press.
Koelble, Thomas A. 1991: *The Left Unraveled: Social Democracy and the New Left Challenge in Britain*. Durham: Duke University Press.
Koestler, Arthur 1969: *The Invisible Writing*, New York: Stein and Day.
Koopmans, Ruud 1990: Bridging the Gap: The Missing Link between Political Opportunity Structure and Movement Action. Paper presented at the Twelfth World Congress of the International Sociological Association, Madrid.
Koopmans, Ruud 1993: The Dynamics of Protest Waves: West Germany, 1965 to 1989. *American Sociological Review*, 58, 637–58.
Koopmans, Ruud 1995: *Democracy from Below. New Social Movements and the Political System in West Germany*. Boulder, CO: Westview Press.
Koopmans, Ruud 1996a: Explaining the Rise of Racist and Extreme Right Violence in Western Europe: Grievances or Opportunities? *European Journal of Political Research*, 30, 185–216.
Koopmans, Ruud 1996b: New Social Movements and Changes in Political Participation in Western Europe. *West European Politics*, 19, 28–50.
Koopmans, Ruud 1997: Dynamics of Repression and Mobilization: The German Extreme Right in the 1990s. *Mobilization*, 2, 149–65.
Koopmans, Ruud and Duyvendak, Jan-Willem 1995. 'The Political Construction of the Nuclear Energy Issue and Its Impact on the Mobilization of Anti-Nuclear Movements in Western Europe.' *Social Problems* 42: 201–18.
Koopmans, Ruud and Rucht, Dieter 1995: *Social Movement Mobilization under Right and Left Governments: A Look at Four West European Countries*, Discussion Paper FS III: 95–106, Wissenschaftszentrum Berlin.
Kornhauser, A. 1959: *The Politics of Mass Society*. Glencoe: Free Press.
Krasniewicz, Louise 1992: *Nuclear Summer. The Clash of Communities at the Seneca Women's Peace Encampment*. Ithaca NY: Cornell University Press.
Kriesi, Hanspeter 1984: *Die Zürcher Bewegung. Bilder, Interaktionen, Zusammenhänge*. Frankfurt am Main: Campus.
Kriesi, Hanspeter 1988a: The Interdependence of Structure and Action: Some Reflections on the State of the Art. In B. Klandermans, H. Kriesi and S. Tarrow (eds), *From Structure to Action*, Greenwich, CT: JAI Press, 349–68.

Kriesi, Hanspeter 1988b: Local Mobilization for the People's Petition of the Dutch Peace Movement. In B. Klandermans, H. Kriesi and S. Tarrow (eds), *From Structure to Action*, Greenwich, CT: JAI Press, 41–82.

Kriesi, Hanspeter 1989a: The Political Opportunity Structure of the Dutch Peace Movement. *West European Politics*, 12, 295–312.

Kriesi, Hanspeter 1989b: New Social Movements and the New Class in the Netherlands. *American Journal of Sociology*, 94, 1,078–116.

Kriesi, Hanspeter 1991: *The Political Opportunity Structure of New Social Movements*, Discussion Paper FS III: 91–103. Wissenschaftszentrum Berlin.

Kriesi, Hanspeter 1992: Support and Mobilisation Potential for New Social Movements. In M. Diani and R. Eyerman (eds), *Studying Collective Action*, Newbury Park/London: Sage, 22–54.

Kriesi, Hanspeter 1993: *Political Mobilization and Social Change. The Dutch Case in Comparative Perspective*. Aldershot: Avebury.

Kriesi, Hanspeter 1995: The Political Opportunity Structure of New Social Movements: Its Impact on Their Mobilization. In J. C. Jenkins and B. Klandermans (eds), *The Politics of Social Protest*, Minneapolis, MI/London: University of Minnesota Press/UCL Press, 167–98.

Kriesi, Hanspeter 1996: The Organizational Structure of New Social Movements in a Political Context. In D. McAdam, J. McCarthy and M. N. Zald (eds), *Comparative Perspective on Social Movements. Political Opportunities, Mobilizing Structures, and Cultural Framing*, Cambridge/New York: Cambridge University Press, 152–184.

Kriesi, Hanspeter and van Praag, Philip 1987: Old and New Politics: The Dutch Peace Movement and the Traditional Political Organizations. *European Journal of Political Research*, 15, 319–46.

Kriesi, Hanspeter, Koopmans, Ruud, Duyvendak, Jan-Willem, and Giugni, Marco 1995: *New Social Movements in Western Europe*. Minneapolis/London: The University of Minnesota Press/UCL Press.

Kumar, Krishan 1995: *From Post-industrial to Post-modern Society*. Oxford/Cambridge, MA: Blackwell.

Lacey, Nicola, Wells, Celia and Meure, Dirk 1990: *Reconstructing Criminal Law. Critical Perspectives on Crime and the Criminal Process*. London: Weidenfeld & Nicolson.

Lalli, Pina 1995: *L'Ecologia del Pensatore Dilettante*. Bologna: Clueb.

Lang, Kurt and Lang, Gladys 1961: *Collective Dynamics*. New York: Thomas & Crowell.

Larana, Enrique, Johnston, Hank and Gusfield, Joe (eds) 1994: *New Social Movements. From Ideology to Identity*. Philadelphia: Temple University Press.

Lash, Scott and Urry, John 1987: *The End of Organized Capitalism*. Cambridge: Polity.

Lash, Scott, Szerszynski, Bron, and Wynne, Brian (eds) 1996: *Risk, Environment, and Modernity*. Thousand Oaks/London: Sage.

Laumann, Edward O. and Knoke, David 1987: The *Organizational State. Social Choice in National Policy Domains*. Madison, WI: University of Wisconsin Press.

Lawson, Robert 1983: A Decentralized but Moving Pyramid: The Evolution and Consequences of the Structure of the Tenant Movement. In J. Freeman (ed.), *Social Movements of the Sixties and Seventies*, London: Longman, 119–32.

Lehmbruch, Gerhard 1977: Liberal Corporatism and Party Government. *Comparative Political Studies*, 10, 91–126.

Lemert, Charles 1994: Dark Thoughts about the Self. In C. Calhoun (ed.), *Social Theory and the Politics of Identity*, Oxford/Cambridge, MA: Blackwell, 100–129.

Lenart, Silvo 1993: *Shaping Political Attitudes. The Impact of Interpersonal Communication and Mass Media*. Thousand Oaks/London, Sage.

Lichterman, Paul 1995a: *The Search for Political Community: American Activists Reinventing Commitment*. Cambridge/New York: Cambridge University Press.

Lichterman, Paul 1995b: Piecing Together Multicultural Community: Cultural Differences in Community Building among Grass-Roots Environmentalists. *Social Problems*, 42, 513–34.

Lidskog, Rolf 1996: In Science We Trust? On the Relation between Scientific Knowledge, Risk Consciousness and Public Trust. *Acta Sociologica*, 39, 31–56.

Lijphart, Arendt 1984: *Democracies*, New Haven: Yale University Press.

Lipset, Seymour M. and Rokkan, Stein (eds) 1967: *Party Systems and Voter Alignments*. New York: Free Press.

Lipsky, Michael 1965: *Protest and City Politics*. Chicago: Rand McNally & Co.

Lipsky, Michael 1970: Introduction. In M. Lipsky (ed.), *Law and Order: Police Encounters*. New York: Aldine Publishing Company, 1–7.

Lo, Clarence Y. H. 1982: Countermovements and Conservative Movements in the Contemporary US, *Annual Review of Sociology*, 8, 107–34.

Lo, Clarence Y. H. 1990: *Small Property, Big Government: Social Origins of the Property Tax Revolt*. Berkeley, CA: University of California Press.

Lodhi, A. Q. and Tilly, Charles 1973: Urbanization, Crime and Collective Violence in 19th Century France. *American Journal of Sociology*, 79, 296–318.

Lodi, Giovanni 1984: *Uniti e Diversi. Le Mobilitazioni per la Pace nell'Italia degli Anni Ottanta*. Milano: Unicopli.

Lodi, Giovanni and Grazioli, Marco 1984: Giovani sul Territorio Urbano: L'Integrazione Minimale. In A. Melucci (ed.), *Altri Codici*, Bologna: il Mulino, 63–126.

Lofland, John 1985a: Becoming a World-saver Revisited. In John Lofland, *Protest. Studies of Collective Behavior and Social Movements*. New Brunswick: Transaction Books, 147–57.

Lofland, John 1985b: Social Movement Culture. In J. Lofland, *Protest. Studies of Collective Behavior and Social Movements*, New Brunswick: Transaction Books, 219–239.

Lofland, John 1995: Charting Degrees of Movement Culture: Tasks of the Cultural Cartographer. In H. Johnston and B. Klandermans (eds), *Social Movements and Culture*, Minneapolis/London: University of Minnesota Press/UCL Press, 188–216.

Lofland, John and Skonovd, Norman 1985: Conversion Motifs. In J. Lofland, *Protest. Studies of Collective Behavior and Social Movements*, New Brunswick: Transaction Books, 158–71.

Lovendusky, Joni 1986: *Women and European Politics: Contemporary Feminism and Public Policy*, Amherst MA: The University of Massachussets Press.

Lovenduski, Joni and Randall, Vicky 1993: *Contemporary Feminist Politics*. Oxford/New York: Oxford University Press.

Lowe, Philip D. and Goyder, Jane M. 1983: *Environmental Groups in Politics*. London: Allen & Unwin.

Lowe, Stuart 1986: *Urban Social Movements. The City after Castells*. London: Macmillan.

Lowi, Theodor 1971: *The Politics of Disorder*. New York: Norton.

Luker, Kristin 1984: *Abortion and the Politics of Motherhood*. Berkeley, CA: University of California Press.

Lyons, Matthew Nemiroff 1988: The 'Grassroots' Network. Radical Nonviolence in the Federal Republic of Germany 1972–1985. *Cornell Studies In International Affairs – Western Societies Papers 20*, Ithaca, NY: Cornell University.

Mach, Zdzislaw 1993: *Symbols, Conflict, and Identity*. Albany, NY: SUNY Press.

Maffesoli, Michel 1995: *The Time of Tribes. The Decline of Individualism in Mass Society*. London/Thousand Oaks: Sage.

Maguire, Diarmuid 1993: Protesters, Counterprotesters, and the Authorities. *The Annals of the AAPSS*, 528, 101–13.

Maguire, Diarmuid 1995: Opposition Movements and Opposition Parties: Equal Partners or Dependent Relations in the Struggle for Power and Reform? In J. C. Jenkins and B. Klandermans (eds), *The Politics of Social Protest. Comparative Perspectives on States and Social Movements*, Minneapolis/London: University of Minnesota Press/UCL Press, 189–207.

Maheu, Louis (ed.) 1995: *Social Movements and Social Classes*, London/Thousand Oaks: Sage.

Manconi, Luigi 1990: *Solidarietà, Egoismo. Movimenti, Buone Azioni, Nuovi Conflitti*. Bologna: il Mulino.

Mannheim, Karl 1946: *Ideology and Utopia*. New York: Harcourt, Brace.

Mannheimer, Renato and Sani, Giacomo 1987: *Il Mercato Elettorale. Identikit dell'Elettore Italiano*. Bologna: il Mulino.

Mansbridge, Jane J. 1986: *Why We Lost the ERA*. Chicago: University of Chicago Press.

Manza, Jeff and Brooks, Clem 1996: Does Class Analysis Still Have Anything to Contribute to the Study of Politics? – Comments. *Theory and Society*, 25, 717–24.

Maraffi, Marco (ed.) 1981: *La Società Neo-corporativa*. Bologna: il Mulino.

Markoff, John 1996: *Waves of Democracy. Social Movements and Political Change*. London/Thousand Oaks: Sage/Pine Forge Press.

Marks, Gary 1989: *Union in Politics. Britain, Germany and the United States in the Nineteenth and Early Twentieth Century*. Princeton: Princeton University Press.

Marks, Gary and Doug McAdam 1998: Social Movements and the Changing Political Opportunity in the European Community. In D. della Porta, H. Kriesi and D. Rucht (eds), *Social Movements in a Globalizing World*, New York/London: Longman.

Marsden, Peter V. and Lin, Nan (eds) 1982: *Social Structure and Network Analysis*. Beverly Hills/London: Sage.

Marshall, Th. 1976: *Cittadinanza e Classe Sociale*. Turin: Utet. (Original edition Citizenship and Social Class. In T. H. Marshall and T. Bottomore, *Citizenship and Social Class*, London: Pluto Press, 1992 [1950], 3–51.)

Martinotti, Guido 1993: *Metropoli. La Nuova Morfologia Sociale della Città*. Bologna: il Mulino.

Marwell, Gerald and Oliver, Pamela 1993: *The Critical Mass in Collective Action. A Micro-Social Theory*. Cambridge/New York: Cambridge University Press.

Marwell, Gerard and Ames, Ruth E. 1979: Experiments on the Provision of Public Goods. I. Resources, Interest, Group Size, and the Free Rider Problem. *American Journal of Sociology*, 84, 1,335–60.

Marx Ferree, Myra 1992: The Political Context of Rationality: Rational Choice Theory and Resource Mobilization. In A. Morris and C. McClurg Mueller (eds), *Frontiers in Social Movement Theory*, New Haven: Yale University Press, 29–52.

Marx, Gary T. 1979: External Efforts to Damage or Facilitate Social Movements: Some Patterns, Explanations, Outcomes and Complications. In J. McCarthy and M. N. Zald (eds), *The Dynamics of Social Movements*, Cambridge MA: Winthrop Publishing, 94–125.

Marx Gary T. and Wood, James 1975: Strands of Theory and Research in Collective Behaviour, *Annual Review of Sociology*, 1, 363–428.

Mayer, Robert N. 1989: *The Consumer Movement. Guardians of the Marketplace*. Boston: Twayne.

McAdam, Doug 1982: *Political Process and the Development of Black Insurgency. 1930–1970*. Chicago: University of Chicago Press.

McAdam, Doug 1983: Tactical Innovation and the Pace of Insurgency. *American Sociological Review*, 48, 735–54.

McAdam, Doug 1986: Recruitment to High-Risk Activism: The Case of Freedom Summer. *American Journal of Sociology*, 92, 64–90.

McAdam, Doug 1988: *Freedom Summer*. New York/Oxford: Oxford University Press.

McAdam, Doug 1994: Culture and Social Movements. In E. Larana, H. Hohnston and J. R. Gusfield (eds), *New Social Movements: From Ideology to Identity*, Philadelphia: Temple University Press, 36–57.

McAdam, Doug 1995: 'Initiator' and 'Spinoff' Movements: Diffusion Processes in Protest Cycles. In M. Traugott (ed.), *Repertoires and Cycles of Collective Action*, Durham, NC: Duke University Press, 217–39.

McAdam, Doug and Fernandez, Roberto 1990: Microstructural Bases of Recruitment to Social Movements. In L. Kriesberg (ed.), *Research In Social Movements, Conflict and Change*, vol. 12, Greenwich, CT: JAI Press, 1–33.

McAdam, Doug and Paulsen, Ronnelle 1993: Specifying the Relationship between Social Ties and Activism. *American Journal of Sociology*, 99, 640–67.

McAdam, Doug and Rucht, Dieter 1993: The Cross-national Diffusion of Movement Ideas. *The Annals of the AAPSS*, 528, 56–74.

McAdam, Doug and Snow, David (eds) 1996: *Social Movements. Readings on Their Emergence, Mobilization, and Dynamics*. Los Angeles: Roxbury.

McAdam, Doug, McCarthy, John D. and Zald, Mayer N. 1988: Social Movements. In N. J. Smelser (ed.), *Handbook of Sociology*, Beverly Hills/London: Sage, 695–739.

McAdam, Doug, McCarthy, John and Zald, Mayer N. (eds) 1996: *Comparative Perspective on Social Movements. Political Opportunities, Mobilizing Structures, and Cultural Framing*. Cambridge/New York: Cambridge University Press.

McAdam, Doug, Tarrow, Sidney and Tilly, Charles 1996: To Map Contentious Politics. *Mobilization*, 1, 17–34.

McAllister, Ian 1983: Social Contacts and Political Behaviour in Northern Ireland, 1968–78. *Social Networks*, 5, 303–13.

McCarthy, John D., Britt, David W. and Wolfson, Mark 1991: The Institutional Channeling of Social Movements by the State in the United States. *Research in Social Movements, Conflict and Change*, 13, 45–76.

McCarthy, John D. 1994: Activists, Authorities, and Media Framing of Drunk Driving. In E. Larana, H. Johnston and J. R. Gusfield (eds), *New Social Movements: From Ideology to Identity*, Philadelphia: Temple University Press, 133–67.

McCarthy, John D. 1996: Constraints and Opportunities in Adopting, Adapting, and Inventing. In D. McAdam, J. McCarthy and M. N. Zald (eds), *Comparative Perspective on Social Movements. Political Opportunities, Mobilizing Structures, and Cultural Framing*, Cambridge/New York: Cambridge University Press, 141–51.

McCarthy, John D. and Wolfson, Mark 1992: Consensus Movements, Conflict Movements, and the Cooptation of Civic and State Infrastructures. In A. Morris and C. McClurg Mueller (eds), *Frontiers in Social Movement Theory*, New Haven: Yale University Press, 273–98.

McCarthy, John D. and Zald, Mayer N. 1987a: The Trend of Social Movements in America: Professionalization and Resource Mobilization. In M. N. Zald and J. D. McCarthy, *Social Movements in an Organizational Society*, New Brunswick: Transaction, 1987, 337–91 (originally published as *The Trend of Social Movements In America*. Morristown: General Learning Press, 1973).

McCarthy, John D. and Zald, Mayer N. 1987b: Resource Mobilization and Social Movements: A Partial Theory. In M. N. Zald and J. D. McCarthy, *Social Movements in an Organizational Society*, New Brunswick: Transaction, 1987, 337–91 (originally published in *American Journal of Sociology*, 1977, 82, 1,212–41).

McCarthy, John, McPhail, Clark and Crist, John 1998: The Emergence and Diffusion of Public Order Management System: Protest Cycles and Police Response. In D. della Porta, H. Kriesi and D. Rucht (eds), *Social Movements in a Globalizing World*, forthcoming, New York/London: Longman.

McCarthy, John, McPhail, Clark and Smith, Jackie 1996: Images of Protest: Dimensions of Selection Bias in Media Coverage of Washington Demonstrations, 1982 and 1991. *American Sociological Review*, 61, 478–99.

McCrea, Frances B. and Markle, Gerald E. 1989: Atomic Scientists and Protest: The Bulletin as a Social Movement Organization. In L. Kriesberg (ed.), *Research in Social Movements, Conflict and Change*, vol. 11, Greenwich, CT: JAI Press.

McFarland, Andrew 1984: *Common Cause. Lobbying in the Public Interest*. Chatham, NJ: Chatham House.

McKay, George 1996: *Senseless Acts of Beauty: Cultures of Resistance since the 1960s*. London: Verso.

McPhail, Clark 1991: *The Myth of the Madding Crowd*. New York: Aldine de Gruyter.

McPhail, Clark, Schweingruber, David and McCarthy, John D. 1998: Policing Protest in the United States: From the 1960s to the 1990s. In D. della Porta and H. Reiter (eds), *Policing Protest. The Control of Mass Demonstrations in Western Democracies*, Minneapolis: The University of Minnesota Press, 49–69.

Melucci, Alberto 1982: *L'Invenzione del Presente. Movimenti, Identità, Bisogni Individuali*. Bologna: il Mulino.

Melucci, Alberto (ed.) 1984a: *Altri Codici. Aree di Movimento nella Metropoli*. Bologna: il Mulino.

Melucci, Alberto 1984b: Movimenti in un Mondo di Segni. In A. Melucci (ed.), *Altri Codici*, Bologna: il Mulino, 417–48.

Melucci, Alberto 1985: The Symbolic Challenge of Contemporary Movements. *Social Research*, 52, 789–816.

Melucci, Alberto 1987: *Libertà che Cambia*. Milano: Unicopli.

Melucci, Alberto 1988: Getting Involved: Identity and Mobilization in Social Movements. In B. Klandermans, H. Kriesi and S. Tarrow (eds), *From Structure to Action*, Greenwich, CT: JAI Press, 329–48.

Melucci, Alberto 1989: *Nomads of the Present*. London: Hutchinson Radius.

Melucci, Alberto 1990: Challenging Codes. Framing and Ambivalence. Paper presented at the workshop, Social Movements: Framing Processes and Opportunity Structure, Berlin, July.

Melucci, Alberto 1991: *L'Invenzione del Presente* (2nd edition). Bologna: il Mulino.

Melucci, Alberto 1994: A Strange Kind of Newness: What's 'New' in New Social Movements? In E. Larana, H. Johnston and J. Gusfield (eds), *New Social Movements. From Ideology to Identity*, Philadelphia: Temple University Press, 101–30.

Melucci, Alberto 1995: The Process of Collective Identity. In H. Johnston and B. Klandermans (eds), *Social Movements and Culture*, Minneapolis/London: University of Minnesota Press/UCL Press, 41–63.

Melucci, Alberto 1996: *Challenging Codes*. Cambridge/New York: Cambridge University Press.

Melucci, Alberto and Diani, Mario 1992: *Nazioni Senza Stato. I Movimenti Etnico-Nazionali in Occidente* (2nd edition). Milano: Feltrinelli.

Mennell, Stephen 1994: The Formation of We-Images: a Process Theory. In C. Calhoun (ed.), *Social Theory and the Politics of Identity*, Oxford/Cambridge, MA: Blackwell, 175–97.

Merelman, R. 1984: *Making Something of Ourselves. On Culture and Politics in the United States*. Berkeley: University of California Press.

Meyer, David S. 1990: *A Winter of Discontent*. New York: Praeger.

Meyer, David S. and Marullo, Sam 1992: Grassroots Mobilization and International Politics: Peace Protest and the End of the Cold War. *Research in Social Movements, Conflict and Change*, 14, 99–140.

Meyer, David S. and Staggenborg, Suzanne 1996: Movements, Countermovements and the Structure of Political Opportunities. *American Journal of Sociology*, 101, 1,628–60.

Meyer, David S. and Whittier, Nancy 1994: Social Movements Spillover. *Social Problems*, 41, 277–98.

Meyer, J. and Rowan, B. 1983: Institutional Organizations: Formal Structure as Myth and Ceremony. In J. Mayer and W.R. Scott (eds), *Organizational Environments: Ritual and Rationality*, Beverly Hill, Sage, 21–44.

Middendorp, C. 1992: Left–right Self-identification and (Post)materialism in the Ideological Space. *Electoral Studies*, 11, 249–60.

Miliband, Ralph 1989: *Divided Societies: Class Struggle in Contemporary Capitalism*. Oxford: Clarendon Press.

Minkoff, Debra C. 1993: The Organization of Survival: Women's and Racial-ethnic Voluntarist and Activist Organizations, 1955–1985. *Social Forces*, 71, 887–908.

Minkoff, Debra C. 1995: *Organizing for Equality: The Evolution of Women's and Racial-ethnic Organizations in America*. New Brunswick, NJ: Rutgers University Press.

Mittdun, Atle and Rucht, Dieter 1994: Comparing Policy Outcomes of Conflicts over Nuclear Power: Description and Explanation. In H. Flam (ed.), *States and Antinuclear Movements*, Edinburgh: Edinburgh University Press, 383–415.

Mizruchi, Mark S. and Schwartz, Michael (eds) 1987: *Intercorporate Relations. The Structural Analysis of Business*. Cambridge/New York: Cambridge University Press.

Moaddel, Mansoor 1992: Ideology as Episodic Discourse: The Case of the Iranian Revolution. *American Sociological Review*, 57, 353–79.

Moore, Barrington Jr 1966: *Social Origins of Dictatorship and Democracy*. Boston: Beacon Press.

Moore, Kelly 1995: Organizing Integrity: American Science and the Creation of Public Interest Organizations, 1955–1975. *American Journal of Sociology*, 101, 1,592–1,627.

Moore, Kelly forthcoming: Political Protest and Institutional Change: The Anti-Vietnam War Movement and American Science. In M. Giugni, D. McAdam, and C. Tilly (eds), *How Movements Matter*, Minneapolis, MI/London: University of Minnesota Press/UCL Press.

Morgan, Jane 1987: *Conflict and Order. The Police and Labour Disputes in England and Wales. 1900–1939*. Oxford: Clarendon Press.

Morris, Aldon 1984: *The Origins of the Civil Rights Movement: Black Communities Organizing for Change*. New York: Free Press.

Morris, Aldon and Herring, Cedric 1987: Theory and Research in Social Movements: A Critical Review. *Annual Review of Political Science*, 2, 137–98.

Morris, Aldon and Mueller, Carol (eds) 1992: *Frontiers in Social Movement Theory*. New Haven: Yale University Press.

Mueller, Carol 1994: Conflict Networks and the Origins of Women's Liberation. In E. Larana, H. Johnston, and J. Gusfield (eds), *New Social Movements*, Philadelphia: Temple University Press, 234–63.

Müller-Rommel, Ferdinand 1985: Social Movements and the Greens: New Internal Politics in Germany. *European Journal of Political Research*, 13, 53–67.

Müller-Rommel, Ferdinand (ed.) 1989: *New Politics in Western Europe: The Rise and the Success of Green Parties and Alternative Lists*. Boulder CO: Westview Press.

Müller-Rommel, Ferdinand 1990: New Political Movements and 'New Politics' Parties in Western Europe. In R. Dalton and M. Kuechler (eds), *Challenging the Political Order: New Social and Political Movements in Western Democracies*, Cambridge: Polity Press, 209–31.

Müller-Rommel, Ferdinand 1993: *Grüne Partein in Westeuropa. Entwicklungsphasen und Erfolgsbedingungen*. Opladen: Westdeutscher Verlag.

Mullins, Patrick 1987: Community and Urban Movements. *Sociological Review*, 35, 347–69.

Nas, Masja 1993: Women and Classes: Gender and the Class Base of New Social Movements in the Netherlands. *European Journal of Political Research*, 23, 343–55.

Neidhardt, Friedhelm 1981: Über Zufall, Eigendynamik und Institutionalisierbarkeit absurder Prozesse. Notizen am Beispiel der Entstehung und Einrichtung einer terroristischen Gruppe. In H. von Alemann and H. P. Thurn (eds), *Soziologie in weltbürgerlicher Absicht*, Opladen: Westdeutscher Verlag, 243–57.

Neidhardt, Friedhelm 1989: Gewalt und Gegengewalt. Steigt die Bereitschaft zu Gewaltaktionen mit zunehmender staatlicher Kontrolle und Repression. In W. Heitmeyer, K. Möller, and H. Sünker (eds), *Jugend-Staat-Gewalt*, Weinheim and Munich: Juventa, 233–43.

Neidhardt, Friedhelm and Rucht, Dieter 1991: The Analysis of Social Movements: The State of the Art and Some Perspectives for Further Research. In D. Rucht (ed.), *Research on Social Movements: The State of the Art in Western Europe and the USA*, Frankfurt/M and Boulder, CO: Campus and Westview Press, 421–64.

Nelkin, Dorothy and Pollack, Michael 1981: *The Atom Besieged. Extraparliamentary Dissent in France and Germany*. Cambridge, MA: MIT Press.

Nevola, Gaspare 1994: *Conflitto e Coercizione. Modelli di Analisi e Studio di Casi*. Bologna: il Mulino.

Noelle-Neumann, Elisabeth 1984: *The Spiral of Silence*. Chicago, IL: University of Chicago Press.

Nolan, Mary 1981: *Social Democracy and Society: Working-class Radicalism in Dusseldorf, 1890–1920*. Cambridge/New York: Cambridge University Press.

Nollert, Michael 1995: Neocorporatism and Political Protest in the Western Democracies: A Cross-National Analysis. In J. C. Jenkins and B. Klandermans (eds), *The Politics of Social Protest. Comparative Perspectives on States and Social Movements*, Minneapolis: University of Minnesota Press, 138–64.

Norris, Pippa 1987: *Politics and Sexual Equality. The Comparative Position of Women in Western Democracy*. Boulder, CO: Riennen.

O'Sullivan See, Katherine 1986: *First World Nationalisms. Class and Ethnic Politics in Northern Ireland and Quebec*. Chicago: University of Chicago Press.

Oberschall, Anthony 1973: *Social Conflict and Social Movements*. Englewood Cliffs, NJ: Prentice Hall.

Oberschall, Anthony 1980: Loosely Structured Collective Conflict: A Theory and an Application. In L. Kriesberg (ed.), *Research in Social Movements, Conflict and Change*, Vol. 3, Greenwich, CT: JAI Press, 45–54.

Oberschall, Anthony 1993: *Social Movements. Ideologies, Interests, and Identities*. New Brunswick/London: Transaction.

Oberschall, Anthony and Kim, Hyojoung 1996: Identity and Action. *Mobilization*, 1, 63–85.

Offe, Claus 1985: New Social Movements: Changing Boundaries of the Political. *Social Research*, 52, 817–68.

Offe, Claus 1990: Reflections on the Institutional Self-transformation of Movement Politics: A Tentative Stage Model. In R. Dalton and M. Kuechler (eds), *Challenging the Political Order: New Social and Political Movements in Western Democracies*, Cambridge: Polity Press, 232–50.

Ohlemacher, Thomas 1996: Bridging People and Protest: Social Relays of Protest Groups against Low-flying Military Jets in West Germany. *Social Problems*, 43, 197–218.

Oliver, Mike and Campbell, Jane 1996: *Disability Politics. Understanding Our Past, Changing Our Future*. London: Routledge.

Oliver, Pamela 1984: 'If You Don't Do It, Nobody Else Will': Active and Token Contributors to Local Collective Action. *American Sociological Review*, 49, 601–10.

Oliver, Pamela 1989: Bringing the Crowd Back In: The Nonorganizational Elements of Social Movements. In L. Kriesberg (ed.), *Research in Social Movements, Conflict and Change*, vol. 11, Greenwich, Conn.: JAI Press, 1–30.

Oliver, Pamela and Marwell, Gerald 1992: Mobilizing Technologies for Collective Action. In A. Morris and C. McClurg Mueller (eds), *Frontiers in Social Movement Theory*, New Haven: Yale University Press, 251–72.

Olson, Mancur 1963: *The Logics of Collective Action*. Cambridge, MA: Harvard University Press.

Olzak, Susan 1992: *The Dynamics of Ethnic Competition and Conflict*. Stanford, CA: Stanford University Press.

Omi, Michael and Winant, Howard 1986: *Racial Formation in the United States: From the 1960s to the 1980s.* New York: Routledge & Kegan Paul.

Omvedt, Gail 1993: *Reinventing Revolution: New Social Movements and the Socialist Tradition in India.* New York: M. E. Sharpe.

Opp, Karl-Dieter 1988: Community Integration and Incentives for Political Protest. In B. Klandermans, H. Kriesi and S. Tarrow (eds), *From Structure to Action,* Greenwich, CT: JAI Press, 83–101.

Opp, Karl-Dieter 1989: *The Rationality of Political Protest.* Boulder, CO: Westview Press.

Opp, Karl-Dieter 1990: Postmaterialism, Collective Action, and Political Protest. *American Journal of Political Science,* 34, 212–35.

Opp, Karl-Dieter and Gern, Christiane 1993: Dissident Groups, Personal Networks, and the East German Revolution of 1989. *American Sociological Review,* 58, 659–80.

Opp, Karl-Dieter, Finkel, Steve, Muller, Edward N., Wolfsfeld, Gadi, Dietz, Henty A. and Green, Jerrold D. 1995: Left–Right Ideology and Collective Political Action: A Comparative Analysis of Germany, Israel, and Peru. In J. C. Jenkins and B. Klandermans (eds), *The Politics of Social Protest. Comparative Perspectives on States and Social Movements,* Minneapolis: University of Minnesota Press, 63–95.

Orfali, Brigitte 1990: *L'Adhésion Au Front Nationale.* Paris: Editions Kime.

Ortoleva, Peppino 1988: *Saggio sui Movimenti del 68 in Europa e in America.* Rome: Editori Riuniti.

Otto, Karl O. 1989: *APO. Die ausserparlamentarische Opposition in Quellen und Dokumenten 1960–1970.* Köln: Pahl-Rugenstein.

Padgett, John F. and Ansell, Christopher K. 1993: Robust Action and the Rise of the Medici, 1400–1434. *American Journal of Sociology,* 98, 1,259–319.

Pakulski, Jan 1988: Social Movements in Comparative Perspective. In L. Kriesberg (ed.) *Research in Social Movements, Conflicts and Change,* vol. 10, Greenwich, CT: JAI Press, 247–67.

Pakulski, Jan 1990: *Social Movements. The Politics of Moral Protest.* London/Melbourne: Longman.

Pakulski, Jan 1995: Social Movements and Class: The Decline of the Marxist Paradigm. In L. Maheu (ed.), *Social Movements and Social Classes,* London/Thousand Oaks: Sage, 55–86.

Pakulski, Jan and Waters, Malcolm 1996: Misreading Status as Class: A Reply to Our Critics. *Theory And Society,* 25, 731–6.

Panebianco, Angelo 1982: *Modelli di Partito.* Bologna: il Mulino.

Papadakis, Elim and Taylor-Gooby, Peter 1987: Consumer Attitudes and Participation in State Welfare. *Political Studies,* 35, 467–81.

Parkin, Frank 1968: *Middle Class Radicalism.* New York: Praeger.

Passerini, Luisa 1988: *Autobiografia di Gruppo.* Florence: Giunti.

Passy, Florence 1998: Supranational Political Opportunities. A Channel of Globalization of Political Conflicts. The Case of the Conflict around the Rights of the Indigenous People. In D. della Porta, H. Kriesi and D. Rucht (eds), *Social Movements in a Globalizing World,* New York/London: Macmillan.

Pearce, Jone L. 1994: *Volontariato. Motivazioni e Comportamenti Nelle Organizzazioni di Lavoro Volontario*. Milano: Cortina. (Original edition *Volunteers*, London/New York: Routledge, 1993.)

Perrow, Charles 1961: The Analysis of Goals in Complex Organizations. *American Sociological Review*, 26, 854–66.

Perrucci, Robert and Pilisuk, Marc 1970: Leaders and Ruling Elites: The Interorganizational Bases of Community Power. *American Sociological Review*, 35, 1,040–57.

Petrosino, Daniele 1991: *Stati Nazioni Etnie. Il Pluralismo Etnico e Nazionale nella Teoria Sociologica Contemporanea*. Milano: Angeli.

Pickvance, Chris G. 1977: From 'Social Base' to 'Social Force': Some Analytical Issues in the Study of Urban Protest. In M. Harloe (ed.), *Captive Cities*, Wiley: Chichester, 175–86.

Pickvance, Chris G. 1985: The Rise and Fall of Urban Movements and the Role of Comparative Analysis. *Society And Space*, 3, 31–53.

Pickvance, Chris G. 1986: Concepts, Contexts and Comparison in the Study of Urban Movements: A Reply to M. Castells. *Society And Space*, 4, 221–31.

Pickvance, Chris 1995: Social Movements in the Transition From State Socialism: Convergence or Divergence? In L. Maheu (ed.), *Social Movements and Social Classes*, London/Thousand Oaks: Sage, 123–150.

Pinto, Louis 1990: Le Consommateur: Agent Economique et Acteur Politique. *Revue Française De Sociologie*, 31, 179–98.

Piore, Michael and Sabel, Charles 1984: *The Second Industrial Divide. Possibilities for Prosperity*. New York: Basic Books.

Piven, Frances F. and Cloward, Richard 1977: *Poor People's Movements*. New York: Pantheon.

Piven, Frances F. and Cloward, Richard 1992: Normalizing Collective Protest. In A. Morris and C. McClurg Mueller (eds), *Frontiers in Social Movement Theory*, New Haven: Yale University Press, 301–25.

Pizzorno, Alessandro 1978: Political Exchange and Collective Identity in Industrial Conflict. In C. Crouch, and A. Pizzorno (eds), *The Resurgence of Class Conflict in Western Europe*, New York: Holmes & Meier, 277–98.

Pizzorno, Alessandro 1981: Interests and Parties in Pluralism. In S. Berger (ed.), *Organizing Interests in Western Europe*, Cambridge: Cambridge University Press, 3–46.

Pizzorno, Alessandro 1983: Sulla Razionalità della Scelta Democratica. *Stato e Mercato*, n. 7.

Pizzorno, Alessandro 1986: Sul Confronto Intertemporale Delle Utilità. *Stato e Mercato*, 16, 3–25.

Pizzorno, Alessandro 1987: Considerazioni sulle Teorie dei Movimenti Sociali. *Problemi Del Socialismo*, 12, 11–27.

Pizzorno, Alessandro 1996: Decisioni o Interazioni? La Micro-Descrizione del Cambiamento Sociale. *Rassegna Italiana di Sociologia*, 37, 107–32.

Pizzorno, Alessandro, Regalia, Ida, Regini, Marino and Reyneri, Emilio 1978: *Lotte Operaie e Sindacato: Il Ciclo di Lotte 1968–1972 in Italia*. Bologna: il Mulino.

Plumb, Lawrence D. 1993: *A Critique of the Human Potential Movement*. New York: Garland.

Poggi, Gianfranco (ed.) 1968: *L'Organizzazione Partitica del PCI e della DC*. Bologna: il Mulino.

Poguntke, Thomas 1993: *Alternative Politics. The German Green Party*. Edinburgh: Edinburgh University Press.

Porter, Gareth and Brown, Janet Welsh 1991: *Global Environmental Politics*. Boulder, CO/London: Westview Press.

Rabehl, Bernd 1998: *Am Ende der Utopie. Die politische Geschichte der Freien, Universität Berlin*, Berlin: Argon Verlag.

Ranci, Costanzo 1992: La Mobilitazione dell'Altruismo. Condizioni e Processi di Diffusione dell'azione Volontaria in Italia. *Polis*, 6, 467–505.

Randall, Vicky 1982: *Women and Politics*. London: Macmillan.

Rapoport, Anatol 1960: *Fights, Games, and Debates*. Ann Arbor: The University of Michigan Press.

Raschke, Joachim 1988: *Soziale Bewegungen. Ein historisch-systematischer Grundriss*. Frankfurt am Main: Campus.

Redhead, Steve (ed.) 1993: *Rave Off: Politics and Deviance in Contemporary Culture*. Aldershot: Avebury.

Regalia, Ida, Regini, Marino, and Reyneri, Emilio 1978: Labor Conflicts and Industrial Relations in Italy. In C. Crouch and A. Pizzorno (eds), *The Resurgence of Class Conflict in Western Europe since 1968*, London: Macmillan, 101–58.

Regini, Marino 1992: *Confini Mobili*. Bologna: il Mulino.

Reiner, Robert 1998: Policing, Protest, and Disorder in Britain. In D. della Porta and H. Reiter (eds), *Policing Protest. The Control of Mass Demonstrations in Western Democracies*, Minneapolis: The University of Minnesota Press, 35–48.

Reiter, Herbert 1998: Police and Public Order in Italy, 1944–1948. The Case of Florence. In D. della Porta and H. Reiter (eds), *Policing Protest. The Control of Mass Demonstrations in Western Democracies*, Minneapolis: The University of Minnesota Press, 143–65.

Richardson, Dick and Rootes, Chris (eds) 1994: *The Green Challenge. The Development of Green Parties in Europe*. London/New York: Routledge.

Rihoux, Benoit and Walgrave, Stefaan 1997: *L'Année Blanche*. Bruxelles: EVO.

Robbins, Thomas 1988: *Cults, Converts and Charisma: The Sociology of New Religious Movements*. London/Newbury Park, CA: Sage.

Rochford, E. Burke 1985: *Hare Krishna in America*. New Brunswick, NJ: Rutgers University Press.

Rochon, Thomas R. 1988: *Between Society and State: Mobilizing for Peace in Western Europe*. Princeton: Princeton University Press.

Rochon, Thomas R. and Mazmanian, Daniel A. 1993: Social Movements and the Policy Process. *The Annals of the AAPSS*, 528, 75–87.

Rohrschneider, Robert 1988: Citizens' Attitudes towards Environmental Issues: Selfish or Selfless? *Comparative Political Studies*, 21, 347–67.

Rohrschneider, Robert 1990: The Roots of Public Opinion toward New Social Movements. *American Journal of Political Science*, 34, 1–30.

Rohrschneider, Robert 1993a: Impact of Social Movements on the European Party System, *The Annals of the American Academy of Political and Social Sciences*, 528, July, 157–170.

Rohrschneider, Robert 1993b: Environmental Belief Systems in Western Europe. *Comparative Political Studies*, 26, 3–29.

Rokkan, Stein 1982: *Cittadini, Elezioni, Partiti*. Bologna: il Mulino. (Original edition *Citizens, Elections, and Parties*. Oslo: Oslo University Press, 1970.)

Rolke, Lothar 1987: *Protestbewegungen in der Bundesrepublik*. Opladen: Westdeutscher Verlag.

Rootes, Christopher 1992: The New Politics and the New Social Movements: Accounting for British Exceptionalism. *European Journal of Political Research*, 22, 171–91.

Rootes, Christopher 1994: Parties and Movements as Alternative Modes of Collective Action: Green Parties and Environmental Movements in Europe, Paper presented at the Thirteenth World Congress of Sociology, Bielefeld, July.

Rootes, Christopher 1995: A New Class? The Higher Educated and the New Politics. In L. Maheu (ed.), *Social Movements and Social Classes*, London/Thousand Oaks: Sage, 220–35.

Rootes, Christopher 1997: Shaping Collective Action: Structure, Contingency and Knowledge. In R. Edmonson (ed.), *The Political Context of Collective Action*, London/New York: Routledge.

Rose, Richard 1988: *L'espansione della Sfera Pubblica*. Bologna: il Mulino. (original edition *Understanding Big Government*, London, Sage, 1984).

Roseneil, Sasha 1995: *Disarming Patriarchy*. Milton Keynes: Open University Press.

Rosenthal, Naomi and Schwartz, Michael 1989: Spontaneity and Democracy in Social Movements. In B. Klandermans (ed.), *Organizing For Change*, Greenwich, CT: JAI Press, 33–60.

Rosenthal, Naomi, Fingrutd, Meryl, Ethier, Michele, Karant, Roberta and McDonald, David 1985: Social Movements and Network Analysis: A Case Study of Nineteenth-century Women's Reform In New York State. *American Journal of Sociology*, 90, 1,022–54.

Rosenthal, Naomi, McDonald, David, Ethier, Michele, Fingrutd, Meryl, and Karant, Roberta 1997: Structural Tensions in the Nineteenth Century Women's Movement. *Mobilization*, 2, 21–46.

Roszak, Theodor 1976: *La Nascita di una Controcultura*, Milan: Feltrinelli.

Roth, Roland 1994: *Demokratie von unten: Neue soziale Bewegungen auf dem Wege zur politischen Institution*. Köln: Bund Verlag.

Rothenberg, Lawrence S. 1992: *Linking Citizens to Government. Interest Group Politics at Common Cause*. Cambridge/New York: Cambridge University Press.

Rucht, Dieter 1984: Zur Organisation der neuen sozialen Bewegungen. In Jürgen Falter et al., *Politische Willensbildung und Interessenvermittlung*, Opladen: Westdeutscher Verlag.

Rucht, Dieter 1989: Environmental Movement Organizations in West Germany and France: Structure and Interorganizational Relations. In B.

Klandermans (ed.), *International Social Movement Research*, vol. 2, *Organizing for Change*, Greenwich, CT: JAI Press, 61–94.

Rucht, Dieter 1990a: The Strategies and Action Repertoire of New Movements. In R. J. Dalton and M. Kuechler (eds), *Challenging the Political Order. New Social Movements in Western Democracies*, Cambridge: Polity Press, 156–75.

Rucht, Dieter 1990b: Campaigns, Skirmishes and Battles: Anti-nuclear Movements in the USA, France and West Germany. *Industrial Crisis Quarterly*, 4, 193–222.

Rucht, Dieter (ed.) 1991a: *Research in Social Movements: The State of the Art*. Frankfurt/Boulder, CO: Campus Verlag/Westview Press.

Rucht, Dieter 1991b: A Critique of Alain Touraine's Intervention Sociologique. In D. Rucht (ed.), *Research in Social Movements: The State of the Art*, Frankfurt/Boulder, CO: Campus Verlag/Westview Press.

Rucht, Dieter 1991c: Das Kräftefeld soziale Bewegungen, Gegenbewegungen und Staat. *Forschungsjournal Neue Soziale Bewegungen*, 2(4), 31–42.

Rucht, Dieter 1992: *Studying the Effects of Social Movements: Conceptualization and Problems*. Paper presented at the Joint Sessions of the European Consortium for Political Research, Limerick, 30 March–4 April.

Rucht, Dieter 1993: 'Think Globally, Act Locally'? Needs, Forms and Problems of Cross-national Cooperation Among Environmental Groups. In J. D. Liefferink, P. Lowe and A. P. J. Mol (eds), *European Integration and Environmental Policy*, London/New York: Belhaven Press/Halsted Press, 75–95.

Rucht, Dieter 1994: *Modernizierung und Soziale Bewegungen*. Frankfurt am Main: Campus.

Rucht, Dieter 1995: The Impact of Anti-nuclear Power Movements in International Comparison. In M. Bauer (ed.), *Resistance to New Technology*. Cambridge: Cambridge University Press.

Rucht, Dieter 1996: The Impact of National Contexts on Social Movements Structure. In D. McAdam, J. McCarthy and M. N. Zald (eds), *Comparative Perspective on Social Movements. Political Opportunities, Mobilizing Structures, and Cultural Framing*. Cambridge/New York: Cambridge University Press, 185–204.

Rüdig, Wolfgang 1990: *Anti-nuclear Movements: A World Survey*. London: Longman.

Rule, James R. 1988: *Theories of Civil Violence*. Berkeley: University of California Press.

Rupp, Leila and Taylor, Verta 1987: *Survival in the Doldrums: The American Women's Rights Movement, 1945 to the 1960s*. Columbus: Ohio State University Press.

Rusconi, Gian Enrico 1992: Etnia: Un Costrutto Polemico. *Polis*, 6, 571–87.

Rusconi, Gian Enrico 1993: *Se Cessiamo di Essere una Nazione*. Bologna: il Mulino.

Ryan, Barbara 1992: *Feminism and the Women's Movement: Dynamics of Change in Social Movements' Ideology and Activism*. New York: Routledge.

Safran, William 1989: The French State and Ethnic Minority Cultures: Policy Dimensions and Problems. In J. Rudolph and R. J. Thompson (eds), *Ethnoterritorial Politics, Policy, and the Western World*, Boulder, CO/London: Lynne Rienner, 115–58.

Sanchez Jankowski, Martin 1991: *Islands in the Street: Gangs and American Urban Society*. Berkeley: University of California Press.

Sartori, Giovanni 1970: Concept Misformation in Comparative Politics. *American Political Science Review*, 56, 1,033–53.

Sartori, Giovanni 1987: Ideologia. In *Elementi di Teoria Politica*. Bologna: il Mulino.

Sartori, Giovanni 1990: Comparazione e Metodo Comparato. *Rivista Italiana di Scienza Politica*, 20, 397–416.

Sassoon, Joseph 1984a: Ideologia, Azione Simbolica e Ritualità: Nuovi Percorsi dei Movimenti. In A. Melucci (ed.), *Altri Codici*, Bologna: il Mulino, 385–415.

Sassoon, Joseph 1984b: Ideology, Symbolic Action and Rituality in Social Movements: The Effects of Organizational Forms. *Social Science Information*, 23, 861–73.

Saunders, P. 1987: Social Theory and the Urban Question. London: Unwin Hyman.

Scharpf, Fritz W. 1984: Economic and Institutional Constraints of Full-Employment Strategies: Sweden, Austria, and West Germany. In J. H. Goldthorpe (ed.), *Order and Conflict in Contemporary Capitalism*, Oxford: Clarendon Press, 257–90.

Scheff, Thomas J. 1994a: *Bloody Revenge. Emotions, Nationalism, and War.* Boulder, CO: Westview Press.

Scheff, Thomas 1994b: Emotions and Identity: A Theory of Ethnic Nationalism. In C. Calhoun (ed.), *Social Theory and the Politics of Identity*, Oxford/Cambridge, MA: Blackwell, 277–303.

Schmitt, Rüdiger 1989: Organizational Interlocks between New Social Movements and Traditional Elites: The Case of the West German Peace Movement. *European Journal of Political Research*, 17, 583–98.

Schmitter, Philippe 1974: Still a Century of Corporatism? *Review of Politics*, 36, 85–131.

Schmitter, Philippe 1981: Interest Intermediation and Regime Governability in Contemporary Western Europe and North America. In Suzanne Berger (ed.), *Organized Interests in Western Europe: Pluralism, Corporatism, and the Transformation of Politics*, Cambridge/New York: Cambridge University Press, 287–327.

Schmitter, Philippe and Lehmbruch, Gerard (eds) 1979: *Trends towards Corporatist Intermediation*. London/Beverly Hills: Sage.

Schumaker, Paul D. 1975: Policy Responsiveness to Protest Group Demands. *The Journal of Politics*, 37, 488–521.

Scotch, Richard K. 1988: Disability as The Basis for a Social Movement: Advocacy and the Politics of Definition. *Journal of Social Issues*, 44, 159–72.

Scott, Alan 1990: *Ideology and the New Social Movements*. London: Unwin Hyman.

Scott, Alan (ed.) 1997: *The Limits of Globalization*. London: Routledge.

Scott, John 1992: *Social Network Analysis. A Handbook*. London/Newbury Park, CA: Sage.

Scott, W. Richard 1981: *Organizations: Rational, Natural and Open System*. Englewood Cliffs: Prentice Hall.

Seligman, Adam 1992: *The Idea of Civil Society*. New York: Free Press.

Sewell, William H. Jr 1992: A Theory of Structure: Duality, Agency, and Transformation. *American Journal of Sociology*, 98, 1–29.

Shah, Ghanshyam 1990: *Social Movements in India: A Review of the Literature*. New Delhi/Newbury Park: Sage.

Sharpe, L. Jim 1988: The Growth and Decentralisation of the Modern Democratic State. *European Journal of Political Research*, 16, 365–80.

Showstack Sassoon, A. 1987: *Women and the State: Shifting Boundaries of Public and Private*. London: Hutchinson.

Siltanen, Janet and Stanworth, Michelle 1984: *Women and the Public Sphere*. London: Hutchinson.

Simmel, Georg [1908] 1955: Conflict. In *Conflict and the Web of Group Affiliations*, translated by K. Wolff. New York: Free Press, 11–123. (Original edition *Die Streit in Soziologie*, München, Duncker und Humblot, 1908.)

Skocpol, Theda 1979: *States and Social Revolutions*. Cambridge/New York: Cambridge University Press.

Smelser, Neil J. 1962: *Theory of Collective Behavior*. New York: The Free Press.

Smelser, Neil J. 1992: Culture: Coherent or Incoherent. In N. J. Smelser and R. Muench (eds), *Theory of Culture*, Berkeley/Los Angeles: University of California Press, 3–28.

Smith, Anthony D. 1981: *The Ethnic Revival*. Cambridge: Cambridge University Press.

Smith, Anthony D. 1986: *The Ethnic Origins of Nations*. Oxford: Basil Blackwell.

Smith, Jackie 1995: Transnational Political Processes and the Human Rights Movement. In L. Kriesberg (ed.), *Research in Social Movements, Conflict and Change*, vol. 17, Greenwich, CT: JAI Press, 185–219.

Smith, Jackie 1998: Global Strategies of Social Protest: Transnational Social Movement Organizations in World Politics. In D. della Porta, H. Kriesi and D. Rucht (eds), *Social Movements in a Globalizing World*, New York/London: Macmillan.

Smith, Jackie, Pagnucco, Ron and Romeril, Winnie 1994: Transnational Social Movement Organisations in the Global Political Arena. *Voluntas*, 5, 121–54.

Snow, David A. and Benford, Robert D. 1988: Ideology, Frame Resonance, and Participant Mobilization. In B. Klandermans, H. Kriesi and S. Tarrow (eds), *From Structure to Action*, Greenwich, CT: JAI Press, 197–218.

Snow, David A. and Benford, Robert D. 1989: Schemi Interpretativi Dominanti e Cicli di Protesta. *Polis*, 3, 5–40.

Snow, David A. and Benford, Robert D. 1992: Master Frames and Cycles of Protest. In A. Morris and C. McClurg Mueller (eds), *Frontiers In Social Movement Theory*, New Haven: Yale University Press, 133–55.

Snow, David A. and Oliver, Pamela 1995: Social Movements and Collective Behavior: Social Psychological Dimensions and Considerations. In K. S. Cook, G. A. Fine and J. House (eds), *Sociological Perspectives on Social Psychology*, Boston: Allyn & Bacon, 571–99.

Snow, David A., Rochford, Burke E., Worden, Steven and Benford, Robert 1986: Frame Alignment Processes, Micromobilization, and Movement Participation. *American Sociological Review*, 51, 464–81.

Snow, David A., Zurcher, Louis A. and Ekland-Olson, Sheldon 1980: Social Networks and Social Movements: A Microstructural Approach to Differential Recruitment. *American Sociological Review*, 45, 787–801.

Snyder, David and Tilly, Charles 1972: Hardship and Collective Violence in France, 1830–1960. *American Sociological Review*, 37, 520–32.

Somers, Margaret R. 1993: Citizenship and the Place of the Public Sphere: Law, Community, and Political Culture in the Transition to Democracy. *American Sociological Review*, 58, 587–620.

Soysal, Yasemine N. 1994: *Limits of Citizenship: Migrants and Postnational Membership in Europe*. Chicago: Chicago University Press.

Staggenborg, Suzanne 1986: Coalition Work in the Pro-Choice Movement: Organizational and Environmental Opportunities and Constraints. *Social Problems*, 33, 623–41.

Staggenborg, Suzanne 1991: *The Pro-Choice Movement: Organization and Activism in the Abortion Conflict*. New York: Oxford University Press.

Stark, Rodney and Bainbridge, William S. 1980: Networks of Faith: Interpersonal Bonds and Recruitment to Cults and Sects. *American Journal of Sociology*, 85, 1,376–95.

Steel, Brent S., Warner, Rebecca L., Stieber, Blair, and Lovrich, Nicholas P. 1992: Postmaterialist Values and Support for Feminism among Canadian and American Women and Men. *Western Political Quarterly*, 45, 339–53.

Stefancic, Jean and Richard Delgado 1996: *No Mercy: How Conservative Think Tanks and Foundations Changed America's Social Agenda*. Philadelphia: Temple University Press.

Stoecker, Randy 1995: Community, Movement, Organization: The Problem of Identity Convergence in Collective Action. *Sociological Quarterly*, 36, 111–30.

Stokman, Frans N., Ziegler, Rolf and Scott, John (eds) 1985: *Networks of Corporate Power: A Comparative Analysis of Ten Countries*. Cambridge: Polity Press.

Strand, David and John W. Meyer 1993: Institutional Conditions for Diffusion. *Theory and Society*, 22, 487–511.

Strauss, Anselm L. 1947: Research in Collective Behavior: Neglect and Need, *American Sociological Review*, 12, 352–4.

Streeck, Wolfgang 1992: *Social Institutions and Economic Performance*. Thousand Oaks/London: Sage.

Swidler, Ann 1986: Culture in Action: Symbols and Strategies. *American Sociological Review*, 51, 273–86.

Swidler, Ann and Arditi, Jorge 1994: The New Sociology of Knowledge. *Annual Review of Sociology*, 20, 305–29.

Szasz, Andrew 1994: *EcoPopulism. Toxic Waste and the Movement for Environmental Justice.* Minneapolis/London: University of Minnesota Press/UCL Press.

Szelenyi, Sonia and Olvera, Jacqueline 1996: The Declining Significance of Class: Does Gender Complicate the Story? – Comments. *Theory And Society*, 25, 725–30.

Szerszinski, Bron 1995: Entering the Stage: Strategies of Environmental Communication in the UK. In K. Eder (ed.), *Framing and Communicating Environmental Issues*, Research Report, Commission of the European Communities, DGXII, Florence/Lancaster: European University Institute/CSEC, University of Lancaster.

Sztompka, Piotr 1993: *The Sociology of Social Change.* Oxford: Basil Blackwell.

Taggart, Paul A. 1996: *The New Populism and the New Politics: New Protest Parties in Sweden in a Comparative Perspective.* New York: St Martin's Press.

Tarrow, Sidney 1983: Struggling to Reform: Social Movements and Policy Change during Cycles of Protest. *Western Societies Paper 15.* Ithaca, NY: Cornell University.

Tarrow, Sidney 1989a: *Democracy and Disorder. Protest and Politics in Italy, 1965–1975.* Oxford/New York: Oxford University Press.

Tarrow, Sidney 1989b. Mutamenti nella Cultura di Opposizione in Italia, 1965–1975. *Polis*, 3, 41–63.

Tarrow, Sidney 1990: The Phantom at the Opera: Political Parties and Social Movements of the 1960s and the 1970s in Italy. In R. J. Dalton and M. Kuechler (eds), *Challenging the Political Order: New Social Movements in Western Democracies*, Cambridge: Polity Press, 251–73.

Tarrow, Sidney 1994: *Power in Movement. Social Movements, Collective Action and Politics.* New York/Cambridge: Cambridge University Press.

Tarrow, Sidney 1995: The Europeanization of Conflict: Reflections from a Social Movement Perspective. *West European Politics*, 18, 223–51.

Taylor, Bron (ed.) 1995: *Ecological Resistance Movements.* Albany, NY: SUNY Press.

Taylor, Charles 1993: *Multiculturalismo. La Politica Del Riconoscimento.* Milano: Anabasi (original edition *Multiculturalism and the Politics of Recognition*, Princeton, NJ, Princeton University Press, 1992).

Taylor, Ian 1996: Fear of Crime, Urban Fortunes and Suburban Social Movements: Some Reflections from Manchester. *Sociology*, 30, 317–37.

Taylor, Verta 1989: Social Movement Continuity: The Women's Movement in Abeyance. *American Sociological Review*, 54, 761–75.

Taylor, Verta and Whittier, Nancy 1992: Collective Identity in Social Movement Communities: Lesbian Feminist Mobilization. In A. Morris and C. McClurg Mueller (eds), *Frontiers in Social Movement Theory*, New Haven: Yale University Press, 104–32.

Taylor, Verta and Whittier, Nancy 1995: Analytical Approaches to Social Movement Culture: The Culture of the Women's Movement. In H. Johnston and B. Klandermans (eds), *Social Movements and Culture*, Minneapolis/London: University of Minnesota Press/UCL Press, 163–87.

Taylor-Gooby, Peter 1986: Consumpion Cleavages and Welfare Politics. *Political Studies*, 34, 592–606.

Tejerina Montana, Benjamin 1992: *Nacionalismo y Lengua*. Madrid: Centro de Investigaciones Sociologicas.

Thompson, Edward H. 1963: *The Making of the English Working Class*. London: Penguin.

Thompson, J. D 1967: *Organizations in Action*. New York: McGraw-Hill.

Tillock, H. M. and Morrison, D. E. 1979: Group Size and Contribution to Collective Action: An Examination of Olson Theory Using Data from Zero Population Growth. In L. Kriesberg (ed.), *Research in Social Movements, Conflicts and Change*, vol. 2. Greenwich, CO: JAI Press, 131–52.

Tilly, Charles 1978: *From Mobilization to Revolution*. Reading, MA: Addison-Wesley.

Tilly, Charles 1984: Social Movements and National Politics. In C. Bright and S. Harding (eds), *State-Making and Social Movements: Essays in History and Theory*, Ann Arbor: University of Michigan Press, 297–317.

Tilly, Charles 1986: *The Contentious French*. Cambridge MA: Harvard University Press.

Tilly, Charles 1987: 'Social Conflict.' *CSSC Working Paper Series 43*. New York: New School for Social Research.

Tilly, Charles 1988: Social Movements, Old and New. In L. Kriesberg (ed.), *Research in Social Movements, Conflict and Change*, vol. 10, Greenwich, CT: JAI Press, 1–18.

Tilly, Charles 1993: *European Revolutions 1492–1992*. Oxford/Cambridge, MA: Blackwell.

Tilly, Charles 1994: Social Movements as Historically Specific Clusters of Political Performances. *Berkeley Journal of Sociology*, 1–30.

Tilly, Charles, Tilly, Louise and Tilly, Richard 1975: *The Rebellious Century 1830–1930*. Cambridge, MA: Harvard University Press.

Todesco, Fabio 1992: Marketing Elettorale e Comunicazione Politica. Il Caso Lega Nord. Dissertation. Università Bocconi, Milan.

Tondeur, Alain. 1997. *La Crise Blanche*. Brussels: Editions Luc Pire.

Touraine, Alain 1977: *The Self-Production of Society*. Chicago: University of Chicago Press.

Touraine, Alain 1981: *The Voice and the Eye. An Analysis of Social Movements*. Cambridge: Cambridge University Press.

Touraine, Alain 1984: *Le Retour de L'acteur*. Paris: Fayard.

Touraine, Alain 1985: An Introduction to the Study of Social Movements. *Social Research*, 52, 749–88.

Touraine, Alain 1987: *The Workers' Movement*. Cambridge/New York: Cambridge University Press.

Touraine, Alain 1991: Commentary on Dieter Rucht's Critique. In D. Rucht (ed.), *Research in Social Movements: The State of the Art*, Frankfurt/Boulder, CO: Campus Verlag/Westview Press, 385–91.

Touraine, Alain 1992: *Critique de la Modernité*, Fayard, Paris.

Touraine, Alain, Dubet, François, Hegedus, Zsuzsa and Wieviorka, Michel 1981: *Le Pays contre L'Etat. Luttes Occitanes*. Paris: Seuil.

Touraine, Alain, Hegedus, Zsusza, Dubet, François and Wieviorka, Michel 1983a: *Anti-nuclear Protest. The Opposition to Nuclear Power in France*. Cambridge: Cambridge University Press.

Touraine, Alain, Dubet, François, Wieviorka, Michel and Strzelecki, Jan 1983b: *Solidarity. The Analysis of a Social Movement: Poland 1980–1981*. Cambridge: Cambridge University Press.

Trigilia, Carlo 1984: *Grandi Partiti e Piccole Imprese. Comunisti e Democristiani nelle Regioni a Economia Diffusa*. Bologna: il Mulino.

Trump, Thomas M. 1991: Value Formation and Postmaterialism. Inglehart's Theory of Value Change Reconsidered. *Comparative Political Studies*, 24, 365–90.

Turk, Herman 1977: *Organizations in Modern Life*. San Francisco: Jossey-Bass.

Turnaturi, Gabriella 1991: *Associati per Amore*. Milan: Feltrinelli.

Turner, Bryan 1988: *Status*. Milton Keynes: Open University Press.

Turner, Ralph 1969: The Theme of Contemporary Social Movements. *British Journal of Sociology*, 20, 390–405.

Turner, Ralph 1994: Ideology and Utopia After Socialism. In E. Larana, H. Johnston and J. Gusfield (eds), *New Social Movements. From Ideology to Identity*, Philadelphia: Temple University Press, 79–100.

Turner, Ralph and Killian, Lewis 1987: *Collective Behaviour*. Englewood Cliffs, NJ: Prentice Hall (original edition *Collective Behaviour*, Englewood Cliffs, NJ: Prentice Hall, 1957).

Urry, John 1995: Rethinking Class. In L. Maheu (ed.), *Social Movements and Social Classes*, London/Thousand Oaks: Sage, 169–81.

Useem, Bert 1980: Solidarity Model, Breakdown Model and the Boston Anti-busing Movement, *American Sociological Review*, 45, 357–69.

van de Hoonaard, Will C. 1991: Numbers and 'Social Forms': The Contribution of Simmel to Social Movements Theory. In L. Kriesberg (ed.), *Research In Social Movements, Conflict and Change*, vol. 13, Greenwich, CT: JAI Press, 31–43.

van der Heijden, Hein-Anton, Koopmans, Ruud, and Giugni, Marco 1992: The West European Environmental Movement. In L. Kriesberg (ed.), *Research in Social Movements, Conflict and Change. Supplement 2*, Greenwich, CT: JAI Press, 1–40.

van Gennep, A. 1983: *I Riti di Passaggio*. Torino: Boringhieri. (original edition *Les Rites de Passage*, Paris, Nourry, 1908).

Van Zoonen, Liesbet 1996: A Dance of Death: New Social Movements and Mass Media. In D. Paletz (ed.), *Political Communication in Action*, Cress Hill, NJ: Hampton Press, 201–22.

Verba, Sydney, Norman H. Nie and Jae-on Kim 1978: *Participation and Political Equality*. Cambridge/New York: Cambridge University Press.

von Beyme, Klaus (ed.) 1988: *Right-wing Extremism in Western Europe*. London: Cass.

von Dirke, Sabine 1997: *All the Power to the Imagination! The West German Counterculture from the Student Movement to the Greens*. Lincoln/London: University of Nebraska Press.

Wacquant, Loic J. D. 1994: The New Urban Color Line: The State and Fate of the Ghetto in Postfordist America. In C. Calhoun (ed.), *Social Theory and the Politics of Identity*, Oxford/Cambridge, MA: Blackwell, 231–76.

Waddington, P. A. J. 1994: *Liberty and Order: Policing Public Order in a Capital City*. London: UCL Press.

Walby, Sylvia 1997: *Gender Transformations*. London: Routledge.

Walker, Jack L. 1991: *Mobilizing Interest Groups in America: Patrons, Professions, and Social Movements*. Ann Arbor: University of Michigan Press.

Wallace, Michael and Jenkins, J. Craig 1995: The New Class, Postindustrialism, and Neocorporatism: Three Images of Social Protest in Western Democracies. In J. C. Jenkins and B. Klandermans (eds), *The Politics of Social Protest*, Minneapolis/London: University of Minnesota Press/UCL Press, 96–137.

Wallis, Roy 1977: *The Road to Total Freedom*. New York: Columbia University Press.

Wallis, Roy and Bruce, Steve 1986: *Sociological Theory, Religion and Collective Action*. Belfast: Queen's University Press.

Walsh, Edward 1988: *Democracy in the Shadows: Citizens Mobilization in the Wake of the Accident at Three Mile Island*. New York: Greenwood Press.

Walsh, Edward and Warland, Rex 1983: Social Movement Involvement in the Wake of A Nuclear Accident: Activists and Free Riders in the TMI Area. *American Sociological Review*, 48, 764–80.

Wasko, Janet and Mosco, Vincent (eds) 1992: *Democratic Communications in the Information Age*. Toronto/Norwood, NJ: Garamond Press/Ablex.

Waters, Malcolm 1995: *Globalization*. London: Routledge.

Watts, Meredith W. 1997: *Xenophobia in United Germany: Generations, Modernization, and Ideology*. New York: St Martin's Press.

Wellman, Barry 1988: Structural Analysis: From Method and Metaphor to Theory and Substance. In B. Wellman, and S. D. Berkowitz (eds), *Social Structures. A Network Approach*, Cambridge/New York: Cambridge University Press, 19–61.

Wellman, Barry and Berkowitz, Steve D. (eds) 1988: *Social Structures: A Network Approach*. Cambridge/New York, Cambridge University Press.

Wellman, Barry, Carrington, Peter J. and Hall, Alan 1988: Networks as Personal Communities. In B. Wellman and S. D. Berkowitz (eds), *Social Structures. A Network Approach*, Cambridge/New York: Cambridge University Press, 130–84.

Whalen, Jack and Richard Flacks 1989: *Beyond the Barricades: The Sixties Generation Grows Up*. Philadelphia: Temple University Press.

White, Harrison 1988: Varieties in Markets. In B. Wellman and S. D. Berkowitz (eds), *Social Structures: A Network Approach*, Cambridge: Cambridge University Press, 226–60.

White, Paul E., Levine, Sol and Vasak, George 1975: Exchange as a Conceptual Framework for Understanding Interorganizational Relationships. In R. A. R. Negandhi (ed.), *Interorganizational Theory*, Kent: Kent State University Press, 182–95.

Whittier, Nancy 1995: *Feminist Generations. The Persistence of the Radical Women's Movement*. Philadelphia: Temple University Press.

Whittier, Nancy 1997: Political Generation, Micro-Cohorts, and the Transformation of Social Movements. *American Sociological Review*, 62, 760–78.

Whutnow, Robert 1987: *Meaning and Moral Order: Explanations in Cultural Analysis*. Berkeley: University of California Press.

Wieviorka, Michel 1995: *The Arena of Racism*. London/Thousand Oaks: Sage.

Wilcox, Clyde 1996: *Onward Christian Soldiers? The Religious Right in American Politics*. Boulder, CO: Westview Press.

Willelms, Helmut, Wolf, Marianne and Eckert, Roland 1993: *Unruhen und Politikberatung. Funktion, Arbeitweise, Ergebnisse und Auswirkung von Untersuchungskommissionen in der USA, Grossbritannien und des Bundesrepublik Deutschlands*. Opladen: Westdeutscher Verlag.

Wilson, Bryan (1982) *Religion in Sociological Perspective*. Oxford: Oxford University Press.

Wilson, Frank L. 1990: Neo-corporatism and the Rise of New Social Movements. In R. J. Dalton and M. Kuechler (eds), *Challenging the Political Order. New Social Movements in Western Democracies*, Cambridge: Polity Press, 67–83.

Wilson, Graham K. 1990: *Interest Groups*. Oxford: Blackwell.

Wilson, James Q. 1973: *Political Organizations*. New York: Basic Books.

Wilson, John 1973: *Introduction to Social Movements*. New York: Basic Books.

Wilson, John 1976: Social Protest and Social Control. *Social Problems*, 24, 469–81.

Winter, Martin 1998: Protest Policing in Germany. In D. della Porta and H. Reiter (eds), *Policing Protest. The Control of Mass Demonstrations in Western Democracies*. Minneapolis/London: The University of Minnesota Press/UCL Press, 188–212.

Wisler, Dominique and Hanspeter Kriesi 1998: Decisionmaking and Style in Protest Policing. The Cases of Geneva and Zurich. In D. della Porta and H. Reiter (eds), *Policing Protest. The Control of Mass Demonstrations in Western Democracies*, Minneapolis/London: The University of Minnesota Press/UCL Press, 91–116.

Woliver, Laura R. 1993: *From Outrage to Action: The Politics of Grass-roots Dissent*, Urbana, IL: University of Illinois Press.

Wood, Michael and Hughes, Michael 1984: The Moral Basis of Moral Reform: Status Discontent vs. Culture and Socialization as Explanations of Anti-Pornography Social Movement Adherence. *American Sociological Review*, 49, 86–99.

Worster, Donald 1994: *Storia delle Idee Ecologiche*. Bologna: il Mulino (original edition *Nature's Economy*, Cambridge/New York, Cambridge University Press, 1985).

Wrench, John and Solomos, John (eds) 1993: *Racism and Migration in Western Europe*. Oxford/New York: Berg.

Wright, Erik O. 1985: *Classes*. London: Verso.

Wright, Erik O. 1996: The Continuing Relevance of Class Analysis – Comments. *Theory and Society*, 25, 693–716.

Yearley, Steven 1988: *Science, Technology and Social Change*. London: Unwin Hyman.

Yearley, Steven 1991: *The Green Case*. London: Routledge.

Yearley, Steven 1996: *Sociology, Environmentalism, Globalization*. London/ Thousand Oaks: Sage.

Yinger, J. Milton 1982: *Countercultures*. New York: Free Press.

Zald, Mayer N. 1970: *Organizational Change: The Political Economy of the YMCA*. Chicago: University of Chicago Press.

Zald, Mayer N. and Ash, Roberta 1966: Social Movement Organizations: Growth, Decay and Change. *Social Forces*, 44, 327–40.

Zald, Mayer N. and Jacobs, David 1978: Compliance/Incentive Classifications of Organizations. Underlying Dimensions. *Administration and Society*, 9, 403–24.

Zald, Mayer N. and McCarthy, John 1980: Social Movement Industries: Competition and Cooperation Among Movement Organizations. In L. Kriesberg (ed), *Research In Social Movements, Conflict and Change*, vol. 3, Greenwich, CT: JAI Press, 1–20.

Zald, Mayer N. and McCarthy, John 1987: *Social Movements in an Organizational Society*. New Brunswick, NJ: Transaction.

Zald, Mayer N. and Useem, Bert 1987: Movement and Countermovement Interaction: Mobilization, Tactics, and State Involvement. In M. N. Zald and J. D. McCarthy (eds), *Social Movements in an Organizational Society*, New Brunswick: Transaction Books, 247–72.

Zincone, Giovanna 1992: *Da Sudditi a Cittadini*. Bologna: il Mulino.

Zirakzadeh, Cyrus E. 1991: *A Rebellious People*. Reno: University of Nevada Press.

Zirakzadeh, Cyrus E. 1997: *Social Movements in Politics. A Comparative Study*. London/New York: Longman.

Zuo, Jiping and Benford, Robert D. 1994: Mobilization Processes and the 1989 Chinese Democracy Movement. *Sociological Quarterly*, 36, 801–28.

Zurcher, Louis A. and Curtis, Russel L. 1973: A Comparative Analysis of Propositions Describing Social Movement Organizations. *Sociological Quarterly*, 14, 175–88.

Index

Contents

The Author
Mollie K. Hughes

Mollie Hughes has long been involved in environmental issues. Since moving to Hanover, N.H., she has played a leading role in identifying the trees on the Dartmouth College campus—a campus she rightly refers to as "an arboretum of northern trees."

She was born in Washington, D.C., and graduated from Wellesley College in 1950. Prior to her marriage to D. R. (Turk) Hughes, she was employed in Washington by the American Meteorological Society as a researcher-writer and was a research assistant on President Dwight D. Eisenhower's Advisory Committee on Weather Control.

For three decades she lived in Dayton, Ohio where she immersed herself in a number of regional environmental issues and public, private and parochial school programs focused on the preservation of natural resources and the planting of trees.

Sponsored by the Kettering Foundation, Mrs. Hughes was sent to Europe to observe and study natural techniques to improve climate, environment and the quality of life in selected cities in Germany and Holland. She and her husband have volunteered on Earth Watch research projects in China, Poland, Venezuela and Costa Rica.

In 1984, they moved to Hanover where she continued to pursue her interests in outdoor activities and especially to focus on Dartmouth campus trees. She has led Study Groups for the Institute for Lifelong Education at Dartmouth (ILEAD), worked as a ski instructor at Killington and the Dartmouth Skiway, and spent seven years as a volunteer teaching handicapped skiers.

Mrs. Hughes was the recipient of the first Governor's Arbor Day Award for the State of Ohio, an honor which singled her out for her many successes in enhancing the quality of life in that state.

Work on *Forever Green* began some years ago when she first became aware of the Dartmouth Class of 1950's Tree Project. *(A.G.M. '50)*

Preface

The campus of Dartmouth College in Hanover, New Hampshire, is honored and treasured as one of the most beautiful in the nation, perhaps in the world. More than 1,750 trees help define this special place and enhance its reputation.

Dartmouth's wealth of trees provides a sequence of color, texture and shape throughout the seasons. Trees complement and soften the lines of architecture. They delineate and preserve precious open space. Unusual species from many parts of the world contribute scientific interest to the academic setting. The presence of trees native to northern New England helps blend the beauty of the College with the character of its surrounding environment.

This book, celebrating those trees, details species included in the *Campus Tree Inventory for Dartmouth College* which was completed in 1999 by Saucier & Flynn, Ltd., Landscape Architects, and the College's Department of Facilities Operation and Management. Even here, far north in the Upper Valley of the Connecticut River, the inventory identifies more than 75 species of trees. Parts of the campus were not inventoried. In those areas, including the Hanover Country Club and around Occom Pond, College Park (which includes Bartlett Tower, Shattuck Observatory and the Bema), and the old cemetery on the west side of campus (the property of the Town of Hanover), additional species such as Aspen, Cottonwood, Gray Birch and American Sycamore can be found. These species are not included in *Forever Green*.

No inventory of trees can be kept constantly up to date. New trees are planted each spring and fall, and established trees succumb and must be removed. Every attempt has been made to include all inventoried species of trees represented on the Dartmouth College campus at the turn of a new century.

M.K.H.
February 2000

Endorsing Comments

"*Forever Green* offers an intriguing stroll through the trees of Dartmouth College and the natural history of New Hampshire. Hughes brings the beauty that surrounds us to life."

—*Jeanne Shaheen, Governor*
State of New Hampshire

"The trees come alive with historical anecdotes, folklore and traditions, all within a framework of scientific accuracy. Though specific to the Dartmouth College campus, the information in this book is applicable to southern Canada and the northern half of the United States east of the Rocky Mountains. I'll return to *Forever Green* again and again."

—*Mary Reynolds*
Urban Forester
State of New Hampshire

"The Dartmouth College campus is a little known but important arboretum of trees hardy in our northern climate. This witty and informative guide is a delightful and welcome addition to the natural history literature for our region."

—*David Goudy, Director*
Montshire Museum of Science
Norwich, Vermont

Introduction

James Wright
President, Dartmouth College

I am delighted to be able to write this introduction to this wonderful book, *"Forever Green,"* by Mollie Hughes. I am pleased also to recognize the Class of 1950 as the sponsor of this book and as Dartmouth's "Tree Class."

The combination of architecture and landscaping makes the Dartmouth campus one of the most attractive anywhere in the world. There is indeed a special sense of place here. But it was not always so. The first impulse of the earliest settlers was to cut down the trees. Before he could establish his college Eleazar Wheelock and his students needed to clear the white pines from the Hanover plain. The fallen trunks of these enormous trees were stacked five feet high, and it was not until the 1830s that the College removed the last of the stumps from the Green. Pictures of Dartmouth in the mid-nineteenth century show a Hanover mostly bereft of trees.

In 1869, Judge Joel Parker, a former trustee of the College, donated 7,500 seedlings to the College to be planted near the observatory. He started a concern for the landscape that continues to this day. In the 1870s, students began work to beautify the whole College Park area and planted many of the trees that still grace that area today.

In *"A Young Birch,"* Robert Frost described a tree:

> *It was a thing of beauty and was sent*
> *To live its life out as an ornament.*

The Class of 1950 has planted many things of beauty that have enhanced Dartmouth's special sense of place. I thank them and Mollie Hughes for providing this descriptive inventory and record.

From my office in Parkhurst Hall, I can see a wonderful American Fountain Elm, which anchors the northwest corner of the Green. The Parkhurst Elm was probably planted around 1870 and has seen a great deal of Dartmouth history pass below its branches. This history includes ten presidents, countless faculty, and one hundred and thirty classes of students. When it was planted, the fence around the Green still existed and the College had neither electricity nor a water system.

The Parkhurst Elm and the many other trees on the Dartmouth campus are more than just things of beauty. They are companions, and they enrich the quality of this place while serving as silent witnesses to our history.

Baker Library

Dartmouth College Class of 1950
The Tree Planting Class

During the 1960s, one after another of the magnificent American Elms on the Dartmouth College campus was stricken by Dutch Elm disease and had to be removed. Two former college roommates, Newcomb Eldredge and the late Stevenson Flemer, suggested that their Class of 1950 initiate an ongoing tree planting program. The idea was enthusiastically adopted as a "natural." Their classmates understood the real and symbolic contribution trees have made to Dartmouth's beauty and tradition.

For almost 40 years, the Class of 1950 Tree Planting Program has provided the College with sufficient varieties to qualify the campus as an arboretum, a natural museum for the enjoyment and study of trees.

Circled numbers on the enclosed maps designate many of the more than 170 trees planted by the Class of 1950. It is the intention of Dartmouth 1950 to gradually turn over the Tree Planting Project to a younger class whose members share their interest and commitment.

Publication of this book, in conjunction with their 50th Reunion in June 2000, has been made possible by the generous financial support of many members of the Class of 1950. Particular recognition is due to David Taylor and Newcomb Eldredge for their faithful involvement with the book from its inception. And, to A. G. (Joe) Medlicott for his editorial assistance, inspiration and enthusiastic counsel to the author and to the production staff.

At this book's printing deadline, these members of the Class of 1950 are acknowledged with gratitude as underwriters of the project:

James G. Birney	Robert M. Kirby
William W. Broadbent	Joel A. Leavitt
William H. Carpenter	Alexander G. Medlicott
William J. Cross	Alan R. Mitchell
H. Newcomb Eldredge	H. Foster Nichols
Mrs. Stevenson Flemer	Bennett H. Shaver
Warren L. Franz	David J. Taylor
Jacques Harlow	Edward Tuck II
John C. Harned	Robert S. Wilkinson, Jr.
Robert D. Kilmarx	

American Elms along College Street, looking across the Green toward Hanover Inn, circa 1900.

Hanover, New Hampshire
A Tree City USA

TOWN *of* HANOVER

For many years, Dartmouth College and the Town of Hanover have cooperated closely in matters concerning trees. This mutual help continues to the present day. The College extends its excellent Elm protection program to Elms on Hanover Town property, and the Town reciprocates by frequently assisting in the removal of trees on College property.

Both Dartmouth and Hanover are keenly interested in and respectful of long range planning and the selection of species. The campus has many species not represented in the Town. The Town boasts at least 12 species not grown on campus. Among those 12, Hanover reports excellent results with the Bur and Shingle Oaks and the American Hornbeam.

For 21 years, Hanover has received the Tree City USA Award, a national honor based on tree planning, funding, planting and preservation.

TREE CITY USA

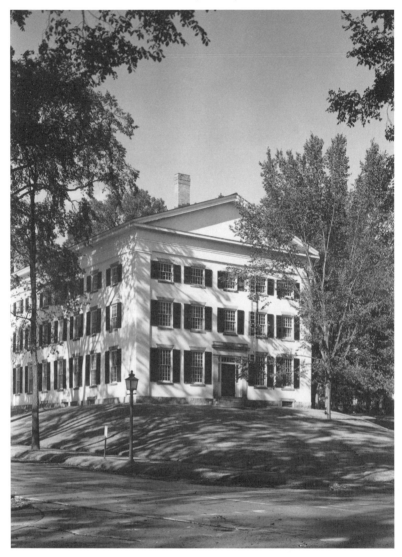

Reed Hall in the 1960s

What's In a Name
Why Trees Have Latin Names

Latin, or scientific, names are consistent throughout the world. Common names vary by region and language. In the extreme, a single tree could bear up to seven consecutive Latin names. Of the Latin names, however, only those designating *genus* and *species* are used in this book.

Latin names always appear in *italics*. For example, *Quercus alba* is the scientific name for the tree we know as the White Oak. The first and capitalized Latin word, *Quercus*, indicates the group of genetically related trees (the genus) to which all Oaks belong. The second Latin word, *alba*, identifies the particular species of Oak, in this case the White Oak.

In some instances, a name in single quotation marks appears after the two Latin words, as in *Acer platanoides* 'Crimson King.' *Acer* stands for the genus which includes all Maples and *platanoides* tells us the tree belongs to the species known as Norway Maple. 'Crimson King' identifies this tree as a cultivar. A cultivar is a variety of a species developed and cultivated by tree experts to emphasize a particular characteristic not always appearing in the species. The 'Crimson King' cultivar of the Norway Maple is cultivated for the deep red color of its foliage.

An "x" between two Latin names identifies a hybrid or cross-breed between two species. An example could be *Aesculus* x *carnea*, a cross between two Horsechestnuts. Some hybrids occur naturally; some are man-made.

Latin names solve many international misunderstandings far more effectively than do political treaties. The British call a certain group of trees Limes while in the United States the same trees are referred to as Lindens. While British and Americans share a common language, strangely enough that language is not English: It's Latin. Tree people in both countries know Limes and Lindens as *Tilia*.

Beauty For All Seasons
A Selection of Colorful Trees

Spring Bloom

Ohio Buckeye
Northern Catalpa
Black Cherry
Oriental 'Kwanzan' Cherry
Crabapples
Cornelian Cherry Dogwood
Fringetree
English 'Toba' Hawthorn
Ruby Red Horsechestnut
Japanese Tree Lilac
Black Locust
'Merrill' Magnolia
Saucer Magnolia
Star Magnolia
Red Maple
European Mountainash
Korean Mountainash
'Bradford' Pear
Downy Serviceberry
Yellowwood

Summer Bloom

Kousa Dogwood
Littleleaf Linden
Amur Maackia
Japanese Pagodatree

Fall Color—Red

Black Cherry
Amur Maple
Red Maple
Pin Oak
Red Oak
Black Tupelo

Fall Color— Orange and Yellow

Green Ash
Birches
Black Cherry
Amur Corktree
Ginkgo
English 'Toba' Hawthorn
Littleleaf Linden
Honeylocust
Larches
Amur Maple
Sugar Maple
Korean Mountainash
Downy Serviceberry

Fall Color— Plum, Wine and Purple

White Ash
Korean Mountainash
White Oak
Downy Serviceberry

Common Hackberry.

Crabapple, Crabapple bloom (inset).

Opposite:Winter beauty. Insets from top left:
Catalpa, Green Ash, Sugar Maple,
Ruby Red Horsechestnut.

Sugar Maple, Red Maple (inset).

Opposite:Winter beauty. Insets from top:
Star Magnolia,White Ash, Maples and Pines.

21

Kousa Dogwood, Kousa Dogwood bloom (inset).

Opposite: Littleleaf Linden. Insets clockwise from top:
Hawthorn, Pin Oak, Fringetree.

22

Yellowwood, Yellowwood bloom (inset).

Stresses and Strains
of Life in the "Big City"

Living with people is not always easy. From the point of view of a tree, even Hanover, N.H., qualifies as an urban location. Given a choice, a tree would probably plant itself in the company and safety of other trees and would search out a location providing its favorite soil. The tree would not choose to position itself beside a street or even on the Dartmouth College campus. Put yourself in the place of a tree removed from its native habitat and planted in an urban area.

Perhaps you're the giant American Elm located in the center of the paved walkway to the Hood Museum of Art. You were growing in that spot long before construction began. Since you have survived, care must have been taken not to sever or expose your roots or alter soil level in your space. Many less fortunate urban trees suffer or die as a result of construction. Being an Elm, you have a fibrous root system which remains close to the surface. That root system is now entirely covered with pavement. Someone considered your water supply and provided openings in the pavement through which water can seep. Rapid runoff, lack of percolation, and interference with the natural water table cause many an urban tree to die of thirst or drown.

Now, think of yourself as the Red Maple planted near the southwest corner of the Green. Thousands of students walk within a few feet of your trunk every day. The soil around you is tightly packed. Water and oxygen cannot reach your roots. Soil compaction frequently spells the doom of urban trees. Being close to a street, you're also plagued by dust, salt and vehicular exhaust. Then there are the friendly dogs who make your life even more difficult by using you as their favorite fireplug. You may not survive.

Or, imagine yourself as a London Planetree, one of the giants of our northeastern trees. Fortunately you were planted in a location with plenty of space to reach your massive maturity. Your relatives have lived more than 500 years. But when you were only 75 years old, a street had to be widened, a sidewalk built, and underground heating pipes relocated. Being a strong and growing "teenage tree," you fought back. Your powerful roots pierced the pipes and threatened the street. Your future does not look bright.

Or, picture yourself as a beautiful White Pine planted between two large buildings. You might find yourself suffering from deep shade, dumped on by snow and ice cascading off a roof, or struggling to survive in an architecturally induced wind-tunnel.

If you're an urban tree, these are but a few of the problems you face. Life for you is not easy. But, you do your best to tough it out and make our urban environment infinitely more beautiful, healthy and livable. You deserve our respect and all the support we can provide.

How Big Is That Tree? Trees and Architecture

From the foundation to the top of the cupola, Dartmouth Hall—the College's most historic building—reaches a height of 85 feet and offers a reference for judging the height of trees as they relate to architecture.

Small
(under 30 feet)

Crabapple
Cornelian Cherry Dogwood
Kousa Dogwood
Pagoda Dogwood
'Camperdown' Elm
Fringetree
'Toba' Hawthorn
Japanese Tree Lilac
'Merrill' Magnolia
Saucer Magnolia
Star Magnolia
Amur Maple
Pissard Plum
Downy Serviceberry

Medium
(30-50 feet)

'Whitespire' Birch
Ohio Buckeye
'Kwanzan' Cherry
Amur Chokecherry
Amur Corktree
White Fir
Thornless Honeylocust
Eastern Hophornbeam
Ruby Red Horsechestnut
Eastern Larch
Amur Mackia
Ashleaf Maple
Norway Maple
European Mountainash
Korean Mountainash
Engelmann Spruce
Black Tupelo
American Yellowwood

Tall
(over 50 feet)

Red Maple
Silver Maple
Sugar Maple
Chestnut Oak
English Oak
Pin Oak
Red Oak
Swamp White Oak
White Oak
Japanese Pagodatree
Austrian Pine
Eastern White Pine
Red Pine
Scotch Pine
London Planetree
Dawn Redwood
Colorado Blue Spruce
Norway Spruce
White Spruce
Black Walnut
'Tristis' Golden Weeping Willow
Japanese Zelkova

American Arborvitae
Green Ash
White Ash
American Beech
Paper Birch
Sweet Birch
Yellow Birch
Butternut
Northern Catalpa
Black Cherry
Kentucky Coffeetree
Douglasfir
American Elm
English Elm
Slippery Elm
Ginkgo
Common Hackberry
Eastern Hemlock
Katsuratree
European Larch
Littleleaf Linden
Black Locust

USDA Plant Hardiness Zone Map

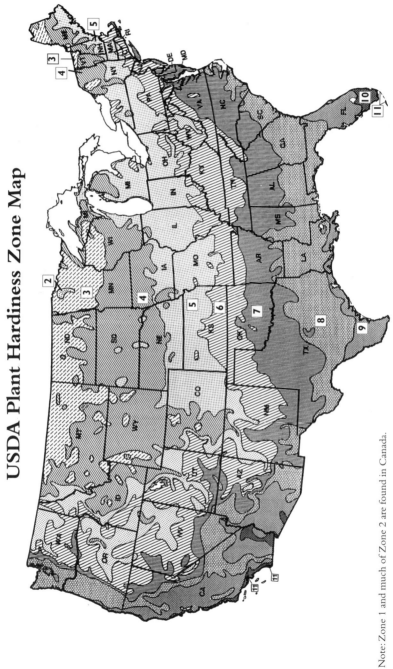

Note: Zone 1 and much of Zone 2 are found in Canada.

28

Surviving Winter in New England

USDA Plant Hardiness Zones

(Minimum temperatures a tree can be expected to withstand)

Zone 1: -50°F and below	Zone 7: 0°F to 10°F
Zone 2: -50°F to -40°F	Zone 8: 10°F to 20°F
Zone 3: -40°F to -30°F	Zone 9: 20°F to 30°F
Zone 4: -30°F to -20°F	Zone 10: 30°F to 40°F
Zone 5: -20°F to -10°F	Zone 11: above 40°F
Zone 6: -10°F to 0°F	

The ability of a tree to live and grow depends on many variables including low and high temperature extremes, light and moisture conditions, soil acidity or alkalinity, location in relation to competing species, and human-related factors such as air pollution and soil compaction. The U.S. Department of Agriculture Tree Hardiness Zones used in this book refer only to minimum temperatures a tree can be expected to withstand.

Trees rated as "hardy," in Zones 1, 2, 3 and 4 should be safe on the campus of Dartmouth College as far as low temperature is concerned. Most Zone 5 trees survive if not planted in extremely exposed locations. Zone 6 trees are experimental but can sometimes be grown successfully if sited in microclimatic areas such as inner courtyards which receive abundant sunshine and afford total protection from wind.

In the New Hampshire and Vermont hills surrounding Hanover as well as in some valley locations where cold air stagnates, lower temperatures necessitate the selection of more hardy trees.

Master List of Trees on the Dartmouth College Campus

Common Name	Scientific Name	Mature Height (Feet)	USDA Hardiness Zones	Tree ID Number on Maps	Profile Page
Arborvitae, American	*Thuja occidentalis*	40-60	2-7	1	37
Ash, Green	*Fraxinus pennsylvanica*	50-60	3-8	2	38
Ash, White	*Fraxinus americana*	50-80	3-9	3	39
Beech, American	*Fagus grandifolia*	50-70	4-9	4	40
Birch, Black (*see* Birch, Sweet)					
Birch, Paper	*Betula papyrifera*	50-70	2-6	5	43
Birch, Sweet	*Betula lenta*	40-55	3-7	6	44
Birch, White (*see* Birch, Paper)					
Birch, 'Whitespire'	*Betula populifolia* 'Whitespire'	40-50	4-7	7	45
Birch, Yellow	*Betula alleghaniensis*	60-75	3-7	8	46
Blackgum (*see* Tupelo, Black)					
Boxelder (*see* Maple, Ashleaf)					
Buckeye, Ohio	*Aesculus glabra*	20-40	3-7	9	47
Butternut	*Juglans cinerea*	40-60	3-7	10	48
Catalpa, Northern	*Catalpa speciosa*	40-60	4-8	11	49
Cedar, White Northern (see Arborvitae, American)					
Cherry, Black	*Prunus serotina*	50-60	3-9	12	50
Cherry, Cornelian (*see* Dogwood, Cornelian Cherry)					
Cherry, Oriental 'Kwanzan'	*Prunus serrulata* 'Kwanzan'	20-35	5-8	13	51
Chokecherry, Amur	*Prunus maackii*	35-45	2-6	14	52
Coffeetree, Kentucky	*Gymnocladus dioicus*	60-75	4-8	15	53
Cork Tree, Amur	*Phellodendron amurensis*	30-45	4-7	16	54

Crabapple	*Malus spp.*	10-25	4-8	17	55
Dogwood, Cornelian Cherry	*Cornus mas*	20-25	4-8	18	56
Dogwood, Kousa	*Cornus kousa*	20-30	5-8	19	57
Dogwood, Pagoda	*Cornus alternifolia*	15-25	3-7	20	58
Douglasfir	*Pseudotsuga menziesii*	40-80	4-6	21	59
Elm, American	*Ulmus americana*	60-80	2-9	22	62
Elm, American 'Liberty' (*see* Elm, American)					
Elm, American 'Princeton' (*see* Elm, American)					
Elm, English	*Ulmus procera*	80-100	4-9	23	64
Elm, Scotch 'Camperdown'	*Ulmus glabra* 'Camperdownii'	20-25	4-8	24	65
Elm, Slippery	*Ulmus rubra*	40-70	3-9	25	66
Fir, Douglas (*see* Douglasfir)					
Fir, White	*Abies concolor*	30-50	3-7	26	67
Fringetree	*Chionanthus virginicus*	12-25	4-9	27	68
Ginkgo	*Ginkgo biloba*	50-80	4-9	28	69
Hackberry, Common	*Celtis occidentalis*	40-60	3-9	29	70
Hawthorn, English 'Toba'	*Crataegus x mordensis* 'Toba'	15-20	4-6	30	71
Hemlock, Eastern	*Tsuga canadensis*	40-70	3-7	31	72
Honeylocust, Thornless	*Gleditsia triacanthos* var. *inermis*	30-35	4-9	32	73
Honeylocust, Thornless 'Imperial' (*see* Honeylocust, Thornless)					
Honeylocust, Thornless 'Sunburst' (*see* Honeylocust, Thornless)					
Hophornbeam, Eastern	*Ostrya virginiana*	25-40	4-9	33	74
Horsechestnut, Ruby Red	*Aesculus x carnea*	30-40	4-7	34	75
Katsuratree	*Cercidiphyllum japonicum*	40-60	4-8	35	76
Larch, Eastern	*Larix laricina*	30-50	2-4	36	77

Master List of Trees on the Dartmouth College Campus

Common Name	Scientific Name	Mature Height (Feet)	USDA Hardiness Zones	Tree ID Number on Maps	Profile Page
Larch, European	*Larix decidua*	70–75	2–6	37	78
Lilac, Japanese Tree	*Syringa reticulata*	15–25	3–7	38	79
Linden, Littleleaf	*Tilia cordata*	60–70	3–7	39	80
Locust, Black	*Robinia pseudoacacia*	30–60	3–8	40	81
Maackia, Amur	*Maackia amurensis*	20–40	4–7	41	82
Magnolia, 'Merrill'	*Magnolia x loebneri* 'Merrill'	15–25	4–8	42	83
Magnolia, Saucer	*Magnolia x soulangiana*	20–30	5–9	43	84
Magnolia, Star	*Magnolia stellata*	15–20	4–8	44	85
Maple, Amur	*Acer ginnala*	15–18	3–8	45	86
Maple, Ashleaf	*Acer negundo*	30–50	2–9	46	87
Maple, Norway	*Acer platanoides*	40–50	3–7	47	88
Maple, Norway 'Crimson King' (*see* Maple, Norway)					
Maple, Red	*Acer rubrum*	40–60	3–9	48	89
Maple, Rock (*see* Maple, Sugar)					
Maple, Silver	*Acer saccharinum*	50–70	3–9	49	90
Maple, Sugar	*Acer saccharum*	60–75	4–8	50	91
Mountainash, European	*Sorbus aucuparia*	20–40	3–6	51	92
Mountainash, Korean	*Sorbus alnifolia*	40–50	3–6	52	93
Oak, Chestnut	*Quercus prinus*	60–70	4–8	53	94
Oak, English	*Quercus robur*	40–60	3–7	54	95
Oak, Pin	*Quercus palustris*	60–70	4–7	55	96
Oak, Red	*Quercus rubra*	60–75	4–7	56	97

Common name	Scientific name				
Oak, Swamp White	*Quercus bicolor*	50–60	3–8	57	98
Oak, White	*Quercus alba*	50–80	3–8	58	99
Osier, Green (*see* Dogwood, Pagoda)					
Pagodatree, Japanese	*Sophora japonica*	50–70	4–7	59	100
Pear, 'Bradford'	*Pyrus calleryana* 'Bradford'	30–50	5–8	60	101
Pine, Austrian	*Pinus nigra*	50–60	4–7	61	102
Pine, Eastern White	*Pinus strobus*	50–80	3–8	62	103
Pine, Red	*Pinus resinosa*	50–80	2–5	63	106
Pine, Scotch	*Pinus sylvestris*	30–60	2–7	64	107
Pine, White (*see* Pine, Eastern White)					
Planetree, London	*Platanus x acerifolia*	70–100	4–8	65	108
Plum, Pissard	*Prunus cerasifera* 'Atropurpurea'	15–30	5–8	66	109
Redwood, Dawn	*Metasequoia glyptostroboides*	70–100	5–8	67	110
Serviceberry, Downy	*Amelanchier arborea*	15–25	4–9	68	111
Spruce, Colorado Blue	*Picea pungens*	30–60	2–7	69	112
Spruce, Engelmann	*Picea engelmannii*	40–50	2–6	70	113
Spruce, Norway	*Picea abies*	40–60	2–7	71	114
Spruce, White	*Picea glauca*	40–100	2–6	72	115
Tamarack (*see* Larch, Eastern)					
Tupelo, Black	*Nyssa sylvatica*	30–50	4–9	73	116
Walnut, Black	*Juglans nigra*	50–75	4–9	74	117
Willow, 'Tristis' Golden Weeping	*Salix alba* 'Tristis'	50–70	4–9	75	118
Yellowwood, American	*Cladastris kentukea*	30–50	4–8	76	119
Zelkova, Japanese	*Zelkova serrata*	58–80	5–8	77	120

Studying beneath a Crabapple tree

Tree Profiles

Personal Stories
of Seventy-Seven Species of Trees
Found on the
Dartmouth College Campus

In Alphabetical Order
from Arborvitae to Zelkova

Structure, Size, Hardiness, Brilliance, Color, Function
Each Tree Makes a Unique Contribution to a Planned Landscape

The Many Shapes of Leaves

Leaf Arrangement

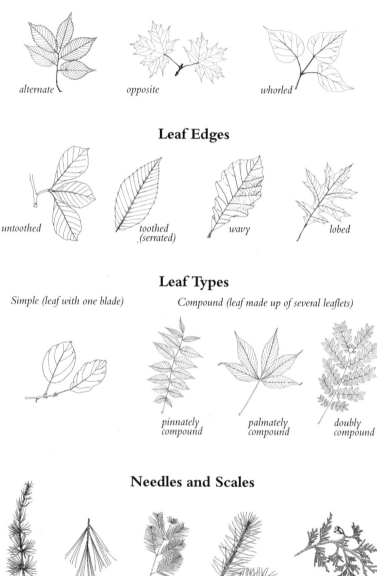

alternate

opposite

whorled

Leaf Edges

untoothed

toothed
(serrated)

wavy

lobed

Leaf Types

Simple (leaf with one blade)

Compound (leaf made up of several leaflets)

pinnately
compound

palmately
compound

doubly
compound

Needles and Scales

cluster of
larch needles

bundle of
pine needles
with sheath

needles in
one plane

needles
encircling
twig

scales of
arborvitae

Eastern Arborvitae

Northern White Cedar, Oo-soo-ha-tah, Canoe Wood

Thuja occidentalis

Need a vitamin fix? Brew some tea from the bark and leaves of the Arborvitae. That's what provided the vitamin C credited with saving Jacques Cartier and his fellow explorers from scurvy in 1536. They named the species 'tree of life' and valued it so highly that they carried living specimens home to Paris, thus making the Arborvitae possibly the first tree transported west to east across the Atlantic. Native Americans had long been aware of the Arborvitae's medicinal value. To them the tree was known as 'canoe wood' for its light weight, water resistant wood that served as frames for their canoes, or as Oo-soo-ha-tah, a name descriptive of its graceful leaf pattern. Arborvitae leaves are flat scales which arrange themselves into feather-like sprays. Measuring a mere 1/16th to 1/8th of an inch in length, they are the smallest leaves on campus. Groups of diminutive, bell-shaped cones develop near the ends of the sprays. When mature, they open to release tiny flying-saucer seeds that travel considerable distances. In the wild, the cone-shaped Arborvitae grows relatively slowly to heights of about 60 feet and often survives several hundred years. It is most frequently found in alkaline soils near rivers and lakes or in swamps. As a landscape tree, Arborvitae can be used as a handsome, free-standing specimen or can be planted as a windbreak or hedge. The cultivar, 'Techny,' is highly recommended for cold climates, because it remains dark green throughout the winter when many other varieties turn an unattractive yellow-brown. Arborvitae is resistant to extreme cold, pollution, and compacted soil. But keep it away from streets and driveways as it does not tolerate salt.

Leaves: Scale-like, evergreen

Map ID #1

Green Ash

Swamp Ash, Water Ash

Fraxinus pennsylvanica

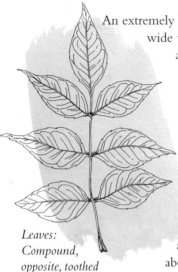

Leaves:
Compound,
opposite, toothed

An extremely hardy, fast-growing tree that is tolerant of a wide variety of soil conditions, the Green Ash is a smaller sibling to the majestic White Ash. Both are easily identifiable by the opposite compound leaf which, among tall trees, is unique to the Ash species, the Ashleaf Maple, and the Amur Cork Tree. Like most siblings, the Green Ash has a personality of its own. Whereas leaves of the White Ash turn a purplish-red in autumn, those of the Green Ash change to a vibrant yellow. The Green Ash takes after its shorter ancestors and tops out at about 60 feet while its larger relative soars above 100 feet. Excellent male cultivars of the Green Ash are widely available and totally free of the clusters of seeds which can label many Ash varieties as litterers. Among those cultivars, one of the most popular is the 'Marshall's Seedless' found in numerous locations on campus. Like the larger White, the Green Ash is a well-shaped tree with dense and luxurious foliage. Sometimes confused with the Red Ash, the Green can be distinguished by its greater height and by its hairless and somewhat shiny twigs. The Green Ash is the most widely distributed of wild Ash trees in the United States. Native Americans tapped the tree to make a sugary, but somewhat bitter, syrup.

Map ID #2

38

White Ash
American Ash, Biltmore Ash, Cane Ash

Fraxinus americana

Brighten the corner where you live. Take some advice from a tree. In a fascinating way, the White Ash improves its own environment. White Ash have large, feather-like leaves consisting of up to nine leaflets. Those leaflets are considered a culinary delicacy by earthworms. When the leaves fall, the worms pull the leaflets into their burrows, devour them and return valuable nutrients in the form of worm droppings to the soil beneath the tree. Of some 30 Ash varieties native to North America, the White Ash is probably the most frequently chosen for landscaping. This handsome, native tree is capable of growing more than 100 feet tall

Leaves: Compound, opposite, toothed or untoothed

and living 150-200 years. The White Ash is a fast grower which is comparatively free of insect and disease problems, particularly when it is planted in colder regions. It adapts well to a broad range of soil conditions. White Ash are trees for all seasons, with rich green foliage in summer, beautiful coloration in autumn, and striking silhouettes in winter. That dramatic splash of purple-red on campus each fall is courtesy of the White Ash. Attractive, but somewhat of a nuisance when they drop, are the large drooping clusters of single, inch-long winged seeds call samara.

Map ID #3

American Beech

Beechnut Tree

Fagus grandifolia

Leaves:
Simple,
alternate,
toothed

Want to know the secret of growing old without wrinkles? Ask an American Beech. It's one of the few trees that retains smooth bark right into old age, and old age can mean 300-400 years. Even in our far northern forests there are Beech trees estimated to be more than 250 years old. Some say the mighty Oak is king of the forest. If so, its close relative, the Beech, must be queen. Tall, majestic, graceful, and wearing a rounded crown, the American Beech is regal at all times of year. Smooth gray bark, lance-like buds, and a handsome silhouette with lower branches that often sweep the ground distinguish the tree in winter, as do long-clinging, translucent leaves the color of undyed deer-skin. In summer, those leaves, dark blue-green above and a lighter green beneath, form a dense canopy that provides welcome shade. Some, but not all, American Beech put on a massive display of golden brown in the fall. It's a tree worth honoring. Give it well-drained soil, lots of space and a location safe from salt and the tread of feet. The American Beech will more than repay you with beauty while providing wildlife with nuts so delicious they might even tempt a black bear to enroll at Dartmouth.

Robert Frost

Robert Frost (1874–1963), the world-renowned poet laureate of the United States, was a member of the Class of 1896 at Dartmouth College. Throughout his life, Frost returned to the College many times to lecture Dartmouth students.

Birches

When I see birches bend to left and right
Across the lines of straighter darker trees,
I like to think some boy's been swinging them
But swinging doesn't bend them down to stay.
Ice-storms do that. Often you must have seen them
Loaded with ice a sunny winter morning
After a rain. They click upon themselves
As the breeze rises, and turn many-colored
As the stir cracks and crazes their enamel.
Soon the sun's warmth makes them shed crystal shells
Shattering and avalanching on the snow-crust—
Such heaps of broken glass to sweep away
You'd think the inner dome of heaven had fallen.
They are dragged to the withered bracken by the load,
And they seem not to break; though once they are bowed
So low for long, they never right themselves;
You may see their trunks arching in the woods
Years afterwards, trailing their leaves on the ground
Like girls on hands and knees that throw their hair
Before them over their heads to dry in the sun.
But I was going to say when Truth broke in
With all her matter-of-fact about the ice-storm
I should prefer to have some boy bend them
As he went out and in to fetch the cows—
Some boy too far from town to learn baseball,
Whose only play was what he found himself,
Summer or winter, and could play alone.
One by one he subdued his father's trees
By riding them down over and over again
Until he took the stiffness out of them,
And not one but hung limp, not one was left
For him to conquer. He learned all there was
To learn about not launching out too soon

And so not carrying the tree away
Clear to the ground. He always kept his poise
To the top branches, climbing carefully
With the same pains you use to fill a cup
Up to the brim, and even above the brim.
Then he flung outward, feet first, with a swish,
Kicking his way down through the air to the ground.
So was I once myself a swinger of birches.
And so I dream of going back to be.
It's when I'm weary of considerations,
And life is too much like a pathless wood
Where your face burns and tickles with the cobwebs
Broken across it, and one eye is weeping
From a twig's having lashed across it open.
I'd like to get away from earth awhile
And then come back to it and begin over.
May no fate willfully misunderstand me
And half grant what I wish and snatch me away
Not to return. Earth's the right place for love:
I don't know where it's likely to go better.
I'd like to go by climbing a birch tree,
And climb black branches up a snow-white trunk
Toward heaven, till the tree could bear no more,
But dipped its top and set me down again.
That would be good both going and coming back.
One could do worse than be a swinger of birches.

Paper Birch

White Birch, Canoe Birch

Betula papyrifera

The flexible trunks of a clump of young Paper Birch might well have been both playground and athletic field for the isolated farm boy in Robert Frost's *Birches* (p. 41). Considered by the experts of Harvard's Arnold Arboretum to be "one of our best native ornamental trees," the Paper Birch can live up to 125 years and grow to a height of 100 feet. To achieve such size, the tree should be protected from strong winds and grown with a single trunk. Also known as the White or Canoe Birch, this striking tree is easily recognized by its peeling white bark that is decorated with horizontal, black lenticels or breathing pores. These breathing pores are vital, because the bark of the Paper Birch is so saturated with resin as to be almost impervious to oxygen and water. Native Americans chose this bark to make canoes light

Leaves: Simple, alternate, toothed

enough to be portaged by one man, but sufficiently buoyant to support heavy loads. Bark was removed from the Birch in long vertical strips, stretched, stitched with the fibrous roots of the Eastern Larch, sealed with Pine or Balsam pitch, and applied inside out over a lightweight frame of Cedar. All these species used for building canoes grow wild in New Hampshire. Leaves of the Paper Birch are egg-shaped with pointed tips and widely spaced veins. Like leaves of other Birches, they turn yellow in the fall. Young trees have smooth, brown bark. As the Paper Birch matures, its bark becomes snow white and starts to peel. At this stage, there is no mistaking this most widely distributed of the world's many Birches. Not only does the Paper Birch thrive in the northland down to temperatures of -50°F, but it grows well in the stony tills and outwash terraces left behind by retreating glaciers.

Map ID #5

Sweet Birch

Black Birch, Cherry Birch

Betula lenta

If you happen to have a passion for chewing on trees, Sweet Birch—or to a lesser degree Yellow Birch—would be the ones to sample. Stems and bark from young trees of these species were once distilled into oil of wintergreen. But, please, if you must eat trees, don't sample one on campus. Go find a tree growing wild where squirrels, rabbits, moose, deer, and grouse will join you in your feast. Not all Birch trees have white or yellow bark. The bark of a young Sweet Birch is reddish-brown and does not peel. That of an old Sweet Birch becomes almost black and fissures into scaly, non-peeling plates. This distinctive bark pattern is one of the few features to help distinguish Sweet from Yellow Birch. Young trees are still very difficult to differentiate. Despite its dark bark, the Sweet species can easily be identified as a Birch by the presence of long, slender, pollen-providing catkins and one-to-one-and-a-half inch cone-like fruits. Under cultivation, the tree grows 50-70 feet in height and develops a rounded, wide-spreading crown. The golden yellow of its fall foliage is perhaps the best among all the Birches. The Sweet, or Black, Birch grows wild in a 200-300 mile wide swath bracketing the Appalachian Trail from southern Maine to northern Georgia. The largest specimens, measuring 80 feet in height with trunks 2-5 feet in diameter, once grew on the moist, west-facing mountain slopes of Tennessee. In addition to oil of wintergreen, alcohol was distilled from the wood of the Sweet Birch. It could be that this tree has some connection with an old folk song which begins, "My brother, Bill, had a still on the hill where he turned out a gallon or two."

Leaves: Simple, alternate, toothed

'Whitespire' Birch

Betula populifolia 'Whitespire'

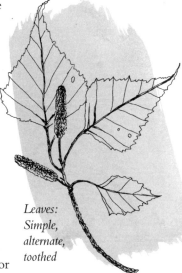

If the Birch trees planted on campus in the spring of 1999 are genuine 'Whitespires,' then they are clones. To be a clone, a tree must have been reproduced vegetatively rather than from seed. In the vegetative reproduction process, a single bud from the parent tree is propagated under sterile conditions in an artificial medium. When this technique is used, the resulting offspring is genetically identical to its parent. The DNA of a true 'Whitespire' Birch exactly matches the DNA of one specified Gray Birch that was raised and is still flourishing in the Longenecker Gardens of the University of Wisconsin Arboretum at Madison. According to Professor Emeritus Edward R. Hasselkus of that University's Department of Horticulture, Gray Birch *(Betula populifolia)* seeds were sent from Exeter, N.H., to the arboretum at Madison, Wis., in 1941. The seeds were planted but all but one of the resulting collection of trees had died by 1966. That tree alone demonstrated unusual tolerance to heat and drought as well as good resistance to the bronze borer, an insect which plagues Birch trees. In 1983, Professor Hasselkus selected the vigorous survivor and introduced it to the world of horticulture. He warns that trees propagated from seed, rather than by means of the vegetative process, are being marketed under the name 'Whitespire.' Such seed grown trees may not demonstrate as completely the admirable qualities for which the original tree was selected. According to Professor Hasselkus, true clones of the original tree should be labeled 'Whitespire Sr.' The 'Whitespire' Birch grows to about 40 feet in height and is lushly clothed in dark green, triangular-shaped leaves which change to yellow in the fall. If Dartmouth's new Birches have inherited the precious resistance to the Birch borer, then the gorgeous white bark of this interesting clone may still grace the campus when the Class of 2050 is ready to graduate.

Leaves: Simple, alternate, toothed

Map ID #7

Yellow Birch

Silver Birch, Swamp Birch

Betula alleghaniensis

Leaves: Simple, alternate, toothed

In the spring of 1999, two old-growth Yellow Birches were discovered on the slopes of Mount Sunapee. The trunks of both trees measured almost three feet in diameter. Their ages were estimated to be between 200 and 300 years. Because Yellow Birches are logged for the beauty, strength, and hardness of their wood, few such magnificent specimens remain. However, the species is still our most abundant native Birch. The Yellow Birch grows wild across southern Canada and the northern United States from the Atlantic to Minnesota, as well as south through the Appalachian Mountains. Like the Paper Birch, the Yellow grows into a tall, handsome tree capable of topping 100 feet. Shiny, pale, golden-bronze bark that peels in thin curly flakes or plates rather than sheets makes this species relatively easy to identify. The Yellow Birch grows well in regions which experience winter temperatures as low as -40°F. Its oval leaves display doubly sawtoothed edges and tightly packed, almost parallel, veins. If you have never seen a Yellow Birch, look for that shining, golden bark. Once you've recognized the species, you'll realize it is one of northern New England's most common trees. Much of the beautiful splash of yellow that adorns the region's hillsides each fall is courtesy of the Yellow Birch.

Ohio Buckeye
Fetid Buckeye
Aesculus glabra

Carry the shiny brown seed of a Buckeye in your pocket and cure your rheumatism. So thought the pioneers. These nuts, which are named for their resemblance to the eye of a buck, still prove irresistible to the young at heart. The Ohio Buckeye grows wild in most areas from Ohio west to Kansas and south to Alabama. So many of the trees were found along the banks of the Ohio River that Ohio was dubbed the Buckeye State. The Buckeyes of North America and the Horsechestnuts of Europe are close relatives which crossbreed frequently. Therefore, the campus Buckeye could be a hybrid.

Leaves: Compound, opposite, toothed

They are the only two species of trees with opposite, compound leaves comprised of leaflets radiating fan-like from a central point. Such a radiating growth pattern of leaflets is called 'palmate.' Neither tree should be confused with the American Chestnut which belongs to a different biological classification. The 20-40 foot Ohio Buckeye with its coarse but attractive structure can be an interesting specimen in a campus or park setting. Don't plant it close to outdoor living areas, because, like the Horsechestnut, it is always dropping some sort of litter, be it

flowers, leaves, or nuts. The tree earns its descriptive nickname, Fetid Buckeye, from the unfortunate fact that, when crushed, its flowers, twigs, and bark emit an unpleasant odor. Buckeye leaves, twigs, and seeds can be toxic to wildlife and livestock. In defense of the Ohio Buckeye, it is hardy, lives up to 200 years, has large upright spikes of yellowish bloom in the spring, and turns shades of orange and yellow in the fall.

Map ID #9

Butternut
Oil Nut, White Walnut
Juglans cinerea

Leaves:
Compound,
alternate,
toothed

Sometimes it's important to help preserve a certain tree by planting it on campuses and in parks and arboreta, because that tree is close to becoming an endangered species. The Butternut is one such example. Native to the entire northeastern quadrant of the United States, this relatively short-lived tree most commonly tops out at 30-50 feet with an open, spreading crown and a short trunk. Although very tolerant of cold temperatures, it is susceptible to ice breakage which often leads to the development of an asymmetric silhouette. A close cousin to the Black Walnut, the Butternut is easy to distinguish from that taller and far more valuable tree. Both have alternate, compound leaves which turn yellow in the fall, but the spring and summer foliage of the Butternut is lighter green, aromatic, and sticky. Also sticky is the greenish husk which covers the football-shaped nut of the Butternut. Native Americans boiled these nuts to obtain oil from which to make a butter-like spread, accounting for the tree's common name. Terminal leaflets are generally present on the Butternut but frequently missing on the Walnut. The famous Swedish botanist, Carolus Linnaeus, classified the Butternut as *Juglans* (for Walnut family) and *cinerea* (meaning ashes) to describe its ashy gray bark. On mature trees the bark develops broad flat ridges. The Butternut is intolerant of compacted soil and salt. Therefore, it is not a good tree to plant in areas of heavy pedestrian traffic or close to streets where salt may be used during the winter. Like the Black Walnut, the roots of the Butternut create an environment toxic to many other plants.

48

Northern Catalpa

Catawba, Hardy Catalpa, Indian Bean, Cigartree

Catalpa speciosa

Big and beany can be beautiful if you don't plant it in a small front yard. A full-grown Catalpa could never be described as graceful but, in a park or campus setting, this species makes a dramatic statement. Forty-foot mature trees develop picturesque, irregular crowns clothed in whorls of 12-inch heart-shaped leaves. When it blooms profusely in June, the Catalpa is at its most beautiful. Clusters of cream-colored blossoms are borne upright at the ends of the branches and are highly visible. Individual flowers with fringed petals and yellow, orange, and purplish markings resemble orchids. If you mentally flatten out a large, blooming Northern Catalpa you can

Leaves: Simple, opposite, whorled, untoothed

imagine the equivalent of a garden plot packed with flowers and measuring approximately 100 by 50 feet. The *raison d'être* of flowers is to produce seeds. In this department, the Catalpa is almost overly efficient. Untold numbers of seed-enclosing bean pods measuring up to 18 inches in length give this species two of its common names, Cigartree and Indian Bean. Fallen bean pods, flower petals and leaves assure the tree's reputation as a litterer. The Northern Catalpa is native to a relatively small region which centers on the confluence of the Ohio and Mississippi rivers. While well able to tolerate heat and drought, this tree, whose relatives are almost entirely tropical, could suffer if not protected from extremes of winter cold.

Map ID #11

Black Cherry

Rum Cherry

Prunus serotina

Leaves: Simple, alternate, toothed

If the birds don't get there first, you can harvest the tiny fruits of this native tree, add a dash of rum, and make yourself a glass of "cherry bounce." The Black Cherry is found throughout most of the eastern two-thirds of the United States as well as in southeastern Canada. Wildlife continues to do its nature-assigned job of "planting" Black Cherry seedlings along roads and fence lines. But those seedlings almost never grow to maturity. Nowadays, chances of finding a 70-80 foot Black Cherry in its native habitat are as unlikely as chances of locating a full-grown Black Walnut. Prime specimens of both species have disappeared because their wood is so valuable for cabinet making. In landscaped settings, the Black Cherry develops a straight trunk and oval crown. It tops out at about 50 feet. Smooth, dark reddish-brown bark, with horizontal lines of breathing pores, helps identify young trees. As the tree ages, this distinctive bark darkens and develops scaly plates. Some tree species bloom early in the spring and display their flowers on bare branches. Other types of trees wait to bloom until after their new leaves have emerged. The Black Cherry's second scientific name, 'serotina,' means "appearing late" and identifies the tree as a member of the late-blooming group. In May, drooping popsicle-like clusters of tiny white flowers contrast attractively with the red glow of new foliage. In summer, miniature red cherries ripen against a background of shining green leaves. And, in autumn, as the cherries darken to almost black, the leaves change to rich tones of red and yellow. Varieties of Black Cherry, with weeping habits and more abundant flowers than found on the wild tree, are available commercially.

Oriental 'Kwanzan' Cherry
Oriental Cherry
Prunus serrulata 'Kwanzan'

Each spring, thousands of tourists flock to our nation's capital to walk around Potomac Park and the Tidal Basin when the Japanese Cherries bloom. The original planting was given to the city in 1912 by the mayor of Tokyo. Many of those greatly admired trees are Kwanzan Cherries, distinguished by a profusion of deep pink, double flowers displayed against smooth, reddish-brown bark. Here, on a northern campus, we can enjoy the same tree because the Kwanzan is able to survive winter temperatures down to -20°F. But even this most cold-hardy of all the double-flowering cherries must be afforded some degree of protection from winter winds and sites where cold air collects and stagnates. Japanese Cherries are not valued

Leaves: Simple, alternate, toothed

for their fruit but for their large, showy blossoms which appear in early spring on bare branches. They are particularly beautiful when planted against a background of graceful Hemlocks or other ground-sweeping evergreens. Kwanzan leaves are reddish when they first emerge. The foliage then changes to green for the summer and turns orange-brown in the fall. The tree is attractive throughout its entire growing season. Branches sweep upward in a vase-shaped pattern from single or multiple trunks. Flowering Cherries are relatively short-lived and highly susceptible to disease and insect attack. But they are worth planting and replanting. Their springtime blooms are welcome and dramatic.

Map ID #13

Amur Chokecherry

Prunus maackii

Leaves: Simple, alternate, toothed

You might not choke on these cherries, but you'll surely pucker up. The Amur Chokecherry is not grown for its fruit. The tiny cherries are extremely bitter. Their seeds are poisonous—hardly a healthy crop. Instead, the tree is planted for the exceptional beauty of its bark and the delicacy of its spring bloom. Both Birch bark and Beech bark are showy and beautiful in a winter landscape. But even more dramatic is the glistening, peeling bark of the Amur Chokecherry. In polished tones ranging from honey-gold through every shade known to maple syrup, the multiple trunks of this Asian import are unforgettable against a background of snow. The word 'Amur' in its name designates this tree as a species that grows wild in the areas of Manchuria and northeastern Siberia that are drained by the mighty Amur River. Trees able to survive the extremes of Siberian winters are not threatened by the cold of New England. This most hardy of all Cherries can withstand temperatures as low as -50° but it is unable to cope with heat. The Amur Chokecherry matures at heights of 35-45 feet with a well-rounded and dense crown. Abundant clusters of tiny white flowers envelop the tree in May.

Kentucky Coffeetree

Coffeenut, Nickertree, Stumptree

Gymnocladus dioicus

Which tree on the Dartmouth campus has the largest leaf? Oak, Maple, and London Planetree leaves can grow up to 10 inches in length while Ash, Buckeye, and Walnut leaves reach 12-24 inches. The Kentucky Coffeetree outdoes them all with leaves measuring up to 36 inches long and 24 inches wide. How can this be? The Kentucky Coffeetree appears to have mere leaflets, no more than a few inches in length. The answer lies in the word "leaflets." Some trees, including the Oak and Maple, have "simple leaves" consisting of a single leaf blade with a soft stalk. That soft stalk, or midrib, attaches directly to a woody twig. Other trees, including the Ash and Walnut, have "compound leaves."

Leaves: Compound, alternate, untoothed

Such leaves are comprised of three or more "leaflets" attached to a soft midrib which in turn attaches to a woody twig. One compound leaf is made up of many leaflets. The Kentucky Coffeetree takes the business of compound leaves one step further. Its leaves are doubly compound. Their soft central stalks branch into several soft side stalks, each of which sprouts many leaflets. Therefore, one leaf of this strange tree can be made up of as many as 60 leaflets, all attached in a fern-like pattern to subdivisions of a single leaf stalk. The huge complex of non-woody material is considered one leaf. The Kentucky Coffeetree is the state tree of Kentucky, but it is also able to survive farther north where temperatures drop to -20°F or lower. Native Americans roasted the seeds from its large pods and ate them as nuts, being very careful to avoid the poisonous, sticky pulp found inside the pod. Early settlers used these same seeds to make a substitute for coffee. Attaining heights of about 100 feet during its 100-125 year life span, the Kentucky Coffeetree is remarkably free from problems associated with insects, disease, wind, ice, soil compaction, salt, and drought. But when its large seed pods and gigantic leaf structures drop, there's a pile of litter.

Map ID #15

Amur Cork Tree

Phellodendron amurense

Leaves:
Compound,
opposite,
untoothed

An exotic new species has joined the Dartmouth family of trees. From 1996 to 1998, extensive tree planting was done north of Maynard Street on land where the original Mary Hitchcock Memorial Hospital once stood. Considerable thought went into the selection and siting of those trees, because long-term plans call for the campus to expand north in that direction. Two of the young specimens are Amur Cork Trees, natives of northern China, Japan, and the Amuria region of far eastern Siberia. Note the specie's Latin name, '*amurense*.' At maturity, the trees should stand 30-45 feet tall with broad-spreading and open crowns. A complex pattern of massive branches, combined with deeply ridged and corky-textured bark, make the Amur Cork Tree especially attractive in a winter landscape. Large and feathery compound leaves, made up of shiny, green leaflets, provide a striking contrast to the mature tree's rugged structure. Compound leaves grow opposite one another on the twigs, a highly unusual characteristic shared on campus with the Ash trees and the Ashleaf Maple. Given well-drained soil and full sun, the Amur Cork Trees should prosper. Winter temperatures pose no problem. The tree has proved cold-hardy down to -35°F.

Crabapple

Malus spp.

Crabapples are Apple Trees which bear fruit two inches or less in diameter. Almost 30 species grow wild throughout the world, but most North American favorites are crossbreeds of Asian trees. Crabapples cross-fertilize with remarkable ease and frequency. New hybrids appear regularly. If these show promising traits, they are raised by nurseries and given new cultivar names. At least 800 cultivars are marketed. More than 200 types of Crabapples grow in Harvard's Arnold

Leaves: Simple, alternate, toothed

Arboretum alone. As a group, Crabapples display tremendous variety. In height, they range from shrub-size to about 25 feet; in shape, from weeping to columnar to spreading. Fruit can be as tiny as a pea or as large as a small plum. In areas of extreme winter temperatures, such as Siberia, central Canada, and the northern midwest of the United States, cold-hardy Crabapples replace regular Apple Trees as a food source. In most parts of the world, however, Crabapples are planted for their spring blossoms which usually appear in May and can be single or double, white, pink, red or purplish-red. Fall-maturing fruits ranging in color from yellow to red provide a second season of beauty and prove irresistible to wildlife. Entire flocks of migrating birds often land in a single tree to enjoy the feast. Like regular Apples, Crabapples are highly susceptible to disease and insect attack. Any good nursery can advise prospective buyers as to the most resistant varieties for use in a particular region. On campus, some favorite cultivars are the 'Indian Summer,' with its rose-red bloom, persisting red apples and bronze-tone foliage; 'Indian Magic,' with its deep pink flowers that open from red buds and its persisting red-to-orange fruit; 'Donald Wyman,' with its handsome branch structure, pink buds, white flowers and persisting fruit; and 'Dolgo,' with its wide-spreading growth habit, pink buds, snowy-white flowers and reddish-purple fruit.

Map ID #17

Cornelian Cherry Dogwood

Cornus mas

Leaves: Simple, alternate, untoothed

Mud season is barely over when profuse bouquets of tiny yellow flowers grace the bare branches of the Cornelian Cherry Dogwood—an early, cheering harbinger of spring. If the weather continues cool, the tree's April bloom can last three weeks. Native to southern and central Eurasia, this rugged, hardy species is closely related to the ground-hugging Bunchberry that blooms so beautifully on New Hampshire's White Mountains from the hardwood forest habitat at 2000-foot levels all the way up into the alpine zones above 5000 feet. The natural growth pattern of the Cornelian Cherry Dogwood is shrub-like with many stems. Timely pruning, however, can lead to a single-trunk pattern and the development of a small tree which matures at 20-25 feet with a round, dense crown. Depending on the variety planted, summertime foliage ranges from gold, yellow, or green with tinges of pink, to variegated green and white. Regardless of their color, all leaves display the curved veins and smooth edges typical of Dogwood. Leaves of some varieties turn reddish in the fall. The species earns its 'Cherry' name from the olive-shaped, edible fruit that matures between July and September and remains on the tree until eaten by wildlife or harvested by humans for jelly-making. The half-inch long fruits are most commonly a shiny scarlet, but (again depending on variety) can also be yellow or white. The intriguing Cornelian Cherry Dogwood is almost maintenance free, for it is highly resistant to attack by either insects or disease.

Kousa Dogwood
Japanese Dogwood
Cornus kousa

Strangely enough, the Dogwood and the Poinsettia share a common characteristic. What appear to be the petals of spectacular blossoms on both plants are actually specialized, colored leaves (bracts) surrounding the true but inconspicuous flowers. Cream-colored bracts of the Kousa Dogwood turn pinkish after several weeks of bloom. When the bracts finally fall, rounded raspberry-like fruits appear and provide a delicious treat for wildlife. Depending on altitude, most of the Hanover area falls within the U.S. Department of Agriculture's cold hardiness zones 3 and 4 (see USDA map, p. 28). The beautiful Flowering

Leaves: Simple, opposite, untoothed

Dogwood *(Cornus florida)* is unable to survive here because of low winter temperatures. But thanks to the Kousa Dogwood, an import from Asia, residents located in the warmer sections of this area are treated to almost a month of bloom in early to mid-summer. The Kousa Dogwood must be protected from extremes of cold and wind. With leaves, which grow opposite to one another rather than in an alternate arrangement, the Kousa belongs to a select group of trees popularly categorized as the MAD HORSES: M for Maple; A for Ash; D for Dogwood; and HORSES for the Horsechestnut and its close

relative, the Buckeye. Growing to about 25 feet with a broad, horizontal branching pattern, the Kousa Dogwood is a handsome specimen for landscape use. Its beauty is not limited to summer bloom. In fall, the Kousa's leaves turn striking shades of scarlet and purplish red.

Map ID #19

Pagoda Dogwood

Pigeonberry, Alternate-Leaf Dogwood, Blue Dogwood, Green Osier

Cornus alternifolia

Leaves: Simple, alternate, untoothed

Stand back to appreciate a Monet. Move in close to enjoy a Bruegel. The same is true for nature's works of art. Appreciate the flaring silhouette of an American Elm from a distance, but take a close look to enjoy the best features of a 25-foot Pagoda Dogwood. The bright yellowish-green leaves of this little-known tree are gracefully detailed with curving veins which parallel the smooth margins. On their undersides, the leaves frequently display a bright orange midrib. Horizontal layers of radiating branches become progressively more narrow toward the top of the tree. Because of this feature, the tree's structure resembles a pagoda. The tiered and tapering branching pattern is handsome in winter and is displayed to good advantage when the tree is positioned to soften the stark vertical lines of buildings. Individually inconspicuous May or early-June flowers mass together to form attractive, flat-headed clumps of cream-colored bloom more similar to Viburnum than to Dogwood. Flowers evolve into the tree's most pleasing feature. By fall, bunches of blue-black berries appear on dramatic red stems. This northern-most native Dogwood is not used extensively for landscaping, but it is worthy of inclusion on a northern campus.

Douglasfir

Douglas Spruce, Douglas Yew, Oregon Pine

Pseudotsuga menziesii var. *glauca*

Naming this magnificent native of the Rocky Mountains and the Pacific Coast has caused an inordinate amount of disagreement among scientists and laymen alike. The scientists finally settled on a Latin name that says the tree looks like, but is not really, a Hemlock and was named in honor of a man by the name of Archibald Menzies. In 1791, Menzies was the first European to "discover" the tree on Vancouver Island. Laymen, on the other hand, call it some sort of a Fir. Or Spruce. Or Yew. Or Pine. The popular names laymen bestow are often prefaced by Douglas, in honor of David Douglas, the Scotsman who introduced the tree to the British Isles. Regardless of what one calls it, this conifer is unquestionably among our most beautiful evergreens. Along the Pacific Coast, 400-1,000 year-old Douglasfirs have been measured at heights of 325 feet with trunks up to 17 feet in diameter. This is only about 30 feet shorter than North America's tallest tree, the Coastal Redwood. The Rocky Mountain Douglasfir (variety *glauca*) is less long-lived, shorter, and slower growing. It is the type planted in the northeast. Under cultivation, this Douglasfir grows up to 80 feet tall and matures into a handsome specimen with a slender,

Needles: Evergreen, soft, flat, bluntly pointed

slightly tapering silhouette. The tree shows relatively good resistance to attack by insects and disease. Young Douglasfirs of the Rocky Mountain variety, with their pleasing shapes and bluish-green, soft, dense foliage, are popular as Christmas trees. The pendulous 2-4 inch cones of the Douglasfir are unique. Long, grass-like leaves, or bracts, protrude from between the scales. The bracts give the cones a shaggy look that distinguishes

them from cones of other familiar evergreens. Also helpful in identifying the species are the sharply pointed, orange-red buds at the tips of the branches. Nurseries have developed varieties of Douglasfir with growth patterns that can be pendulous, dwarf, or columnar and with slight variations of needle color. Such specialized cultivars can be difficult to find.

Map ID #21

The Parkhurst Elm

The Parkhurst Elm

By Everett W. Wood

In front of Parkhurst Hall stands a towering elm—perfect in form, rendering shade in summer and golden hues in fall. Hundreds walk by it every day without giving it a glance. If they but knew what odds that elm has overcome to be what it is today, they would gaze at it in awe.

To grow from a seedling to a 130 year old tree—under ideal conditions—is extraordinary for an elm. To do so jammed between a sidewalk and Hanover's North Main Street is virtually impossible.

The hurricane of 1938 leveled elms all over town. The Parkhurst Elm stood firm.

In the 1950s Dutch elm disease decimated Dartmouth's remaining proud "shade trees." The Parkhurst Elm survived.

In 1979, the east roots of the Parkhurst Elm were cut away to improve the drainage under North Main Street. And it still grew and grows—now measuring more than 14 feet in circumference and 94 feet tall.

In 1989 I led a French-speaking tour on campus. Approaching the Parkhurst Elm, the visitors saw an amazing sight. The elm's root flair, uncovered a foot underground, was encircled by a plastic tube connected to a maze of "injection tees" inserted in the roots. Additional paraphernalia included a huge tank attached to an electric pump.

"What's that?" asked a matronly observer. "Intravenous feeding of a tree?"

"Exactly," I replied. "Our tree expert, Robert Thebodo, inoculates all infected elms with fungicide. If this tree will absorb, under pressure, 60 gallons of fluid within two days, it will resist the fatal elm disease for three years. If not, it is beyond help and must be destroyed. The next two days will tell."

The matron looked wistfully at the elm before speaking: "Please tell Monsieur Thebodo I shall pray for this tree tonight."

It must have helped. That was nine years ago, and the Parkhurst Elm keeps growing, in defiance of all the odds.

This article by Everett W. Wood, Dartmouth Class of 1938, appeared in the October 1998 edition of the Dartmouth Alumni Magazine. *As the 21st century begins, the Parkhurst Elm continues to defy the odds.*

American Elm

White Elm, Soft Elm, Water Elm, River Elm

Ulmus americana

*Leaves:
Simple,
alternate,
toothed*

The fountain Elms of Dartmouth: Only those who knew the College and the town before the mid-1950s can recall their stately magnificence. Upward-arching branches of trees, planted on opposite sides of streets around the Green, embraced 50 or more feet above the ground, creating tunnels of cool, filtered light. Planted during the administration of Dartmouth President Nathan Lord (1828-1863), the handsome tree on Main Street in front of Parkhurst Hall survives from those glory days of the American Elm. Shortly before 1930 a killer-fungus, concealed within a shipment of Elm logs from Europe, arrived in New York. The stage was set for the devastation of America's favorite street tree by the incurable Dutch Elm disease. Almost 100 million American Elms would die. Carried by Elm bark beetles, that tunneled through the bark, or spread underground from root to root, the fungus killed by crippling a tree's vascular system. By 1948, untold numbers of American Elms were dead or dying in Connecticut and Massachusetts. Twenty cases of the disease were confirmed in Vermont. Hanover and Dartmouth escaped until 1950. Then the tell-tale wilted and discolored leaves began to appear on many of the area's more than 3,000 potential victims. As a town and campus species, the American Elm had proved itself hard to beat. The tree is fast-growing, long-lived, and relatively tolerant of soil compaction, drought and pollution. It's adaptable to a broad range of growing conditions and is able to survive the coldest of New England winters. A straight, sturdy trunk and upward sweeping branches produce a vase-like silhouette which complements large buildings without concealing their facades. Champion specimens have reached heights of 150 feet and lived well over 200 years. Unfortunately, the American Elm has many enemies, the Dutch Elm and the phloem necrosis diseases being the most serious. To combat problems caused by insects and disease, a regular program of Elm pruning, fertilization, and injection with fungicide is carried out at Dartmouth. This has led to the survival of about 100 of the College's American Elms, probably the largest number to be found today on any campus in the United States.

Map ID #22

The Fountain Elms of Dartmouth in 1948

A 1998 inventory of College trees indicated that Elms were growing larger and living longer than most other campus species, including the Sugar Maple. For this reason, it seemed logical to continue planting American Elms, but only if young trees could be found which had an excellent chance of proving resistant to the Dutch Elm disease. Fortunately, intense scientific research aimed at producing just such cultivars of the American Elm has been in process for many years at the Elm Research Institute in southern New Hampshire, the Princeton Nursery in New Jersey, the University of Wisconsin at Madison, and the National Arboretum outside Washington. Already established on campus are two new American Elms, the 'Princeton,' developed at the Princeton Nursery, and the 'Liberty,' a product of the Elm Research Institute of New Hampshire. The disease-resistant 'New Harmony' and 'Valley Forge' varieties, developed by the National Arboretum and presently under cultivation on a farm in Vermont, will undoubtedly find their way to Dartmouth.

English Elm

Ulmus procera

In the mythology of northern Europe, human beings were said to have emerged from two trees, the Ash and the Elm. The English Elm was probably that mythological Elm. Native to Western Europe and England, this stately species was introduced to North America during early colonial times. Now the tree can be found growing wild in the northeastern United States and along the Pacific Coast. Unfortunately, the English Elm, like its indigenous cousin the American Elm, is susceptible to the Dutch Elm disease. But, it does exhibit stout resistance to urban stress in the form of pollution, soil compaction, and drought. The survival of large specimens on the Dartmouth College campus is undoubtedly due to the constant surveillance and aggressive maintenance afforded all local Elms. Capable of growing to heights above 100 feet, the English Elm develops a mature silhouette quite different from that of the flaring American Elm. The lower branches of this imported species reach out almost horizontally while its upper branches grow vertically. Leaves of the English Elm are almost stemless, doubly-toothed, frequently rough to the touch, and asymmetric. Fold a leaf in half and the two halves will never coincide. Foliage remains on the tree longer in the fall than it does on the American Elm. Some experts claim that the English Elm is a true and distinct species. Others suspect it may be a hybrid or cross-breed between two different Elms.

*Leaves:
Simple,
alternate,
toothed*

Scotch 'Camperdown' Elm

Ulmus glabra 'Camperdown'

Near the end of Tuck Drive, a road curves left toward the River Cluster dormitories. There stands one of the strangest trees on campus— a mushroom mound of dense foliage in summer, a stubby-trunked tangle of twisted, pendulous branches in winter. Who would guess that such a tree could possibly be an Elm? It's a 'Camperdown' Elm, a variety of the Scotch Elm. Nature created the top of this unique specimen, and nature created its sturdy trunk. But nature did not plan that these two sections should be joined. The 'Camperdown' Elm is literally "man-ufactured." A cutting, or scion, from one tree has been grafted to the trunk and root system of another. In the grafting process, a ¼- or ½-inch diameter twig is cut from a tree selected for its special beauty or unique shape. The trunk and root

Leaves: Simple, alternate, toothed, lobed at times

system are provided by a closely related species that has proved rugged and vigorous, although not necessarily beautiful. The trunk diameter of the donor tree must match the diameter of the scion, or cutting, which will become its new upper section. Both top and trunk cuttings are trimmed diagonally, notched, and bound together in such a way that their ultra-thin layers of growth cells (cambium cells) touch. The cambium layers gradually merge, and a callous or swelling appears around the trunk where it has been joined to the scion. Each section of the grafted tree maintains its own identity and performs its own duty. The roots send minerals and water to the tree top by way of the trunk. The large, rough, asymmetric leaves then produce the food which nourishes both trunk and root system. What has become the upper section of the 'Camperdown' Elm was originally found growing wild in Scotland as a low, sprawling plant. When grafted several feet up on the trunk of another Elm, it matures into a 20-25 foot tall, round-headed tree with ground-sweeping branches. The 'Camperdown' is susceptible to attack by insect and disease but is worth planting for its distinctive shape.

Map ID #24

Slippery Elm

Red Elm, Moose Elm, Soft Elm

Ulmus rubra

Leaves: Simple, alternate, toothed

In the early 1930s, woods and hedgerows were relatively plentiful in northern New England. But dollars were mighty scarce. Many of the young American Elms planted at that time around Dartmouth's newly completed Baker Library started life as wild seedlings. Crews were sent out to locate and dig up handsome young American Elms and haul them back to campus. Among those transplanted wild trees, possibly included by mistake, was at least one Slippery Elm. A close relative of the treasured American Elm, the Slippery could well have been found growing wild on the floodplain of the Connecticut River or among other hardwoods on higher, drier hillsides. People today consider it a weed tree, but this species of 'ellum' was sought after and highly valued by early settlers. It was probably from the Native Americans that they learned to chew, soak or make a powder of the tree's slimy inner bark for use in the preparation of medications to treat scurvy, cholera and flesh wounds. The Slippery Elm matures at heights of 40-70 feet with a long trunk and a flat to somewhat rounded crown which differs slightly from the vase-shape of the American Elm. The tree is capable of living for 150 to 200 years—not bad for a weed. The large leaves of the Slippery are rough to the touch and display the doubly-serrated edges and asymmetrical bases typical of the Elm family.

White Fir

Concolor Fir

Abies concolor

When choosing a Christmas tree, don't hesitate to take home a Fir. The needles won't puncture your fingers and they'll stay where you want them—on the branches rather than on the floor. For landscaping purposes, however, be very careful in selecting a tree of this type. Firs mature into narrow, stiffly pyramidal specimens. Being native to high mountain terrain, most require cool moist environments. Of the group, the White Fir is probably the best choice. Although native to the Sierra and Rocky Mountains at altitudes where moisture is readily available, the White Fir is able to survive brief periods of drought and heat. It tolerates shade, severe cold, moderate pollution, and attack by disease and

Needles: Evergreen, flattened, pointed or rounded

insects. But don't tread heavily on its surroundings. It does not like compacted soil. The smooth, thin bark of young White Firs becomes deeply furrowed and more than half a foot thick on mature trees, making the 100-foot tall giants of the western mountains relatively fireproof. That protection helps them survive in their native habitat for up to 350 years. White Fir trees in landscaped sites live far shorter lives and rarely exceed 50 feet in height. On campus, there are only two true Firs, the Balsam Firs and the White Firs. On both of these species, the cones stand erect. Their scales fall

off when the seeds are released. The so-called Douglasfir is not really a Fir. Its cones hang downwards, and its Latin name designates it as a pseudo-Hemlock.

Fringetree

Old Man's Beard, Grancy Gray-Beard

Chionanthus virginicus

We all know that Francophiles love everything French, and bibliophiles are devoted to books. But who ever heard of *Chionanthus*-philes? What's their common denominator? They happen to be an enthusiastic bunch who sing the praises of the Fringetree. According to Elbert L. Little of the National Audubon Society, this native plant of the southeastern United States is "one of our most beautiful small trees." Going one step further, the renowned horticulturalist, Michael A. Dirr, ". . . would like to make a case for (the Fringetree) as the national shrub, for even Dogwood does not carry itself with such refinement, dignity and class when in flower." If that's not enough, British *Chionanthus*-philes consider the Fringetree "one of the finest American plants introduced into their gardens." With a short trunk that divides into several thick, upward-curving limbs, the Fringetree most commonly reaches a height of 12-20 feet. Dwarf varieties exist which mature at 3-4 feet and are classified as shrubs. The Fringetree more than compensates for its habit of being one of the last trees to leaf out by covering itself in late spring with a profusion of delicate, sweet smelling, white flowers which hang gracefully in clusters. Blue, grape-like fruits mature in late summer and remain on the tree into the winter, providing a favored treat for wildlife. In autumn, the long leaves of the Fringetree turn bright yellow.

Leaves: Simple, alternate, untoothed

Ginkgo
Maidenhair Tree
Ginkgo biloba

No other tree on earth is quite like the Ginkgo. Take a close and admiring look at this "living fossil." Notice its tapered trunk, spike-like branch pattern, and uniquely fan-shaped leaf. The Ginkgo is the sole surviving species of a large family of trees which was widespread 200 million years ago. Those were the days of the giant dinosaurs. About 350 million years ago, plants improved their reproductive processes by producing seeds. Among the first seed-producers were the fan-leafed Ginkgo and the needle-leafed Spruce, Larch, Pine and other similar conifers. Over 500 species of ancient conifers have survived to this day. But, of the ancient broad-leafed, seed-producing trees, only the Ginkgo remains. It was

Leaves: Simple, clustered or alternate, untoothed, lobed

obviously a well-designed model. Great high-latitude forests of Ginkgo-related trees were obliterated, possibly by glacial advances. Luckily, a few of the trees survived in the warmer forests of what is now China. Nowhere in the world do representatives of this magnificent family of trees grow wild today. Only because it was kept alive in the sacred temple groves of China, Japan and Korea does one, and only one, species of Ginkgo, the *Ginkgo biloba*, survive. Some individual trees in those sacred groves are thought to be almost 1,000 years old. In landscape plantings, the Ginkgo grows from 50-80 feet tall with a crown spread of about 40 feet. Only male specimens should be planted, because the plum-like fruit of the female tree has a most unpleasant odor. The Ginkgo is highly resistant to urban pollution, insect damage, disease, fungus and drought. In autumn it puts on a dramatic display of gold and yellow.

69

Map ID #28

Common Hackberry

Sugarberry, Nettletree

Celtis occidentalis

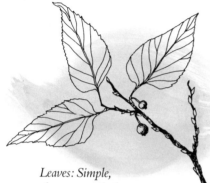

Leaves: Simple, alternate, toothed

You might call this one the Halloween Tree. Unless a resistant variety such as 'Prairie Pride' is planted, the Hackberry is liable to develop random clusters of superfluous twigs known as "Witches Brooms." Their presence actually helps us identify the Hackberry, and it does not prevent these rugged, fast-growing native trees from surviving 200 years or longer. It's feasible that a Hackberry, planted in 1797 to celebrate the founding of the Dartmouth Medical School, could still be living. Actually, there are no venerable Hackberries on today's campus, but the species has been planted as one possible replacement for the stricken American Elms. The Hackberry grows 75-100 feet tall with a comparably spreading canopy. Its leaves are smooth-edged for a short distance above their asymmetric bases and then outlined with sharp teeth all the way to their pointed tips. Blue-green leaves of summer turn pale yellow in the fall at the same time that the tree bears cherry-like, purplish brown to deep orange fruit loved by game birds, songbirds and small mammals. The Hackberry is a member of the Elm family. A workhorse of a tree, it's able to grow in disturbed sites and is tolerant of drought, pollution, severe cold and some degree of soil compaction. This species is a good choice for planting close to streets and sidewalks, because its deep root system does not lift pavements.

English 'Toba' Hawthorn

Crataegus laevigata 'Toba'

So much depends on one's point of view. Consider the word "haw." To a donkey, it's the second half of a "hee." To a workhorse, it's the opposite of a "gee." In Anglo-Saxon, it's a hedge or fence. But, to a botanist, "haw" is the colorful fruit of a Haw-thorn. Hawthorns are a confusing group of shrubs and small trees which interbreed, or hybridize, with exceptional frequency. The result is the existence of up to 1,000 variations in North America, perhaps 100 of which grow into 25-30 foot trees. Hawthorns are frequently multi-trunked and generally wide-spreading with a dense branching pattern. Their small, tooth-edged leaves turn shades ranging from brown to bronze-red in autumn. Leaves of different shapes often appear on the same tree. In the wild, Haw-

Leaves:
Simple,
alternate,
toothed,
lobed

thorns are thorny plants, a feature that adapts them well for use in hedge-rows. Numerous cultivated varieties have been developed which eliminate the thorns, vary in shape from broad to columnar, and offer flowers and fruits in a range of colors. In May, flowers similar to apple blossoms appear in flat clusters near the ends of Hawthorn branches. Individual blossoms can be double or single in tones of red, pink or white. White is the dominant color. All Hawthorn trees bear decorative red-to-orange fruits in the fall. Birds rely heavily on these fruits as a source of winter food. Most frequently planted on campus, the 'Toba' is a hybrid of English Hawthorn with dou-ble, fragrant flowers which start out white and then change to pink. The 'Toba' is considered one of the most attractive and hardy of the Hawthorns, but even it must be monitored for signs of a leaf blight which can cause defoliation.

Map ID #30

Eastern Hemlock

Canada Hemlock, Hemlock Spruce

Tsuga canadensis

Needles: Flat, evergreen

If you're thinking of planting an Eastern Hemlock, be sure to protect it from strong winds and provide it with well-drained soil and a ready supply of water. The tree could reward you and many future generations by growing over 150 feet in height and living 1,000 years. That's a record, of course. Much shorter lives and heights of 60-80 feet are more common. One of the loveliest of our large evergreens, the Hemlock is distinguished by its feathery appearance. To help identify this tree, look at the "leader" or topmost growth. On a Hemlock, that leader will droop rather than pointing stiffly skyward as on a Pine, Fir or Spruce. Hemlocks are distinguished by short, flat needles arranged in almost a single plane, and by tiny, downward-hanging cones. When mature, the reddish-brown cones open to release winged seeds which spiral to the ground. Four of the ten surviving species of this ancient tree are native to North America, while the other six are found in the Himalayas, Japan and China. No Hemlocks grow wild in Europe today, but there is fossil evidence indicative of their prior existence. Varieties of the versatile Hemlock display growth patterns ranging from dwarf, to weeping, to ground covering. When closely planted, the tree can be pruned into a handsome hedge. The Hemlock is not a good choice for intensely urban settings because of its sensitivity to drought, heat, salt, soil compaction and pollution. But, it's a beauty in parks and residential areas and on campuses. In the forest, wildlife rely on the Hemlock for cover and food. Thick, cinnamon-colored bark increases the wild tree's chances for longevity by protecting it from forest fire. That same bark, however, cost many Hemlocks their lives when humans discovered its value in the production of leather. Monitor your precious Hemlocks with care. An Asian insect now threatens this previously highly resistant species.

Common Thornless Honeylocust

Gleditsia triancanthos var.*inermis*

The 'Imperial' and 'Sunburst' varieties of the Common Honeylocust are both found on campus. As legumes, or members of the pea family, they belong to the third largest group of seed-bearing plants in the world. Their "cousins by the dozens" include the Kentucky Coffeetree, the Black Locust and the Yellowwood. Back in the 1950s, varieties of Honeylocust showed great promise as replacements for the disease-stricken American Elm. Thousands were planted as specimen and street trees. The Honeylocust had a reputation of being fast-growing, disease-resistant, easy to transplant, adaptable to a wide range of soils, and highly tolerant of salt. Because of its fern-

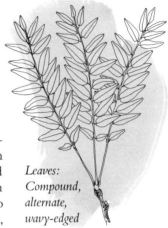

*Leaves:
Compound,
alternate,
wavy-edged*

like compound leaves and open branching pattern, light passes through and creates a filtered shade which allows grass to grow easily beneath the tree. When the small, narrow leaflets drop in the fall, almost no raking is needed. That feature alone would make a deciduous tree popular. The Common Honeylocust was so successful that nurserymen cultivated many varieties which preserved the good features of the parent while demonstrating different growth characteristics. Among these cultivars are Dartmouth's 'Imperial' and 'Sunburst.' The 'Imperial' is a fast-growing, graceful and thornless 30-35 foot tree which produces very few of its parent's undesirable, large seed pods. The 'Sunburst' matures into a tree of comparable height, but with a more pyramidal shape. Its specialized feature is its leaf color—golden in early spring, yellow or yellowish-green during the summer, then gold again in the fall. Unfortunately, the Honeylocust story has an unhappy ending. This once desirable and successful group of trees is no longer recommended for landscape usage because it has become highly susceptible to attack by insects and disease.

Map ID #32

Eastern Hophornbeam

Ironwood, American Hophornbeam

Ostrya virginiana

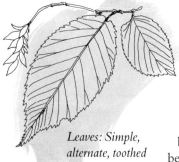

Leaves: Simple, alternate, toothed

The Hophornbeam is a small, graceful tree with a cumbersome name. "Hop" refers to the tree's fruits, which appear as hanging clusters of seed-enclosing sacks and resemble the hops from which beer is made. "Hornbeam" is descriptive of the tough, heavy wood that was once used to make oxen yokes. There is some confusion between the Eastern Hophornbeam and the American Hornbeam, mostly because of the similarity of names. The two trees belong to the Birch family, but each is a distinct species. Both display pendant, pollen-bearing male blossoms, or catkins, similar to those seen on a Birch tree. The brown bark of the Hophornbeam is rough and sheds in narrow strips, whereas the blue-gray bark of the Hornbeam is smooth. The Hophornbeam is the larger of the two trees. Introduced into North America just 70 years after the Mayflower dropped anchor, the Hophornbeam adapted to its new home so well that it now grows wild throughout almost all of the eastern half of the United States and southeastern Canada. Egg-shaped leaves, measuring between two and six inches in length, have slightly heart-shaped bases, pointed tips, and doubly saw-toothed margins. The dark yellow-green foliage of summer fades to an undramatic yellow in the fall. Although it grows slowly to its mature height of about 50 feet, it's a hardy tree which has proved highly resistant to damage from wind, ice, insects and disease. One of the tree's admirable talents is its ability to thrive in urban settings where it can survive compacted soil. It has even been grown successfully in planters.

Map ID #33

74

Ruby Red Horsechestnut

Aesculus x carnea 'Brioti'

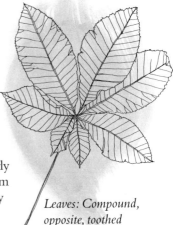

You've seen it happen with humans. A none-too-handsome couple produces a beautiful child. That's the case with the Ruby Red Horsechestnut, a hybrid tree which turned out to be more attractive than either of its parents. Many years ago, probably somewhere in Germany, two species of Horsechestnuts crossbred and produced an offspring with a broad crown, dense foliage and spectacular pinkish red bloom. That hybrid, the Ruby Red Horsechestnut, proved particularly successful and capable of reproducing itself from seed, an unusual talent among hybrids. A century later, a cultivar called 'Brioti' was developed which bore even larger upright clumps of bloom in a dramatic shade of deep red. It is that

Leaves: Compound, opposite, toothed

cultivar which is found on campus. Like the Austrian Pine and the Norway Spruce, the Ruby Red Horsechestnut grows twice as tall in Europe as it does in North America. This difference is probably due to climate. Here in the northeastern United States, a Ruby Red grows slowly and tops out at about 40 feet. The leaflets of the tree's compound leaf radiate from a common point like spokes on a wheel or lines on the palm of your hand. Botanists designate such a leaf pattern as "palmately compound." Fall leaf color of the Ruby Red is nondescript, but that drawback is more than counterbalanced by the spectacular bloom in late spring.

Map ID #34

Katsuratree

Cercidiphyllum japonicum

Leaves: Simple, opposite, wavy edged

Some of our most dramatic trees literally trace their roots to the Far East. Among Asian trees which have been introduced into North America are the Katsuratree, several Maples, numerous conifers (evergreens), the unique Dawn Redwood, and many species treasured for the beauty of their flowers. The Katsura, of China's largest deciduous trees, is a broad-crowned shade tree with a multi-trunked growth pattern. As the Katsura ages, this feature can make it subject to breakage, especially in regions of heavy snow. The tree can be trained to a single trunk pattern. When so pruned, its trunk will be stronger but its crown will be less broad spreading. The Katsura adapts particularly well to locations where the soil is moist. Don't plant it where people take short cuts, because it will not thrive in heavily compacted soil. And, it does not like drought and heat. The Katsura's distinctive, heart-shaped, blue-green leaves turn yellow to scarlet in the fall. If you're looking for an unusual, rugged, fast growing and relatively pest-free tree, an excellent choice would be a Katsura.

Eastern Larch
Tamarack, Hackmatack, American Larch

Larix laricina

A real denizen of the north, the Eastern Larch, or Tamarack, loves cold and hates heat. Notice on the master list of campus trees that this species is one of only nine campus trees rated as able to survive in Zone 2 where temperatures fall as low as -50°F. The native range of the Tamarack reflects that ability, extending across Canada, into Alaska, and throughout northern New England and the Great Lakes region. The tree tolerates growing conditions ranging from relatively dry, loamy hillside soils to wet, soggy swamps. Pure stands of Eastern Larch are often found in drained beaver ponds or in peat bogs associated with prior glaciation. The slow-growing Eastern Larch attains heights of about 50 feet in its 150-180 year life span. On campus, most of the Larch trees are European rather than Eastern. Tell them apart by the size of their cones: tiny cones of the Eastern Larch measure only ½ to ¾ inch in length. Those of the European Larch are twice as large. Both species are susceptible to attack by insects. Like the imported species, the Eastern Larch drops its needles every fall. Neither tree is a thing of beauty during the winter. But the annual reappearance of delicate, clustered needles on the Larches is one of the true joys of spring in the north country. Railroad ties made from the moisture-resistant wood of the Eastern Larch have played a part in many an autumn Dartmouth Night bonfire on the Green.

Needles:
Deciduous, clusters

European Larch

Common Larch

Larix decidua

Not all "evergreens" are ever green. Both European and Eastern Larches bear cones and needles, as do the Hemlock, Spruce and Pine trees. But Larches shed their needles and remain bare and shaggy throughout the winter. On campus, only they and the Dawn Redwood lose their needles every fall. Because of that behavior, these three species are classified as deciduous conifers. Similar in deciduous habit is the Bald Cypress, native to southern swamps but never seen in New England. The European Larch was brought to North America in the 17th century from cold, mountainous regions of Europe. The tree soon escaped from cultivation and established itself in the wild. It is more frequently chosen as a landscape specimen than is its native cousin. Most Larches on campus are of the European species. One-to-one-and-a-half inch cones of the European Larch are almost twice as large as cones of the Tamarack, or Eastern Larch, a feature which is helpful when distinguishing between the two trees. Both species are at their most beautiful in springtime when delicate clusters of soft green, newly-emerged needles encircle their branchlets.

Of the two Larches, the European develops a broader crown, is taller and faster growing. Because of its shallow root system, it can be easily transplanted. The European Larch grows best in a sunny location with well-drained, acidic soil. Cultivars with growth habits ranging from pendulous to columnar are available.

Needles:
Deciduous, clusters

Japanese Tree Lilac

Syringa reticulata

Certain flowering trees, such as Japanese Cherries and Star Magnolias, owe much of their beauty to the fact that they bloom on bare branches before springtime leaves emerge. The exact opposite is true for the Japanese Tree Lilac. Its fully developed green leaves provide a dramatic background for bouquet-like clusters of creamy-white blossoms. These masses of tiny, four-petaled flowers are highly visible, because they are borne close to the ends of the branches. Clusters can be a foot long and 10 inches wide. Japanese Tree Lilac blossoms appear in mid-June and emit a fragrance similar to that of privet. Bloom often lasts for up to two weeks. The tree is closely related to a species native to the climatically extreme Amur region of northern Manchuria. With such genes, it has no trouble coping with wintertime temperatures on the Dartmouth campus. The Japanese Tree Lilac matures into a graceful, 20-30 foot tall specimen with a rounded crown. Shiny, cherry-like bark and persistent, pale brown seed capsules make the tree an attractive addition to the winter landscape. It is the most resistant of all the lilacs to disease and insect attack and demonstrates good tolerance to both heat and drought. 'Ivory Silk' and 'Summer Snow' are popular and frequently recommended cultivars of the Japanese Tree Lilac.

Leaves: Simple, opposite, untoothed

Map ID #38

Littleleaf Linden

Small-leaf Linden, European Linden

Tilia cordata

Leaves: Simple, alternate, toothed

"Super Linden." That's the title bestowed upon *Tilia cordata* in 1997 by a group of German scientists. For 10 years, they tested many varieties of Lindens for resistance to a spectrum of urban stress ranging from air and dog pollution to drought. The Littleleaf Linden out-performed all others. In usage along city streets, the tree had already proved itself cold-hardy, easy to transplant, able to grow in poor soils, and highly tolerant of urban pollution. A smaller relative of the American Linden or Basswood, the Littleleaf Linden was brought to North America from Europe more than two centuries ago. If you see a neatly tailored tree with dark bark and a symmetrical branching pattern, a tree that is clothed in two tones of green throughout its leaf season, chances are good that you've found a Littleleaf Linden. Rounded, dark green leaves with heart-shaped bases are densely packed and create excellent shade. "Unter den Linden" in Berlin designates a famous boulevard. "Unter den Linden" on the Dartmouth campus means "under a Linden tree," a cool place to study during the summer term. The tree's two-tone appearance results from the presence of pale green bracts, or modified petal-like leaves, to which the flowers and subsequent fruit of the Linden are attached. These distinctive bracts persist throughout the growing season and most of the winter. Drooping clusters of small fragrant, yellowish-white flowers cover the tree in early July when little else in the tree world is blooming. Numerous varieties of Littleleaf Lindens, displaying slightly differing patterns of growth, have been cultivated and distributed by nurseries. It's probable that several such varieties grow on campus, one of which is called the 'Greenspire.' For mapping purposes, they will all be grouped as Littleleaf Linden.

Map ID #39

Black Locust

Yellow Locust, White Locust, Common Locust

Robinia pseudoacacia

Everyone loves an Oak. But not everyone loves a Locust. Enthusiasts proclaim the Black Locust a splendid urban tree because of its fast growth, fragrant spring bloom, and tolerance of pollution, salt, heat, drought, and cold. Detractors label it as weedy and beany, an alley cat of a tree. Even alley cats have some redeeming features. They're supremely adaptable. The Black Locust thrives on soils at which many other trees turn up their arboreal noses. Like the Gray Birch, it is a natural "bandaid" for eroded, strip-mined, or depleted soils. While clinging tenaciously to such sites with its widespreading fibrous root system, this member of the pea family enriches its own environment by adding nitrogen to the soil. The Black Locust has been planted successfully in almost every state. In Europe cultivars, such as 'Frisia' with its dramatic yellow foliage, are popular. The compound leaves of the Black Locust consist of 7-19 oval leaflets attached in feather-like fashion to a central stem. People who live up north have seen leaves of Mountain Laurel and Rhododendron curl tightly when temperatures drop. For some strange reason, Black Locust leaves curl on rainy days and as light fades in the evening. On campus, this tree earns its keep. Although it seldom tops 70-80 feet and lives less than 100 years, the Black Locust blooms beautifully in the spring. Graceful, hanging clusters are comprised of elegant little flowers, creamy white with just a splash of yellow. Bloom is followed by the development of seeds enclosed in flat pods about four inches long. While one person sees the tree as "beany," another applauds it as one of nature's wind chimes. Dried pods cling to its branches throughout the winter and rustle pleasantly in the wind. On the down side, it should be mentioned that Black Locust is susceptible to attack by insects, won't grow in poorly drained soils, spreads like a weed, and has thorns. Native Americans fashioned bows from the wood of the Black Locust and early settlers prized the lumber for its strength and ability to withstand contact with soil. It made great fence posts. Try to search out a Black Locust when it's blooming.

Leaves: Compound, alternate, untoothed

Amur Maackia

Maackia amurensis

Leaves: Compound, alternate, untoothed

Among the more than 70 species of trees on campus, the Amur Maackia is certainly one of the two or three least familiar. This native of the borderlands between northern China and Siberia is a member of the legume (pea/bean) family. As such, it is a distant cousin of the Yellowwood and Black Locust. Like those two campus trees, the Amur Maackia has graceful clusters of pea-like blossoms and compound leaves comprised of numerous small leaflets attached to a central stem. It's about the size of the Yellowwood, topping out between 30 and 45 feet. Whitish-green springtime foliage darkens to an intense green in summer, but does not change color in the fall. Dartmouth's first Amur Maackia trees were planted in the spring of 1999. At least one was included in the interesting grove of new species requested by the Department of Biological Sciences. Campus trees are chosen for many different reasons. All must be able to survive temperature extremes and other local climatic conditions. Some, like the Elm, are selected for the ways in which their shape, structure and color enhance the appearance of buildings near which they are sited. Others, such as the Locust, must be able to cope with difficult conditions of soil, drainage, and pollution. Lesser known species, such as the Amur Maackia, are planted to give the campus an arboretum-like quality worthy of an academic institution. Each tree makes a unique contribution to the whole. Special features of the Amur Maackia are its amber-colored bark and its mid-July bloom. Only the Japanese Pagoda Tree blooms as late.

'Merrill' Magnolia

Magnolia x loebneri 'Merrill'

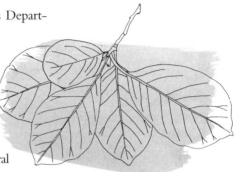

At the suggestion of Dartmouth's Department of Biological Sciences, another Magnolia has been added to the campus. The 'Merrill' Magnolia is part of an interesting collection of trees planted in the late 1990s near the south entrance of Gilman Hall. In addition to the 'Merrill' Magnolia, there are several other species new to campus, including the Dawn Redwood, Engelmann Spruce, Amur Maackia, London Plane-tree, Northern Catalpa and Douglasfir. One tends to think of Magnolias as southern trees—and with good reason. Ninety-foot specimens growing in the Gulf States are among the most magnificent flowering trees in the world. Scientific study of their blossom structure, combined with paleobiological evidence, reveals that Magnolias are almost as ancient as those living fossils, the Ginkgo trees. As indicated by the 'x' in its Latin name, the 'Merrill' Magnolia is a cross-breed. In the late 1930s, botanists at Harvard University's Arnold Arboretum developed the new hybrid. The 'Merrill,' as it was named, proved to be larger, faster growing, younger flowering, and slightly more resistant to cold than either of its parents. If the Gilman Hall group of three reaches its height potential of close to 50 feet, the early spring display of four-inch wide, fragrant white flowers will be spectacular. 'Merrill' Magnolias show good resistance to attack by disease and insects. They do their best when protected from extreme cold, salt spray, shade, drought and either poorly drained or compacted soil.

Leaves: Simple, alternate, untoothed

Map ID #42

Saucer Magnolia

Magnolia x soulangiana

Leaves: Simple, alternate, untoothed

Almost 200 years ago, blooming in a garden not far from Paris, were two species of Asiatic Magnolias. Along came the birds. Or perhaps it was the bees. The following spring, a tiny hybrid magnolia appeared. Fortunately, the gardener did not pull it up as a weed. Instead, he allowed the small tree to grow for several years until it produced its first flowers. The new crossbreed species, now known as the Saucer Magnolia, turned out to be highly attractive and different from either parent. By means of cuttings, the plant was preserved and propagated. Fossil records indicate that Magnolias as a group are ancient trees which, before the Ice Age, were native to semi-tropical regions throughout the Northern Hemisphere. They are still warm weather trees which can exceed 100 feet in height where they grow wild in the Gulf States. In the north, the Saucer Magnolia grows to about 25 feet and is winter-resistant to only -10°F. So, how can it possibly survive here in the Upper Valley where temperatures have been recorded at -30°F? The answer lies in careful siting. Dartmouth's only Saucer Magnolia is planted in a highly protected corner, snug up against the College heating plant. The tree has reached a height of about 20 feet in spite of some splitting caused by ice. In years when late frosts do not damage the sensitive buds as they unfold, large fragrant flowers adorn the tips of the Magnolia's bare branches. Displaying colors ranging from pale pink to rosy purple, the dramatic blossoms open fully into saucer shapes measuring 4-8 inches across. The extensive planting along Commonwealth Avenue in Boston is most probably Saucer Magnolias. In that location, the cold-sensitive trees are afforded some protection by their proximity to buildings and by the warmer temperatures characteristic of urban heat islands. Magnolias grow best in well-drained soils and may require spraying against insect attack.

Star Magnolia

Magnolia stellata

When the Star Magnolia blooms, it's as though a beautiful Japanese painting had come to life. In the latter half of April—well ahead of other blossoming species which will later enliven the campus—fragrant white flowers grace the Star Magnolia. The effect is dramatic. Before the leaves have emerged, star-shaped, double flowers glow in sharp contrast to the plant's smooth and attractive gray bark. Flower buds open successively, so the welcome display of early spring bloom sometimes lasts three weeks. This native of Japan can be grown as a round and dense shrub or it can be pruned when young and encouraged to grow into a 10-20 foot tree with an open, multi-trunked silhouette. The Star Magnolia is more toler-ant of cold than is the Saucer Magnolia, but even the Star must be afforded some protection from winter extremes. Siting in an inner courtyard of the Hop-kins Center provides protection for one of Dartmouth's Star Magnolias. Many excellent cultivars of the plant have been developed, among the most popular being 'Royal Star' and 'Centennial.'

Leaves: Simple, alternate, untoothed

In choosing a Star Magnolia, be sure to find out if the one you'd like to plant will be able to survive winter temperatures in your area. The Star is highly resistant to insect and disease problems and adapts well to a wide range of soils as long as the soil is well drained. Search out a Star Magnolia when it's at its best—announcing the arrival of spring.

Map ID #44

Amur Maple

Siberian Maple

Acer ginnala

The Amur Maple is sometimes called the Siberian Maple because it is native to the area of northeast Asia where the mighty Amur River flows. The tree is almost as well adapted to the far north of our continent as is an Inuit. A fast-growing and pest-free small tree, it is capable of surviving winter temperatures as extreme as -50°F. Trees are sometimes defined as "woody, perennial plants with single stems called trunks." The Amur Maple with its multiple trunks and shrub-like growth pattern is an obvious exception to that definition. But, take a close look at its beautifully shaped, small leaves and its "give-away" pairs of winged seeds. There's no doubt you've found a Maple. Those winged seeds mature in varying tones of pinks and reds, providing a lovely contrast with the green of late summer foliage. It's not a bad idea to plant an Amur Maple a short distance from your bird feeder. The winged seeds remain on the tree throughout the winter and prove irresistible to birdseed-guzzling red squirrels. In good Maple fashion, the Amur is capable of putting on a dazzling display of orange and red in the fall. The variety known as 'Flame' is particularly colorful.

Leaves: Simple, opposite, toothed, lobed

Ashleaf Maple

Boxelder, Manitoba Maple

Acer negundo

Because we're familiar with the beautiful flag of Canada, most of us think we know how a Maple leaf should look. The Ashleaf Maple, more commonly known as the Boxelder, is obviously classified as a Maple, being listed with all other Maples as belonging to the species *Acer*. But its leaves resemble poison ivy more closely than they do the leaf on the flag of our neighbor to the north. The Boxelder, or Ashleaf Maple, is the only Maple that does not have simple, single-bladed leaves. Its leaves are compound and consist of 3-5 leaflets attached to a shared stem. The entire group of leaflets and their stem is considered a single leaf. Like all other Maples, these leaves, though compound, grow opposite one another. Seeds are the typical winged pairs.

Leaves: Compound, opposite, toothed, slightly lobed

Native to regions west and south of New England, the Boxelder was introduced into this area because, like the Gray Birch and Black Locust, it will grow happily on disturbed and barren soil. Unfortunately, the Boxelder feels right at home in New England. It has established itself in the wild and is spreading like a weed. It is cold-hardy, fast-growing, resistant to pollution, able to survive compacted soil, and tolerant of both flood and drought, although it prefers wet feet to dry. At maturity, the Boxelder can reach a height of 50 feet with a short trunk and a broad but often irregular crown. Grosbeaks and other wildlife feast on its seeds. Botanists often work wonders with weed trees. Because the Boxelder will thrive in locations where few other trees are able to grow, and because it has several redeeming features to recommend it as a landscape specimen, nurserymen have developed numerous cultivars of the tree. One cultivar has yellow leaves all summer and another turns red in the fall.

Map ID #46

Norway Maple

Acer platanoides

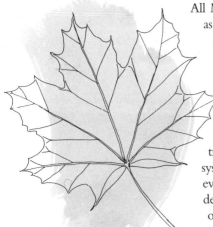

All Maples have pairs of winged seeds known as keys or samara. Those of the Norway Maple are the most distinctive. Two seeds are attached in a wide-spreading pattern that resembles the wings of a hawk in flight or the legs of a cheerleader performing a split jump. Some urban foresters believe that the Norway Maple should no longer be planted as a street tree, because its extensive and shallow root system lifts pavements. Carefully sited, however, the Norway grows into a handsome, dense shade tree. Varieties have been developed with silhouettes ranging from columnar to globular and with leaves of different colors. Leaves of the 'Crimson King' cultivar are dark red throughout the spring and summer. In general, leaves of Norway Maples resemble a shiny, leathery version of a Sugar Maple leaf with less deep indentations between lobes and numerous sharp points along the margins. Native across Europe from Norway to Turkey, this fast-growing tree has proved remarkably tolerant of automobile pollution, smoke, dust, salt, poor soil and moderate drought. It is also relatively resistant to attack by fungus and insects. The Norway Maple is an arboreal immigrant which is being assimilated into our native tree culture. It escapes from landscape plantings to adjacent fields and hedge rows where it establishes itself in the wild. There is some concern that the Norway Maple may be crowding out native Maples in their natural habitat. For landscaped settings in northern regions, the Norway Maple can be an asset because it provides a welcome display of greenish yellow bloom quite early in the spring. Leaves emerge early, turn bright yellow in the fall, and remain on the tree later than do leaves of many other species.

Leaves: Simple, opposite, untoothed, lobed

Red Maple

Swamp Maple, Scarlet Maple, Soft Maple, Water Maple

Acer rubrum

*The flaming red of New England's fall
The seasonally reddest tree of all.*

With red buds in winter, a profusion of tiny red flowers in spring, red leaf stems in summer, and red fruit and foliage in autumn, the Red Maple accessorizes itself brilliantly in all seasons. Lumbermen call it a weed tree. But, what a spectacular weed. The Red Maple can reach 130 feet or more under ideal conditions and live up to 150 years. This handsome, moisture-loving shade tree grows wild from southern Canada as far south as the Everglades of Florida, and from the East Coast west to slightly beyond the Mississippi River. Nurseries have developed varieties of the Red Maple with more intense fall color and more resistance to cold than the wild tree. They have also increased the tree's speed of growth and sculpted its shape to meet specific landscape demands. The Red Maple is

Leaves: Single, opposite, toothed, lobed

an excellent choice for poorly drained sites. Because of its deeper root system, it can survive a greater degree of soil compaction than can other Maples. Both Red and Sugar Maples have opposite leaves with 3-5 lobes. The leaf of the Sugar Maple has smooth edges and smooth curves between its lobes. Leaves of the Red Maple have saw-toothed edges and sharp angles between their lobes. In the fall, if warm sunny days are followed by cold nights, the sugar manufactured in Red Maple leaves remains in the leaves rather than moving to other parts of the tree. Leaf chemistry then utilizes that accumulation of sugar to produce large quantities of the pigment which causes leaves to turn red. Touches of yellow and orange appearing in the leaves are due to the season-long presence of another pigment. That pigment only becomes visible as the leaves slow down and finally cease their production of the chlorophyll which makes them green all summer. Few other species can compete with the blazing autumn display staged by a Red Maple.

Map ID #48

Silver Maple

White Maple, Soft Maple, River Maple, Silverleaf Maple

Acer saccarinum

The three largest trees on the Dartmouth College campus are Silver Maples. Each has a trunk measuring more than five feet in diameter. The oft-maligned Silver Maple has performed well here in the North Country. Ice damage, which can present problems with this species, has been minimal and specimens have achieved impressive size and longevity. But, of the more than 60 Maples native to the Western Hemisphere, Silver Maple is not the best choice to plant in your backyard. It takes a lot of space and drops a lot of litter. The tree frequently tops out at more than 100 feet but it is susceptible to a fungus disease which can hollow out its trunk and limbs. In the wild, that's a plus for small animals and birds in search of a home. But, close to a private residence, why risk the possible weakening of trunk and limbs? Lace-like leaves of the Silver Maple are deeply indented between their lobes and irregularly toothed along their margins. They become doubly interesting when the wind blows and reveals their pale undersides. A relatively short trunk, with scaling bark, divides into massive, upward sweeping branches.

Leaves: Simple, opposite, toothed, lobed

Sugar Maple
Hard Maple, Rock Maple, Sugartree

Acer saccharum

Check out those five big beauties on the Green across from the Hanover Inn. They're Sugar Maples, one of New England's favorite trees. The smaller trees at each end of the row are Red Maples. Sugar Maples put on a brilliant show of orange, yellow and red in the fall and provide the precious sap for maple syrup and maple sugar in the spring. An average large tree yields some 15-20 gallons of sap, but it takes up to 35-50 gallons to boil down into one gallon of syrup. That means these five trees, when mature, could yield about two gallons of syrup annually if someone were willing to invest considerable time and hard work. A large group of Sugar Maples being used for sap production is known as a sugar bush. Upward sweeping branches, a five-lobed leaf, delicate pointed buds and double-winged seeds identify the species. In May, when the Sugar Maple appears intensely yellow green, take a close look. You'll discover the tree is in bloom. Flowers rather than emerging leaves account for the dramatic coloration. About 10 miles north of Hanover, not far from the town of Thetford, Vermont, there's a Sugar Maple that's thought to be about 250 years old. The five trees planted along the south end of the Green are very young in terms of a tree's life. They were planted in 1969 by members of the Class of 1950, Dartmouth's "Tree Planting Class" for over 30 years. When this class celebrated its 50th reunion in the year 2000, the trees were somewhere between 35 and 40 years old. With a little bit of luck, good care and a minimum of nearby construction, the five Sugar Maples should still be hale and hardy in the year 2050. That's the year when men and women of the Class of 2000 return to campus for their 50th reunion.

Leaves: Simple, opposite, lobed, untoothed

91

Map ID #50

European Mountainash

Rowan Tree, Small-fruited Mountainash

Sorbus aucuparia

Leaves: Compound, alternate, toothed

Mountainashes aren't even Ashes. Ashes belong to the olive family, whereas Mountainashes are members of the rose family. They boast about 2000 relatives worldwide, most of which are known for their blossoms and fruit. Hikers, willing to do battle with the black flies still rampant in mid-June in the White Mountains of New Hampshire, will find the wild American Mountainashes in bloom. Halfway up the Gale River Trail, which leads to the Galehead Hut on Mount Garfield, there's a ravine filled with their showy white blossoms. The berries those native trees produce are extremely important to wildlife. For landscaping, however, the European Mountainash is more frequently planted. The tree was brought from Europe and Asia in the 17th century and now grows wild all the way across the northern United States and southern Canada. It is the only introduced species which has naturalized itself in Alaska. The Korean Mountainash, also found on campus, has simple leaves, whereas the European has compound leaves with as many as 15 or more small, stemless leaflets attached to a central stalk. As on all trees with compound leaves, the entire complex of leaflets and stalk comprises a single "leaf." European Mountainashes bloom in early June, close to the time of commencement. Trees display 3-6 inch clusters of white flowers which mature into bright orange-red berries. The alternate name, "Rowan Tree," derives from the Scandinavian for "red." Young trees are compact but become much more graceful and open when they approach their mature heights of 20-40 feet. Fall color is highly variable, ranging from yellow to red to purple. Mountainashes are showy, decorative specimens, but they must be constantly protected from disease and insect attack.

Korean Mountainash

Sorbus alnifolia

In the late 19th century, horticultur-
ists at Harvard University learned
about this native of Asia, realized
its potential for use in North
America, and brought it to
the Boston area where they
cultivated it under the excellent
growing and maintenance conditions provided by the Arnold Arboretum.
Mountainashes grow wild in both North America
and Europe but it is the Asian species that has
proved the most beautiful. A round tree with

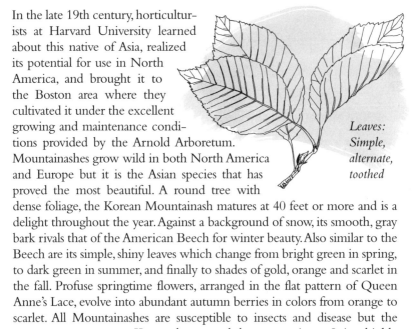

*Leaves:
Simple,
alternate,
toothed*

dense foliage, the Korean Mountainash matures at 40 feet or more and is a
delight throughout the year. Against a background of snow, its smooth, gray
bark rivals that of the American Beech for winter beauty. Also similar to the
Beech are its simple, shiny leaves which change from bright green in spring,
to dark green in summer, and finally to shades of gold, orange and scarlet in
the fall. Profuse springtime flowers, arranged in the flat pattern of Queen
Anne's Lace, evolve into abundant autumn berries in colors from orange to
scarlet. All Mountainashes are susceptible to insects and disease but the
Korean has proved the most resistant. It is a highly
desirable tree.

Map ID #52

Chestnut Oak
Rock Oak, Mountain Oak, Basket Oak, Cow Oak
Quercus prinus

Sometime between the Norman conquest of England (1066) and the granting of the Magna Carta (1215), a squirrel buried an acorn on the bank of the Hudson River. The chosen site was about 80 miles north of present-day New York City. Perhaps it was a mild winter. Or, perhaps, the squirrel forgot where he stashed his treasure. Whatever happened, a seedling Chestnut Oak sprouted the following spring. For 800 to 1000 years it grew until it was 100 feet in height with a trunk 22 feet around. It was known as the "Washington Oak." In the shade of its massive crown, General George Washington would mount his horse and ride to review the troops near Fishkill, New York. On Dartmouth's campus, there is one sizable Chestnut Oak, doing well but not destined to rival the Hudson River giant. The tree could live several hundred years, but will probably top out at a height not exceeding 60-70 feet. Although the largest examples of this species grow in well-drained, moist locations, the Chestnut Oak is most commonly found in dry, rocky soils where few other trees can survive. It grows wild throughout a large part of the eastern United States, from southern Maine west to southern Michigan and south into Georgia. For its native habitat in all three northern New England states, the Chestnut Oak chooses areas where winter temperature extremes are moderated slightly by the influence of water. In Maine and New Hampshire, it is most often found in Atlantic Coast areas, and in Vermont on the warmer Lake Champlain side of the Green Mountains. Four-to-nine inch long egg-shaped leaves with wavy edges distinguish this Oak. The similarity of its foliage to that of the American Chestnut gives the species its name. Shiny, dark to yellowish-green leaves of summer change to bronze-orange in the fall. In roughly five-year cycles, the Chestnut Oak produces a bumper crop of acorns which are relished by cows, kids and wildlife.

Leaves:
Simple,
alternate,
wavy edged

Map ID #53

94

English Oak
European Oak, Truffle Oak, Pedunculate Oak

Quercus robur

It's the late 17th century. A sailing vessel, not much larger than the Mayflower, is beating its way across the North Atlantic with settlers headed for the colonies. There's little space for baggage. All but the smallest reminders of previous lives have been left behind. But, one man has brought along memories of a favorite tree. In his pocket are 8-to-10 acorns, collected beneath a massive Oak that towered 100 feet over the edge of his field in southern England. That tree was so old that 20 generations of children might have climbed in its branches. Records show that the English Oak arrived in North America in early colonial times. Perhaps it really did come in someone's pocket. Also called the European Oak, the tree grows wild in northern Africa, Asia and Europe as well as in the British Isles. Like several other intro-duced trees, this Oak grows larger and lives longer in its native lands than it does

Leaves: Simple, alternate, lobed

in the Western Hemisphere. Specimens in the United States generally top out at no more than 60 feet. Smooth-lobed leaves and acorns that fully ripen in one year indicate that the English Oak belongs to the white, rather than the red, group of Oaks. The unusual, ear-lobe shaped base of many of its leaves is helpful when identifying the species. Green leaves of the English Oak cling to the branches late into the fall before finally turning brown and dropping. The Arnold Arboretum warns that large specimens of this tree have been known to die suddenly for no apparent reason. In 1998, considerable dead wood had to be removed from the crown of Dartmouth's large English Oak that grows just south of Reed Hall. The tree now seems to be doing well. This species hybridizes with great ease and frequency. The campus tree could possibly be a cross-breed, but its dominant characteristics are unquestionably those of an English Oak. Numerous cultivars have been developed by nurseries. The New Hampshire Division of Forests and Lands recommends the increased usage of a tall, slender variety of English Oak called the 'Fastigiata.'

95

Map ID #54

Pin Oak
Swamp Oak, Spanish Oak

Quercus palustris

Leaves: Simple, alternate, lobed

The Pin Oak can't seem to figure out which way its branches should grow. With this species, it's a case of swoop and droop. The upper branches swoop skyward, the middle branches are horizontal, and the lower branches droop earthward. In spite of this strange pattern—or perhaps because of it—the Pin Oak is one of the most popular of some 30-40 varieties of Oaks sold by North American nurseries. As a young or middle-aged tree, the Pin Oak is pyramidal. In old age, it often loses its lower branches and becomes more rounded in outline. Its shiny, dark green leaves are slender and have 5-7 sharply tipped lobes divided by spacious, rounded sinuses. In fall, the leaves of one Pin Oak could be scarlet, of another reddish brown, and of a third, brown. Growing wild in acidic soils from southern New England west to Illinois and south into Arkansas, Tennessee and North Carolina, the Pin Oak is usually found in moist, flat areas, along clay ridges, and close to swamps. Its scientific name, *palustris*, is derived from the Latin word meaning swamp. The common name "Pin" describes its abundance of short, pin-like side branches as well as the prickly tips of its leaves. The Pin Oak is easy to transplant, has dense foliage and a graceful shape, is a fast grower, supplies good shade, and is relatively tolerant of pollution. Although frequently used as a street tree, it should only be planted where its downward hanging lower branches will not interfere with traffic and pedestrians. The almost-round, squat little acorns of the Pin Oak are appealing. Broader than tall, they are set into shallow saucers measuring about ¼-inch in depth.

Map ID #55

96

Red Oak

Northern Red Oak, Gray Oak

Quercus rubra

Among the mighty Oaks, there are two categories: the whites which grow wild all around the Northern Hemisphere and the reds (or blacks) which are native only to North America. The two types of Oaks are differentiated in large part by the color of their wood. Fortunately, tree enthusiasts can distinguish between the white and the red Oak groups without resorting to an ax. The white group leaf margins, whether lobed or just wavy, are always smooth. Leaves of Oaks in the red group are

Leaves: Simple, alternate, lobed

bristly, with veins which protrude right through their tips. On campus, the White, Swamp White, Chestnut and English Oaks are members of the white Oak group. Representing the red group are the Pin and Red Oaks. Like other species of Oaks, the Red Oak grows to be a rugged, noble tree when planted in deep, well-drained soil and afforded adequate light as well as space for its root system to spread unimpeded. As a youngster, this fastest growing of all oaks is quite homely. But, when the Red Oak reaches its mature height of 75 feet or more, its heavy, twisted, upward-slanting limbs create a handsome, rounded crown with a spread which often exceeds its height. It's a magnificent shade tree with dense foliage which turns tones of red and brown in the fall. Red Oaks are relatively free of insect and disease attack, highly resistant to winter cold, easy to transplant, and tolerant of urban conditions. Some sources classify Red Oaks and Northern Red Oaks as the same species, whereas others call the latter *Quercus borealis*.

Map ID #56

Swamp White Oak

Swamp Oak

Quercus bicolor

In the wild, plants which survive most successfully have generally found the one environmental niche best suited to their needs. For the Swamp White Oak, that niche lies along the edges of swamps or other lowlands with poorly drained, acidic soil. In such locations, the tree has proved itself able to tolerate cold, heat, shade, diseases, insects and natural breakage. Native throughout the northeast quadrant of the United States and extreme southeastern Canada, the Swamp White is a rugged survivor that has been known to live 300-350 years. When used as a landscape specimen, the Swamp White grows and looks best in spacious areas such as parks and campuses rather than in front yards of private homes. In urban or semi-urban areas, it should not be planted along streets because of its intolerance to pollution and salt. For an Oak, it is a fast grower and is relatively easy to transplant. The 5-6 inch long leaves are halfway between those of the Chestnut Oak and those of the White Oak in appearance. From a narrow, pointed base, the Swamp White's leaves broaden and become blunt or slightly rounded at the tip. One leaf, or different leaves on the same tree, can display edges that are wavy, have shallow rounded lobes, or include an occasional pointed lobe. Acorns suspended on stems longer than the leaf stems help identify the Swamp White Oak. A fringe of branches hanging downwards from the upper trunk is another, but less reliable, identifying feature.

Leaves: Simple, alternate, lobed, wavy edged

White Oak

Stave Oak, Forkleaf White Oak, Ridge White Oak

Quercus alba

Good things are worth waiting for. The King of the Oaks—the White Oak—may be a slow grower, but champion specimens have lived 800 years and grown to heights and breadths in excess of 100 feet, with trunks eight feet in diameter. Heights of 50-80 feet and lives of 200-300 years are more common. A magnificent shade tree, the White Oak is often considered the best of over 400 species of Oaks. Transplant it when it is very young because it will soon develop a deep tap root that makes moving the tree almost impossible. That tap root enabled the White Oak to survive the violence of the 1938 hurricane which downed American Elms and many other trees on campus. The dark green to bluish-green leaves of the White Oak have rounded lobes separated by deep sinuses. In the fall, the tree puts on a long-lasting display of color ranging from purplish red to deep wine. Many Oak leaves, particularly on inner branches, persist throughout the winter and drop off shortly before new leaves emerge. Early Europeans deemed the Oak blessed, because the gods chose to strike it with lightning more frequently than they did any other tree. Lightning was considered sacred fire. A burning tree from which man could steal fire was an awe-inspiring, holy gift. Between 1000 and 1100 A.D., Scandinavians could well have been influenced by that pagan belief when they chose a European cousin of the North American White Oak with which to build their earliest stave churches. When planting a White Oak, honor it with rich, well-drained and slightly acidic soil, and provide it with a spacious site free from the tread of many feet. Planted in the year 2000 on the Dartmouth College campus, a White Oak could very well witness the graduation of several hundred undergraduate classes.

Leaves: Simple, alternate, lobed

99

Map ID #58

Japanese Pagodatree
Chinese Scholartree
Sophora japonica

In May and June, the Dartmouth campus is bedecked with blossoming trees. Crabapples, Bradford Pears, Hawthorns, Yellowwoods, Mountainashes, Tree Lilacs, Fringetrees, Dogwoods, Cherries and several other species stage a breathtaking display. It's a rare tree that waits to bloom until mid-summer. On the Dartmouth campus, one such exception is the Japanese Pagodatree. In late July or early August it sports an abundance of cream-colored flowers displayed in large, upright clusters. The flowers gradually evolve into yellow seed pods that are constricted between the seeds in such a way that they resemble little strings of beads. The pods remain on the tree throughout the winter and, in combination with a touch of yellow-green in both bark and twigs, impart to the bare tree a subtle golden glow. Young Pagodatrees need protection from severe cold. A specimen

Leaves: Compound, behind Fayerweather Hall is well sited because it is
alternate, untoothed shielded from the blasts of winter and is planted halfway down a hill where temperatures tend to be more moderate. Once established, the tree is relatively tolerant of cold, heat, drought and pollution and shows good resistance to attack by insects and disease. Japanese Pagodatrees belong to a group of species (a genus) known in Latin as *Sophora*. In North America, the genus *Sophora* is represented by only two tree species, both of which are true southerners, able to grow wild no further north than Oklahoma. Their more cold-hardy cousin, the Japanese Pagodatree that thrives on the Dartmouth campus, is a native of China and Korea. It was introduced into North America in the mid-18th century at a time when botanists were actively transporting seeds and samples of plant materials from one part of the world to another. Mature specimens top out at 50-75 feet with broad, round crowns. Lesser heights are seen this far north. Compound leaves, comprised of handsome, medium-to-dark green leaflets, resemble those of the Black Locust, and, in locust-like fashion, allow filtered light to reach grass growing beneath the tree. This tree is worthy of discovery and deserving of more frequent inclusion in landscape plans.

Map ID #59

Bradford Pear

Pyrus calleryana 'Bradford'

Like some people, certain trees can be rugged individuals. In the fall, as the days grow shorter and the sun's rays less intense, leaves on most campus trees slow down production of the chlorophyll that gives them their green summer color. Those trees begin to change color. Not so the Bradford Pear. Somewhere, this little offspring of a tree native to Korea and China must have misplaced its time clock. When the first snow falls, just before or just after Thanksgiving, snowflakes collect on the still-green leaves of the Bradford Pear. Not until late November do these leaves change to yellow, orange, red and scarlet. Finally they drop, but not until about the first week of December. Further south, the color change is more dramatic and lasts longer. Because of its profusion of white spring bloom, its glossy

Leaves: Simple, alternate, toothed

summer foliage, brilliant fall coloration, symmetrical growth pattern, and resistance to fungal infection, the Bradford Pear became extremely popular

in this country. Overplanting resulted. As those trees have aged, a pronounced tendency to splitting has become a serious problem. The Bradford can be a treasure for perhaps 20-25 years, but arborists now recommend researching alternative varieties of blossoming Pears before deciding which to plant.

Map ID #60

Austrian Pine

Black Pine, European Black Pine

Pinus nigra

*Needles:
Evergreen, two
per bundle*

The Austrian Pine was brought to the American Colonies in 1759, only 10 years before Dartmouth College was founded in the wilderness of northern New England. A native of Asia Minor, as well as of southern and central Europe, this handsome conifer has proved to be a valuable import. The fast-growing, pyramidal young Austrian Pine evolves into a broad-crowned, mature specimen in 20-30 years. Like the Norway Spruce, the Austrian Pine grows far taller in its native Europe than in its adopted North America. In Austria, for example, trees of 100-150 feet are common and are a valuable source of lumber. In the United States, Austrian Pines planted as ornamentals or for screens and windbreaks seldom exceed heights of 60 feet. The tree is unusually tolerant of urban problems such as dust, salt, pollution, smoke and compacted soil. Dwarf and columnar varieties are available to solve specific site requirements. If moisture is adequate, Austrian Pines will grow in a wide range of soil types, including even the fairly heavy clay of the "Hanover Plain" which was laid down some 10,000 years ago on the bottom of a large lake formed when the glaciers were retreating. Almost every feature of this Pine is solid. Its branches are strong, its 3-6 inch pairs of needles are stiff, and the scales of its broad-based tapered cones are thick and prickly.

Eastern White Pine
Soft Pine, Pumpkin Pine, Sapling Pine, Weymouth Pine

Pinus strobus

The White Pine as a Landscape Specimen

Under cultivation, the White Pine is a fast grower. It can reach heights up to 100 feet if planted in moist, well-drained soil, protected from extremes of wind and sited a safe distance from highway salt and pollution. Long flexible needles, 6-8 inch pendulous cones, and a whorled branching pattern are identifying features. The White Pine is the only native Pine east of the Continental Divide to grow needles in bundles of five—one needle for each letter in its first name. Nurseries and research centers have developed a large number of cultivars of the species. In growth patterns, these range from dense and low-spreading, to weeping, to open and pyramidal. The tall, slender 'Fastigiata' is a particularly graceful selection. Tallest of all eastern conifers, the White Pine is a confirmed North American. In the late 16th and early 17th century, the tree was planted in France and England, but it refused to thrive on foreign soil.

Needles: Evergreen, five per bundle

103

The Old Pine in 1885

Eastern White Pine

The White Pine in History and Tradition

From 1769 to 1895—"By the light of many thousand sunsets"—the Old Pine stood watch over the traditions, aspirations, and memories of Dartmouth College. Celebrated in song and story, that beloved tree was a White Pine. For more than a century, it clung tenaciously to the granite of New Hampshire and grew to become the symbol of "Dartmouth undying." Even after the damage done by wind and lightning necessitated its removal in 1895, the Old Pine lives on as the icon of the College. The stylized image of a White Pine appears today on Dartmouth publications and on the College flag which flies above the Green. On the Baker Tower windvane, a White Pine provides shade in which Dartmouth's founder, Eleazar Wheelock, is seen teaching a Native American student. When Wheelock first laid eyes on the Hanover plain, he proclaimed it "a horrid wilderness." The ground beneath the dense forest of towering trees was damp, dark and foreboding. Where students now cross a sunlit Green, there once stood some of the largest White Pines in North America. These old-growth giants, with trunks five feet in diameter, reached heights above 220 feet. They were so tall that four of them lying on the ground, arranged in a square, would enclose an acre. The size and straightness of their trunks dictated that these trees—and all others like them—be blazed with a broad arrow and designated as "the King's Pines." By law, such trees were claimed by King George III and destined to become masts of British ships of the line. Severe penalties were imposed on private individuals who dared to cut or sell them. In northern New England, the tree laws led to as much pre-revolutionary unrest as did the Stamp Act and Tea Tax. Significantly, the first flag of the American revolutionary forces bore an image of a White Pine. Dartmouth's Old Pine was one of the few local trees to escape being cut and floated down the Connecticut River. Its twisted trunk and lesser height rescued it from a life at sea. This tree of tradition grew alone in an exposed and unforgiving location above the almost clearcut College Park. Its stump can be seen today on the hilltop near the College observatory. In 1969, members of the Class of 1927 planted the New Dartmouth Pine close to the entrance of the Bema.

Red Pine

Norway Pine

Pinus resinosa

Needles: Evergreen, two per bundle

The Ice Ages were a boon to the Red Pine. Wherever receding glaciers dumped deposits of sand and gravel in southern Canada, New England and the Great Lakes region, this magnificent conifer flourishes. Champion Red Pines have been known to live more than 300 years and grow to heights of 140 feet with straight trunks clothed in reddish gray bark. In landscaped sites, heights of 60-100 feet and life spans of 200 years or less are more common. To distinguish one Pine from another, it helps to count the needles per bundle and to take a close look at the cones. Up north, the Red Pine is our only native Pine with two needles per bundle. That can still be confusing because at least two other Pines on campus display needles in bundles of two. However, the two-per-bundle needles of the imported Austrian Pine are stiffer and not quite as long as needles of the native Red Pine. And, those of the imported Scotch Pine are short and twisted. While flexible and up to six inches long like those of the White Pine, Red Pine needles have sharper points and grow in bundles of two rather than five. Stalkless cones, single or paired, mature in the fall of their second season and resemble perky, two-inch tall Christmas trees. Scales of pine cones can be quite distinctive. Those of the Red Pine have no thorns, are slightly thickened, and display tiny "keels" on their undersides. The hardy Red Pine can tolerate temperatures ranging from -50°F to +100°F, but it definitely prefers the cold. That preference is fortunate for birds and mammals of the far north which feast on its seeds and browse its needles and twigs. Mistakenly dubbed the Norway Pine by early settlers, especially those living in the vicinity of Norway, Maine, the Red Pine is a native of North America and not of Scandinavia.

Scotch Pine

Scots Pine, Scotch Fir

Pinus sylvestris

Although this conifer is named for Scotland where it grows wild, it is also a native of Scandinavia, most of northern Europe and a large segment of Asia. The Scotch Pine is dominant in the great forests of Norway, Sweden, Germany and Russia. In its native lands, the tree can grow to 150 feet and has long proved a valuable source of lumber. Early colonists in North America dreamed of using the Scotch Pine to help satisfy their need for building materials. They imported the tree. But their dreams turned to nightmares. In its new home, the straight-trunked, slender tree of Eurasia developed a crooked bole and grew only 30-60 feet with a broad, umbrella-like crown. Native North American trees far surpassed the imported species for lumber. Young Scotch Pines can be pruned to symmetrical shapes which make them popular as Christmas trees. But, it turns out to be the misshapen,

Needles: Evergreen, two per bundle

but highly picturesque, structure of the mature tree which has made it so appealing as a landscape specimen. Scotch Pines are relatively free of disease and insect attack and tolerate a broad spectrum of climatic and soil conditions. Bluish-green needles of the Scotch Pine are sheathed in bundles of two, measure 1½-3 inches in length and are slightly twisted. Dramatic cinnamon-to-orange bark on the upper trunks and branches of older Scotch Pines helps identify the species.

London Planetree

Platanus x acerfolia

*Leaves: Simple,
alternate, lobed*

Somewhere in 17th century England, a little mutt of a tree appeared. It turned out to be a natural cross between a Euro-Asian Planetree and an American Planetree, or Sycamore. Luckily, the tiny hybrid survived. It was destined to become one of the two or three most important urban street trees in the Western World. The London Planetree, one of very few trees able to survive the atmospheric urban soup of air polluted by coal dust, took its name from the City of London where it was extensively planted. Severely pruned London Planetrees still line the streets of many European cities. Extreme pruning is almost a requisite when the tree is growing in a confined location. Left unpruned, the London Plane (like the American Sycamore), can grow to heights of 100 feet with a rugged branch pattern spreading out as much as 80 feet. The scientific name, *Platanus*, derives from the Greek word for "broad." No other trees in the eastern United States can rival the massive trunks of the two Planetrees, the London and the Sycamore. It would take three or four tall men to reach around a champion specimen of either. To distinguish a London Planetree from an American Sycamore, look closely at the fruits and leaves. Both species produce "button-balls" which hang from stems several inches long. These fruits, made up of numerous seeds encased in nutlike shells, grow singly on the Sycamore, but they appear most commonly in twos and three on the London Planetree. Both trees have leaves 8-10 inches wide. London Planetree leaves have smoother edges and are more deeply lobed. Their resemblance to Maple leaves gives the London Planetree its second Latin name, *acerfolia*, meaning "maple-leafed." The calico bark of this tree rivals even the Birch and the Beech for winter beauty. Outer layers flake off to reveal a patchwork of brown, green, gray and yellow tones. Overplanting has made the London Planetree, like so many other trees, increasingly susceptible to attack by insects and disease. More resistant cultivars are now being developed. Take care where you plant this magnificent tree. It's a beauty, but the powerful roots can invade storm sewers and damage the foundations of buildings.

Pissard Plum

Cherry Plum, Myrobalan Plum

Prunus cerasifera 'Atropurpurea'

Sometime in the latter half of the 19th century, when Persia was still Persia, the Shah's gardener was pruning a Plum tree. He noticed that the leaves on one branch were an attractive reddish-purple, a color quite different from leaves on the rest of the tree. What he observed is known as a "branch sport," a genetic mutation which causes the affected branch to develop unique characteristics. Being a trained horticulturist, the gardener realized that in the mutated branch he might have the raw material to use in propagating a variety of the parent species. A cutting, or scion, was taken from the branch and carefully grafted onto the young root system of another tree. The graft was successful and the tree grew to produce foliage of the desired color. The new cultivar was named 'Atropurpurea' or

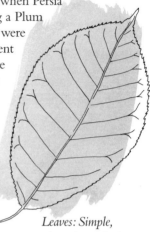

Leaves: Simple, alternate, toothed

Pissard Plum. The tree proved so successful that it was exported to France, from which it made its way to the Western Hemisphere. All Plums belong to a large group of flowering plants known as the Rose family. Other family members on the Dartmouth College campus include Cherries, Hawthorns, Crabapples, Mountain-ashes and Serviceberries. The Pissard Plum is one of the earliest local trees to bloom. It produces a profusion of small, pink blossoms in late April or early May. Upright and somewhat slender in its growth pattern, the tree matures at heights from 15 to 30 feet. Smooth, brownish-gray bark heavily marked with horizontal rows of lenticels, or breathing pores, identify it as a close relative of the Cherry tree. Although the Pissard Plum is short-lived and susceptible to insect and disease problems, it is worth planting and replanting for the beauty of its bloom and the color of its foliage.

Map ID #66

Dawn Redwood

Metasequoia glyptostroboides

Needles:
Deciduous,
flat

Two hundred and fifty dollars saved an ancient tree from extinction. As recently as the early 1940s, the Dawn Redwood was known only to paleo-botanists. Fossil records indicated that the tree might have existed as long ago as 150 million years—the age of the dinosaurs. No scientist had ever seen a living example of such a tree. Therefore, it was considered extinct. In the mid-1940s, about 25 unusual trees were found growing in remote areas of China along the provincial border between Szechuan and Hupeh. With China's large population, those few trees were in immediate danger of being cut down for firewood and lumber. Chinese botanists, seeing samples from the trees, suspected they might be looking at a miracle. But China was in political upheaval, and there was no funding available for further investigation. A tree-saving coincidence occurred. The director of one of China's biological institutes had received his doctorate at Harvard and had trained at the Arnold Arboretum. The Harvard University botanists working at the Arboretum were keenly interested in the mysterious trees that had been found growing in China. A gift of $250 from a Harvard graduate, combined with some exemplary international scientific cooperation, was all that was needed to send a small expedition to bring out seeds. The Arnold Arboretum successfully propagated a large number of seedlings and shared seeds with arboreta throughout the world. By 1948, the long-lost Dawn Redwood was safely back in cultivation. This last living species of an ancient group of related species had survived centuries of coexistence with humans primarily because it was associated with Todee, the god of the land. It was rescued just in time from the pressures of modern population growth and almost certain extinction. The Dawn Redwood was worth saving. It's a graceful, pyramidal conifer with bright green needles which turn shades ranging from brown to apricot in the fall. Like the Larch and Cypress, the Dawn Redwood is deciduous and sheds its needles annually. The tree is a fast grower that can reach 50 feet in its first 20 years. It can live several hundred years to top out above 100 feet with a trunk seven feet in diameter. The Dawn Redwood has proved itself cold-hardy down to -30°F near Boston and grows in Sweden within 200 miles of the Arctic Circle. Protected locations are advised because late spring and early fall freezes pose a serious threat to this species. It seems to require a fairly long growing season. Tree men and biology professors alike are watching Dartmouth's first Dawn Redwood with considerable interest.

Map ID #67

Downy Serviceberry

Juneberry, Shadbush, Servicetree, Sarvistree, Shadblow

Amelanchier arborea

In early spring, when the Shad struggle up river to spawn, the Downy Serviceberry (alias Shadbush or Shadblow) bursts into bloom. Showy, pendulous clusters of delicate, five-petaled flowers appear close to the tips of the branches before, or just as, new leaves emerge. The tree is small, but its bloom is dramatic against a background of evergreens and bare deciduous trees in a wild or naturalized landscape. When the Downy's leaves are young, they wear a Pussy Willow blanket of soft white hairs. This covering disappears within a few weeks as the pointed, egg-shaped leaves mature and turn medium to dark green. In the fall, the Downy Serviceberry puts on a show of color that ranks with the very best among small trees. Its leaves can

Leaves: Simple, alternate, toothed

vary in shade from yellow, through rich orange, to dark red and purple bronze. Numerous cultivars of the plant are now available, providing a choice of flowering habits, fall coloration, and resistance to low temperatures. In early summer, tiny apple-like fruits turn a deep reddish purple. Some say they make a delicious "blueberry" pie. But pies are few, because songbirds usually beat humans to the harvest. The native habitat of the Downy Serviceberry blankets almost the entire eastern half of the United States plus southeastern Canada. The tree grows in a wide range of soil and drainage conditions but shows a definite preference for moist locations. As a cultivated specimen, the Downy can be raised as a large, rounded shrub or pruned and trained as a multi-stemmed tree which grows to heights of 15-25 feet.

Map ID #68

Colorado Spruce

Colorado Blue Spruce, Blue Spruce, Silver Spruce

Picea pungens

Needles:
Evergreen,
stiff

What gives the needles of Colorado Spruce a silvery-blue cast while those of other types of Spruce trees are green? New-growth needles of the Colorado Spruce are coated with a fine, white powder. These young needles retain their silvery color for 2-4 years, after which their powdery coating sloughs off revealing the bluish-green beneath. Only the outermost needles of the Colorado Spruce give the tree its distinctive color. Needles farther in on the branches have lost their silver tone. This gorgeous tree is native to a relatively limited area and altitude, specifically the central Rocky Mountains of Colorado, Utah and New Mexico at elevations above 6,000 feet. In its natural habitat, the Colorado Spruce grows up to 100 feet tall and can live well over 500 years. Rocky Mountain climate, below the tree's preferred elevation, is too dry for seedlings of this species to survive. But, given sufficient water, well-drained soil, and full sun, young Colorado Spruces are raised successfully all across the northern United States, regardless of altitude. Once established, the tree becomes relatively resistant to drought. Varieties are available with weeping growth patterns and colors ranging from light, silvery-blue through intense blue to blue-green. With its lush foliage, pyramidal symmetry and beautiful color, the Colorado or Blue Spruce makes a dramatic statement. Unfortunately, when the tree ages beyond about 35 years, its crown begins to thin out and it loses its lower branches. In a forest setting, where the Colorado Spruce grows in proximity to other conifers, this inability to age gracefully matters little. But, for use in a planned landscape, it can become a serious problem.

Engelmann Spruce

Columbian Spruce, Mountain Spruce

Picea engelmannii

When you're all "spruced up," you're decked out in your Sunday best—neat and tidy as a young Spruce tree. Like other Spruces, the Engelmann is dense and pyramidal in growth habit during its early years. After that, its ground-hugging lower branches gradually drop off and the tree assumes the bare-trunked, church-steeple configuration of maturity. Ride a chairlift in the Rocky Mountains and you'll be flanked by slender, cone-bedecked Engelmann Spruce all the way up to the timberline—which can be as high as 12,000 feet in Arizona and New Mexico. Sometimes names of tree species honor the scientist who originally described them. George Engelmann, a well-known botanist, was the first to identify this magnificent conifer of the Cascades and Rockies. In its native habitat, the tree grows more than 100 feet tall and lives up to 500

Needles: Evergreen, four-sided, sharp

years. A few of today's magnificent wild specimens could have been seedlings when Columbus first laid eyes on America. In landscaped locations, considerably shorter lives and heights of about 40 feet are the norm. Given a sufficient supply of water, this hardy evergreen should thrive on campus. Winter temperatures will not be a problem. A single specimen was planted in 1999 south of Gilman Hall as one of a selection of interesting species requested by the Dartmouth Department of Biological Sciences. Recognize the "neat and tidy" young Engelmann Spruce by its sharp, bluish-green needles.

Map ID #70

Norway Spruce
Common Spruce
Picea abies

The Norway Spruce is a musical tree. Both it and its campus cousin, the White Spruce, play in the Dartmouth Symphony Orchestra. Wood from Spruce trees is among the best for creating the sounding boards of musical instruments. An imported native of northern and central Europe, the Norway Spruce is most easily identified by its pyramidal shape and its graceful branches, luxuriantly fringed with downward hanging foliage. Unique to the species are the 4-7 inch cones, the largest found on any Spruce tree. Maturing in one growing season, the cones open early in their second year to release naked seeds with long wings. Four-sided, dark green needles encircle the twigs of the Norway Spruce. For reasons probably associated with climate, the tree rarely reaches 100 feet in height in North America but has been known to tower above 200 feet in Europe. In spite of this growth limitation, the Norway Spruce is widely planted in southern Canada and the northern United States wherever there is sufficient moisture. In favor of the Norway Spruce are its attractive shape, retention of branches all the way to the ground, medium to fast rate of growth, and ability to withstand cold temperatures. Negative qualities include susceptibility to insect damage and a tendency of the foliage on older trees to become ragged and sparse.

Needles: Evergreen, pointed, four-sided

White Spruce

Cat Spruce, Canadian Spruce, Skunk Spruce

Picea glauca

Of the seven species of Spruce native to North America, the White Spruce is one of the two most widely distributed. It grows wild throughout a great arc that sweeps from east to west across Canada and north into Alaska, embraces northern New England and the Lake States, and extends down into the Rocky Mountains of Montana. Three hundred year old specimens, more than 100 feet in height, have been found growing in moist, well-drained soil on the slopes of the Canadian Rockies. In a planned landscape, the White Spruce makes a bold statement. Its graceful, pyramidal shape is defined by horizontal whorls of long branches which curve upwards at their ends. Older trees display a fringe of downward-hanging branchlets similar in

Needles: Evergreen, four-sided, pointed

pattern to the Norway Spruce. Sharp, four-sided needles, which tend to curve upwards, grow all the way around the twigs but are more densely concentrated on their upper sides. The White Spruce is best sited away from streets because of its intolerance to pollution. However, the tree is

able to withstand extreme cold, a wide range of soil conditions, and some degree of drought and heat. When Jacques Cartier sailed up a tributary of the St. Lawrence River in 1535, he marveled at the beauty of the virgin forest. Cartier proclaimed the White Spruce and the other northern trees amongst which it grew to be "some of the finest trees in the world."

Map ID #72

Black Tupelo

Black Gum, Sour Gum, Pepperidge

Nyssa sylvatica

Humans tend to grow shorter as they grow older. So does this tree. In its dotage, the Black Tupelo dies from the top down, a rare negative characteristic in an otherwise glorious, but often unrecognized, species. Few trees rival the spectacular fall color of the beloved Red Maple. The Black Tupelo, or Black Gum, is one that not only rivals but can even surpass the Red Maple. Shiny surfaced, leathery leaves evolve from the deep green of summer through mottled patterns of yellows, oranges and reds to their final glowing scarlet. When the brilliantly colored leaves drop, the tree reveals a horizontally branched structure that is handsome throughout the winter. Native Americans named the Black Tupelo "tree of the swamp." They knew it well as a tree that grew wild in boggy locations throughout most of eastern North America from southern Canada to the Gulf states.

Leaves: Simple, alternate, untoothed

The tree's fanciful, scientific name translates as "water nymph of the forest" and derives from Greek mythology. Although a member of the Dogwood family, the Black Tupelo produces only inconspicuous, greenish flowers. Those flowers, however, mature into an abundant crop of bluish-black, fleshy fruits that look like olives hanging from long stems. In a landscaped setting, the fruits are highly decorative. In the wild, they are relished by birds and animals despite their bitter flavor. When the Black Tupelo matures at heights ranging from 30 to more than 75 feet, its dark, corky bark fissures into a block-like pattern that resembles the hide of an alligator. Campus specimens of this tree are young and have many years to grow before they develop this handsome feature. Because of their deep tap roots, trees of this species transplant safely only when they are small. They should be sited in moist, acidic soil, well away from sources of polluted air and the tread of many feet.

Black Walnut
Eastern Black Walnut, American Walnut

Juglans nigra

Legend has it that the Roman god, Jupiter, loved to snack on Black Walnuts. The Latin name, *Juglans*, means "acorn of Jupiter." We humans also enjoy the flavor of Black Walnut in candies and icings. But for straight nut-eating, we search out the Persian or English Walnut. Mice and squirrels, on the other hand, share the taste of the gods. Magnificent Black Walnut trees, 150 feet tall and a man's height in diameter, once grew wild where soils were rich and deep. They were so abundant that farmers even built fences of Walnut. Today it's extremely rare to find a large Black Walnut growing anywhere within its vast native habitat. The wood became the most sought after variety by cabinet-makers and producers of gun stocks. Easy to work, fine grained, and richly beautiful when finished, it often proved stronger than White Oak. Don't choose a Black Walnut to be your backyard shade tree. The toxicity of its root system creates a soil

Leaves: Compound, alternate, toothed

environment in which many other plants such as White Pines and Crab-apples find it impossible to live. Then there's the litter problem. While the fruit or nut of the Black Walnut is newly fallen, its outer covering or husk is light green and slightly fleshy. When cut or crushed, that husk becomes the source of many a stained hand or item of clothing. Because of its abundant fruit and intolerance to salt, the Black Walnut should not be planted close to a street. With all these negatives, why include it on campus? The Black

Walnut is a handsome remnant of our native forest that deserves to be preserved. With the space afforded in a park or campus landscape plan, it can live for over 200 years and mature into a massive specimen with a crown spread almost equal to its height.

Map ID #74

'Tristis' Golden Weeping Willow

'Tristis' White Willow

Salix alba 'Tristis'

> *On a tree by a river, a little Tom Tit sang*
> *Willow-tit-willow-tit-willow.*

Chances are that Gilbert and Sullivan imagined their lovesick little bird clinging to the waving branch of the most beautiful of all Weeping Willows, the Babylon. That species cannot cope with the winter cold of northern New England. But, fortunately, there is another Willow of similar weeping habit which survives temperatures as low as -30°F. That tree is the Golden Weeping Willow. You'll find it planted in the moist soil it prefers, flanking a little stream north of the Dartmouth Medical School. Willows belong to a prolific group of plants which mature at heights ranging all the way from one inch to 100 feet. Some are capable of growing at latitudes well beyond the Arctic Circle. At least 100 species of Willows are found in North America alone.

Leaves: Simple, alternate, toothed

Of these, about one-third are tall enough to be classified as trees. The 'Tristis' Golden Weeping Willow growing on campus is a cultivated variety, or cultivar, of a species brought from Europe to this hemisphere in the 17th century. While the tree is subject to disease and breakage, it is worth planting for the beauty of its shape, the golden glow of its twigs in winter, the early spring appearance of lush green leaves, and the yellow color display of autumn.

American Yellowwood

Virgilia, Gopher Wood, Yellow Locust

Cladastris kentukea

The Yellowwood is to the giant Oaks and Pines as the 5-foot, 8-inch guard is to the towering forwards and center on a basketball team. Both the guard and the Yellowwood are relatively small but they make the team because they're loaded with talent. This excellent, 30-50 foot shade tree, with its unusually bright green leaves, has a broad crown, handsome limb structure and attractive smooth gray bark similar to the Beech. When established trees bloom, they are covered with fragrant, foot-long clusters of white flowers resembling Wisteria in their pendulous habit. Yellowwoods usually bloom every year but the most abundant bloom occurs every second or third year. A pink flowering variety called 'Rosea' is now available at some nurseries. Blossoms evolve into bean-like pods by fall. Being a member of the legume family,

Leaves: Compound, alternate, untoothed

this tree enriches its own soil through a process by which bacteria in nodules on its roots remove nitrogen from the atmosphere and add it to the soil. Perhaps that process helps the tree survive up to 160 years. Though native to North Carolina, Kentucky and Tennessee, the Yellowwood has proved hardy in northern climates and is highly resistant to insect damage and disease. Just be sure not to prune it in winter or early spring, because it will "bleed" profusely. Yellowwood owes its name to the yellow color of its newly cut heartwood. This jewel of a tree is becoming so popular it is sometimes difficult to find in nurseries or garden centers.

Map ID #76

Japanese Zelkova

Keaki

Zelkova serrata

Leaves:
Simple,
alternate,
toothed

When thousands of magnificent American Elms fell victim to Dutch Elm disease, the search began for trees that could, at least in part, replace one of the best urban trees ever known in North America. Because of its resistance to the Elm leaf beetle, the Zelkova tree, an Asian relative of the Elm, was a strong contender. As a young tree, this native of Japan displays the vase-shaped growth pattern of the American Elm. But, by the time it reaches a mature height of 50-80 feet, the Zelkova has lost that flaring shape and developed a more rounded crown. The tree is attractive throughout the year, an important characteristic in northern regions where deciduous trees remain leafless for up to six months. Smooth, somewhat scaly gray bark and a handsome structure contribute to winter beauty. A dense canopy of dark green, sharply toothed and tapered leaves makes the Zelkova a good summer shade tree. In fall the leaves turn shades ranging from purple to red-bronze. Although borers can be a problem, the Zelkova is a relatively low maintenance tree that is resistant to wind, ice, drought and disease. True to its Asiatic origin, the tree has been known to attract Japanese beetles. The Zelkova tolerates a range of soil conditions from acidic to alkaline but grows best in moist soil and full sunlight. At least two varieties are offered by nurseries, the upright 'Green Vase' and the more spreading and cold hardy 'Village Green' that is the Zelkova planted on campus.

Touring the Campus

Maps of the
Dartmouth College Campus
that Locate
the Trees Profiled in
Forever Green

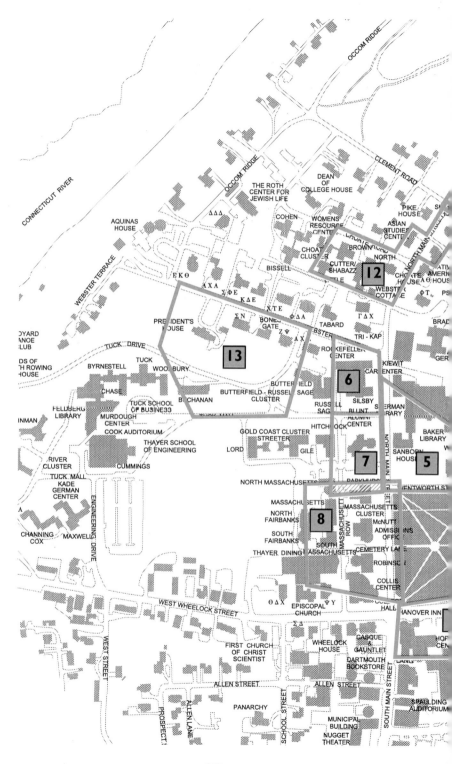

CONNECTICUT RIVER

OCCOM RIDGE

CLEMENT ROAD

OCCOM RIDGE

THE ROTH CENTER FOR JEWISH LIFE

DEAN OF COLLEGE HOUSE

PIKE HOUSE

AQUINAS HOUSE

COHEN

WOMENS RESOURCE CENTER

ASIAN STUDIES CENTER

CHOATE CLUSTER

BROWN

NORTH

CUTTER/ SHABAZZ

CHOATE HOUSE

AMERICA

ΑΘ HOUSE

WEBSTER COTTAGE

ΦΤ

PSI

ΔΔΔ

ΕΚΘ

ΑΧΑ

ΣΦΕ

ΚΔΕ

ΧΤΕ

ΦΔΑ

ΓΔΧ

TABARD

BRA

BISSELL

WEBSTER TERRACE

PRESIDENT'S HOUSE

ΣΝ

BONES GATE

ΖΨ

ΑΧ

WEBSTER

TRI-KAP

GER

ROCKEFELLER CENTER

KIEWIT

DYARD ANOE LUB

TUCK DRIVE

CARPENTER

6

DS OF H ROWING HOUSE

BYRNESTELL

TUCK

WOODBURY

BUTTERFIELD CLUSTER

BUTTERFIELD- RUSSELL SAGE

SILSBY

GERMAN RARY

13

CHASE

TUCK SCHOOL OF BUSINESS

BUCHANAN

RUSSELL SAGE

BLUNT

FELDBERG LIBRARY

MURDOUGH CENTER

ALUMNI CENTER

BAKER LIBRARY

INMAN

COOK AUDITORIUM

GOLD COAST CLUSTER STREETER

HITCHCOCK

THAYER SCHOOL OF ENGINEERING

LORD

GILE

SANBORN HOUSE

W

RIVER CLUSTER

CUMMINGS

7

5

TUCK MALL

KADE GERMAN CENTER

NORTH MASSACHUSETTS

PARKHURST

WENTWORTH ST

CHANNING COX

MAXWELL

ENGINEERING DRIVE

MASSACHUSETTS

NORTH FAIRBANKS

MASSACHUSETTS ROW

MASSACHUSETTS CLUSTER

McNUTT

ADMISSIONS OFFICE

8

SOUTH FAIRBANKS

THAYER DINING

SOUTH MASSACHUSETTS

CEMETERY LANE

ROBINSON

NORTH MAIN STREET

COLLIS CENTER

WEST WHEELOCK STREET

ΘΔΧ

EPISCOPAL CHURCH

ΨΥ

HALL

HANOVER INN

ΣΑ

WEST STREET

FIRST CHURCH OF CHRIST SCIENTIST

WHEELOCK HOUSE

CASQUE & GAUNTLET

HO CEN

DARTMOUTH BOOKSTORE

SOUTH MAIN STREET

ALLEN STREET

ALLEN STREET

PROSPECT

ALLEN LANE

PANARCHY

SCHOOL STREET

MUNICIPAL BUILDING

NUGGET THEATER

SPAULDING AUDITORIUM

122

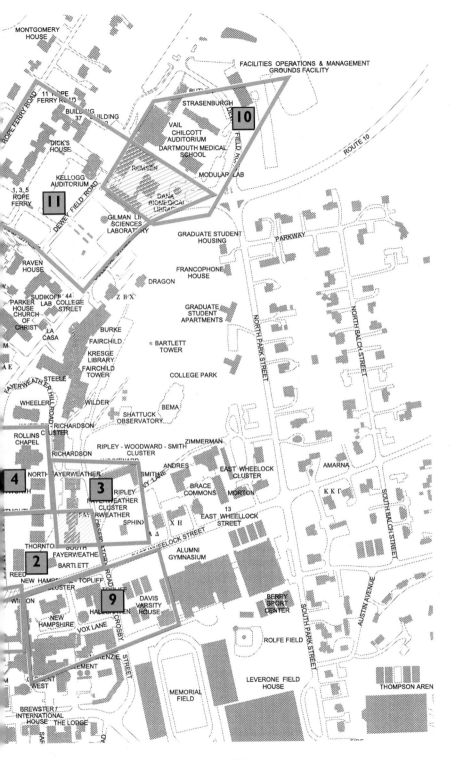

Dartmouth Hall in winter

Center Campus Tree Walk

Fifty Trees in Fifty Minutes

The Center Campus Tree Walk is designed to introduce the walker/ visitor to the many different types of trees that contribute to the beauty of Dartmouth College. Of the 77 different species planted throughout the campus, fully two-thirds can be observed within close proximity to the Green.

The Center Campus Tree Walk can be completed in less than an hour but participants may enjoy being more leisurely. Several short detours are included for those interested in seeing additional species. Along the way, you may notice a new tree which is not mentioned. A better example will be pointed out later in the walk.

In this book, campus trees are numbered alphabetically by their common names. These identifying numbers appear consistently from map to map. For example, the number "56" always indicates a Red Oak; "22" means an American Elm; and "3" is a White Ash. Keys to tree identification numbers are included with each map.

For further information on any type of campus tree, refer to the Tree Profiles section (pages 37-120) where one-page accounts of each species are arranged alphabetically by common names.

Maps 1-8 are segments of the Center Campus Tree Walk. Maps 9-13 lead you to 26 additional species not found on the Center Campus Tree Walk. Composite maps are included to show where smaller maps are located in relation to the entire campus.

The mapping of all 1,750 individual campus trees is beyond the intention of this book. Such information can be found in the Campus Tree Inventory for Dartmouth College.

Text for the Center Campus Tree Walk begins on page 128. Your travels will start at the "Hiker's Elm" on the corner of the Green opposite the Hanover Inn and finish within a few yards of the same tree.

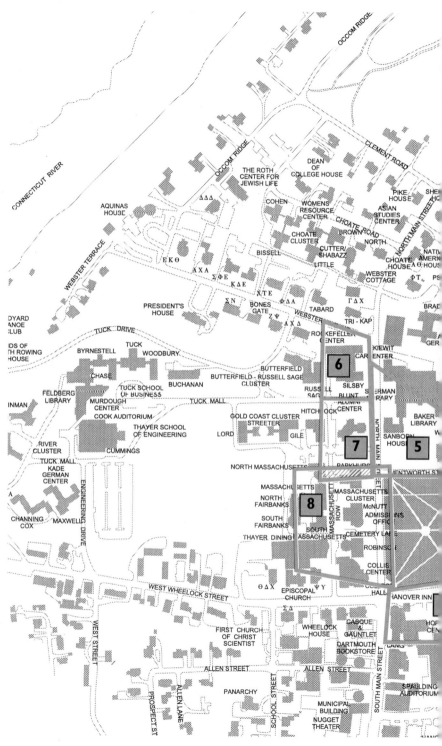

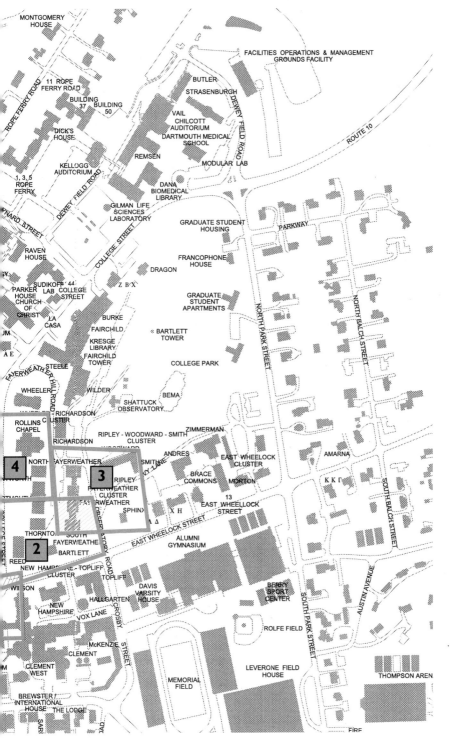

MONTGOMERY
HOUSE

FACILITIES OPERATIONS & MANAGEMENT
GROUNDS FACILITY

BUTLER
STRASENBURGH

11 ROPE
FERRY ROAD

BUILDING
37   BUILDING
50

VAIL
CHILCOTT
AUDITORIUM
DARTMOUTH MEDICAL
SCHOOL

ROUTE 10

DICK'S
HOUSE

REMSEN

MODULAR LAB

KELLOGG
AUDITORIUM

1, 3, 5
ROPE
FERRY

DANA
BIOMEDICAL
LIBRARY

GILMAN LIFE
SCIENCES
LABORATORY

GRADUATE STUDENT
HOUSING

PARKWAY

RAVEN
HOUSE

FRANCOPHONE
HOUSE

DRAGON

SUDIKOFF 44
PARKER LAB COLLEGE
HOUSE   STREET
CHURCH
OF
CHRIST

Z B X

GRADUATE
STUDENT
APARTMENTS

NORTH PARK STREET

NORTH BALCH STREET

LA
CASA

BURKE

FAIRCHILD

BARTLETT
TOWER

KRESGE
LIBRARY

FAIRCHILD
TOWER

COLLEGE PARK

STEELE

WHEELER

WILDER

BEMA

SHATTUCK
OBSERVATORY

RICHARDSON

ROLLINS
CHAPEL

CLUSTER

RICHARDSON

ZIMMERMAN

RIPLEY - WOODWARD - SMITH
CLUSTER

ANDRES

EAST WHEELOCK
CLUSTER

AMARNA

4 NORTH FAYERWEATHER

SMITH

3 RIPLEY
FAYERWEATHER
CLUSTER
FAYERWEATHER

BRACE
COMMONS   MORTON

K K Γ

SPHINX

13
EAST WHEELOCK
STREET

SOUTH BALCH STREET

X H

Δ

THORNTON

SOUTH
FAYERWEATHER

EAST WHEELOCK STREET

ALUMNI
GYMNASIUM

2 BARTLETT

REED

NEW HAMPSHIRE - TOPLIFF
CLUSTER

TOPLIFF

WILSON

DAVIS
VARSITY
HOUSE

BERRY
SPORT
CENTER

AUSTIN AVENUE

NEW
HAMPSHIRE

HALLGARTEN

VOX LANE

CROSBY

ROLFE FIELD

SOUTH PARK STREET

McKENZIE

CLEMENT

CLEMENT
WEST

LEVERONE FIELD
HOUSE

THOMPSON AREN

BREWSTER /
INTERNATIONAL
HOUSE   THE LODGE

MEMORIAL
FIELD

FIRE

ROPE FERRY ROAD

DEWEY FIELD ROAD

COLLEGE STREET

DEWEY FIELD ROAD

FAYERWEATHER HILL ROAD

IVY LANE

TUCK DRIVE

127

Center Campus Tree Walk Map 1

On the southwest, traffic light corner of the Green stands the large "Hiker's Elm," clearly marked with double white blazes. White specifies the Appalachian Trail and the double blaze tells hikers to turn a corner. To begin your 50-50 Tree Walk, follow the Appalachian Trail as it crosses Wheelock Street towards the Hanover Inn. The Trail continues south along Main Street, but you should turn left along Wheelock, go to the walkway just past the Inn's underground parking ramp, and turn right.

This is **Stop A**. Look left at a rugged **Swamp White Oak (57)**, a tree that grows wild in New England. The plaque at its base identifies it as a "dedicated" tree. If it's early to mid-summer, detour down the steps. Immediately on your right a **Kousa Dogwood (19)** may be in bloom. To your left is a spring-blooming **Bradford Pear (60)**.

Continue briefly on the walkway toward Hopkins Center to **Stop B** beside the **Chestnut Oak (53)**. Notice its slender, wavy-edged leaves, so different from the lobed leaves of more familiar Oaks. As you start walking toward **Stop C**, look to your right at the graceful **Eastern Hemlocks (31)**, effectively sited to help provide a transition of scale between the Hopkins Center and the adjacent sunken garden.

At **Stop C** on the entry plaza of the Hopkins Center, admire the naturally sculptured shape of the young **Littleleaf Linden (39)**. The two-tone effect of this tree is caused by the presence of slender, pale green bracts, or differentiated leaves, to which the blossoms and subsequent fruits are attached.

A short detour will lead you to the **Star Magnolia (44)**. Enter the Hopkins Center, descend the steps and turn right into a broad hallway. On your left will be an enclosed courtyard. Tucked into the corner of the courtyard closest to where your hallway makes a left turn is the **Star Magnolia (44)**. Return to **Stop C** on the Hopkins Center entry plaza.

From **Stop C**, you have a sweeping view of the Green with Baker Tower in the background. Along the end of the Green nearest you is a row of seven Maples. The five larger ones are **Sugar Maples (50)**, native trees of New England famous for providing spectacular color in the fall and precious sap for Maple syrup in early spring. The smaller trees anchoring either end of the row are **Red Maples (48)**, struggling to survive in soil compacted by the tread of thousands of passing feet. Their fall leaf color is a spectacular crimson.

At **Stop C**, before proceeding down the steps, glance up at the classic, flaring silhouette of the magnificent **American Elm (22)**. "Percolating pavement" has been placed on its uphill side to help water and air reach the tree's root system. Stop just before the crosswalk at Wheelock Street. To your right is a **Red Oak (56)**, rugged native of the far north. Used extensively on campus, the Red Oak has large leaves with veins which penetrate the tips of the lobes. Cross Wheelock Street, turn right a few feet and walk diagonally left up the wider of the two paved pathways to **Stop D**. Turn to **Map 2**.

Map 1

Area includes: Hanover Inn, Hopkins Center, Hood Museum of Art, Wilson Hall, Dartmouth Green (south side).

Route: Start at the "Hikers Elm" on southwest corner of the Green. Finish at second crossing of East Wheelock Street.

Trees discussed appear in GREEN.

Trees CIRCLED identify those given by the Dartmouth College Class of 1950, including memorial or honorary trees given by Class members or friends.

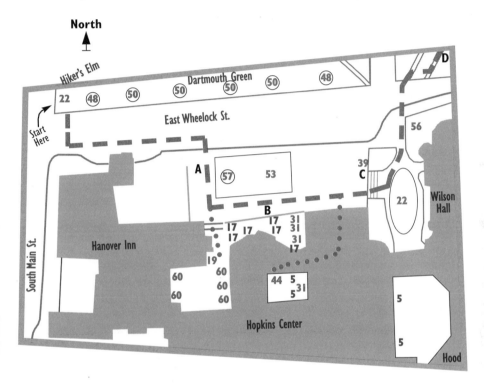

Tree ID Numbers Key

5	Paper Birch	48	Red Maple
17	Crabapple	50	Sugar Maple
19	Kousa Dogwood	53	Chestnut Oak
22	American Elm	56	Red Oak
31	Eastern Hemlock	57	Swamp White Oak
39	Littleleaf Linden	60	"Bradford" Pear
44	Star Magnolia		

Center Campus Tree Walk Map 2

You are now at **Stop D**. About 50 feet to your left (toward the Green) is a very small tree with pendulous branches. Believe it or not, it also is an Elm, a **Camperdown Elm (24)**, created by grafting a scion from one tree onto the root stock of another. Close to the south end of Reed Hall is a large-trunked **English Oak (54)**. This Oak is used extensively in Europe and Great Britain but is somewhat experimental here because of its questionable tolerance to severe cold. Walk uphill a few feet to **Stop E**, located just before the pathway left to the basement entrance of Reed Hall.

To your right, toward Bartlett Hall, is a tall, narrow **Scotch Pine (64)**. The orange tone of its upper trunk and branches adds color to the winter landscape. Before leaving **Stop E**, look uphill at the next deciduous tree on your left. That tree is a **'Crimson King' Norway Maple (47)**, planted for the color contrast provided by its dark foliage.

Now continue uphill to the intersection of walkways at **Stop F**. Slightly left of straight ahead and beyond the large Red Oak, is a well-shaped example of a very young **American 'Liberty' Elm (22)**.

Turn right and walk downhill to **Stop G**. To your right as you face East Wheelock Street is a young shapely **White Spruce (72)**, with sharply pointed needles encircling the twigs. Adjacent to the Spruce is a storm-damaged specimen of a **European Mountainash (51)**. Its early June clusters of white blossoms mature into showy clumps of orange-red berries in the fall.

To see an example of the "King of the Oaks," look slightly uphill. If not disturbed, this well-sited **White Oak (58)**, near the corner of Fayerweather Hall, could live 300 years and top out at a height of 80 feet. Its leaves turn a deep wine color in the fall.

Just beyond **Stop G**, on your right, is a half-grown **Eastern White Pine (62)**, the only Pine east of the Rockies with needles in bundles of five. "The lone Pine above her" in Dartmouth's *Alma Mater* was an Eastern White Pine.

On your way to **Stop H**, you'll pass three tall evergreens, or conifers, on your right—**Norway Spruce (71)**. Branchlets that hang downwards from the branches give these trees a fringed appearance.

So far on your Tree Walk, you've seen five different species of Oak trees. Starting from **Stop H**—if you would like to see the sixth and last species represented on campus—follow the dotted line detour down to Wheelock Street and look to your right, toward the Green. The first street-side tree is a good example of a **Pin Oak (55)** with its downward swooping lower branches and deeply lobed leaves.

If you've taken the detour, backtrack to **Stop H**. Turn to **Map 3**.

Map 2

Area includes: Reed, Thornton, Bartlett, South Fayerweather Halls, Dartmouth Green (east side).

Route: Start at Stop "D" after crossing East Wheelock Street from Wilson Hall. Finish at Stop "H."

Trees discussed appear in GREEN.

Trees CIRCLED identify those given by the Dartmouth College Class of 1950, including memorial or honorary trees given by Class members or friends.

North

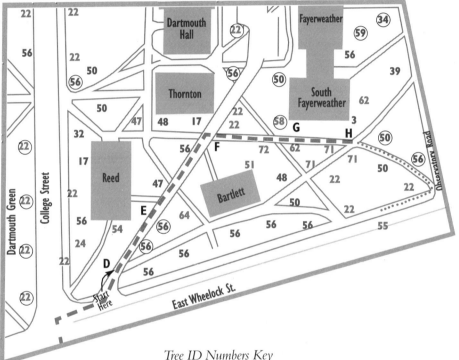

Tree ID Numbers Key

3	White Ash	51	European Mountainash
17	Crabapple	54	English Oak
22	American Elm	55	Pin Oak
24	'Camperdown' Elm	56	Red Oak
32	Honeylocust	58	White Oak
34	Ruby Red Horsechestnut	59	Japanese Pagodatree
39	Littleleaf Linden	62	Eastern White Pine
47	'Crimson King' Norway Maple	64	Scotch Pine
48	Red Maple	71	Norway Spruce
50	Sugar Maple	72	White Spruce

Center Campus Tree Walk Map 3

You are still at **Stop H**. Up to your left, near the corner of Fayerweather Hall, is a **White Ash (3)**. On the branches which overhang the walkway, you can easily see its compound leaves. Each leaf consists of many small leaflets attached to a single stem. To your left, as you proceed downhill toward **Stop I,** you will pass a Red Oak, a tall White Pine and a handsome Little Leaf Linden.

Stop I is on the island in the roadway. Planted here is a **Yellow Birch (8)**. Notice its golden-bronze bark, so different from the bark of the Paper Birch. Beyond the Birch slightly downhill, is a row of young **Austrian Pines (61)**, a good choice for creating a large, dense screen. Towering above and behind the Austrian Pines are three mature **European Larches (37)**, deciduous conifers which shed their needles each fall.

Across the narrow lane from the Austrian Pines is an extremely "long-legged" **Colorado Blue Spruce (69)**. Unfortunately, it is an excellent example of the fact that Blue Spruce are not known for their ability to age gracefully.

Walk uphill to **Stop J**. Close to the right hand side of the street is a densely branched **Katsuratree (35)**. The unusual, heart-shaped leaves will help you identify a much more attractive Katsura later in the Tree Walk.

At **Stop J**, as you look up the service road to the back entrance of Fayerweather Hall, the larger of two small trees on your left is a **Japanese Pagodatree (59)** which blooms in August, a unique feature among the trees on campus. While still facing Fayerweather Hall, look to your right. Beyond the large Red Oak is an **American Beech (4)**, with its identifying smooth, gray bark. The American Beech is a New England native, well adapted to severe cold and capable of living over 200 years. From **Stop J**, walk uphill just beyond North Fayerweather, turn left and continue to **Stop K** near Wentworth Hall. Turn to **Map 4**.

Map 3

Area includes: Fayerweather Cluster, Ripley-Woodward-Smith Cluster
Route: Start at Stop "H," southeast corner of South Fayerweather Hall.
Finish at Stop "K."
Trees discussed are in GREEN.
Trees CIRCLED identify those given by the Dartmouth College Class of 1950, including memorial or honorary trees given by Class members or friends.

North

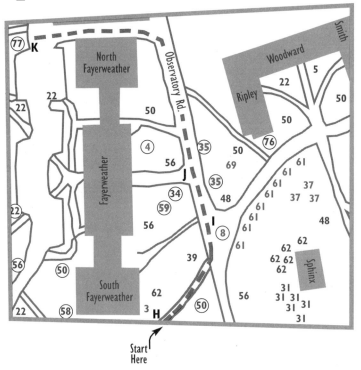

Tree ID Numbers Key

3 White Ash	48 Red Maple
4 American Beech	50 Sugar Maple
5 Paper Birch	56 Red Oak
8 Yellow Birch	58 White Oak
22 American Elm	59 Japanese Pagodatree
31 Eastern Hemlock	61 Austrian Pine
34 Ruby Red Horsechestnut	62 Eastern White Pine
35 Katsuratree	69 Colorado Blue Spruce
37 European Larch	76 Yellowwood
39 Littleleaf Linden	77 Japanese Zelkova

Center Campus Tree Walk Map 4

You are now at **Stop K**. On your left as you face the Green is a **Japanese Zelkova (77)**, often planted as a replacement for American Elms stricken by the Dutch Elm disease.

Follow the sidewalk downhill toward the Green to **Stop L** just past the second tree on your right. As you face the round window of Rollins Chapel, to your right will be a **Korean Mountainash (52)**, considered the best of the Mountainashes for blossoms, berries and fall leaf color. To your left is a smooth-barked **Yellowwood (76)** which in spring is covered with fragrant, foot-long clusters of white flowers. Directly behind you, in front of Wentworth Hall, is a shapely Sugar Maple, displaying the upward-sweeping branch structure so beautiful in the winter.

Continue downhill to **Stop M** at the North College Street sidewalk. To your left is a **Thornless Honeylocust (32)**. This variety of Honeylocust has yellowish-green, compound leaves made up of many tiny leaflets.

Now face the center of the Green. The first street tree to the left of the pathway leading to the center is a **Common Hackberry (29)**, a hardy urban tree with a deep root system that does not tend to lift pavements.

Don't cross North College Street at your present location. Turn right and walk in front of Rollins Chapel to the next painted crosswalk. This is **Stop N**. Diagonally to your right as you look north along the street toward a white church steeple, are three interesting species. The evergreen with the scale-like foliage is an **Arborvitae (1)**, or Northern White Cedar. Native Americans knew this species to be an excellent source of vitamin C.

Beyond the Arborvitae is a **Crabapple (17)** of the 'Liset' variety which displays single-type red blossoms in the spring. Many different kinds of Crabapples provide the campus with spectacular bloom in the spring, colorful fruit in the fall, and structural beauty in the winter when snow adorns their branches. Across the walkway to the left of the Crabapple is a **Ruby Red Horsechestnut (34)**. A mature, 40-foot tree of this species is a gorgeous sight in the springtime when covered with large clumps of pinkish-red blossoms.

Cross College Street at the crosswalk and pause at **Stop O**. If it's color season, be sure to look north toward the church steeple. In front of the brick fraternity house (SAE) stands a Sugar Maple that is magnificent every fall. Turn to **Map 5**.

Map 4

Area includes: Dartmouth Hall (north), Wentworth Hall, Rollins Chapel, Dartmouth Green (east side).
Route: Start at Stop "K" on the northeast corner of Dartmouth Hall.
Finish at Stop "O."
Trees discussed appear in GREEN.
Trees CIRCLED identify those given by the Dartmouth College Class of 1950, including memorial or honorary trees given by Class members or friends.

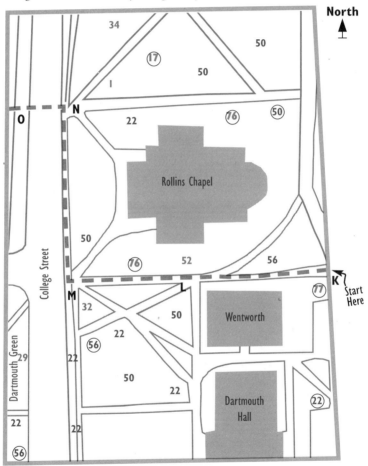

Tree ID Numbers Key

1 Arborvitae	50 Sugar Maple
17 Crabapple	52 Korean Mountainash
22 American Elm	**56 Red Oak**
29 Common Hackberry	76 Yellowwood
32 Thornless Honeylocust	77 Japanese Zelkova
34 Ruby Red Horsechestnut	

Center Campus Tree Walk Map 5

From **Stop O,** walk behind Webster Hall (Rauner Library) and across the lawn of Baker Library to the intersection of the walkways near the corner of Sanborn House. As you face toward North Main Street, the stairway into Sanborn House is on your right.

Follow the diagonal walkway to your left and pause at **Stop P** which is found at the intersection of the diagonal walkway and an unpaved path. Two large Elms stand between you and North Main Street. The right hand Elm, closer to Sanborn House, is an American Elm that shows the result of severe damage it suffered from a windstorm in 1999. The left hand tree is a **Slippery Elm (25)**. Its slippery inner bark was the source of medicines used by Native Americans and early settlers.

Turn right and follow the unpaved path that leads to the Main Street corner of Sanborn House. This is **Stop Q** beside a small **Crabapple (17)** that displays yellow fruit in the fall. Follow the Main Street sidewalk, heading away from the Green, and bear right on a walkway just beyond Sanborn House.

You've reached **Stop R**. To your right, tucked into a little courtyard bounded by Sanborn and Baker Library, is a handsome **Hawthorn (30)**, which bears clusters of white blossoms in the spring and shiny red fruit in the fall. This specimen is a Washington Hawthorn rather than the 'Toba' Hawthorn which has been more frequently planted on campus in recent years.

As you walk toward the Library steps, you'll notice that both sides of the Main Street entrance to the Library are flanked by sizable Crabapples and Arborvitae. The former provide spring bloom and fall berries, and the latter remain green throughout the winter.

At **Stop S**, there's an old, declining American Elm. Beneath it is an interesting plaque dedicating the tree to a member of the Dartmouth Class of 1879.

Cross North Main Street with care to **Stop T**. Turn to **Map 6**.

Map 5

Area includes: Baker Library (south), Sanborn House, Baker Lawn, Dartmouth Green (north side), Webster Hall/Rauner Library.
Route: Start at Stop "O."
Finish after crossing North Main Street to Stop "T."
Trees discussed appear in GREEN.
Trees CIRCLED identify those given by the Dartmouth College Class of 1950, including memorial or honorary trees given by Class members or friends.

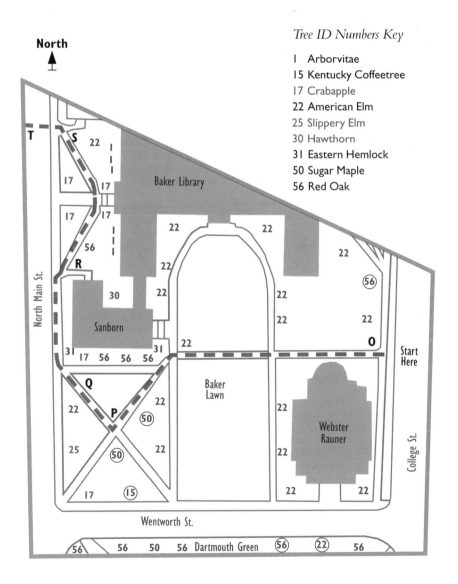

North

Tree ID Numbers Key

1 Arborvitae
15 Kentucky Coffeetree
17 Crabapple
22 American Elm
25 Slippery Elm
30 Hawthorn
31 Eastern Hemlock
50 Sugar Maple
56 Red Oak

Center Campus Tree Walk Map 6

Stop T is located at the intersection of the North Main Street sidewalk and the walkway along the Tuck Drive side of Silsby Hall. With Main Street behind you, look left at a tree close to Tuck Drive. It's a **Black Walnut (74)**, injured in the summer storm of 1999. Many trees such as White Pines and Crabapples are unable to survive if planted too close to this valuable North American native.

Follow the walkway beside Silsby Hall until you reach **Stop U** at the brick walk. To your left toward Tuck Drive is the well-shaped **Katsuratree (35)** which was mentioned back at **Stop J**.

From **Stop U**, you can consider a short detour.

If it's late spring, you may want to turn right between Silsby and Russell Sage Halls. Follow the brick walk toward the archway of Rockefeller Hall. On your left will be one Hawthorn and several Crabapples, all of which provide spring bloom and fall fruit.

Beyond the arch, the last two trees on your left before Webster Street are young **'Kwanzan' Cherries (13)**. These trees are famous in Washington, D.C., for their profusion of deep pink, double flowers.

Return to **Stop U**. Turn to **Map 7**.

Tree ID Numbers Key

13 Kwanzan Cherry	35 Katsuratree
17 Crabapple	47 'Crimson King' Norway Maple
22 American Elm	50 Sugar Maple
30 Hawthorn	55 Pin Oak
32 Honeylocust	74 Black Walnut

Map 6

Area includes: Rockefeller Center, Silsby Hall, Russell Sage Hall (east end)
Route: Start at Stop "T" after crossing North Main Street from Baker Library. Finish
    at Stop "U."
Trees discussed appear in GREEN.
Trees CIRCLED identify those given by the Dartmouth College Class of 1950,
including memorial or honorary trees given by Class members or friends.

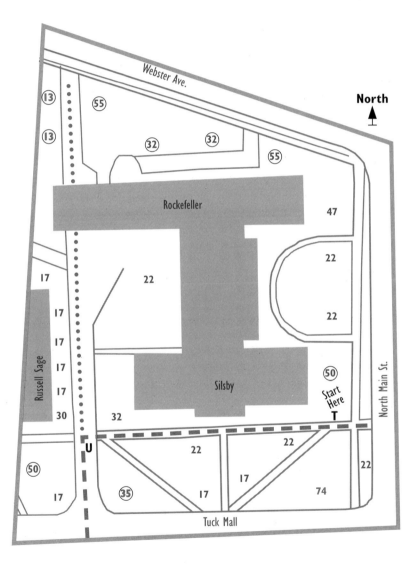

Center Campus Tree Walk Map 7

From **Stop U**, cross Tuck Drive and enter Massachusetts Row Lane between Hitchcock Hall on the right and the white Blunt Alumni Center on the left. Turn left on the walkway beside Blunt and proceed a very short distance to **Stop V**.

Straight ahead of you, just left of the walk, is an aging **Sweet Birch (6)**. Oil of wintergreen was once distilled from the stems and bark of this species. Between Blunt and Tuck Drive, there are four tall trees in a row. The huge, shaggy-barked tree farthest left is a **Silver Maple (49)**, one of the three largest trees on campus.

To the right of the huge Silver Maple, there's a large tree with uniquely fan-shaped leaves. You're looking at the oldest **Ginkgo (28)** on campus. The Ginkgo is the only surviving species of many kinds of broad-leafed trees that thrived during the days of the dinosaurs.

To the right of the Ginkgo stands a Red Oak. Towards Main Street from the Red Oak is a tall **Kentucky Coffeetree (15)** with a shaggy silhouette. Measuring up to 36 inches in length, its compound leaves are the largest on campus.

Continue walking towards Main Street. On your right, just before you turn right along Main toward the Green, is a half-grown **Green Ash (2)**. Like the Coffeetree, it has compound leaves made up of several leaflets arranged feather-like along a central stem.

Turn right on the Main Street sidewalk and continue to the walkway on your right which leads to the entrance of the Blunt Alumni Center. This is **Stop W**. Flanking the columns on the Main Street end of Blunt are two multi-trunked **Japanese Tree Lilacs (38)**. Their large white springtime blossoms, displayed against deep green leaves, are a beautiful complement to the white building. Also well chosen to enhance the attractiveness of this architecture are the graceful clumps of **Paper Birch (5)** sited near the entrance. Continue walking toward the Green along the sidewalk to **Stop X**. Turn to **Map 8**.

Tree ID Numbers Key

2	Green Ash	38	Japanese Tree Lilac
5	Paper Birch	47	Norway Maple
6	Sweet Birch	49	Silver Maple
15	Kentucky Coffeetree	52	Korean Mountainash
17	Crabapple	50	Sugar Maple
22	American Elm	56	Red Oak
24	Camperdown Elm	62	Eastern White Pine
27	Fringetree	76	Yellowwood
28	Ginkgo		

Map 7

Area includes: Blunt Alumni Center, Parkhurst, Hitchcock.

Route: Start by crossing Tuck Mall from Rockefeller Center toward Blunt. Finish at Stop "X" by the circular walkway to Parkhurst Hall.

Trees discussed appear in GREEN.

Trees CIRCLED identify those given by the Dartmouth College Class of 1950, including memorial or honorary trees given by Class members or friends.

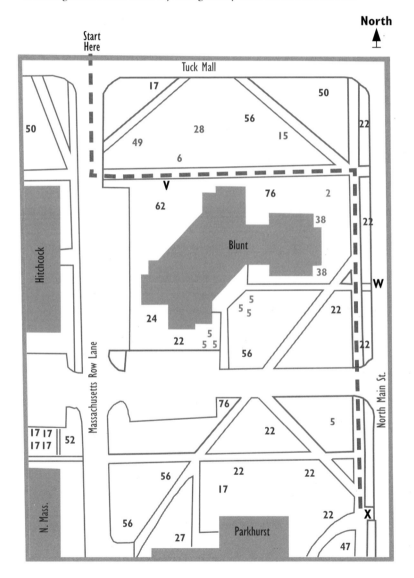

Center Campus Tree Walk Map 8

Stop X is by the circular walkway to Parkhurst Hall. Immediately to your right is a **Norway Maple (47)**. At **Stop E** we saw an example of the 'Crimson King' variety of this species with its rusty-red leaves. The common form of Norway Maple seen here has broad, green leaves with a hint of red in their stems.

Continue walking along Main Street beneath the famous Parkhurst Elm which is at least 130 years old, 14 feet around, and more than 90 feet tall.

Stop Y is just after you turn right on the walkway between Parkhurst and McNutt Halls. Close to you on the McNutt side of the walk is a large **English Elm (23)**. See how its branch pattern differs from the upward-sweeping silhouette of the Parkhurst American Elm. Ahead of you on the right is a **Fringetree (27)**. If the tree is in bloom, sit down on the bench close by and enjoy its delicate beauty and fragrance.

Follow the walkway away from the Green toward the Massachusetts Row dormitories. Turn left on the roadway and walk a very short distance until the covered passageway between Massachusetts Hall and South Massachusetts Hall is to your right. A detour through that passageway will lead you to the **Pissard Plum (66)**, planted to the right of the stairway of Fairbanks North. Return through the passageway, turn right and walk just beyond Thayer Hall to **Stop Z**.

With your back to Collis Center, you'll notice a wing on the left side of Thayer Hall. Topping the roof line of the wing is a **Black Locust (40)**. It may be called a weed tree, but it can grow in soils and locations where most other species have no chance of survival.

You've now met about two-thirds of the tree species on the Dartmouth College campus. All other species are located for you on additional maps in this book (see pages 145-157). Complete your Center Campus Tree Walk by passing between Robinson Hall and Collis Center back to Main Street. You'll find yourself almost across from the "Hiker's Elm" where the Tree Walk started.

Tree ID Numbers Key

2	Green Ash	34	Ruby Red Horsechestnut
3	White Ash	40	Black Locust
5	Paper Birch	47	Norway Maple
17	Crabapple	50	Sugar Maple
22	American Elm	55	Pin Oak
23	English Elm	56	Red Oak
27	Fringetree	62	Eastern White Pine
30	Hawthorn	66	Pissard Plum
32	Honeylocust	76	Yellowwood

Map 8

Area includes: Parkhurst, McNutt and Robinson Halls, Massachusetts Row, Thayer Dining Hall, Collis Center, Dartmouth Green (west side).

Route: Start at Stop "X" in front of Parkhurst. Finish on the North Main Street side of Collis Center across from the "Hiker's Elm."

Trees discussed appear in GREEN.

Trees CIRCLED identify those given by the Dartmouth College Class of 1950, including memorial or honorary trees given by Class members or friends.

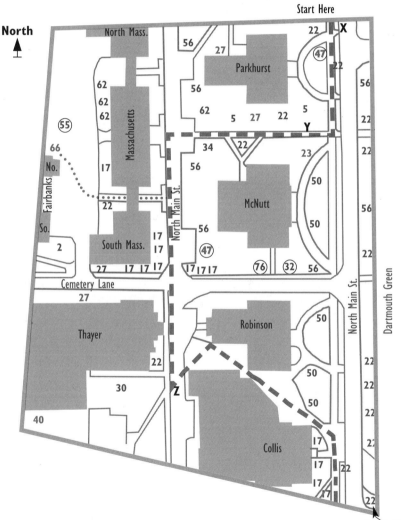

Trees Not Included on the Center Campus Tree Walk

The 26 Dartmouth College campus trees listed below are not included on the Center Campus Tree Walk (Maps 1-8). To locate examples of each of these trees, refer to Maps 9-13 on the following pages.

ID Number	Common Name	Map Number
7	'Whitespire' Birch	13
9	Ohio Buckeye	12
10	Butternut	10
11	Northern Catalpa	11
12	Black Cherry	13
14	Amur Chokecherry	13
16	Amur Cork Tree	11
18	Cornelian Cherry Dogwood	12
20	Pagoda Dogwood	13
21	Douglasfir	11
26	White Fir	10
30	English 'Toba' Hawthorn	11
33	Eastern Hophornbeam	11
36	Eastern Larch	10
41	Amur Maackia	11
42	'Merrill' Magnolia	11
43	Saucer Magnolia	9
45	Amur Maple	12
46	Ashleaf Maple	13
63	Red Pine	9
65	London Planetree	11
67	Dawn Redwood	11
68	Downy Serviceberry	11
70	Engelmann Spruce	11
73	Black Tupelo	11
75	'Tristis' Weeping Willow	10

On Maps 9-13, the trees listed above are identified by their Tree Identification numbers. Dots are used to designate the position of other trees in the area.

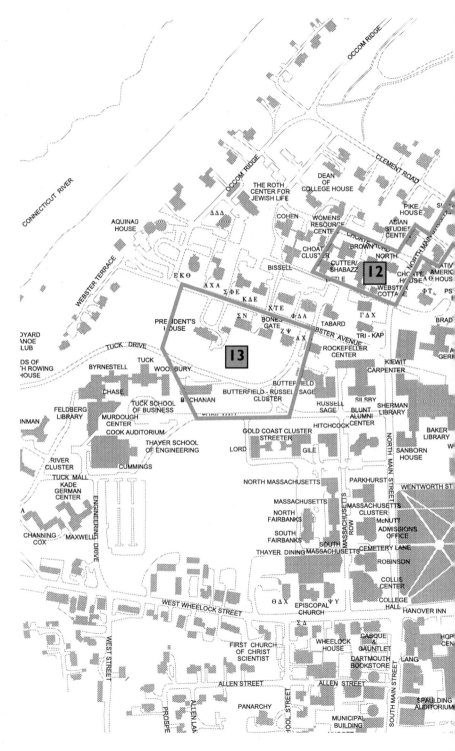

CONNECTICUT RIVER

OCCOM RIDGE

CLEMENT ROAD

OCCOM RIDGE

THE ROTH
CENTER FOR
JEWISH LIFE

DEAN
OF
COLLEGE HOUSE

PIKE
HOUSE

AQUINAS
HOUSE

COHEN

WOMENS
RESOURCE
CENTER

ASIAN
STUDIES
CENTER

Δ Δ Δ

CHOATE ROAD

BROWN

CHOATE
CLUSTER

NORTH

ΕΚΘ

BISSELL

CUTTER/
SHABAZZ

CHOATE
HOUSE

AMERICAN
HOUS

WEBSTER
TERRACE

ΑΧΑ

ΣΦΕ

ΦΤ

PS

12

ΚΔΕ

WEBSTER
COTTAGE

ΧΤΕ

OYARD
ANOE
LUB

PRESIDENT'S
HOUSE

ΣΝ

BONE
GATE

ΦΔΑ

ΓΔΧ

BRAD

DS OF
H ROWING
HOUSE

TUCK DRIVE

ΖΨ

TABARD

WEBSTER AVENUE

ΑΧ

TRI-KAP

GERI

BYRNESTELL

TUCK

WOODBURY

13

ROCKEFELLER
CENTER

KIEWIT

CHASE

TUCK SCHOOL
OF BUSINESS

BUCHANAN

BUTTERFIELD
BUTTERFIELD-RUSSELL SAGE
CLUSTER

CARPENTER

RUSSELL
SAGE

SILSBY

SHERMAN
LIBRARY

INMAN

FELDBERG
LIBRARY

MURDOUGH
CENTER

BLUNT
ALUMNI
HITCHCOCK CENTER

BAKER
LIBRARY

COOK AUDITORIUM

GOLD COAST CLUSTER
STREETER

SANBORN
HOUSE

THAYER SCHOOL
OF ENGINEERING

LORD

GILE

RIVER
CLUSTER

CUMMINGS

NORTH MAIN STREET

TUCK MALL
KADE
GERMAN
CENTER

NORTH MASSACHUSETTS

PARKHURST

WENTWORTH ST

MASSACHUSETTS

MASSACHUSETTS
CLUSTER

CHANNING
COX

MAXWELL

ENGINEERING DRIVE

NORTH
FAIRBANKS

MASSACHUSETTS ROW

McNUTT

ADMISSIONS
OFFICE

SOUTH
FAIRBANKS

CEMETERY LANE

THAYER DINING

SOUTH
MASSACHUSETTS

ROBINSON

COLLIS
CENTER

WEST WHEELOCK STREET

ΘΔΧ

EPISCOPAL
CHURCH

ΨΥ

COLLEGE
HALL

HANOVER INN

WEST STREET

ΣΔ

FIRST CHURCH
OF CHRIST
SCIENTIST

WHEELOCK
HOUSE

CASQUE
&
GAUNTLET

HOP
CEN

DARTMOUTH
BOOKSTORE

LANG

ALLEN STREET

ALLEN STREET

SOUTH MAIN STREET

PANARCHY

SCHOOL STREET

ALLEN LANE

PROSPE

MUNICIPAL
BUILDING

SPAULDING
AUDITORIUM

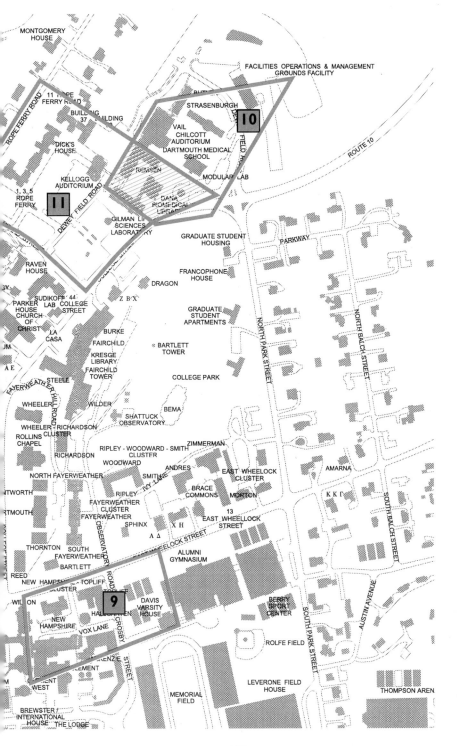

MONTGOMERY HOUSE

FACILITIES OPERATIONS & MANAGEMENT GROUNDS FACILITY

11 ROPE FERRY ROAD

BUILDING 37

BUILDING

STRASENBURGH

VAIL
CHILCOTT AUDITORIUM
DARTMOUTH MEDICAL SCHOOL

10

DICK'S HOUSE

REMSEN

MODULAR LAB

ROUTE 10

KELLOGG AUDITORIUM

1, 3, 5 ROPE FERRY

11

DEWEY FIELD ROAD

GILMAN LIFE SCIENCES LABORATORY

DANA BIOMEDICAL LIBRARY

GRADUATE STUDENT HOUSING

PARKWAY

RAVEN HOUSE

DRAGON

FRANCOPHONE HOUSE

SUDIKOFF 44
PARKER LAB COLLEGE
HOUSE STREET
CHURCH OF CHRIST
LA CASA

Z B X

BURKE

GRADUATE STUDENT APARTMENTS

FAIRCHILD

BARTLETT TOWER

KRESGE LIBRARY
FAIRCHILD TOWER

COLLEGE PARK

STEELE

WHEELER

WILDER

BEMA

SHATTUCK OBSERVATORY

WHEELER RICHARDSON
ROLLINS CHAPEL
CLUSTER

RICHARDSON

RIPLEY - WOODWARD - SMITH CLUSTER

ZIMMERMAN

WOODWARD

ANDRES

NORTH FAYERWEATHER

SMITH

IVY LANE

EAST WHEELOCK CLUSTER

AMARNA

TWORTH

RIPLEY

FAYERWEATHER CLUSTER
FAYERWEATHER

BRACE COMMONS

MORTON

K K Γ

SOUTH BALCH STREET

RTMOUTH

SPHINX

X H

13 EAST WHEELOCK STREET

A Δ

THORNTON SOUTH FAYERWEATHER
BARTLETT

OBSERVATORY ROAD

WHEELOCK STREET

ALUMNI GYMNASIUM

REED

NEW HAMPSHIRE TOPLIFF
CLUSTER

WIL ON

9

HALL

DAVIS VARSITY HOUSE

BERRY SPORT CENTER

AUSTIN AVENUE

NEW HAMPSHIRE

VOX LANE

CROSBY STREET

ROLFE FIELD

SOUTH PARK STREET

KENZIE STREET

EMENT

WEST

MEMORIAL FIELD

LEVERONE FIELD HOUSE

THOMPSON AREN

BREWSTER / INTERNATIONAL HOUSE
THE LODGE

NORTH PARK STREET

NORTH BALCH STREET

Tree Map 9

Area includes: New Hampshire Hall; Topliff Hall; Heating Plant; Tennis courts west of Alumni Gymnasium; North end of Memorial Field.

Two trees not identified on the Center Campus Tree Walk can be found on Map 9.

Saucer Magnolia (43)

The location of this tree in a protected corner close to the Heating Plant allows it to survive northern winters.

Red Pine (63)

Inside the fence along the north end of Memorial Field there's a row of young Pines. The larger trees on either end are Red Pines. Between the Red Pines are Austrian Pines. A tall Red Pine and a tall Scotch Pine can be seen close together near the west end of Alumni Gymnasium.

Map 9

North

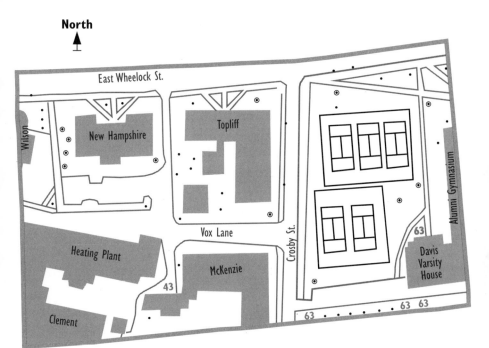

Tree ID Numbers Key

43 Saucer Magnolia
63 Red Pine

Trees CIRCLED identify those given by the Dartmouth College Class of 1950, including memorial or honorary trees given by Class members or friends.

Tree Map 10

Area includes: Part of Dartmouth Medical School complex; Part of area north of Medical School.

Four trees not identified on the Center Campus Tree Walk can be found on Map 10.

Butternut (10)

Close to being classified as an endangered species, the Butternut is a relative of the more handsome Black Walnut.

White Fir (26)

Firs are closely related to Pines but have flat needles with rounded tips rather than sharp needles in bundles.

Eastern Larch (36)

Most people know this deciduous conifer as a Tamarack. Extreme cold doesn't bother the Tamarack, but the tree cannot survive sustained periods of heat.

'Tristis' Weeping Willow (75)

This cultivated variety of a Weeping Willow should thrive in its streamside location.

Tree ID Numbers Key

10 Butternut
26 White Fir
36 Eastern Larch
75 'Tristis' Weeping Willow

Map 10

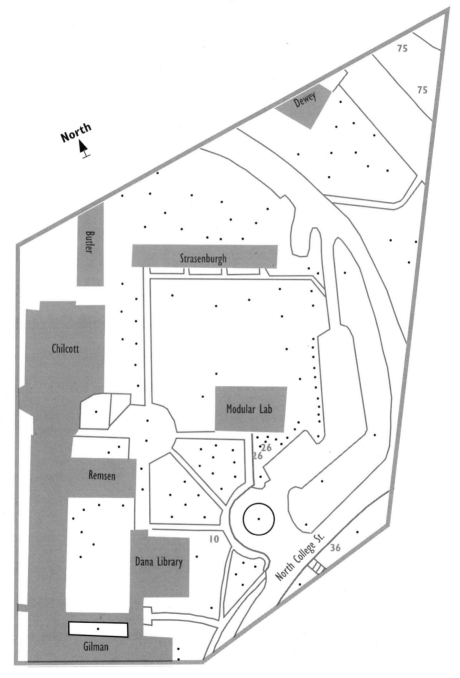

Tree Map 11

Area includes: Gilman Life Sciences Laboratory and Kellogg Auditorium; Dick's House and the Rope Ferry Road buildings; Maynard Lot, bounded by Rope Ferry Road, Maynard Street and North College Street.

Thanks to the interest and guidance of Dartmouth's Department of Biological Sciences, this area of recently planted trees is a gold mine of varied species. Twelve trees not identified on the Center Campus Tree Walk can be found on Map 11.

Northern Catalpa (11)
Orchid-like blossoms of the Catalpa are dramatic in the springtime.

Amur Corktree (16)
At maturity, this Siberian native develops a massive structure and handsome bark.

Douglasfir (21)
The Douglasfir is not a Fir. For an explanation, see page 59.

'Toba' Hawthorn (30)
The 'Toba' is a highly successful cultivar of the Hawthorn with blossoms which gradually change from white to pink.

Eastern Hophornbeam (33)
The Hophornbeam is a small, graceful tree with uniquely shaped seed clusters.

Amur Maackia (41)
The name "Amur" refers to the Amur River drainage basin in northeast Asia and assures us that the tree is hardy in cold climates.

'Merrill' Magnolia (42)
The group of trees to which this cross-breed Magnolia belongs is thought to have existed on earth almost as long as the Ginkgo.

London Planetree (65)
A giant among eastern trees, the London Planetree could grow 80-100 feet tall.

Dawn Redwood (67)
Read the story of this fascinating species on page 110.

Downy Serviceberry (68)
This small tree ranks among the best when it comes to fall color.

Engelmann Spruce (70)
Rocky Mountain specimens have been known to live 500 years.

Black Tupelo (73)
In autumn, the Black Tupelo puts on a show of variegated color that can equal the brilliance of a Red Maple.

Map 11

North

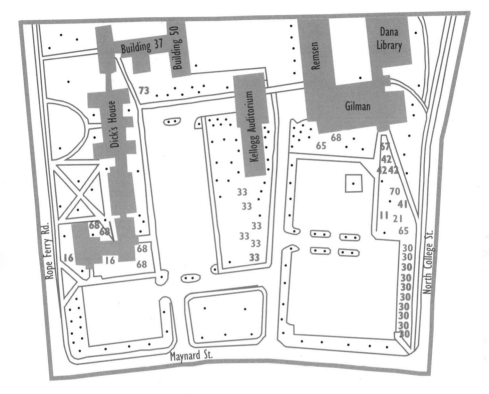

Tree ID Numbers Key

11	Northern Catalpa	42	'Merrill' Magnolia
16	Amur Corktree	65	London Planetree
21	Douglasfir*	67	Dawn Redwood
30	'Toba' Hawthorn	68	Downy Serviceberry
33	Eastern Hophornbeam	70	Engelmann Spruce
41	Amur Maackia	73	Black Tupelo

*A replacement Douglasfir is planned at this site in 2000.

Tree Map 12

Area includes: North Main Street including Native American House, Choate House, Cutter, Brown, North and Little Halls, Webster Cottage.

Three trees not identified on the Fifty-Fifty Tree Walk can be found on Map 12.

Ohio Buckeye (9)

The campus specimen could be a crossbreed between an Ohio Buckeye and a Horsechestnut, but its leaves and nut closely resemble those of the Buckeye.

Cornelian Cherry Dogwood (18)

It's a small, shrub-like tree that more than earns its keep by producing masses of tiny yellow blossoms in the early spring.

Amur Maple (45)

The Amur Maple is one of the lesser known gems of autumn, capable of putting on a dazzling display of orange and red.

Map 12

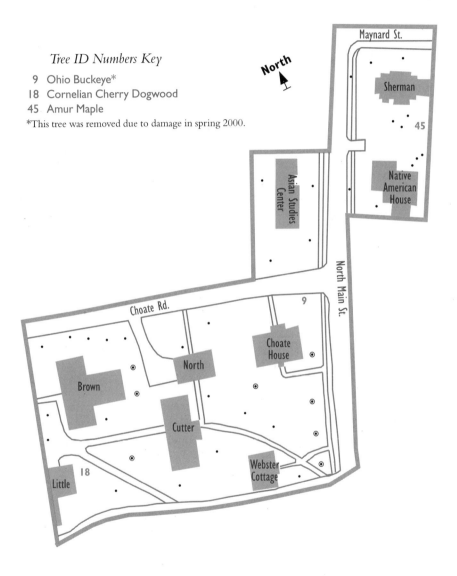

Tree ID Numbers Key

9 Ohio Buckeye*
18 Cornelian Cherry Dogwood
45 Amur Maple

*This tree was removed due to damage in spring 2000.

Trees CIRCLED identify those given by the Dartmouth College Class of 1950, including
memorial or honorary trees given by Class members or friends.

Tree Map 13

Area includes: Webster Avenue and Tuck Drive including the President's House and the east end of the Tuck School campus.

Note: Among the five trees on Map 13, three—the 'Whitespire' Birch, the Amur Chokecherry and the Pagoda Dogwood—are located on the grounds of the President's House and may be viewed on community tours scheduled during June and July. Dates and times of tours are found in the calendar of events appearing in the June-July issues of "Vox of Dartmouth," a biweekly College news publication.

Five trees not identified on the Center Campus Tree Walk can be found on Map 13.

'Whitespire' Birch (7)

The 'Whitespire' Birch, at the President's House, is a clone of a disease-resistant Birch raised at the University of Wisconsin.

Black Cherry (12)

A multi-talented tree, the Black Cherry provides valuable lumber, cough syrup, attractive blossoms and an abundance of food for wildlife.

Amur Chokecherry (14)

Another rugged native of northeast Asia, the Amur Chokecherry has handsome, copper-colored bark. In addition to the species located at the President's House, a beautiful example of this tree can also be seen in front of the Nugget Theater on Main Street, Hanover.

Pagoda Dogwood (20)

Of the three species of Dogwood on campus, the Pagoda is the northernmost native. The black fruit of this species, located at the President's House, is an important food source for wildlife.

Ashleaf Maple (46)

Often considered a weed tree, the Ashleaf Maple, or Boxelder, is able to grow where most other trees have little chance of surviving.

Map 13

North

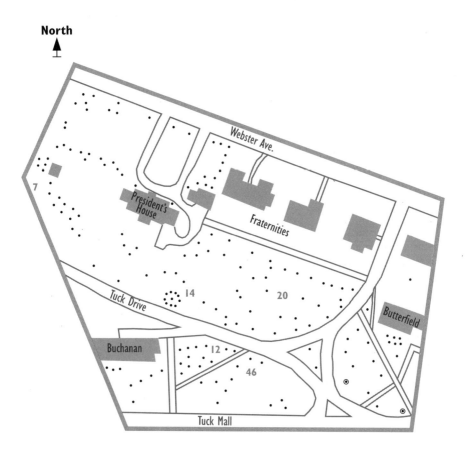

Tree ID Numbers Key

  7 'Whitespire' Birch
12 Black Cherry
14 Amur Chokecherry
20 Pagoda Dogwood
46 Ashleaf Maple

Trees CIRCLED identify those given by the Dartmouth College Class of 1950, including memorial or honorary trees given by Class members or friends.

157

Tree Trivia
Fascinating Facts About the Trees of Dartmouth

The *Inventory of Trees on the Dartmouth College Campus* identifies over 1750 trees, representing more than 75 species. Campus plantings include four species of Birch, three of Dogwood, four of Elm, three of Magnolia, six of Maple, five of Pine, four of Spruce and six of Oak.

Three Silver Maples, with trunks measuring over five feet in diameter, are the largest trees on campus. Next largest are several American Elms.

New cultivars of the American Elm, such as the 'Liberty' and 'Princeton,' have already been planted on campus. At Dartmouth's organic farm, seedling American 'Liberty' Elms are being raised for future use.

The Old Pine, removed in 1895 due to wind and lightning damage (the repaired stump remains on Observatory Hill near Bartlett Tower), and the Parkhurst Elm, which was planted about 1870 beside North Main Street and still stands tall near Parkhurst Hall, are two trees that span the entire history of Dartmouth College.

Larches in the Bema are thought to be the tallest in New England.

The largest leaf on campus, a doubly compound leaf measuring up to 36 by 24 inches, belongs to the Kentucky Coffeetree.

The smallest leaves on campus are the 1/8-to-1/4 inch long scales of the Arborvitae. These tiny scales join together to create the tree's fan-shaped foliage.

Large trees on campus that display the most dramatic bloom include the Yellow-wood, the Catalpa, the Littleleaf Linden, the Black Locust and the Sugar Maple.

Trees native to the Amur River region of Siberia have no trouble surviving winter temperatures in New Hampshire. On campus, representing that region, are the Amur Maple, Amur Corktree, Amur Chokecherry, and Amur Maackia.

Eastern White Pines taller than Baker Tower (210 feet) once grew on the Green. "The Lone Pine above her," celebrated in Dartmouth's *Alma Mater*, was a White Pine.

The Ginkgo is the sole surviving broad-leafed species that dates from the time of the dinosaurs, but all of Dartmouth's evergreens (conifers) date back to that era.

There are 14 different species of needle or scale-leafed "evergreens" on campus.

"Evergreens" should really be called "conifers." Three of Dartmouth's conifers, the Eastern Larch (Tamarack), European Larch, and Dawn Redwood, are deciduous. Each loses its needles in the fall and regrows them in the spring.

Trees not rated as cold-hardy in northern New England can sometimes be planted successfully on campus if carefully sited in warmer mini-climatic locations such as the inner courtyards of the Hopkins Center.

In late October, the leaves of the Ginkgo fall en masse. Dartmouth students have been known to hold a lottery to pick the day when the Ginkgo leaves fall.

Glossary of Tree Related Terms

Alternate leaves—Leaves arranged along a twig in a staggered, non-opposite pattern, e.g., Elm.

Bark—Outer protective tissue of woody root, trunk or branch

Berry—Fruit with soft flesh covering a seed, e.g., Cherry, Hawthorn.

Blade—The broad, flat, thin portion of a leaf attached to a stem or petiole.

Bract—A leaf modified in color, shape or texture, e.g., Dogwood, Linden.

Branch—A woody, secondary limb from a main trunk.

Branch sport—A genetically mutated branch which develops unique characteristics, such as leaf color, e.g., Pissard Plum.

Cambium—The thin layer of cells between the inner bark and the sapwood of a tree, where new cells are produced and older cells differentiate and become cells of either bark or sapwood.

Clone—A genetically identical copy; a tree propagated asexually from a single original.

Clustered—Crowded groups of leaves or needles, e.g., Larch.

Columnar—Fastigiate, slender and tall, e.g., English Oak 'Fastigiata.'

Compacted soil—Soil so tightly compressed that it partially or completely prevents oxygen and water from reaching the root systems of trees.

Compound leaf—Composed of three or more leaflets attached to a single midrib. The entire complex is considered one leaf, e.g., White Ash.

Cone—Woody fruit with stiff, overlapping scales that protect the seeds.

Conifer—A cone-bearing tree, e.g., Spruce, Pine.

Crown—The branches and foliage portion of a tree.

Cultivar—A named and cultivated variety of a species, e.g., English Hawthorn 'Toba.'

Deciduous—A tree which sheds its leaves or needles annually, e.g., Mountainash, Dawn Redwood.

Doubly compound—A compound leaf with a primary stem which branches into lateral stems, e.g., Kentucky Coffeetree; Honeylocust.

Doubly serrated—Leaf margins on which teeth are subdivided into smaller teeth; doubly toothed, e.g., Hophornbeam.

Doubly toothed—See Doubly serrated.

Evergreen—Holding green leaves of any type throughout the year, e.g., Pine, Arborvitae.

Exfoliating—Bark which flakes or peels, e.g., Birch, London Planetree.

Family—A closely related group of genera, e.g., the Beech family which includes the Beech genus and the Oak genus.

Fastigiate—See Columnar.

Fissure—Long, deep crack in bark.

Genus—Closely related group of species; the first and capitalized word of the scientific name, e.g., *Abies* as in *Abies concolor*.

Grafting—The joining of a cutting (scion) from one tree species to the rootstock of another species, e.g.,'Camperdown' Elm.

Hardiness—A tree's ability to withstand extremes of heat and cold, e.g., a Larch which is cold-hardy.

Hardiness Zone—In this book, only cold hardiness is considered. A cold Hardiness Zone is the area throughout which winter temperature extremes can be expected to fall within a specified range such as -20° to -30°F. Hardiness zones can also be defined in terms of highest summer temperatures.

Hybrid—A tree resulting from the crossbreeding of parents belonging to different species, e.g., Ruby Red Horsechestnut, Saucer Magnolia.

Intolerance—See Tolerance.

Leaf—The food-producing unit of foliage that is attached by a non-woody stem to woody branches or twigs.

Leaflet—One of the leaflike subdivisions which together make up a compound leaf.

Legume—Member of the pea/bean family; trees with pea-like flowers and pods, e.g., Pagodatree, Black Locust.

Lenticel—Corky growth on young bark through which air passes into twigs or branches, e.g., Cherry.

Lobes—Sizable projections on the leaf margin which are divided by sinuses, e.g., Maple, Oak.

Margin—The edge of a leaf which can be described as toothed, untoothed, wavy, lobed etc.

Midrib—The mid-vein of a leaf or leaflet.

Naturalized—Referring to a non-native tree which seeds itself and grows wild among native trees.

Needle—The slender leaf of many conifers, e.g., Spruce, Fir.

Node—A point on a stem at which a leaf or cluster of leaves is attached.

Nut—Fruit in a husk, e.g., Black Walnut, Butternut.

Opposite leaves—Leaves growing in pairs opposite one another along a twig or branch, e.g., Dogwood.

Ovule—A small structure in the cell of an ovary containing the egg. When fertilized it becomes a seed.

Paleobotanist—A scientist who uses fossil records to study ancient plants.

Palmately compound—A leaf with leaflets radiating fan-like from a common point, e.g., Ohio Buckeye.

Petiole—Non-woody stem or stalk of a leaf, flower or fruit.

Pinnately compound—A leaf with leaflets arranged featherlike on opposite sides of a stem, e.g., Ash.

Pod—The dry, linear fruit of a legume.

Root system—The underground supporting segment of a tree.

Rootstock—The root system and lower trunk portion of one tree onto which a cutting (scion) from another tree is grafted.

Samara—Seed with a membranous wing, e.g., Maple, Ash, Elm.

Scion—A cutting from one tree which is grafted onto the root system of another tree.

Seed—A fertilized and mature ovule, containing an embryonic tree.

Serrated—See Toothed.

Sheath—A tubular envelope which binds together bundles of needles, e.g., Pine.

Simple—Referring to a leaf with a single blade.

Sinus—The space betwen two lobes of a leaf, e.g., Oak, Maple.

Species—A group of plants that resemble each other closely and that interbreed freely; the second and non-capitalized word in the scientific name, e.g., *palustris* in *Quercus palustris*.

Stalk—See Petiole.

Taproot—The primary descending root, often large and long, e.g., White Oak.

Terminal leaflet—The single end leaflet of a compound leaf, e.g., Butternut (often missing on Walnut).

Tolerance (intolerance)—A tree's ability (inability) to withstand specific stresses such as poor or compacted soil, wind, salt, air pollution and temperature extremes.

Toothed—Leaf margins broken into small, sharp-pointed serrations, e.g., Beech, Elm.

Tree—Tall woody plant that frequently grows with a single trunk.

Trunk—The woody main stem of a tree.

Untoothed—Leaves or leaflets with smooth, non-serrated margins, e.g., Magnolia, Yellowwood.

Variety—See Cultivar; terms used interchangeably in this book.

Wavy-edged—Leaf margin with undulating, relatively shallow indentations, e.g., Katsura Tree.

Weeping—Tree crown pattern with secondary branchlets hanging or drooping, e.g., Willow.

Whorled branches—Roughly horizontal layers of branches encircling trunk, e.g., Pagoda Dogwood.

Whorled leaves—A pattern in which three or more leaves encircle a twig at the same node, e.g., Catalpa.

Winged seeds—See Samara.

Witch's Broom—Broom-like masses of superfluous shoots or stems which grow along a tree's branches as a result of a fungus infection or an infestation by insects, e.g. Hackberry.

Dartmouth College Class of 1950

Memorial and Honorary Trees

Since the late 1960s, when its Tree Planting Program was established, the Class of 1950 has given about 175 trees to Dartmouth College. Among them are many that have been given, as memorial or honorary trees, by members of the Class or by individuals or organizations regarded as friends of the Class.

The Class of 1950 has not been directly involved in all of these gifts of memorial or honorary trees. The committee that has directed publication of *Forever Green* believes, after careful research of Class and College records covering a period of about 40 years, the following list to be accurate and regrets any omissions that may have occurred.

Donor(s)	*Dedicated to*
Eleanor Batty	W. L. (Larry) Batty, Jr. '50
William H. Carpenter '50	Russell P. Carpenter '23
Jacques Harlow '50	Allison Ann Murphy Harlow
	Reneé B. and John M. Harlow '15
John C. Harned '50	John E. MacDonald '50
Alexander C. Hoffman '50	
Raymond T. King '50	
Frank L. Harrington, Jr. '50	Frank L. Harrington '24
Larry Huntley '50	Robert Karman '50
Clifton A. Mauk '50	Stanley M. Mauk '19
Robert M. Mauk '50	
Norman E. McCulloch, Jr. '50	Theodore F. Prime '50
Joy Shaver	Bennett H. Shaver '50
Jennifer, Mary, Robin, Sarah	Anthony R. Terrace '50
and Steven Terrace	
David J. Taylor '50	John D. Taylor '23
Edward Tuck II '50 and family	John Tuck, Jr. '54
James. D. Vail III '50	Franklin N. Corbin, Jr. '20
	Albert W. Frey '20
	Foster D. McGaw '20
	James D. Vail, Jr. '20
Mollie K. Hughes and	Ruth and Joel A. Leavitt '50
D. R. (Turk) Hughes P'79, P'84	
Friends and Classmates	Gordon S. Pinkham '50
Dartmouth Club of Chicago	Rudolph Horky, Jr. '40

Index of Tree Species by Common Names

Index of Tree Species by Scientific Names

Notes

Bibliography

Clark, Robert B., *Flowering Trees*, D.Van Nostrand Co., Inc., 1963.

Collingwood, G.H. and Brush, Warren D., *Knowing Your Trees*, American Forestry Association, 1964.

Crockett, James U., *Trees, Time-Life Encyclopedia of Gardening*, Time-Life Books, Inc., 1972.

Dame, Lorin L. and Brooks, Henry, *Handbook of the Trees of New England*, Dover Publications, Inc., 1972.

Dirr, Michael A., *Dirr's Hardy Trees and Shrubs, An Illustrated Encyclopedia*, Timber Press, 1997.

Dirr, Michael A., *Manual of Woody Landscape Plants, 4th edition*, Stipes Publishing Co., 1990.

Elias, Thomas S., *The Complete Trees of North America Field Guide and Natural History, Outdoor Life-Nature Books*, Van Nostrand Reinhold Co., 1980.

Feininger, Andreas, *Trees*, Viking Press, 1968.

Frost, Robert, *The Poetry of Robert Frost,* edited by Edward Connery Lathem, Copyright 1944 by Robert Frost, Copyright 1916, Copyright 1969 by Henry Holt and Company, Inc.

Graham, Robert C., *The Dartmouth Story,* Summer Hill Books, 1990.

Hasselkus, Prof. Emeritus Edward R., correspondence, Department of Horticulture, University of Wisconsin, Madison, Wis.

Herman, Prof. Dale E., correspondence, Department of Plant Sciences, North Dakota State University, Fargo, N.D.

Hightshoe, Gary L., *Native Trees, Shrubs and Vines for Urban and Rural America*, Van Nostrand Reinhold Co., 1988.

Jonas, Gerald, *North American Trees,* Reader's Digest Association, Inc., 1993.

Landgren, Craig R., *The Trees of the Middlebury Campus,* Middlebury College Press, 1981.

Lawrence, Gale, *Guide to Fall Foliage,* Vermont Life, 1984.

Little, Elbert L., *National Audubon Society, Field Guide to North American Trees, Eastern Region,* Alfred A. Knopf, 1997.

Nehring, William and Leighton, Roger, *Trees and Shrubs in New Hampshire,* University of New Hampshire Press, 1967.

Petrides, George, *A Field Guide to Trees and Shrubs,* Houghton Mifflin Co., 1958.

Princeton Nurseries, *The Princeton Elm,* 1998.

Reynolds, Mary K. and Boivin, Raymond M., *Selecting Trees for Urban Landscape Ecosystems; Hardy Species for Northern New England Communities,* State of New Hampshire, Department of Resources and Economic Development, Division of Forests and Lands, 1994.

Rogers, Mary Earl, *Tree Species Selector and Planting Guide for the Urban Dayton Area,* City of Dayton, Ohio, 1980.

Saucier & Flynn, Ltd., Landscape Architects, and Dartmouth College Department of Facilities Operation & Management, *Campus Tree Inventory for Dartmouth College,* June 1999.

Taylor, Norman, *Taylor's Guide to Trees,* Houghton Mifflin Co., 1988.

Trees, Time-Life Gardener's Guide, Time-Life Books, Inc., 1988.

Wyman, Donald, *Trees for American Gardens,* Macmillan Co., 1972.

Zion, Robert L., *Trees for Architecture and the Landscape,* Reinhold Book Corporation, 1968.

FOUNDING OF DARTMOUTH COLLEGE.

Photo Credits

Joseph Mehling, Dartmouth College Photographer: 17-24, 60; Adrian Bouchard: 63; Dartmouth College Archives: 10, 12, 14, 34, 63, 104, 124, 158, 168.